STUDIES IN ETHNOMET
AND CONVERSATION
No. 3

PAUL TEN HAVE and GEORGE PSATHAS
Editors

# SITUATED ORDER

## Studies in the Social Organization of Talk and Embodied Activities

1995

International Institute for Ethnomethodology and Conversation Analysis &
University Press of America
Washington, D.C.

**University Press of America®, Inc.**
4720 Boston Way
Lanham, Maryland 20706

3 Henrietta Street
London WC2E 8LU England


Printed in the United States of America
British Cataloging in Publication Information Available

Copublished by arrangement with the
International Institute for Ethnomethodology and
Conversation Analysis

**Library of Congress Cataloging-in-Publication Data**

Situated order : studies in the social organization of talk and embodied activities / edited by Paul ten Have and George Psathas.
p. cm. — (Studies in ethnomethodology and conversation analysis ; no. 3)
All but one of the papers in this vol. were presented at the International Conference on Current Work in Ethnomethodology and Conversation Analysis, which was held July 1991, University of Amsterdam.
Includes bibliographical references and index.
1. Conversation analysis—Congresses. 2. Ethnomethodology—Congresses. 3. Oral communication—Congresses. I. Have, Paul ten. II. Psathas, George. III. International Institute for Ethnomethodology and Conversation Analysis. IV. International Conference on Current Work in Ethnomethodology and Conversation Analysis (1991 : University of Amsterdam) V. Series.
P95.45.S557 1994 302.3'46—dc20 94–19520 CIP

ISBN 0–8191–9625–8 (cloth : alk. paper)
ISBN 0–8191–9626–6 (pbk. : alk. paper)

The paper used in this publication meets the minimum requirements of American National Standard for Information Sciences—Permanence of Paper for Printed Library Materials, ANSI Z39.48–1984.

**Studies in Ethnomethodology and Conversation Analysis**

is co-published by the

**International Institute for Ethnomethodology and Conversation Analysis**

**&**

**University Press of America, Inc.**

# Contents

# Acknowledgements

The preparation of this book has passed through many phases in which we incurred many debts. We would like to acknowledge here the support of a number of institutions and individuals.

With one exception, the papers in this volume were first presented at the International Conference on Current Work in Ethnomethodology and Conversation Analysis at the University of Amsterdam, July 1991. This conference was organized by the senior editor, with the help of Hanneke Houtkoop and Harrie Mazeland. We were lucky to have the assistance of Eddie Appels for the audio-visual equipment, and of Norbert van Bemmel, Chris van Dijke, Martin Gerrebrands, Joanne Swabe, Nicoline Wolthuis, and Janneke Wijfels for many practical details. Personnel of the Faculty of Political and Social-Cultural Sciences and the Department of Sociology at the University of Amsterdam were also very helpful.

The support in grants from the following institutions is gratefully acknowledged.

The Faculty of Political and Social-Cultural Sciences at the University of Amsterdam and the Royal Dutch Academy of Science provided major grants, while the Department of Sociology and the Department of Science Dynamics at the University of Amsterdam, the Amsterdam Center for Comparative European Social Studies (ACCESS), and the University for Humanistic Studies in Utrecht furnished smaller ones. Kluwer Academic Publishers in Dordrecht, publishers of *Human Studies*, offered a reception. The Conference was co-sponsored by The International Institute for Ethnomethodology and Conversation Analysis. The organizers are very grateful to the 100 participants from 16 different countries, and especially those who presented their work, for making the conference a success.

As to the book itself, we have appreciated the work of those participants who sent us their papers. We could not accept all. The contributors worked hard to meet our deadlines and incorporate our editorial suggestions. The copy editing and further work on the book has been done in Boston. We gratefully acknowledge the careful and attentive transformation of the manuscript into consistent word processing formatting by Laura M. Carpenter who also managed all the final editing as well as the production of the Index.

A collection of original papers represents the collaborative work of many and we are especially indebted to all the authors for their outstanding contributions.

Paul ten Have
George Psathas

# Introduction

Paul ten Have and George Psathas

Titles are meant to convey, in a general way, the orientation of a particular set of studies which they collect. This book collects studies of practical activities, including talk, in a variety of settings: an emergency dispatch center, a software engineering lab, courtrooms, a survey interviewing company, and therapy sessions, as well as "mundane conversation."[1]

"Situated order" is a reasonable gloss for the kinds of phenomena studied here in the sense that "order"*[2] is a locally occasioned matter, locally accomplished in and constitutive of that self-same setting. The local accomplishment of order can be analyzed in terms of the "work" of participants to make their activities "fit" the setting as well as to show that the setting is being (re-)constituted in that work.

The subtitle, "Studies in the social organization of talk and embodied activities," is also meant to call attention to an interest in various other phenomena, in addition to talk, such as laughter, hand movements, telex communications, and the work of computer programmers.

This volume, thus, comes as part of a series of collections, published in various places and formats over the last twenty years. When their titles are examined we find that apart from ethnomethodology and conversation analysis, "interaction" is the most frequently used collector, with "language" (or "talk" or "text") as a frequent second.

The programmatic motives that are inferable from these titles include the notion that ethno/CA studies focus on interactional phenomena, i.e., the "local" accomplishment of order, and the "methods" or "procedures" used in that accomplishment. Furthermore, some of the major findings of the studies concern the role of "talk" in that respect. Some recent collections stand out from the rest by the fact that specific attention is given to issues concerning the "connection" of such "local" phenomena to "larger" ones, glossed by terms like "social structure," "context," or "institutional setting" (e.g., Boden and Zimmerman, 1991, *Talk and Social Structure*; Watson and Seiler, 1992, *Text and Context*; Drew and Heritage, 1992, *Talk at Work*). These studies show that the relation can be conceived of in a variety of ways. Most resist the traditional sociological temptation to see larger structures as determining interaction. In fact, even such terms as "larger" and "restricted" and the associated macro/micro imagery may be avoided. What is conceded, however, is that settings and "institutional" identities, in ways that can be analyzed, may "constrain" actions undertaken in those "institutional" settings. Alternative courses of action will have alternative sets of consequences for designated parties in the interaction depending on specific conventionalized "institutional" episodes and identities. The basic mechanism that does the work of such constraints is seen to be an inferential one; i.e., competent participants make inferences (and assume that others do so as well) concerning the selection, use and outcomes of particular options.

What settings, structures, contexts, etc., "do" is to provide members with "frames" to take into account and to orient to when designing their own activities and assessing those of others. Settings provide members with sets of resources for the design and interpretation of action.

The specific studies in this volume each demonstrate the ways in which contexts of various sorts are taken up in the production of local, situated order.

## Studies in phenomena of situated order

Schegloff's paper is a fine example of a data-based consideration of some basic properties of talk-in-interaction, in this case the significance of numbers for turn-taking. He shows that it is not just the mere fact of the number of participants present, or the conventional meanings of the ways in which they can be seen as a party's members, that "determines" their structured activities.

Rather, the activities themselves are designed to demonstrate how numbers or types of alignments are relevant on a moment-by-moment basis. For example, when Reuben announces "Hey we got good news," he constitutes himself to be a member of a party of the informed, as regards the to-be-announced topic -- note the use of "we" in this respect. In so doing, he proposes a way in which the company can be seen as composed of a set of parties, only to find it being liable to a "correction" in the next slot. As Schegloff writes:

> the number of parties into which those participants may be seen to be organized (because they see *themselves* so to be organized, and embody that stance in their conduct) can change continuously as the contingencies of the talk change, contingencies most centrally supplied by the participants themselves and the nature of the talk which they undertake with one another.

Phillip Glenn's contribution takes off from some of Gail Jefferson's earlier work on laughing in conversational settings, focusing on the shifting alignments that are produced in and through such activities, i.e., from affiliative laughing "with" to a distancing laughing "at" and vice versa. Glenn's analysis shows the possibilities for shifting alliances among conversational partners and suggests that:

> By transforming laughing *at* to *with* (or vice versa), participants may accomplish a micro-transformation of social structure.... the *with/and* possibilities stand as microcosms of, and ways of enacting, cybernetic adjustments common to all relationships.... Thus conversational laughter plays a fundamental role in the organization of human interactions (italics added).

In other words, local conversational negotiations can produce "results," i.e., "joking" relationships and identities of "being a joker," that enter participants' lives on a more permanent basis.

Robert Hopper similarly examines shifts in conversational "play," this time as part of an emerging playfully sexual "contest." His main argument concerns what he calls "trajectories," which can be constructed through the negotiated use of "turning-points" in terms of a play/serious dialectic. His example concerns the rather conventionalized setting of a televised talk show, which structurally involves a live audience as an essential party. Participants not only rely on their local identities as "host" and "guest," but also on their "larger" ethnic and gender ones, which are playfully underscored as they go along.

> The trajectories ... are neither clearly purposeful, nor only emergent. The (given) descriptions have emphasized emergent accidence in the episode. Yet much of the analysis would not change were we to learn that these actors had carefully rehearsed this episode's course. Furthermore, even the most emergent trajectories usually get constructed from relatively pre-fabricated subroutines -- especially in sexual banter.

In the next chapter, Marek Czyzewski shifts to the rather more serious context of psychotherapy to study the functions of response tokens in that setting. His analysis addresses the everyday interactional competencies involved in therapeutic work, as displayed in the selective use of various types of "mm hm" devices. Some of these usages are similar to those deployed in ordinary conversation, while one other seems to be a professionally adapted use of what Jefferson (1984), referring to conversation, has called the "'perverse' passive." The choice of one or the other set of devices seems to be connected with the professional orientation of the therapist (i.e., Rogerian versus psychoanalytic) and helps to sustain different interactional formats (i.e., monological versus dialogical). A very interesting observation concerns crying episodes. At these tense moments, the therapist is seen to temporarily abandon her usual "mm hm" work routine. In other words, professional conduct may involve a selective and setting-adapted use of various conversational devices, depending on theory-based work styles, but exceptional circumstances may lead to a temporary renunciation of those same routines, as a display of what Czyzewski calls "responsibility of the Other."

A similar theme of competent shifting from professional to conversational formats, and vice versa, is taken up in Hanneke Houtkoop-

Steenstra's study of computer-directed telephone survey interviews. Professional survey interviewers are under obligation to read questions exactly as worded by the designers and in the order in which they appear on their screen; furthermore, they should not provide any answers themselves, nor should they suggest a "preference" for one or another alternative. In the instances that Houtkoop-Steenstra quotes, however, we see them doing all of these things and for very good, locally relevant conversational reasons. When earlier exchanges have established a certain state of interactional knowledge, for instance, interviewers turn their questioning on those topics into a reading out loud of a pre-defined question. Her findings suggest that interviewers are able to shift back and forth between their general, "audience designed" script, and locally motivated "recipient designed," corrections on and adaptations of that script. In some cases, interviewers and respondents arrive at a collaborative format of filling out the form together. In other words, Houtkoop-Steenstra's analysis suggests that really effective interviewing requires an unofficial, generally unacknowledged, but still professional competence to shift between questionnaire and conversational frames as the situation requires. Pre-given scripts are practically used as materials to be locally adapted to situated sequential circumstances in order to produce "facts" that, in aggregated form, are used later to represent fields of action for policy makers.

Martha Komter's paper takes us to another rather formal setting, the courtroom. She analyzes the ways in which participants in that setting rely on generally held presuppositions, regarding the knowledge of the interactional parties involved in the criminal activities under discussion and how these are used strategically. This includes knowledge about "facts," about "inner states" and about the inferences that can be drawn from various versions of what happened. Her analysis shows how both the availability of some element of knowledge to the speaker and his supposed interests in various versions, as well as the inferences that can be drawn from these, play a role in the extent to which his testimony will be taken seriously or not. At the same time, the self-interested nature of the defendant's testimony is not explicitly attended during the interaction itself.

> The consistency of statements about "the facts" is taken as an indication of them being true. Inconsistent statements on the other hand require an explanation. Inconsistencies are taken up by the judges as elicitation techniques that invite the defendants to solve these "puzzles." The underlying idea is that the exact details of the criminal events can be verbally "replayed" in the courtroom, and that there can be only one true report of what has happened.

Criminal court hearings, then, not only depend on institutional specifications of procedure, but also on cultural presuppositions regarding the availability and trustfulness of knowledge claims, in relation to the party's involvements in both the reported events and the current negotiations concerning guilt or innocence. The parties to the proceeding often seem to deny, however, that their preferred "readings" of the facts that are being established, depend on a pre-existing belief in the guilt or innocence that they are trying to prove. Within the situated order of the court, pre-established knowledge is tested locally, while persistent general assumptions about knowledge and interests are brought to bear on unique case materials to ground decisions with serious direct and indirect consequences.

Paul McIlvenny introduces us to a social world that is at the same time different and familiar to us: the one inhabited by Deaf people. It is familiar in the sense that there too a social order is constituted continuously by the use of shared devices. But it is different in that the interactional devices available to participants are limited to ones not based on hearing, which leads to an increased use of those relying on sight and touch. McIlvenny's explorations not only provide a description of how people with limited possibilities have created their own natural order of communication, but also serve to create another moment of "estrangement" as regards the taken-for-granted order of the worlds of seers-hearers-speakers, as a non-experimental device to make common sense presuppositions and seen but unnoticed procedures visible and analyzable.

The final set of papers concerns phenomena of situated order in worlds in which technological innovations extend the possibilities for the production of order, as compared to "mundane conversation." At the same time, technology may play a decisive role in pre-structuring available action opportunities, in connecting the local situation to other ones, or even in creating the "field" in which a situated order can be built in the first place (cf. Button, 1992, for more ethnomethodological studies of technological work).

Alan Firth examines how employees of widely separated business enterprises -- in Denmark and Saudi Arabia respectively -- use a variety of technical means, including telephone and telex, to "tele-negotiate" a commercial settlement. His analysis shows that these means are not equivalent in terms of accountability. The telephone can be used to build the agreement -- and to talk about the weather -- but the deal needs to be confirmed by telex.

> The result is that, despite the multiplicity of modes employed, the spatio-temporally disjoined communications transcend the separation of modes, space, and time, to evince coherent, orderly discourse activity. In this light, we may be justified in referring to the observed configurations of communication ... as a particularized "activity system"...

This "system" is built on a three-part "purchasing sequence" which:

> while emergent in and through action on each and every occasion, is rendered meaningful and coherent firstly by locally managed discourse actions, and secondly by the parties' ongoing orientations to who they relevantly are and what they are doing together....

This last phrase rather elegantly sums up one of the ways in which studies like those collected here deal with issues of "larger structures": the "problem" is respecified as one of members' orientations from within the situations observed.

Marjorie Harness Goodwin's paper is one of a series of reports on a three year collaborative project at Xerox PARC, called The Workplace Project (cf. among others: Brun-Cotton, 1990/1991; Suchman, 1992). She discusses aspects of the ways in which airline employees, as part of their job, collaboratively "assemble a response" to either another employee's, or a customer's, request. Her detailed analyses demonstrate how workers routinely combine material and bodily "technologies" to bring off such collaborations. In some settings, they have various electronic devices at their disposal to construct larger or more restricted participation states on a moment-by-moment basis, while in others ellipses can be used to "hide" collaboration from outsiders. In addition to that, workers rely on an extended set of conversational devices, including intonation, body posture and various "registers," to display their informational needs of the moment. "Situated activity systems," as well as "participation frameworks," are highly flexible and shifting "units," created and dismissed on the spot according to participants' needs of the moment.

> Speech acts are thus not the product of isolated individuals; they are rather assembled achievements emerging from the collaborative work-web of co-present workers who constantly monitor on-going interaction for their possible involvement in it, non-present participants whose work is made relevant through electronically transmitted messages and documents, as well as the tools in their work spaces (such as video monitors positioned at gates) which provide access to information of various sorts.

Jack Whalen analyzes an episode in which an emergency call-taker coordinates her talking on the phone with typing at the keyboard of a computer-aided dispatch system. In a fashion similar to the situation studied by Houtkoop-Steenstra, this system both grounds and constrains her talking-and-typing-as-work. She has to attend to both the talk-situation and the typing-situation, as well as to trying to understand the situation that is being reported, in anticipation of possible police assistance. As Whalen writes:

> ... the call-taking face sheet is clearly more than "just a form" for recording information; ... it serves as a kind of "methodological scheme" for doing the work of call-taking ... the form functions as a textual idealization of the organizational agenda ... while simultaneously providing a convenient framework for the specific practical actions by which that agenda can be more or less realized....

Button and Sharrock, finally, have studied the work of people who produce the so-called soft parts of the technological environments used in modern societies, i.e., computer programmers. It is argued that the intelligibility of that work, for both readers and writers of computer "code," depends on the professional community's requirements of logic and elegance, in a way similar to those found in other forms of artful practice. These involve keeping the structure of the code visible by starting from "the simplest possible case," temporally "naming" variables and functions, using sensible names generally, and using lay-out practices. This latter device is often built into the facilities that programmers use, i.e., screen-structure editors and "pretty printing" devices. This fact is taken, by the authors, as a demonstration that the computer science community acknowledges not just formal but also "vulgar" competencies involved in writing "good code." This acknowledgment might provide, they suggest, a basis for having ethnomethodological work accepted more easily in this field than in many others, such as those of the natural and social sciences.

## Ethnomethodology and conversation analysis: Living traditions

In the final section of this introduction, we would like to put the papers collected in this volume in a larger theoretical perspective. They were all written under the auspices of what may be called the "living traditions" of ethnomethodology and conversation analysis. Based on the brilliant initiatives of Harold Garfinkel and Harvey Sacks, and their collaborators, these traditions have drawn growing numbers of researchers from most Western/Northern countries. Although basically sociological enterprises, there are many researchers from other disciplines who have contributed to the corpus of such studies, including anthropologists, linguists and communication scientists.

The concept of "living tradition" is meant to evoke a tension between, on the one hand, the essential problematics, presuppositions, and methods -- in short the "vision" -- of its originators and, on the other, the fact that later contributors inevitably will do the work in their own evolving ways. The conference at which these papers were first presented was titled "Current Work in Ethnomethodology and Conversation Analysis" and was chosen to invite recent explorations in the field, while still connecting to the primary visions that made the later work possible.

There is now a substantial literature on how this work relates to the discipline of sociology and the other social sciences. And there is a much smaller, although growing number of remarks on the relationships of the two traditions of ethnomethodology and conversation analysis to each other. There is no question that they are related and that ethnomethodology was and is "first," in the sense of it being the earlier and more general and basic endeavor. But apart from that, disagreement prevails.

We believe that the next chapter of this volume, by Clayman and Maynard, will make an important contribution to this debate. It is a revised version of the opening lecture at the conference. They discuss ethnomethodology and conversation analysis as related, as well as contrastive enterprises, stressing a need for complementarity. At the deeper levels of assumptions and sensibilities, the two traditions are linked, but:

> Substantively, ethnomethodology's broad concern with diverse forms of practical reasoning and embodied action contrasts with the conversation analytic focus on a comparatively restricted domain of talk-in-interaction and its various constituent activity systems.... Methodologically, Garfinkel's recent advocacy of investigators achieving the *bona fide* competence of an insider departs from the conversation analytic use of recorded data which anyone, whether a member of the setting or not, can inspect and review for its organizational features.

Clayman and Maynard have organized their discussion of the ethnomethodology/CA relationship under the themes of the use of "disorder" to study the work of order creation, a focus on the study of natural language use, and a stress on achieved organization. What their sensible and sensitive overview seems to amount to, is that CA is the more "productive" tradition of the two, while ethnomethodology is more "radical." CA researchers produce a large corpus of accumulative "results," i.e., findings on the sequential organization of talk-in-interaction in various settings, while ethnomethodologists combine an urge to uncover the "radical phenomena" of "lived experience," while being wary of any concrete "rendering" of those phenomena. Rather than seeing this contrast as a stalemate, Clayman and Maynard urge the two approaches to seek for "complementarity," although not in the sense of a synthesis or a combination of two "perspectives" on the "same" domain.[3]

In what sense, one might ask, are the papers in this volume able to fulfill this hope? We may start by noting that all papers are either clearly conversation analytic in focus or written by researchers who have done such work in the past. There are no contributions from non-CA ethnomethodologists. So we can only take a look at the ways in which the dilemmas sketched by Clayman and Maynard are taken up from the CA side.

Most of the work represented here stays focused on sequential organization of talk-in-interaction, including for the moment issues of turn-taking and body movement. There is, however, a sustained interest in larger sequences and in the ways in which sequences are embedded in, constituted by and constitutive of institutional settings of various sorts. There is much less stress on "conversation" as a basic format, as there was in the '70s and '80s. In a sense, the Atkinson/Heritage model (Atkinson, 1982; Heritage, 1984) -- criticized by Bjelic and Lynch (1992) as CA's "foundationalism" and still prominent in the Boden and Zimmerman (1991) and Drew and Heritage (1992) volumes -- is less central here. Instead, Schegloff's notion of talk-in-interaction is increasingly used to de-focus the conversation/institutional contrast. Video analysis and studies of complex work settings reinforce a trend for "exemplary" analyses, rather than the corpus-based structure-oriented researches that were for quite some time seen as the core type of CA-analysis.

Contributions like those of Marjorie Goodwin and Jack Whalen can be seen to use the sensitivities and findings of CA to study setting-specific practices in a way that comes closer to fulfilling Garfinkel's "unique adequacy requirement" than has been found in earlier CA studies of institutional interaction. Their kinds of analyses might also be related to the debate raised by Michael Moerman (1988) on the use of "ethnography" to complement and "ground" CA analyses (cf. Hopper, 1990/91). Moerman's argument that one has to "know the culture," by doing ethnography, in order to be able to discern what utterances mean to participants, can be countered by saying that he conflates two rather incompatible language games (cf. Watson, 1992), ethnography being much less rigorous and "data-driven" than CA. Goodwin's and Whalen's papers, however, while not using "ethnography" as a loosely invoked independent "resource," demonstrate in their analysis of recorded data that they know much more about the local requirements, practices and routines than an outsider, using the same data, could imagine. In different ways, Hanneke Houtkoop-Steenstra, Martha Komter and Alan Firth also use "ethnographic" knowledge and/or documents other than recordings of interactions, to ground their analyses of setting-specific talk-as-work.

The final chapter, written by Graham Button and Wes Sharrock, comes closest to the ethnomethodological studies of work program. In their analysis of computer programmers' work, there is no use of recorded interaction or sequential analysis at all. They do, however, focus on the "vulgar competencies" that are used and relied upon to do that work. As a concept, "vulgar competencies" seems remarkably close to the stuff CA has been unearthing from recordings. The use of "lay out" by computer programmers may be likened to the use of singsong announcements that Goodwin speaks about, the "conversational" adaptations of an "audience designed" interview script as analyzed by Houtkoop-Steenstra, or the cultural presuppositions about knowledge and interest discussed by Komter.

Thus, these studies include what has been referred to as talk-in-interaction within an "institutional" or "organizational" setting where the focus is on the collection of data which show some of the types of interactional structures which are endogenously produced in these settings and describe how talk-in-interaction is embedded in and constitutive of the setting. In addition, some study other forms of interaction and examine how the particular work of the "organization," "institution," or categories of incumbents achieves its organization.

It seems to us that these studies supplement and enhance each other; there are no serious incompatibilities between them. They reflect the variety of work to be found in ethnomethodological/conversation analytic research. There are differences of emphasis, of problem selection and formulation, of methodological preference, and of focus, e.g., on talk, on talk-in-interaction, on embodied actions, on practical reasoning, on the methods of work organization, etc. But all studies share a foundational position with regard to the effort to discover/describe/analyze everyday, naturally occurring activities, by preserving their *in situ* order and organization as phenomena of study.

---

[1] Earlier versions of the papers, with one exception, were presented at the International Conference on Current Work in Ethnomethodology and Conversation Analysis, co-sponsored by the International Institute for Ethnomethodology and Conversation Analysis and the University of Amsterdam, in Amsterdam, 15-19 July, 1991.

[2] "Order" refers to the original Parsonian inspiration of Garfinkel's work and has recently been invoked by him as "order*", where the "*" is added to indicate that it is a "a collector and a proxy for any and every topic of logic, meaning, method, reason, and order" (Garfinkel and Wieder, 1992: 202; cf. Garfinkel, 1991).

[3] To picture the field as consisting of two "camps" is a simplification, of course, since a number of other strands might be mentioned, including for instance the work of Jeff Coulter, James Heap, and Lena Jayyusi, which do not participate in this "debate" as such (cf. Psathas, 1992).

# 1

# Ethnomethodology and Conversation Analysis*

Steven E. Clayman and Douglas W. Maynard

Of the various forms of research inspired by Harold Garfinkel's *Studies in Ethnomethodology* (1967), perhaps the most prominent has been the enterprise initiated by Harvey Sacks in collaboration with Emanuel Schegloff and Gail Jefferson that has come to be known as conversation analysis. While it has long been recognized that the initial development of conversation analysis was related to Garfinkel's ongoing program of ethnomethodological research, the precise nature of this relationship has only recently begun to receive attention within the literature. Heritage (1984: Chapter 8) reviews the central methodological principles and substantive findings of conversation analytic research within the framework of a broader discussion of ethnomethodology, although the relations between them remain largely implicit in his account. Schegloff (1992a) also touches on this topic in a wide-ranging discussion of Sacks' intellectual development that encompasses various influences on his work but does not focus on the ethnomethodological heritage per se. Our aim is to specify some central points of contact between ethnomethodological and conversation analytic forms of inquiry, although in the course of this discussion we will also touch upon some ways in which they differ.

Our primary objective presupposes that there are indeed continuities to be found between ethnomethodology and conversation analysis. This is a matter of some controversy, however, as scholars have recently devoted substantial attention to specifying points of divergence (Garfinkel and Wieder, 1992; Lynch, 1985: 8-10; Bjelic and Lynch, 1992: 53-55; Lynch and Bogen, 1990). As Schegloff (1992a: xii-xxvii) has noted, Harvey Sacks was influenced by a wide range of intellectual sources in addition to Harold Garfinkel. These include Erving Goffman (one of Sacks' teachers while a graduate student at Berkeley), Wittgenstein's ordinary language philosophy, Chomsky's transformational grammar, Freudian psychoanalysis, anthropological field work, and research by Milman Parry and Eric Havelock on oral cultures. Moreover, the subsequent development of conversation analytic research indicates that, in terms of both substance and method, it has a character and a trajectory that is partially independent of ethnomethodology. Substantively, ethnomethodology's broad concern with diverse forms of practical reasoning and embodied action contrasts with the conversation analytic focus on the comparatively restricted domain of talk-in-interaction and its various constituent activity systems (e.g., turn taking, sequencing, repair, gaze direction, institutional specializations, and the like). Methodologically, Garfinkel's recent advocacy of investigators achieving the *bona fide* competence of an insider departs from the conversation analytic use of recorded data which anyone, whether a member of the setting or not, can inspect and review for its organizational features.

Despite these differences, bonds between the two approaches run deep. Garfinkel and Sacks had an ongoing intellectual and personal relationship that began in 1959 and was sustained through the early 70s (Schegloff, 1992a: xiii), a period when foundational research in both areas was being developed. Moreover, they co-authored a paper (1970) on an issue that is central to both ethnomethodology and conversation analysis: the properties of natural language use.[1] Given this extended relationship, it would be surprising if Garfinkel's ongoing program of ethnomethodological research did not inform the development of conversation analysis and vice versa. As we explore the two enterprises, however, we will see that their commonalities are not to be found in terms of specific topics of interest or methodological techniques, about which there are clear differences. Linkages are most evident at deeper levels where one can discern common theoretical assumptions, analytic sensibilities, and concerns with diverse phenomena of everyday life.

We will organize our discussion around these points of convergence between ethnomethodology and conversation analysis, first in overview and then with reference to more specific issues. Accordingly, we are not attempting a comprehensive review of either discipline, nor are we proposing a formal synthesis. Our discussion, in focusing on aspects of ethnomethodology which have been intertwined with the development of conversation analysis, is avowedly selective with regard to particular themes.

## Ethnomethodology and Conversation Analysis in Overview

We begin with a brief and highly general characterization of the ethnomethodological program of theory and research.[2] Ethnomethodology offers a distinctive perspective on the nature and origins of social order. It rejects "top-down" theories that seek to explain social order in terms of cultural or social structural phenomena which are conceived as standing outside of the flow of events in everyday life. Adopting a thoroughly "bottom-up" approach, ethnomethodology seeks to recover social organization as an emergent achievement that results from the concerted efforts of societal members acting within local situations. Central to this achievement are the various methods which members use to produce and recognize courses of social activity and the circumstances in which they are embedded. The mundane intelligibility and accountability of social actions, situations, and structures is understood to be the outcome of these constitutive methods or procedures.

This distinctive perspective on the foundations of social order originated in Garfinkel's encounter with Talcott Parsons, with whom Garfinkel studied while a graduate student at Harvard (Garfinkel, 1988; Heritage, 1984: Chapter 2). In *The Structure of Social Action* (1937: 27-42) Parsons observed that members' sense of the world is necessarily mediated by conceptual structures; through such structures, otherwise "raw streams of experience" are ordered and rendered intelligible. Just as conceptual structures organize ordinary experience for lay members of society, they are also essential for scientific inquiry. Thus, Parsons held that a first step for social science is the development of a descriptive frame of reference capable of segmenting the complex flux of social activity. This involves analytically specifying certain abstract elements of action that permit empirical generalization and explanation (1937: 727-775). To this end, he developed the well-known "action frame of reference" consisting of the unit act, the means, ends, and material conditions of action, normative constraints on action, and the "analytic elements" or variable properties of action. Subsequent theorizing then focused on explaining patterns of social action by reference to institutionalized norms and more general value systems whose internalization ensures actors' motivated compliance with the normative requirements of society.

As a student and admirer of Parsons' "penetrating depth and unfailing precision," Garfinkel (1967: ix) nevertheless discerned a range of issues that were not addressed in Parsons' approach to the analysis of social action. For Parsons, research and theorizing proceeds from a prespecified analytic construct -- namely, the unit act and its components -- instead of those concrete actions that form the substance of the ordinary actor's experience of the world (Schegloff, 1980: 151; 1987a: 102). Correspondingly, Parsons' emphasis on how actors become motivated to act in normatively standardized ways diverts attention from the real-time process through which intelligible courses of action are produced and managed over their course (Heritage, 1984: 22-33). Finally, Parsons' analytic frame of reference forestalls appreciation of the indigenous perspectives of the actors themselves who, as purposive agents in social life, use forms of common sense knowledge and practical reasoning to make sense of their circumstances and find ways of acting within them. Indeed, it is through such reasoning practices, and the actions which are predicated upon them, that actors collaboratively construct what are experienced as the external and constraining circumstances in which they find themselves. Garfinkel's response was to place these matters involving the local production and indigenous accountability of action, matters which were peripheral for Parsons, at the center of an alternate conception of social organization.

While ethnomethodology thus embodies elements of a distinctive theory of social organization, that theory was not developed independently of empirical research. Indeed, it is a feature of the theory that propositions about social organization cannot be divorced from ongoing courses of inquiry in real settings. Since the intelligible features of society are locally produced by members themselves for one another, with methods that are reflexively embedded in concrete social situations, the precise nature of that achievement cannot be determined by the analyst through a priori stipulation or deductive reasoning. It can only be *discovered* within "real" society (in its "inexhaustible details"), within "actual" society (in the endlessly contingent methods of its production), and within society "evidently" (in analytic claims that are assessable in terms of members' ongoing accounting practices) (Garfinkel, 1988). Accordingly, Garfinkel's theoretical proposals were developed in conjunction with his own empirical studies (1963; 1967), and they have inspired diverse streams of research which are united by the common goal of investigating a previously unexamined domain of social practice (for an overview, see Maynard and Clayman, 1991).

Like ethnomethodology, conversation analysis (henceforth, CA) adopts a thoroughly "bottom-up" approach to research and theorizing. Although conversation analysts are not averse to advancing theoretical claims, often of a highly general nature (Wilson and Zimmerman, 1980: 67), every effort is made to ground such claims in the observable orientations that interactants themselves display to one other. Within this framework, CA has developed its own relatively focused set of substantive concerns. While CA retains an interest in forms of common sense reasoning, these are analyzed as they are put to use within the specific arena of talk-in-interaction. Hence, conversation analysts have developed a distinctive interest in how various orderly characteristics of talk -- regular patterns of turn taking, activity sequencing, institutional specializations, and the like -- are accountably produced by interactants via procedures which are implemented on a turn by turn basis. Despite this focus it is clear that, at least in their broad contours, ethnomethodological and conversation analytic approaches to research and theorizing have much in common.

## Methodological Continuities: Breaching Experiments and Deviant Case Analysis

The first specific point of contact to be discussed is methodological in character, and concerns the relationship between Garfinkel's early breaching experiments and what has come to be known as "deviant case analysis" within CA.

A methodological problem that Garfinkel initially faced was how to make forms of common sense reasoning available for empirical research. Within the phenomenological tradition, Schutz (1962) had emphasized that the constitutive operations of perception, cognition, and reasoning are normally taken for granted in everyday life. Actors confront a world that is eminently coherent and intelligible, and they adopt a thoroughly pragmatic orientation to their affairs in the world thus experienced. Within that orientation, common sense serves as a tacit resource for the pursuit of practical ends, but is not ordinarily an object of conscious reflection in its own right. Thus, Garfinkel (1967) wrote of the "seen-but-unnoticed background features" of social settings, features which are essentially "uninteresting" to the participants themselves. For the analyst, this creates what ten Have (1990: 29) has aptly characterized as "the problem of the invisibility of common sense." How can "invisible" practices be made accessible to systematic empirical scrutiny?

As a first step, Garfinkel stipulated that although such practices may originate within consciousness, they are sociologically meaningful only insofar as they are consequential for, and are observable in, public forms of behavior (1963: 190). Hence, their analysis does not require a *verstehende* method, for they may be investigated exclusively by "performing operations on events that are 'scenic' to the person" (1963: 190). Moreover, Garfinkel proposed that the "scenic operations" that might best reveal the existence and nature of order-productive reasoning procedures are operations that, ironically, generate disorder rather than order. The strategy, as he put it, was:

> to start with a system of stable features and ask what can be done to make for trouble. The operations that one would have to perform in order to produce and sustain anomic features of perceived environments and disorganized interaction should tell us something about how social structures are ordinarily and routinely being maintained (1963: 187).

Garfinkel thus dealt with the invisibility of common sense by approaching the phenomenon indirectly in situations where it had ostensibly broken down. Successfully disrupted situations should enable one to infer the absence of some essential procedure and, by working backward, elucidate its constitutive import in normal circumstances. Thus, Garfinkel's ingenious solution to the problem of the invisibility of common sense methods was based upon the insight that they remain "invisible" only so long as they "work;" if they can somehow be inhibited or rendered inoperative, the entropic social consequences should be both predictable and observable.

In light of these considerations Garfinkel developed the well-known breaching experiments that would serve as "aids to a sluggish imagination" in the analysis of common sense (1967: 38). For inspiration as to what the procedures of common sense might consist of, he drew on Schutz' analysis of the assumptions which comprise "the natural attitude of everyday life" (1962; 1964; 1966) and Gurwitsch's discussion of the use of contextual knowledge in the manner suggested by a phenomenology of perception informed by Gestalt principles ([1959] 1966; 1964).[3] To inhibit these common sense and contextualizing procedures, he instructed his confederates to demand that subjects explain and clarify the meaning of their most casual remarks, to act as boarders in their own homes, to act on the assumption that subjects had some hidden motive, and so on. Although he was hesitant to use the term "experiment" in reference to such studies, preferring to characterize them more modestly as "demonstrations" (1967: 38), Garfinkel's approach was very much reminiscent of the earlier incongruity experiments of Asch (1946; 1951) and Bruner and his associates (Bruner and Postman, 1949; see also Bruner, 1961). Garfinkel's demonstrations, however, were designed to be not merely incongruous with subjects' expectations, but also massively senseless.

The experimental outcomes were indeed dramatic, although not precisely as Garfinkel initially anticipated. Instead of yielding a state of bewilderment or "cognitive anomie," subjects typically reacted with marked hostility, displaying acute anger, sanctioning the confederates, and attributing various negative motivations to them. The main exception to this pattern of hostility occurred when subjects departed from the order of everyday life and assumed that some extraordinary circumstance was operating -- for instance, some kind of game -- which enabled them to "normalize" the anomalous action as a move within a game. Taken together, these reactions served as evidence that societal members tacitly use and orient to these methods of reasoning in ordinary life. Moreover, the hostile reactions suggested that, within the domain of everyday life, sense-making procedures have an underlying moral dimension (Heritage, 1984: Chapter 4). That is, use of the procedures is not merely an empirical regularity, but a moral obligation that societal members enforce on one another; the procedures are treated as mutually relevant and binding. This moral orientation, which Garfinkel initially referred to under the rubric of "trust" (Garfinkel, 1963), constitutes a basic frame of reference in terms of which societal members encounter their fellows. Thus powerful sanctions can be mobilized against those who violate these relevances and the trust that they embody. Garfinkel concluded that

> The anticipation that persons *will* understand, the occasionality of expressions, the specific vagueness of references, the retrospective-prospective sense of a present occurrence, waiting for something later in order to see what was meant before, *are sanctioned properties of common discourse* (1967: 41) (emphasis added).

Since Garfinkel's early breaching experiments, ethnomethodologists have continued to pay close attention to disruptions of perceivedly "normal" states of affairs on the assumption that such events can illuminate otherwise invisible order-productive practices. However, more recent work has tended to avoid experimentally contrived disruptions in favor of seeking out disruptions that arise naturally and spontaneously within social situations. Garfinkel's own case study of Agnes (1967: Chapter 5), who "passed" as a female despite seemingly masculine elements of her anatomy and biography, is an early exemplar of a naturally occurring disruption. More recent examples include Pollner's (1975; 1987) use of reality disjunctures in traffic court to explore the parameters of mundane reasoning, Wieder's [1974] (1988) use of departures from official routines in a halfway house as a resource for exploring the reflexive relationship between norms and the instances of conduct that they are seen to regulate, and Lynch's (1982; 1985) use of research artifacts to explore the material and praxiological foundations of scientific findings.

Naturally occurring disruptions of seemingly "normal" states of affairs have also played an important role in conversation analysis, where investigators examine "deviant" cases as a routine methodological practice. Thus, after locating and initially describing some interactional regularity, analysts commonly search through their data for incongruous cases in which the proposed regularity was not realized. For instance, in Schegloff's (1968) pioneering analysis of conversational openings, a single deviant case is central to his analysis, and he cites Garfinkel for the inspiration that normal scenes can be illuminated by considering disruptions of them (1968: 1077).

This is not to say that conversation analysts have straightforwardly imported this aspect of Garfinkel's method without altering it. In keeping with the naturalistic spirit of CA, and in concert with more recent ethnomethodological studies, disruptions are not engineered experimentally but are found by examining interactional records for spontaneously occurring instances. There are, of course, distinct advantages to this more recent approach. Beyond the obvious benefit of enhanced external validity, spontaneous disruptions are produced by ordinary actors themselves in accordance with thoroughly endogenous considerations. Accordingly, they can be analyzed as specimens of social action, as describable "doings" in their own right, rather than vehicles of social disorganization which are revealing of practices exogenous to the disruption itself.

Moreover, the conversation analytic use of deviant cases has expanded beyond its role in Garfinkel's experiments. For Garfinkel, the primary purpose of the breaching experiments was to test for and to explicate otherwise "invisible" constitutive procedures. Within CA, deviant cases often serve a similar function, but that is subsidiary to the more general goal of producing analytic formulations that can account for the widest range of instances within a corpus of data. Thus, "deviant case" in CA is generally an *analyst's* characterization which may or may not turn out to be, in addition, a characterization that the *interactants* might make; the term usually references events which seem to be inconsistent with an initial analytic formulation of how things work. Investigators aggressively search for such cases because serious consideration of them tends to enrich and deepen an initial analysis by making it account for both the regular patterns of talk as well as those singular instances that run off differently. In this respect, the methodology of CA is formally similar to what has elsewhere been termed "analytic induction," a qualitative research methodology that can be traced to Znaniecki's *The Method of Sociology* (1934) and which seeks to produce, through the systematic analysis of deviant cases, a relationship of perfect correspondence between an empirical phenomenon and the analytic apparatus postulated to explain its various manifestations within a corpus of data (Katz, 1983). Beyond this the similarity ends, for analytic induction has traditionally been concerned with the formulation of causal laws, while conversation analysis has a different objective: namely, to explicate the reasoning principles that guide, and are displayed within, interactional conduct.[4]

Conversation analysts typically deal with deviant cases in one of three ways, only the first of which is directly related to Garfinkel's approach. First, some deviant cases are shown, upon analysis, to result from interactants' orientation to the same considerations that produce the "regular" cases. In the analysis of adjacency pairs, for example, the regular occurrence of certain paired actions (e.g., question-answer, request-response, etc.) is explained by reference to the property of conditional relevance, which stipulates that the production of a first pair-part makes a corresponding response both relevant and expectable (Schegloff, 1968; 1972; Schegloff and Sacks, 1973). How, then, do we account for instances where the relevant response was not immediately produced? In many cases it can be shown that even though the item was not produced then and there, the interactants were nonetheless acting in accordance with the assumption that it should properly be forthcoming. For instance, the recipient may provide an account to explain and justify the nonproduction of a relevant response; alternatively, if no account is forthcoming, the initiator of the sequence may after a pause attempt to elicit the relevant item and thereby "repair" the unfinished sequence. Also relevant here are "insertion sequences" (e.g., question-answer sequences intervening between an adjacency pair initiation and the called-for response) in which the recipient seeks to elicit information necessary to provide an appropriate response. In any case, through such actions the parties display an orientation to the very same principles that are postulated to underpin the production of straightforward adjacency pair sequences (Heritage, 1984: 248-53). This line of reasoning both confirms the initial analysis regarding conditional relevance and enriches it by showing how the same principles operate within, and thereby generate, a nonstandard course of action. Moreover, the line of reasoning is formally similar to Garfinkel's approach in the breaching experiments, where a proposed common sense procedure is confirmed and explicated by examining the consequences of its absence. And just as Garfinkel's demonstrations revealed a morality attached to sense-making procedures, departures from conversational procedures sometimes engender strong negative sanctions, suggesting that at least some of the latter also have an underlying moral dimension.

A second way of handling a deviant case is to replace the initial analysis with a more general formulation that encompasses both the "regular" cases and the "departure." Perhaps the clearest example of this can be found in Schegloff's (1968) analysis of telephone call openings. In a corpus of 500 telephone calls, Schegloff found that a straightforward rule -- "answerer speaks first" -- adequately described all but one of the call openings; in that 500th case, the caller spoke first. Rather than ignoring this instance or explaining it away in an ad hoc fashion, Schegloff argued that this case together with the other 499 could be explained in light of a prior interactional event and its sequential implications: namely, the ring of the telephone, which constitutes the first sequential "move" in any telephone interaction. A ringing phone functions as the first part of a summons-answer sequence, the components of which are linked by the property of conditional relevance. Against this backdrop, the "rule" that answerer speaks first actually reflects the more general principle that once a summons (in the form of a ringing phone) has been issued, an appropriate response is relevant. The deviant case can also be explained in light of the summons and its sequential implications; in that case the ring was followed by silence, which for the caller represented the absence of the relevant response, and this prompted the caller to speak first by reissuing the summons to solicit a response and thereby "repair" the unfinished sequence. Accordingly, the initial rule was shown to be derivative of more general principles that were postulated to account for both the regular cases and the troublesome variant.

If these approaches fail, a third option is to produce a separate analysis of the deviant case, one which treats it as bringing about, in effect, an alternate sequential "reality." Thus, the investigator may describe how the apparent "departure" differs from the "regular" cases, analyze what distinctive activity is being accomplished in and through the departure, and specify how this seemingly atypical course of action alters or transforms the interactional circumstances. A prominent example here is Jefferson and Lee's (1981) analysis of departures from a proposed "troubles-telling sequence." When personal troubles are expressed in conversation, recipients commonly respond with affiliative displays of understanding. However, recipients may also offer advice and thereby transform the situation from a "troubles-telling" to a "service encounter" implicating different discourse identities and activities. This approach, unlike the previous two, does not result in a single analytic formulation which can account for both the "regular" and "deviant" cases. But it does embody an effort to come to terms with apparently atypical courses of action, and thereby incorporate such cases within a comprehensive analysis of the available data. And while this method is not directly related to Garfinkel's breaching experiments, the idea of sequential departures as context-transforming or "frame-breaking" activities is analogous to the way in which some subjects analyzed the breaches as moves to reshape the interaction as a "joke" or "game." It is also reminiscent of Goffman's observation that "a rule tends to make possible a meaningful set of non-adherences" (1971: 61), and his corresponding practice of analyzing such non-adherences in terms of the activities that are accomplished thereby. Within CA this approach has been used more frequently in recent years as researchers have begun to venture away from small, closely ordered sequences such as adjacency pairs and toward the analysis of larger episodes of talk which appear to be more loosely organized, are not sanctionable in the same way, and thus routinely permit a variety of sequential trajectories (e.g., Heritage and Sefi, 1992; Jefferson and Lee, 1981; Jefferson, 1988; Schegloff, 1986; Whalen, Zimmerman, and Whalen, 1988).

In summary, CA has developed a data-driven methodology that places a high priority on working through individual cases to obtain a comprehensive analysis of the available data. In several ways, coming to grips with deviant cases has been part of the methodology. While ethnomethodology has not been as committed to particular methodological strategies, at least one way of reasoning about deviant cases is deeply indebted to Garfinkel's insight that the common sense expectancies underlying perceivedly normal events can be illuminated by considering situations in which that normality is disrupted.

## Natural Language as a Phenomenon: Indexical Expressions and Sequential Organization

Both ethnomethodology and conversation analysis have been concerned with the use of natural language in everyday life. The capacity to categorize and describe persons, activities, and social situations is, of course, a central resource for the conduct of social scientific inquiry. However, this resource is by no means the exclusive province of the professional social scientist; it is derived from natural language capacities possessed by all competent members of society, capacities that play a pervasive and constitutive role in the everyday activities of both laypersons and professionals. For this reason ethnomethodologists of various stripes have sought to investigate what had previously been an unexplicated analytic resource. This theme arose early on in Garfinkel's work; his studies of jury deliberations (1967: Chapter 4) and psychiatric intake practices (1967: Chapter 6), as well as some of the breaching experiments discussed previously, came to focus substantial attention on the oral and written accounts produced by members in various settings. For Sacks this theme was even more central and is the primary focus of his earliest published writings (Sacks, 1963). Thus, he likened society to a machine that produced both a steady stream of *activities* and corresponding stream of *accounts* those activities, a machine with both "doing" and "saying" parts. He then criticized sociologists for excluding the "saying" part of the societal machine from analysis; that is, for producing more refined natural language accounts of activities without attempting to examine language practices as activities or "doings" in their own right. This attitude is broadly congruent with the ordinary language philosophy of John Austin, the later Wittgenstein, and their respective associates, although ethnomethodology developed independently and offers an empirical rather than a philosophical approach to the analysis of language practices.

The interest in natural language use came into focus for both Garfinkel and Sacks via the phenomenon of indexical expressions and their properties, which is the subject of their only published collaboration -- the oft-cited paper "On Formal Structures of Practical Actions" (Garfinkel and Sacks, 1970). Garfinkel and Sacks characterize indexical expressions as utterances whose sense cannot be determined without reference to the person talking, the time and place of talk, or more generally the occasion of speech or its "context" (1970: 348-49). Examples include expressions containing what linguists call *deictic* words or phrases: pronouns, time and place adverbs like "now" and "here," and various grammatical features whose sense is tied to the circumstances of the utterance (Levinson, 1983: 54). Hence, the meaning and understandability of any indexical expression, rather than being fixed by some abstract definition, depends upon the environment in which it appears.

For philosophers concerned with the formal analysis of language, and for social scientists seeking to produce propositions about the organization of society, indexical expressions are treated as a nuisance to be remedied. Thus, every effort is made to render scientific propositions (e.g., hypotheses, ideal types, interview schedules, coding formats, and so on) in abstract terms that will retain a determinate sense across the varied situations where such expressions are intended to apply. Despite these efforts, the best laid categories, descriptions, and explanations always leave something out, need fudging, or contain inconsistencies that remain to be addressed on an ad hoc basis. It seems that language is *necessarily* indexical, so that any attempt to remedy the circumstantiality of one statement by producing a more exact rendition will preserve that very feature in the attempt. The phenomenon is thus truly unavoidable (Garfinkel, 1967: 4-7).

Instead of treating the indexical properties of expressions as a nuisance to be remedied, an alternative approach is to examine them as phenomena. After all, however "flawed" indexical expressions may seem when semantic clarity is entertained as an abstract ideal, in everyday life societal members are somehow able to produce, understand, and deal with such expressions on a routine basis. Hence, Garfinkel and Sacks (1970: 341) argue that the properties of indexical expressions are ordered, socially organized, properties; such orderliness, moreover, "is an ongoing, practical accomplishment of every actual occasion of commonplace speech and conduct." As we shall see, far from being a problem, for lay members of society the indexical properties of everyday language can be a resource for broadly social ends.

What, then, comprises the orderliness of indexical expressions? As one instance, Garfinkel and Sacks (1970) discuss "formulations" through which members describe, explain, characterize, summarize, or otherwise "say in so many words" what they are doing or talking about. Formulations are socially organized in that they may arise when the determinate gist of a potentially multi-faceted conversation has become problematic, and they regularly invite confirmation or denial (Heritage and Watson, 1979). As another instance of the orderliness to indexical properties, Garfinkel and Sacks (1970) discuss "glossing practices" and a collection of examples. One of these is "a definition used in first approximation." An author, at the beginning of an article, may offer a loose definition of some term, subsequently developing arguments and exhibits to elaborate the definition. At the end, the author will supply a second and more precise definition of the term, which formulates the features and connections among the exhibits, arguments, and definitions (Garfinkel and Sacks, 1970:364).

Neither formulations nor glosses, which are themselves indexical, can provide the essential means for rendering natural language expressions intelligible, however. Sacks [1967] (1992a: 720) takes up this very problem in his lectures on spoken interaction:

> If... somebody produced an utterance and you figured that a way to show that you understood it was to produce an explication of it, then that explication would pose exactly the task that the initial utterance posed. And one can see how rapidly that would become an impossible procedure, and in any event would involve some sorts of

constant, and possible indefinitely extended "time outs" in a conversation.

While the sense of an utterance cannot be achieved solely via its explicative potentiality, i.e., from formulations or glosses, Sacks argues that the mechanism of tying one utterance to another through "pro-terms" is an economical way of accomplishing intelligibility (cf. Watson, 1987). Pronouns, which may refer to some other noun or category on whose behalf they stand, are characteristic tying devices, as are what Sacks [1967] (1992a: 717) calls "pro-verbs":

> an interchange like, "Did John and Lisa go to the movies last night?" "They did." There, via "They did," we have tying within a pair.

Tying practices provide for the accomplishment of mutually intelligible interaction in two distinct ways. On the one hand, utterances which are tied to previous ones may be understood by attending to the prior course of talk (Sacks, [1967] 1992a: 717-718). Thus, in the above example the referent of the pro-verb ("did") is readily available from what preceded it ("go to the movies last night"). But in addition to facilitating understanding, tying is also a crucial means by which interactants display their understandings of antecedent utterances to one another. Because pronouns and pro-verbs must be selected to fit what came before, the production of an utterance tied to some prior utterance "is the basic means of showing that you understood that utterance" (Sacks, [1967] 1992a: 718; see also Sacks, Schegloff, and Jefferson, 1974: 728-9). In short, by relating adjacent utterances to one another, interactants can efficiently understand such utterances, display their understandings to one another, and see that they were understood, all without recourse to formulations, glosses, or other regressive explications.

Tying is not the only means by which participants relate utterances to one another to provide for their intelligibility, because understanding interaction involves far more than grasping the lexical meaning of pro-terms or other deictic words. Also relevant is the issue of what a given utterance is *doing* in the service of some recognizable *social action*, such as insulting, requesting, apologizing, joking, reporting some item of news, or whatever. Interactants can relate utterances to one another in terms of the actions they perform; hence, by *positioning* their talk in relation to some antecedent utterance, or in relation to some larger interactional trajectory, interactants can accomplish identifiable activities. Thus, Sacks [1972] (1992b: 530) commented on how the positioning of an utterance can provide in part for what it is doing, due to the "why that now" orientation of interactants (see also Schegloff and Sacks, 1973: 313):

> ... consider for example, that when you say "hello" at the beginning of a conversation, the account for saying "hello" is that it's the beginning of the conversation. So by putting an utterance like that where you put it, you provide an explanation for why you said that

thing. And there are whole ranges of ways whereby parties position their utterances. By "position" I mean that they show, in an utterance's construction, that they know where they're doing it, and why they're doing it then and there.

The phenomena of tying and positioning imply that the *sequential features* of interaction are pervasively operative in the processes by which participants produce, understand, and exploit indexical expressions of every sort. In this sense, the conversation analytic investigation of sequential phenomena -- from simple adjacency pairs to the overall structural organization of a conversation -- can be seen as an extended analysis of the "ordered and socially organized" properties of indexical expressions that Garfinkel, in his own writings as well as his collaboration with Sacks (1970), nominated for study.

This domain of organization, moreover, is a thoroughly local and endogenous production, rather than, say, operating on behalf of some externally-based social structure, such as class, gender, or ethnicity. In that participants relate utterances to one another, a recipient who wishes to speak to whatever topic is on the floor is required to listen not just to some utterance-in-progress, but to the spate of previous talk, for it is in terms of this previous talk that the current utterance itself makes sense.[5] Additionally, when taking a turn of talk, a current speaker is required to demonstrate its relationship to an immediately previous utterance and, indirectly, to the utterances preceding it (Sacks, [1967] 1992a: 716-21).

Although sequential organization is a thoroughly local production, it is also a central means by which interactants, on a moment-by-moment basis, invoke larger interpersonal relationships and patterns of social "distance" and "intimacy" (Button, 1991; Goodwin, 1987; Jefferson, Sacks, and Schegloff, 1987; Maynard and Zimmerman, 1984). For instance, one can show that some current conversation is a developmental moment in the accomplished history of a relationship by connecting the current with a last meeting. Examples that Sacks [1970] (1992b: 193) provides are "You put up your hair" (as a remark when returning to somebody's house) and "How's your mother?", both of which show attention to "...that part of 'us' that is involved in our last interaction."[6]

Thus, in a variety of ways, utterances and their indexical properties provide a window through which to gaze upon the bedrock of social order. Actors produce mutually intelligible courses of talk, and achieve all manner of relationship, interdependence, and commitment (Rawls, 1989a) through the design and placement of single utterances in relation to the immediate environment of vocal and nonvocal activities. The investigation of this domain of organization is, then, one substantive bond between ethnomethodology and conversation analysis.

Since we started this section with a discussion of the Garfinkel and Sacks (1970) paper, it is appropriate to end there as well, for the paper also provides a clue as to what significantly differentiates ethnomethodology and conversation analysis, a subject that we will pursue further later on. While the paper demonstrates that the properties of indexical expressions are achievedly ordered ones and thereby establishes a hitherto overlooked topic for sociological inquiry, it is mainly illustrative. How investigators are to decompose these indexical properties to lay bare the social organization of talk, and indeed what that organization might consist of, remains largely unspecified. This tendency toward illustration is characteristic of early ethnomethodology, and it encouraged many rediscoveries of what came to be called "indexicality," as well "reflexivity," "embodied action," and other core ethnomethodological concepts, in each new setting that the investigators entered (e.g., Baccus, 1986). Early textbooks, such as Handel's (1982: 40-45) and Leiter's (1980: 107-116) devoted entire sections to such topics. With regard to "indexicality," the textbook pattern was to show how it is an invariant feature of talk, and, following Cicourel (1974; 1981), to suggest that members' use their knowledge of the *ethnographic context* to understand otherwise ambiguous utterances. While this approach clearly demonstrated the pervasiveness of "indexicality" and the relation of talk to its context in a general way, it was less successful in setting forth a systematic program for explicating the orderliness of indexical phenomena.

Instead of relying on vague notions of "context" and relatively uncontrolled recourse to ethnographic description in the service of providing illustrative studies and demonstrations, Sacks identified a principle, that of sequential organization, which is pervasively implicated in the processes by which interactants exploit the indexical properties of utterances, achieve local understandings of them, and display such understandings to one another. This form of organization embodies investigable practices through which parties to an interaction precisely time and place their talk so as to both demonstrate one's heed for another's activity and to claim others' attention to one's own in the collaborative building of a course of action.

Having identified sequential organization as a phenomenon, conversation analysis also offers a programmatic way of studying interactionally situated language practices. In a sense, conversation analysis reverses the usual ethnomethodological practice of treating what have been "resources" for sociological inquiry (e.g., indexical expressions) as "topics" of investigation. Garfinkel and Sacks (1970), in arguing that the properties of indexical expressions are achievedly ordered, called attention to a previously unexamined phenomenon and thus made it available for sociological study. When Sacks went beyond this to identify a particular ordering principle -- namely, sequential organization -- he not only established this domain as a topic but provided a resource for continuing research into the turn by turn process by which members perform ordinary social activities. As research has progressed, the investigation of sequential phenomena has become an objective in its own right, and is now pursued in partial independence of the earlier ethnomethodological interest in indexical properties. The task of what Schegloff (1984: 50) refers to as "explicating the various sequential organizations of conversation, and interaction, and, importantly, their integration" has become a well-established program of research; conversation analysts are collectively engaged in the task of identifying types of sequences, analyzing their organizational properties, documenting modifications in institutional settings, and the like. For the moment, then, we wish to note that Sacks initiated a more definitive and potentially cumulative empirical program than was previously available. That programmatic inquiries also might have inherent limitations is a matter to which we will return.

## Achieved Organization: Rules and Sequential Organization

The empirical productivity of CA might seem to represent a fundamental departure from the analytic attitude of ethnomethodology, which has a strong "nonconstructive" or "deconstructive" character. Ethnomethodology may be understood as a form of inquiry which avoids making claims about the substantive character of social life, and investigates instead how social phenomena, whatever their character, are accountably achieved in local environments of action. It is because of this stance that ethnomethodologists have traditionally remained "indifferent" to the results of classical sociological research and theorizing (Garfinkel and Wieder, 1992: 186). Conversation analytic inquiry, by contrast, does seem to render positive characterizations of social phenomena, characterizations that encompass not only the underlying *processes* of interaction but its accountable *products* as well. Research on turn taking, for example, began by specifying the organization of turn taking in ordinary conversation (Sacks, Schegloff, and Jefferson, 1974), and this has served as a foundation for investigating patterns of turn taking in a range of institutional settings, including classroom lessons (McHoul, 1978), trial examinations (Atkinson and Drew, 1979), news interviews (Greatbatch, 1988), and doctor-patient interactions (Frankel, 1990). Correspondingly, descriptions of specific sequences and their organizational properties continue to accumulate.

These developments have generated unease among some ethnomethodologists; in particular, turn taking analyses have been criticized for their formalism (cf., Liberman, 1985; Lynch, 1985: Chapter 5; Molotch and Boden, 1985; O'Connell, et al., 1990; Peyrot, 1982). For instance, Livingston (1987: 73) argues that descriptions of abstract rules for turn taking fail to capture the embodied work by which conversationalists exhibit and ensure that their talk is accountably being done turn-by-turn. We shall argue that although conversation analytic inquiries are in a sense "constructive" and seek to produce formal descriptions of interactional structures, such inquiries show continued attention to the situated practices through which interactional structures are incrementally achieved. This focus on achieved organization thus represents another point of contact between ethnomethodology and conversation analysis.

Within ethnomethodology, the emphasis on achieved organization is perhaps clearest in studies that challenge rule-based models of social action characteristic of classical sociological theory and research (Wilson, 1970). This aspect of ethnomethodology has been extensively discussed elsewhere (e.g., Heritage, 1984: Chapter 5; 1987: 240-248; Maynard and Clayman,

1991: 390-91), so we will only briefly review some of the main issues involved. Garfinkel has consistently criticized the received view propounded by Parsons and others that norms, conventions, or other rules of conduct operate as explanatory agents in the determination of courses of action. A major difficulty with normative theories of action lies in the unresolved relationship between abstract rules and the concrete real-world circumstances in which societal members must act. While rules provide rather general formulations of appropriate conduct, social situations have idiosyncratic features which distinguish them from one another. This raises the problem of how actors come to know whether the particular situation in which they find themselves falls within the domain of a given rule, and hence whether that rule should relevantly come into play. This problem is irremediable in just the way in which indexical expressions are irremediable; no matter how elaborate a normative formulation might be, it cannot encompass all possible circumstantial contingencies. This problematic is the focus of Garfinkel's discussion of the followability of coding instructions (1967: 18-24), in which he observes that coders' decisions are inevitably contingent on a range of ad hoc considerations which are not specified in the coding rules and which cannot be eliminated by elaborations of those rules. Similarly, jury decisions concerning guilt or innocence are not determined by prespecified legalistic criteria (Garfinkel, 1967: Chapter 4).

It would be incorrect to conclude from this that rules are irrelevant to the organization of social action. For societal members, social life is experienced as anything but arbitrary; activities are generally perceived as highly patterned and regular, and such regularities are frequently explained by members in terms of norms of various sorts. Garfinkel treats the apparent rule-governedness of action as a phenomenon, an endogenous achievement in which rules serve not as causal agents in the determination of action but as resources that members use when making sense of action. Here, Garfinkel's discussion of the documentary method of interpretation (1967: Chapter 3), which specifies how particulars and contexts within a perceptual field mutually elaborate one another, may be applied to understand the co-constitutive relationship between rules of conduct and situated actions (Zimmerman, 1970; Wieder, [1974] 1988). For jurors, or coders, or anyone in "common sense situations of choice," rules of various sorts provide for the intelligibility and accountability of social action. As members assemble and orient to relevant aspects of the circumstances at hand (e.g., the categorical identities of the interactants, the type of social or institutional setting in which they are situated, etc.), they understand and describe actions in terms provided by the norms and conventions which are presumed to be operative within those circumstances. In some cases, actions may be accountable as deviations from those rules, and are supplied with "secondarily elaborative" explanations (Heritage, 1987: 246) involving special motives or other contingencies. For both perceivedly "normal" and "deviant" actions, then, norms play an important role in the process by which members grasp what a given behavior is "doing." Moreover, by persistently accounting for the range of actions within a setting either in terms of some primary norm or a range of exceptional circumstances, that norm is preserved across "entropic" events which might otherwise threaten its experiential reality (Heritage, 1987: 246-247). A rule, therefore, does not stand outside of social settings as an exogenous ordering principle, and it cannot in itself provide for the orderliness of social life. Rather, rules are used and applied by societal members themselves (together with other ordering practices) within social settings as a way of making sense of and explaining their own activities. It is this situated accounting work that particularizes and reconciles abstract rules with the details of actual conduct and thus provides for the maintenance of accountable patterns of social life.

Against this backdrop, conversation analytic findings -- such as procedures for turn taking, various sequence organizations, and the like -- may at first glance seem to be rule-like formulations of proper interactional conduct. Sacks may have unwittingly fostered this impression by his use of mechanistic metaphors; he often referred to "the technology" or "the machinery" of conversation and characterized his program of research as an attempt to isolate and describe "the machinery" through which interactions are generated (Sacks, 1984a: 26-27; 1984b: 413-414). However, this terminology was used metaphorically rather than literally, mainly in the context of lectures to students where it served a necessary pedagogical function. Sacks was seeking to overcome the deeply entrenched tendency to view the details of interaction as random or disorderly, or to dismiss them as mere "manners of speaking." By means of the "conversational machinery" rubric, Sacks encouraged his students to assume the opposite; that is, to treat every interactional event, no matter how seemingly small or trivial, as a potentially orderly phenomenon. Perhaps indirectly, Sacks was also addressing his colleagues within the social sciences (e.g., 1984a: 22), who tended to neglect the study of talk-in-interaction in favor of what were generally perceived as "bigger" or "more important" issues. In anthropology and sociology, interest in the structural properties of cultures and social systems greatly overshadowed social interaction as an object of study, and the few attempts to take on the topic of social action (e.g., Weber, Parsons, and Bales) dealt not with concrete activities but with abstract typologies and properties of action that could be readily linked to structural, historical, or other "macro" levels of analysis. And within linguistics, the analysis of language as a formal, self-contained, system of competences (a la Chomsky) forestalled inquiry into how speakers acquire linguistic competences and put them to use in real circumstances. Accordingly, Sacks' use of the "conversational machinery" rubric must be viewed in the context of his efforts to justify inquiry into a domain that had been marginalized and was often regarded -- by both students and colleagues alike -- as a messy "garbage can" of errors, accidents, and random processes.

Conversation analytic investigations have sought to document the orderly, sequential structures of interaction, but in classic ethnomethodological fashion the locus of order is the situated work of the interactants themselves rather than abstract or disembodied rules. This emphasis is manifest in a number of ways, but perhaps the most fundamental is the familiar practice within CA of building analyses out of singular fragments of actual, naturally occurring talk.

Thus, Sacks has observed that although conversation analysts seek to specify the generic "technology of conversation,"

> we are trying to *find* this technology out of actual fragments of conversation so that we can impose as a constraint that the technology actually deals with singular events and singular sequences of events (Sacks, [1970] 1984b: 414).

Analysis thus begins with a given interactional form as it is enacted within, and thereby organizes, some concrete situation. By proceeding on a case by case basis, analysts approach a more general understanding of how the form operates across diverse situations. This way of working produces findings which are neither Weberian ideal types nor Durkheimian averages (Sacks, 1963), findings which can be reconciled with, and are thus answerable to, singular instances of conduct. Correspondingly, the approach specifies a given sequential form in terms of the situated practices out of which instances are composed, rather than in terms of pristine rules of conduct.

Hence, far from being immutable Platonic forms, the sequential structures of CA are comprised of flexible social practices which are highly sensitive to changing circumstances. In the analysis of deviant cases (discussed previously) substantial attention is devoted to courses of talk that *do not* run off canonically due to problematic local contingencies. Such cases reveal that interactants guide their speaking practices in accordance with, and as a constitutive feature of, the particular circumstances at hand, even as they sustain and reproduce more general interactional forms. For example, studies of turn taking have devoted extensive attention to cases where the parties find themselves to be talking in overlap (Sacks, Schegloff, and Jefferson, 1974: 723-724; Jefferson and Schegloff, 1975; Jefferson, 1973; 1986; Lerner, 1989; Schegloff, 1987). Overlapping talk is plainly incongruous with the way in which turn taking is usually managed. It can also disrupt subsequent talk insofar as it interferes with a recipient's capacity to analyze and understand the talk in progress as a prerequisite for determining when and how to speak next (Schegloff, 1987). As it turns out, overlapping talk is by no means a rare event, but it is usually short-lived, in part because at least one of the parties will stop talking in mid-utterance, before a turn constructional unit is completed. Moreover, the speaker who emerges in control of the floor may subsequently take steps to retrieve what was lost in overlap (Jefferson and Schegloff, 1975; Schegloff, 1987). For example, the speaker may cut off and restart his or her turn in such a way as to absorb the overlap from a competing speaker and thus produce a full unit of talk unfettered and in the clear (Schegloff, 1987). These responses to overlapping talk operate to preserve the intelligibility of what is currently being said. In so doing, they also restore regular patterns of turn taking, but they do so only by momentarily disrupting -- through cut-offs and restarts -- the canonical progression of turn constructional units.

Speakers also abort and restart units of talk in other circumstances. Goodwin (1981: Chapter 2) has shown that when the speaker of a turn-at-talk notices a recipient's gaze begin to wander, that speaker will frequently cut off and restart the turn-in-progress, a move that regularly prompts the intended recipient to gaze back toward the speaker. Hence, what might initially seem to be a speech error or disfluency resulting from a problem in the thought processes presumed to underly speech, is in fact a methodical social practice, one that has orderly consequences for ongoing patterns of turn taking and displays of recipiency.

Accordingly, interactants do not enact the turn taking system, or any organization of talk, in a mechanical fashion. While the preceding examples were drawn from studies of turn taking and gaze direction, studies of sequences exhibit the same concern with specifying organizational forms in terms of the situated practices through which they are enacted.[7] The analysis of deviant, problematic, or incongruous cases demonstrates that interactants inevitably act in ways that are sensitive to, and part and parcel of, emergent circumstances and conditions within the local environment of action.

Sequential structures of talk are achieved not only during problematic cases. From an ethnomethodological point of view, even courses of action which run off "routinely" must be regarded as "achievements arrived at out of a welter of possibilities for preemptive moves or claims, rather than a mechanical or automatic playing out of pre-scripted routines" (Schegloff, 1986: 115). To respecify interactional routines as achievements, there has been a strong emphasis on comparative analyses of various kinds: analyses which compare not only "canonical" with "deviant" cases, but also alternate ways of interacting in different contexts. As a consequence, analysts remain sensitive to what interactants do, as well as what they refrain from doing, in order to realize a given course of action.

Consider, for example, how interactants produce stories and other extended courses of talk involving multiple turn constructional units. Within ordinary conversation, story forms cannot be realized unless the turn taking system for conversation is modified to allow the story-teller (or in some instances two or more story-tellers; see Lerner, 1992) primary access to the floor for an extended period. This modification is set in motion when the speaker initially projects that an extended telling is forthcoming (for instance by producing a story preface; see Sacks, 1974). This is by no means the end of the process, however; also essential to the realization of a story are the other interactants, who align as story recipients (or take up other interactional identities in relation to the story; see Goodwin, 1984) by withholding a range of turn types (Sacks, 1974) and by engaging in specific forms of body movement and posturing (Goodwin, 1984) while the story is unfolding. Similarly, news interviews regularly consist of journalists asking questions and public figures responding (Greatbatch, 1988). However, since journalists often produce one or more statements as a way of leading up to the question, question-answer sequences are achieved only insofar as public figures withhold speaking in response to these statements until the question is delivered. This is just one instance of an "institutional" form of talk which is constituted in part by reductions in the range of practices which are available for use in ordinary conversation (e.g., Clayman, 1989; Heritage, 1985; Heritage and Greatbatch,

1991; Whalen and Zimmerman, 1987). In each of these cases, a given sequential form is constituted in part by the *systematic absence* of talk at points where such talk might otherwise be relevant.[8] These absences provide for the accountable achievement of the organizational form in question in two distinct ways. First, the absences show that the interactants treat each unit of talk as one component of a larger sequence-in-progress, and are thus oriented to that larger sequence-in-progress on a moment-by-moment basis. Secondly, such absences facilitate the realization of the sequence as an accomplished fact.

Finally, it should be noted that CA studies are not confined to cases where sequential forms are successfully achieved, maintained, or repaired. Substantial attention has also been paid to cases where such forms are subverted or transformed by interactants in pursuit of some local interactional work or objective. Thus, interactants may remain silent following a question or a summons as a way of accountably "snubbing" an interactional coparticipant (Schegloff, 1968). Or they may depart from standard turn taking procedures by beginning to speak a bit "early," before the current unit of talk is complete, as a way of displaying recognition or independent knowledge of what is being said (Jefferson, 1973). To take one final example, interactants may say "uh huh," which usually occurs *within* an extended story and serves as a display of passive recipiency, at the *completion* of a discourse unit, where it accountably "resists" a more substantive response (Jefferson, 1984). Also relevant here are cases where highly specialized institutional forms of talk "break down" in spectacular ways (Clayman and Whalen, 1988/89; Schegloff, 1988/89; Whalen, Zimmerman, and Whalen, 1988). In many of these cases the transformative action acquires its sense in part by reference to the organizational form from which it departs; for example, the production of "uh huh" cannot be heard as "resistant" unless the stronger forms of receipt are tacitly oriented to as potentially relevant.

It should now be apparent that while conversation analysts seek to isolate and describe sequential forms of a highly general nature, these forms are specified in terms of the concrete situated practices through which they are contingently realized, rather than in terms of abstract rules of conduct. Thus every effort is made to avoid general or ideal-typical characterizations of interactional procedures in favor of attending to specific instances as they unfold within, are shaped by, and in turn organize, concrete circumstances. Correspondingly, rather than treat any particular sequence of activities as a *fait accompli*, investigators seek, through comparative analyses, to remain alive to the various possibilities for action that branch out from successive junctures within interaction as it develops. By these various means CA, consistent with its ethnomethodological heritage, seeks to recover the constitutive processes involved in the production and maintenance of seemingly "natural" and "routine" conversational patterns.

## Achieved Organization: Sequential Component Production

While CA retains a lively sense of sequential structures as achievements, what about the singular activities that comprise sequences? How are these activities assembled, recognized, and thus rendered consequential within a developing course of talk? This problem of sequential *component production* can be elaborated by juxtaposing two investigations of a most mundane event in daily life: the opening of a telephone call. As we have already noted, Schegloff's (1968) study of telephone openings revealed that they are managed through a distinct type of adjacency pair: the summons-answer sequence. Because the sequence components are linked by the property of conditional relevance, and because its completion projects further talk by the initiator of the sequence, this sequence enables parties to coordinate entry into conversation. Schegloff's elegant analysis demonstrates an achieved, unitary solution to the problem of coordinated entry that operates across a variety of settings, across vocal and non-vocal activities, and even across the duration of a single conversation. Nevertheless, there is further orderliness to conversational openings than a strictly sequential analysis provides. In addition to the logic and organization of sequences, there is also the question of how the actions that set sequences in motion (e.g., summonses) are recognizably constituted. This topic has been investigated within both conversation analysis and ethnomethodology, and the way it has been approached provides insight into further aspects of their relationship.

1. Conversation Analysis

Schegloff's early work on telephone openings (1968, 1970, 1986) focuses attention not only on summons-answer sequences and their sequelae, but also on summonses as phenomena in their own right. Thus, Schegloff (1968: 376) observes that the ringing of a telephone achieves the properties of a summons as a result of social and interactional processes.

> The activity of summoning is not intrinsic to the items that compose it; it is an assembled product whose efficacious properties are cooperatively yielded by the interactive work of both summoner and answerer.

Consider that "who" a ringing phone is summoning depends upon how an actor, in concert with others, forges the social environment in which that event occurs. This process can include:[9] (a) how one *categorizes and orients to* the environment -- as one's own office or home, or someone else's office or home, or a public domain, and so on; (b) the *spatial positionings and activities* of members of an office or household vis a vis one another and the telephone -- for instance, the person who is nearest to a ringing phone, or is not presently "working" or otherwise engaged, may be treated as the "summoned" party; (c) the *expectations* that result from relationships, routines, and arrangements which enable one party to anticipate that the other will call one just here, just now -- for example, "my wife's parents call every Thursday night about this time"; (d) the *informings* that are available prior to or during the phone-ring, such as "Jane should be calling soon," or "That's Jane"; (e) whether one is using a phone and calling someone else, such that the ringing represents an "outgoing" summons on the other end of the line, or is merely in the vicinity of an inert phone that commences to ring with a bell or other noise that can be taken as an "incoming" summons.

Consider also that there is, loosely speaking, a "proper" number of rings to a summoning phone -- not too few and not too many -- which a summoned party and others may work to achieve (Schegloff, 1986: 118-119). Thus, in addition to those items listed above, (f) persons who are close by the phone often let it ring several times before answering. Apart from whatever psychological factors might lie behind this tendency, one interactional consideration is that quick-answering is something that can be topicalized, as in "you were sitting by the phone," or "waiting for someone to call," etc. Such topicalization can then taken on its own dynamic, requiring determinate effort to exit, and may well be avoided by allowing some rings to pass. Correspondingly, (g) persons far from the phone sometimes rush to it. Obviously, this is in part because the recipient knows that the caller might make the inference that no one is home and thus hang up before the connection is made. But multiple rings are also vulnerable to topicalization in the way that few rings are; there may be inquiries about where the summoned party was so that a call recipient has to explain the delay in answering, and thus answering a summoning phone "late" may also be something to avoid. Finally, (h) answerers sometimes await the end of a ring or until the next ring has just started before picking up the phone. In light of such observations, Schegloff (1986: 120) concludes that "the actually heard rings [of a summoning phone] are not a random or mechanical matter, but are the product of distinct and methodical forms of conduct by the participants" (Schegloff, 1986: 120).

There is, then, within conversation analysis, concern not just for sequencing and turn taking as such, but also for how the components of these organizations are socially assembled, orderly objects in their own right. However, with respect to conversation analytic work on component production, the preceding analysis of summonses is somewhat atypical, in part because it is based on research done in the late 1960s and early 1970s, before conversation analysis attained its present form. Thus, Schegloff combines conversation analytic methods based on recorded data with more traditional ethnographic data to shed light on how summonses are assembled. Sacks' early lectures on how members "do" specific activities so as to be recognizable as such, and his work on membership categorization devices, are similarly eclectic (e.g., Sacks 1972). More recent conversation analytic work on sequential component production entails a more sustained focus on naturally occurring practices which are available on recorded materials and transcripts of them. Some studies examine various details of utterance design as they figure in the achievement of specific activities (e.g., Boden, in press: Chapter 3;

Drew, 1984; Maynard, 1984: Chapter 3; Pomerantz, 1980; Schegloff, 1988; 1992b; Watson, 1990) and as they impart subtle nuances to activities (Heritage, 1990; Heritage and Sorjonen, 1992). Others examine how turns are shaped by recipients' activities and are thus, in a literal sense, interactionally constructed (C. Goodwin, 1979, 1981; Lerner, 1991). Still others concentrate on sequential and institutional positioning as it figures in the process by which activities are recognized and understood; we reviewed some of this work in our earlier discussion of indexical expressions and sequential organization (e.g., Schegloff, 1984; Whalen and Zimmerman, 1987; Wilson, 1991).

Despite this attention to sequential components and their assembly, within CA the investigation of sequencing remains the primary focus of attention. By comparison, component production has been only intermittently addressed, often in the context of papers that deal mainly with sequencing, or in papers that use sequential positioning as a way of approaching the problem of component production. Insofar as this problem is taken up, it is addressed in classic CA fashion by way of naturally occurring examples, although these have been analyzed from somewhat different perspectives.[10]

2. Ethnomethodology

We turn now to consider what an ethnomethodological approach, based on contrived demonstrations like the breaching experiments discussed earlier, has to offer. While Garfinkel has not been concerned with sequential organization as such, he does discuss the matter of component production in his "summoning phone" exercise, which seeks to penetrate and decompose the utter familiarity of a ringing telephone. Students are asked to gather tape recordings of ringing phones that are (a) hearably summoning just them, (b) hearably summoning someone else, (c) simulating hearably summoning just them, (d) simulating hearably summoning someone else, and (e) just ringing rather than "summoning." Students are to keep detailed ethnographic notes as to how they made these collections, the conversations they engaged in to achieve their objectives, and so on. A brief explication of this exercise, which demonstrates how "methodic procedures" render lived experience and its intrinsic orderliness into "signed objects" whose interpretation necessarily loses a grasp of such orderliness, is now published in Garfinkel and Wieder (1992). We draw on that paper plus our participation in seminars at the University of Wisconsin when Garfinkel was a visiting professor in 1988 and 1990. While such participation provides a more adequate understanding than does a written account, we hope to harvest several points in the ensuing pages. Interested readers can experience the exercise first-hand by following the instructions outlined in Garfinkel and Wieder (1992), and gain deeper appreciation of the argument.

Products of the exercise include recordings and extensive notes regarding the collection of those recordings. The aim is to recover the "more, other, different" details that are ignored and yet depended upon in the response to a ringing or summoning phone (Garfinkel and Wieder, 1992: 203). Ordinarily these details remain invisible to the participants, but the exercise renders them conspicuous in a surprising way. We wish to consider two examples of properties that inhere in such seen-but-unnoticed details. First, the *background* from which a phone-ringing emerges depends upon an actor selecting some high-pitched frequency from a heretofore differently constructed ambiance that immediately has the character of silence out of which the just-now hearable phone-ring emerged. That phone-ringing, in other words, is heard via its functional relationship to the prior silence it simultaneously composes as "preceding" the ring (Garfinkel and Wieder, 1992: 195). This aspect of ringing phones is partly revealed by the simulation, where one might call another person to obtain a call-back that "hearably simulates" summoning the originator. In the simulated case there is a moment of anticipation anterior to the first ring, rather than a "preceding silence" composed simultaneously with the onset of ringing. In other words, "waiting-for-the-first-ring-according-to-the-agreement" is a part of the background that distinguishes the simulation from the actual episode, which is revealed to have a taken-for-granted background of "no telling when."

A second property of summoning phones is the *directionality* of the ring. In order to determine whether a phone is "hearably summoning" oneself, the potential answerer seeks to determine where the ring originates. Wherever the hearer might be, he or she seeks to determine if the ringing is coming from close or far, to the right or left, from in front or behind, and so on. As Garfinkel and Wieder (1992: 197) remark:

> Experimental perception studies are thick with demonstrations that the direction from which a sound is heard is a detail with which the listened to sound is recognized and identified as a sounded doing.

The property of directionality, while unnoticed in the daily routine of answering phones, emerges from Garfinkel's exercise as participants begin to distinguish how a phone can be hearably summoning a particular someone -- i.e., either the experimenter or another party. It is partly through imbuing a ringing sound with spatial attributes that one decides what the sound is and whether and how to respond.

When examined for such properties as its background and directionality, the "functional significance" (Gurwitsch, 1964: 114-122) of each summoning phone, or group (such as those "hearably summoning me" vs. those "simulating hearably summoning me") is essentially unique, a quiddity, or, as Garfinkel and Wieder (1992: 202) put it, an "assemblage of haeccities." Such quiddities or haeccities, *along with their structures of detail*, are collapsed, eviscerated, suppressed, or otherwise lost whenever, through some "methodic procedure," such as a recording technology or rule for counting, investigators represent a summoning episode through a depiction, illustration, categorization, classification, description, label, name, or any other "signed object." Signed objects give the original event an "interpreted significance," and it is the bane of analysis to be committed to such interpretation:

> ... the signed object exhibits the episode as a publicly verifiable object; it exhibits the episode's topical elaboration and exhibits what

> the episode's proper topics could be; it exhibits reasoned discourse about the episode; it exhibits the episode's observable, detectable, demonstrable, discourseable rational properties -- i.e., its calculability, its strategic efficacy, just what about it is available to the consequences of its occurrence, its predictability, its reproducibility, etc.; it provides for what the episode's topics as matters of rational discourse could consist of; it provides for the episode's topics specified as data; it exhibits in the foregoing practical aspects the episode's transcendental orderliness; it exhibits the foregoing in established terms for competent members in a natural language. (Garfinkel and Wieder, 1992: 200).

Signed objects are inclusive of terms such as "summonses" and "answers." To refer to a summons-answer sequence, in other words, can hide from analytic appreciation the lived work of participants producing soundings that emerge for them as this or that particular "summons" to be handled in some specific way.

This point, rather than marking a difference between ethnomethodology and conversation analysis, converges with Schegloff's observation that summoning is an "assembled product." What is distinctive about the ethnomethodological approach is, first, a concern to unlock the unseen, the unnoticed, the invisible, but to do so through some contrivance rather than observing naturally occurring processes or records thereof. In this respect, the summoning phones exercise is reminiscent of early ethnomethodological investigative strategies.

The second distinguishing feature, not found in previous ethnomethodological research, is the concept of "unique adequacy." The idea is that the phenomena of everyday life, without exception, already possess whatever methods they require for their own observation, recognition, collection, and analysis (Garfinkel and Wieder, 1992: 182-84). Summonses might be first pair parts that make answers conditionally relevant, and thus serve to initiate a conversational sequence through which participants can coordinate and make accountable their entry into conversation, but those summonses are also phenomena of orderly achievement, with an in vivo coherence and endogenously affiliated methods for assembly and detection as accountably namable objects. The unique adequacy principle also applies to any and all order-productive practices that an ethnomethodologist might identify. Thus, items (a) through (h) on the preceding list of summons-constitutive practices, as well as the "background" and "directionality" of a ringing phone, are themselves glosses for in situ accomplishments involving infinite depths of detail. *Any* principle by which it is possible to analytically order the phenomenal detail of everyday life is a detail of order that recursively permits appreciation of itself as an organized accomplishment. Such accomplishments are recoverable through the analyst's participation as a competent practitioner in and of the phenomenon being studied (Garfinkel and Wieder, 1992: 182).

The ethnomethodological approach has a third feature which distinguishes it from conversation analysis, and that is the posing of an additional topic for investigation. One purpose of the summoning phone exercise, and related exercises, is to penetrate the familiarity of everyday objects to reveal the "developing contexture of recognizable constituent significations" (Garfinkel and Wieder, 1992: 206) which comprise the object as it is embedded in lived experience. Regularly, however, the "skillful, analytic methods" of classic sociological studies turn this structure of detail, this achieved organization -- i.e., lived experience and its intrinsic orderliness -- into signed objects whose interpretation necessarily loses grasp of such orderliness. Classical studies do this in and through a practice that Garfinkel calls "the rendering theorem," which concerns the relationships between (a) the actually-experienced and collaboratively-produced coherence of objects, (b) a methodic procedure for appropriating such coherence into (c) a collection of signs or an account, which gives actual coherence its "interpreted significance" (Garfinkel and Wieder, 1992). While classical studies are necessarily committed to (b) and (c) and thus to *renditions* of social life rather than the actuality of that life, ethnomethodologists confront the work whereby members produce the naturally accountable objects of everyday life (that is, (a) above). But in addition to this topic, ethnomethodologists also examine the rendering theorem itself as an endemic organizational feature of society (cf., Hilbert, 1992). By means of this theorem, members are perpetually engaged in the task of dismissing the lived, embodied work of accomplishing the most ordinary worldly things, including such humble activities as "summoning." Thus, while both ethnomethodology and conversation analysis are concerned with the achieved organization of component activities, only ethnomethodology poses as a topic of order the ubiquity of the rendering theorem as it operates across lay and professional modes of discourse.

As is characteristic of his overall body of work, Garfinkel's summoning phones exercise is vigorously and insistently suggestive in its probing of the ordinariness of an object of common experience. Nevertheless, the form of research portended by this exercise -- and the article in which it is presented (Garfinkel and Wieder, 1992) -- can be elusive. On the one hand, ethnomethodology continues to be cast as a form of empirical inquiry oriented toward a phenomenal domain of order-productive practices. At the same time, specific "policies and methods" appear to pull the enterprise in a more "radical" direction whose contours remain largely unspecified (cf., Pollner, 1991), although it does seem to forestall the accumulation and codification of research findings. For instance, a strict interpretation of the rendering theorem would seem to preclude analysis *in any form*, because that would be a "rendering" and hence incompatible with an enterprise that claims to be confronting the actuality of lived processes -- including processes of rendering -- in particular settings. It is difficult to grasp what form of inquiry might follow from such principles; what its findings might look like; and in what form they might be conveyed to colleagues within a scholarly community. This unresolved tension between what might be termed "social scientific" and "radical" tendencies (cf., Wilson, 1992) is not necessarily cause for alarm, however. It is precisely this tension that gives ethnomethodology its distinctive intellectual cast, and is arguably responsible for some of the unique insights that ethnomethodology has bequeathed to the social sciences. The insistence on "radical inquiry" is also a reminder that sociological investigation should periodically return to the everyday world to explicate features that cannot be reduced to "practices" or "methods" of whatever sort. As Garfinkel (1988) has argued, organizational features of everyday life require *discovery*, and investigators must be willing to bracket received "methodic procedures" of every sort in order to unearth that which is most fundamental to the orderliness of lived experience.

## Conclusion

In tracing the linkages between ethnomethodology and conversation analysis, we have purposely avoided pejorative statements regarding either enterprise. The field is not lacking in such statements; some ethnomethodologists have directed broadsides against the conversation analytic enterprise. Livingston (1987: 85) has criticized the "received" version of conversation analysis, Lynch and Bogen (1990) object to conversation analytic "foundationalism," and Garfinkel and Wieder (1992: 201) refer to "canonical" conversation analysis. We know of no comparable conversation analytic criticisms of ethnomethodology, although a reading of the literature might suggest that conversation analysts, by selective citations, at times neglect the ethnomethodological groundwork to which they are indebted. To the extent that they exist, we think the broadsides and neglect are unnecessary and counterproductive, for they obfuscate important interrelationships. Making explicit these interrelationships -- in theory, in method, and in substance -- helps to distinguish both endeavors from conventional social scientific practice and facilitates recognition of the ways in which each endeavor offers progressive insights into the foundations of social organization.

Specifying interrelationships also helps define the relative strengths of each mode of investigation and suggests what can be yielded from complementary studies. To be sure, ethnomethodology provides an impetus for exploring radical phenomena, but with the exception of recent studies in a particular substantive domain -- namely, work in the discovering sciences (e.g., Bjelic and Lynch, 1992; Garfinkel, Lynch, and Livingston, 1981; Lynch, 1982; 1985) -- practitioners have had difficulty in advancing a coherent program for explicating these phenomena. As Garfinkel and his colleagues publish work that has existed primarily in lecture form, however, this state of affairs will undoubtedly change. For its part, conversation analysis has established a focused and productive research program based in part on ethnomethodological principles, and has generated substantive findings which build upon one another in a cumulative manner and which have had considerable influence on cognate disciplines (Heritage, 1987: 256). This is due in part to the remarkable "teachability" of conversation analysis, which does provide an almost paradigmatic array of data-gathering methods, analytic techniques, and exemplars for research, including the conversational foundation with which to specify constitutive procedures in and of various institutional settings.[11] Admittedly, any inquiry that sets a definitive trajectory, such as examining sequential organization, does run the risk that Livingston (1987: 78) has discussed as "objectifying" conversational structures. This tendency can be avoided with more emphasis on investigating sequential component production along the lines of Schegloff's early work on summonses, and more generally by retaining a continuing ethnomethodological sense of the "more and other" to sequences and other practices of talk-in-interaction. Otherwise, there is a danger of rendering the actuality of spoken interaction as "signed objects" which forestall further inquiry into interactants' constitutive practices. However, ethnomethodology is also susceptible to this tendency; inquiry can involve endless rediscoveries of essential phenomena, such as "reflexivity," "indexicality," "local historicity," and the "rendering theorem," so that ostensibly ethnomethodological investigations furnish produced objects with an "interpreted significance" rather than documenting the various indigenous methods of their achievement.

If ethnomethodology and conversation analysis face similar dangers, and assuming that both are empirical enterprises seeking to explicate a domain or domains of organizational phenomena, it would seem that there is much to be gained by explicit recognition of the potential for complementarity (e.g., Whalen, 1992; this volume). The overriding objective is to advance our knowledge of the inner workings of social life, and superior research in either area transcends the limitations of received concepts and established ways of working in pursuit of this goal. In proposing a complementarity between ethnomethodology and conversation analysis, we are far from suggesting a formal synthesis or from intimating that they are different "perspectives" on the "same" domain of social facts.[12] We simply mean that, without a conversation analytic branch, ethnomethodology might miss the opportunity for a directed line of inquiry and a focus that provides sustenance for at least some who carry a genuine commitment to the ethnomethodological sensibility and seek a way of actualizing it systematically. Without attending to its ethnomethodological roots, however, conversation analysis might overlook subtle and yet crucial aspects of interactional organization. In short, if we can continue the botanical metaphor, conversation analysis without ethnomethodology risks proliferating findings that are detached from their roots in members' ongoing constitutive activities. Ethnomethodology without its conversation analytic branches risks becoming root-bound, probing ever more deeply into the autochthonous ordering of society, but lacking an analytic apparatus that reaches for the sky.

* We would like to thank Paul ten Have, John Heritage, George Psathas, Manny Schegloff, and Tom Wilson for their comments and feedback on this paper.

1 We discuss the implications of "On Formal Structures of Practical Action" (Garfinkel and Sacks, 1970) below.

2 For more extended general discussions of ethnomethodology, see Boden (1990), Heritage (1984; 1987), Livingston (1987), Maynard and Clayman (1991), Sharrock and Anderson (1986), and Wilson and Zimmerman (1980). For discussions of conversation analysis in particular, see ten Have (1990), Heritage (1984: Chapter 8), Lee (1987), Whalen (1990), and Zimmerman (1988).

3 The Schutzian inspiration is most prominent in Garfinkel's early discussion of the breaching experiments (see Garfinkel, 1963), where the latter are presented as designed to violate specific assumptions of the natural attitude of everyday life as outlined by Schutz (e.g., the assumption of the congruency of relevances, the interchangeability of standpoints, etc.). However, when Garfinkel discusses these experiments several years later in his book (1967: Chapter 2), Schutz figures less prominently in the discussion. Although Gurwitsch is not cited in that chapter, his influence is broadly acknowledged in the preface (1967: ix).

4 On the distinction between causal/statistical laws and conversation analytic structures, see Heritage (1984: 245-53). In a somewhat different vein, see Coulter's (1983) discussion of the distinction between the "logical" structures of CA and the "contingent" structures derived from statistical or distributional investigations.

5 As one final example, consider Goodwin's (1986) analysis of gestures that are often paired with prototypical indexical or deictic terms such as "this" or "that." Through such pairings, a speaker can solicit the gaze of a recipient who is looking elsewhere. Once again, indexical expressions turn out to be significant for the maintenance of mutual involvement of an ongoing course of interaction.

6 For the possibility that such utterances are "micro events" that can comprise what Collins (1981) refers to as "interaction ritual chains," see Hilbert (1990). For an alternative view which is more appreciative of the autonomous ordering of utterances, see Rawls (1989).

7 See our earlier discussion of how adjacency pairs are realized when second pair parts are not initially forthcoming.

8 Systematic absences are somewhat different from what have been called "official absences" within CA (Schegloff, 1968: 1083ff). An item is "officially absent" when its nonoccurrence is noticed and explicitly oriented-to by the interactional coparticipants. By contrast, an item can be characterized as "systematically absent" when the investigator can: 1) formally characterize the sequential environment at hand, 2) show that the item in question regularly

occurs at that sequential juncture in other situations, and 3) show that in the present class of situations the item is regularly withheld.

9 Discussion of components such as those on the following list can be found in Schegloff (1968, 1970, 1986). The list of examples was also informed by taped and written comments of participants in seminars on ethnomethodology and conversation analysis at the University of Wisconsin.

10 For example, see Zimmerman's (1984) analysis and Schegloff's (1991) rejoinder.

11 For a general discussion of this point, see Drew and Heritage (1992), Heritage (1984: 280-290; 1987: 261), and Zimmerman and Boden (1991). For a sampling of empirical work, see Atkinson and Drew (1979), Clayman (1989), Greatbatch (1988), Maynard (1991), and Whalen and Zimmerman (1987).

12 For a penetrating critique of such perspectivism, see Watson and Sharrock (1991).

# 2

# Parties and Talking Together: Two Ways in Which Numbers Are Significant for Talk-in-Interaction*

Emanuel A. Schegloff

## I

Among sociology's intellectual ancestors, it was Georg Simmel who first brought sustained analytic attention to bear "On the significance of numbers for social life," in a classic essay bearing that title and in other essays on the theme "Quantitative aspects of the group" (in Simmel, 1950: 87-177). Of course, what Simmel introduced was a particular set of significances which numbers could have for social life. Some of the themes to which he called attention were subsequently developed within "mainline" social psychology, for example a preoccupation with coalitions and coalition formation in interaction (Caplow, 1968). Other themes were developed in directions bearing more on social structural concerns (e.g., Blau, 1977). Whatever the thematic direction of development, tracing the import of numbers is regularly accompanied by the sense of a bedrock analytic undertaking, a conviction that something with a first-order significance for the domain under examination is being engaged.

With the so-called "linguistic turn" in studies of the domain which was previously the prerogative of social psychology, occasions of interaction were increasingly referred to globally as "dialogues," little respecting the underlying semantic connation of "two"-ness in that term's Greek roots. And occasions which *were* dialogic, i.e., composed of two participants, came often to be referred to generically as "conversation" or "interaction." But the detailed technical organization of talk in interaction is sensitive to the number of participants because those participants can and do design their conduct and understand one another's conduct as shaped in part by reference to numbers of participants.

Here I mean to take up two somewhat related matters bearing on this theme. The first concerns one way in which variation in the number of participants is systematically dealt with in the organization of talk-in-interaction (the more general term which I will prefer to "conversation"). The second concerns the bearing which number of participants has on the forms which *simultaneous* talk can take when it occurs in talk-in-interaction, and in "ordinary conversation" in particular.

Both of these topics involve us in reflections on the organization of turn-taking in talk-in-interaction. This is in some ways unfortunate, because too many people believe that turn-taking is the only aspect of talk in interaction which conversation-analysts focus on, and it would be good to dispel this mis-impression. However, the most direct bearing of numbers on interaction concerns the organization and distribution of participation; *what* one does in interaction by virtue of the numbers of participants clearly depends upon one having an opportunity to do *something* in the first place. And, with respect to participating via *talk*, this implicates the organization of turn-taking. And so to the first of my topics.

## II

Unlike most other prevalent efforts to characterize the organization of the distribution of opportunities to talk, which are designed for two person interaction (e.g., Duncan, 1972; Duncan and Fiske, 1977; Jaffe and Feldstein, 1970; Cappella, 1979, 1980; Cappella and Planalp, 1981), the model of turn-taking proposed in the 1974 paper by Sacks, Schegloff and Jefferson (henceforth SSJ) presumes an unspecified number of participants. Indeed, one of Sacks' originating observations (Winter, 1965; cf. Sacks, 1992: Vol. I, p.95; but not explicitly addressed in the ensuing paper) was that the allocation of turns among more than two participants cannot be derived by extrapolation from the pattern characteristic for two -- namely, a pattern of alternation. For two, the pattern is ABABAB...; for three it is *not* ABCABCABC..., nor does there appear to be any determinate or formulaic pattern for three or more. Rather, as the SSJ paper claimed, there is a set of procedures by which participants, any number of participants, can organize the allocation of participation among themselves, on *that* occasion, honoring whatever relevant aspects of the occasion or the participants they find themselves constrained or disposed to honor given their culture, their attributes, etc. The turn-taking organization's design thus appears to be for "n" participants, with a special pattern for two participants deriving from it. The solution to the generic organizational problem of turn-taking, we proposed, was *procedural*, not formulaic; *interactional and contingent*, not stipulated or derivative from other aspects of social or cultural organization (although its realization on particular occasions could surely be made sensitive to such features of context). It seems clear enough that, although no limitation on numbers is *built in* to this mode of organizing participation, some actual limitations *do* turn out to operate. Above a certain number of participants, conversations become vulnerable to "schism," to division into a number of separate conversations, each of which is self-organized in the same way as the progenitor of the schism, into which the several separate conversations may subsequently remerge.

But there *is* an important provision which bears on number of participants which I have left out of this account so far, and which, although by no means new, I want to foreground as my first point here. And that is that the turn-taking system as described in SSJ organizes the distribution of talk not in the first instance among persons, but among *parties*. Now not uncommonly, of course, parties are composed of persons -- *single* persons. But on some occasions, or for some particular phase or topic or sequence *within* some occasion of talk-in-interaction, the aggregate of persons who are, as Erving Goffman called them, "ratified participants," are organized into parties, such that there are fewer parties than there are persons. Sometimes, these parties coincide with units of social organization which can be claimed to have a persistence and reality quite apart from the interaction -- for example, couples or families or economic or political associates. But they form a party in interaction not by virtue of this extra-interactional tie (they regularly do conduct themselves as separate parties, after all) but by virtue of interaction-specific contingencies and conduct. This can involve their relative alignment in current activities, such as the co-telling of a story or siding together in a disagreement, or their several attributes relative to a momentarily current interactional contingency, for example, whether they are host or guest, whether -- as a new increment is being added to a number of interactional participants -- they are the newly arrived or pre-present. Or the interactional contingencies can make their extrainteractional linkage relevant -- as when three couples discuss plans for the evening *as* three couples rather than as six persons.

The point is that, on the model of turn-taking with which I am operating, what is organized is the distribution and sizing of opportunities to participate among *parties*. If there are multi-person parties in the interaction, the turn-taking organization does not *necessarily* provide for the selection of a person to speak for the party, nor does it provide procedures for doing so (aside from a procedure, or device, for resolving overlapping talk if/when it arises, about which more in a moment).

Consequently, in understanding the interactional significance of simultaneous talk-in-interaction, and in appreciating its relevance to the assessment of models of turn-taking, one important discrimination will be between simultaneous talk between coincumbents of a single party on the one hand, and between separate parties on the other. One characteristic finding which results from close examination of a spate of talk in which a fair amount of simultaneous talk occurs is that much, and often all, of the simultaneous talk is between participants who, at that moment in the conversation, are co-incumbents of a party. Here I can offer only one exemplar of this quite characteristic occurrence.

Frieda and Reuben have come to have dinner at old friends Dave and Kathy's apartment, and on the way have stopped at a hospital to visit a mutual friend who is suspected of having cancer. They bring to the dinner what they think are good tidings, that the friend instead has a "giant fullicular lympho-blastoma" (which will eventually turn out to be cancer). On arrival, after an initial round of greetings and remarks about the apartment, the following transpires:

#1. KC-4:3

```
Reuben:  Hey we got good news.
 Kathy:  [I know.                                <---- a
  Dave:  [What's the good news.                  <---- a
Frieda:  [Ya heard it?                           <---- b
Reuben:  [Oh ya do?                              <---- b
         (0.5)
  Dave:  (What's-)
Reuben:  Oh good.
         (0.8)
  Dave:  Oh yeah, mmhmm
         (1.0)
 Kathy:  'xcept I don' know what a (0.2) giant
         fullicular:: lympho: blastoma is.
Reuben:  Who the hell does, ex[cept a] doctor.
 Kathy:                       [ Well ]
  Dave:  Mm.
 Kathy:  (I d'nno-)=
Frieda:  =This is nice=did you make this?
```

What I want to note about this is very simple. Although Reuben and Frieda on the one hand and Dave and Kathy on the other can be characterized in various ways, each of which would group them together -- for example, as married couples, as guests and hosts respectively, etc. (as well as in ways that would group them differently and separately, e.g., via gender), for the purposes of this sequence as it is initially projected they are respectively "the informed" and "the uninformed," the announcers and the news recipients -- a casting which is no less relevant for being factually incorrect (i.e., Kathy has spoken to the hospitalized friend after Reuben and Frieda visited him). Although two successive turn-positions are occupied by simultaneous talk, note that in each case the simultaneous talkers are co-incumbents of a same party of a sort directly relevant to the conversational business which is at that moment in progress.

In announcement sequences, of which this is designed to be an instance, as is projected by Reuben's "pre-announcement" (i.e., “Hey, we got good news;” cf. Terasaki, 1976), there is generally likely to be some sort of expression of “surprise.” What qualifies some bit of information for delivery in such a sequence is that it is figured by its teller to be not known to the targetted recipient(s) and hence potentially news. Either it will be, or the teller will react to its failure in this regard as itself news and/or a surprise. And that is what happens here.

Note then the following few points.

The first overlap (at the arrows marked "a") involves Dave and Kathy. They are cast as the news recipients in this projected and in-progress announcement sequence; in that regard they are co-incumbents of a party (their couple-hood and host status are not demonstrably relevant to the conduct of this sequence). Note that their co-incumbency is *not* based on their taking up similar stances toward the sequence in progress, for they do not do so. Although they talk simultanously, and although they both talk as projected news recipients, thereby showing their orientation to *that* as the basis for their talking at that point, they take up *opposite* alignments toward the projected news -- one claiming already to know it and thereby blocking progress by the teller from pre-announcement to announcement, the other validating the premise of not knowing the news item and forwarding the projected sequence to its next, announcement, phase.

Similarly, the second overlap (at the arrows marked "b") which directly follows is composed of members of the other party relevant to the currently ongoing sequence -- the news deliverers. Although only Reuben speaks in initiating the announcement sequence, he turns out to be a member of a party whose other incumbent is equally privy to the news and its potential telling (cf. Lerner, 1992). Both members of this party display the second sort of surprise which I mentioned a moment ago -- surprise that their projected news is already known. Note that each independently selects the same one of the preceding simultaneous and divergent turns as the one to be addressed -- namely Kathy's turn which blocked the progress of the announcement sequence.[1] Each addresses that turn and its move from the same stance -- prospective news deliverer, and adopts a similar alignment toward it -- surprise at the claim/fact of already knowing the news.[2]

So that is my first point, or cluster of points. Turn-taking is organized for any number of participants, but the number of participants is directly organized into number of parties. Both can change; people can come and go in the course of talk-in-interaction, but, more directly consequential, even if that number stays the same, the number of parties into which those participants may be seen to be organized (because they see *themselves* so to be organized, and embody that stance in their conduct) can change continuously as the contingencies of the talk change, contingencies most centrally supplied by the participants themselves and the nature of the talk which they undertake with one another.

Understanding this should affect efforts to understand the organization of turn-taking and our assessment of the adequacy of that understanding. In assessing the adequacy of the SSJ model of turn-taking, such considerations will be important, for without them we will not properly appreciate the character of different kinds of simultaneous talk for the participants, and therefore their different bearing on assessment of the model.

## III

The second matter I want to take up also concerns simultaneous or overlapping talk. The points to which I will draw attention are considerations preliminary to a systematic account of how simultaneous or overlapping talk is managed in talk-in-interaction -- a model of an "overlap-resolution device." I cannot deal here with that set of practices itself,[3] but one important set of preliminary considerations bears on numbers of participants. It concerns the sort of materials for which a model should in the first instance be built and be adequate, the sorts of materials which can properly be taken to exemplify the general case.

As a first step in taking up that question, I want to exclude from the materials relevant to my concerns here certain types of episodes of overlapping talk -- primarily those types in which the simultaneous speakers do not appear to be contesting, or even alternative, claimants for a turn space. In these cases, that is, the conduct of the participants does not show these occurrences to be taken as problematic by them, and that governs their treatment by us as analysts. There are four types of these occurrences of simultaneous talk which do not appear to be "problematic" with respect to turn-taking.

First there are so-called "terminal overlaps" in which one speaker appears to be starting up by virtue of a prior speaker's incipient finishing of a turn (although this may turn out to have been an inaccurate hearing).

Second are "continuers" (Schegloff, 1982; C. Goodwin, 1986), by which a participant shows precisely the understanding that another is in the course of an extended turn at talk which is not yet complete, and which is alternative to an independent and competitive spate of talking (here excluding, therefore, the shift-implicative tokens; cf. Jefferson, 1984).

Third, there are various phenomena which can be collected under the rubric "conditional access to the turn," in which a speaker of a not possibly completed turn-in-progress yields to another, or even invites another to speak in their turn's space, conditional on the other's use of that opportunity to further the initial speaker's undertaking. The most familiar instances are those of the word search in which recipient may be invited to participate, and collaborative utterance construction in which one participant initiates an utterance and provides for another to complete it. Both of these phenomena, initially formed up as research topics by Sacks, have been recently made the topics of penetrating accounts -- the former by the Goodwins (1986) and the latter by Gene Lerner (1987, 1991). Again, in each case, should the initial and subsequent speaker end up talking at once, this is generally treated (by them) as noncompetitive and non-problematic.

Fourth, I wish to exclude that set of forms of talk which we can refer to as "chordal" or "choral" in character. By these terms I mean to call attention to forms of talk and activity which are treated by interactional co-participants as not to be done serially, one *after* the other, but simultaneously. There is first of all laughter, whose occurrence, Jefferson has shown (1979), can serve as an invitation for others to laugh, but whose elicited product is done in concert with other laughter, and not after it. Otherwise, there are such various activities as collective greetings and leave-takings, congratulations in response to announcement of personal good news, and the like. Such activities in multi-person settings are regularly produced "chorally," and not serially; and the choral production is done and heard as consensual, not agonistic. Here again, as in all the classes of occurrence which I mean to exclude from the ensuing discussion, the several overlapping participants do not appear to be, or to conduct themselves as, alternatives or competitors, but as properly simultaneous occupants of the floor -- either as a permissible matter (as with overlapping continuers, for example) or as a mandated one (as in choral congratulations, for example).[4]

These classes of overlap aside, in the materials drawn from ordinary talk-in-interaction with which I am familiar, it turns out with very great regularity that when more than one person is talking at a time, *two* persons are talking at a time and not more, and this is more or less invariant to the number of participants in the interaction. There is no time here to explicate this finding; I introduce it as a necessary ingredient for the theme I mean to take up. And keep in mind that I am speaking of single conversations, and not circumstances in which several conversations are going on in one ecological area.

Now in general there are three patterns which overlapping talk by two speakers can take. They may be characterized schematically as follows:

#2.

```
#1.   A -> B          #2.    A -> B        #3.  A <->  B
           |
           v                      ^
                                  |
           C                      C                 C
```

In pattern #1, A is talking to B and B is talking to C. In pattern #2, A is talking to B and C is talking to B. In pattern #3, A is talking to B and B is talking to A.

As with my first topic, I want to offer only a very few observations about these patterns of simultaneous talk. The first observation (more the product of casual though careful observation than of systematic analysis of video materials) is that deployment of the body, and especially gaze direction, appears to figure differently in the three. In pattern #2, the gaze direction of B is likely to feature centrally. A and C can be understood to be competing for a recipient, *this* recipient, and gaze direction can be an indication of which of the competitors this recipient is favoring. Commonly, if B directs gaze at A, C will drop out of the competition, and B can thereby be understood to have decided the matter. But, on occasion, C can respond by competing for the recipient more vigorously -- talking louder still, at higher pitch, etc. Although almost certainly the body can be deployed in a manner relevant to overlap in pattern #3, it does not appear to figure as centrally in that circumstance.

A second observation is that, although these appear to be three discrete and different patterns of overlapping talk, #1 and #2 can naturally alternate under the operation of the turn-taking system. Begin with pattern #1: A is talking to B and B is talking to C. Then one "natural" next phase is that, on possible completion of B's turn, C -- properly -- responds to B. If C does so, then pattern #2 is brought into existence: A is talking to B and C is talking to B. And when C comes to a possible completion, B may appropriately address C again, and pattern #1 is again brought into existence. These two patterns are, in that sense, natural alternators.

Lest this be thought a merely theoretical, logically generated possibility, let me hasten to provide an instance of the sort of empirical material it is meant to characterize.

The material was collected by Richard Frankel in a used furniture store in the Bronx about fifteen years ago. Mike works in the furniture store; Vic and James are janitors in nearby apartment houses. Earlier in the day, a window was broken in James' building while he was away. Mike found out about it, told Vic, and Vic cleaned up the broken glass, encountering the likely culprit while doing so. Upon James' return, the story of the incident is told and retold. James mainly wants to know who did it; Vic mainly wants credit for cleaning up.[5]

#3. US:43

```
01       James:  But dis [person thet DID IT,
02         Vic:          [If I see the person,
03       James:  -IS GOT TUH BE:: ·hh taken care of. You
04               know what  [I mean,
05         Vic:             [Well Ja:mes, [if I see duh person=
06       James:                           [Yeh right. e(hh) !e(hh)!
07         Vic:  =[en you happen tuh be th- by me,
08       James:  =[Yeauh.
09       James:  Yeuh.
10         Vic:  Or if I see  [the person,  [(stannin=
11       James:               [Yeh.         [I dus    =
12         Vic:  =[outside                  ) by you (I'll- y'know I'll
13       James:  =[wantuh know who (dih-)
14->>    Mike:   =[The least they coulda do:ne wz-
15->>    Mike:   Well the least he c'd=
16               =[do is letchu know it happened.
17       James:  =[I DIS WANTUH KNOW DIH- WHO BROKE
18               THAT GLASS [OUT. That's all.
19->>    Mike:              [The least he coulda=
20               =[done wz letchu know it happened?
21         Vic:  =[He might come by still en-[.hh
22       James:                              [Hu  [h?
23->>    Mike:                                     [Th-
24         Vic:                                    [You know I
25               cut  [myself on yo'=
26->>    Mike:        [Th'least they c'd do-
27         Vic:  =[freakin gla:ss,
28->>    Mike:    [Th' least they coulda do:ne,
```

29 James: [Ye:h
30->> Mike: [Least he coulda done [wz come do:wn en=
31 James: [e(hh)h!
32 Mike: =letchu know what happened hey [look yer=
33 James: [Tha:t-
34 Mike: =gla:ss broke,
35 James: Yeh dass ri:ght,

Seven times Mike tries to say his piece (marked by the arrows at lines 14, 15-16, 19-20, 23, 26, 28 and 30-32-34,). Four of these tries are abandoned before possible completion as Mike finds himself talking simultaneously with another. The tries initiated at lines 15 and 19 are pressed to completion, but in each case Mike finds them ineffective, that is, not sequentially implicative or consequential, by virtue of their involvement in overlap. Only the last try, starting at line 30, is said substantially in the clear, and is acknowledged by a recipient.

Let us identify Mike with "A" in our patterns of overlap, and James (who is the "you" of Mike's "The least they could have done is let *you* know it happened") with "B". Then note that at Mike's tries at lines 14 and 15, James is talking to Vic (B is talking to C), and at the try at line 19-20 Vic is responding to James (C is talking to B). At the tries at lines 23 and 26 and 28, Vic is talking to James as Mike is also addressing him (C to B, A to B) and in the try at line 30, James is responding to Vic.

So we have here just the circumstance described schematically. There is a colloquy in progress between B and C, here James and Vic, into which A is trying to break, here Mike. And these two patterns, #1 and #2, alternate as A's repeated efforts to gain B as a recipient run into an alternation in the conversation between B and C.

Of course it is unusual to find as extended a series of efforts as this, which displays so clearly the alternation of these two patterns, which shows them to be alternate "values" of a single form of organization. It allows us to appreciate that much briefer episodes, ones in which either pattern #1 or pattern #2 is observed, are moments caught in a potential stream of conduct which has this potential trajectory, but which the involved parties ordinarily arrest before it gets to this point. The competition for B's eyes which I remarked on earlier can thus be seen to have a history and/or a future -- it will be enmeshed in an ongoing or prospective effort to prevent a colloquy from forming or to intervene in one already in progress.

Clearly occurrences of the sorts described by patterns 1 and 2 are *not* the *general* cases of overlap. For one thing, they necessarily involve three participants. If we want to understand in the most general way how simultaneous talk comes to occur and how it is resolved, we should examine occurrences structured like pattern #3. It requires for its occurrence only that which talk-in-interaction *per se* appears to require -- two participants. And that is the number who generally are talking if more than one is talking. It is surely possible that overlapping talk between two participants to one another will be dealt with differently, by them, when there are other ratified coparticipants than when those two are the only present company. But it does appear that the mechanism, the practices of conduct, by which overlapping speakers deal with their simultaneous talk is formed up in the first place for talk by two, and to one another. If things are different when more are present, it appears that this involves modifications to those practices. What these overlap management practices are, however, cannot be taken up here.[6]

One last point, however, needs to be mentioned concerning these three "patterns." I have offered them here to characterize alternative possible forms which simultaneous talk can take. Quite independently, Gene Lerner (1987: 213-215) has formulated quite similar patterns in characterizing the contexts for collaboration between several participants in producing a turn at talk. Lerner has been finding that aspects of the form which a collaborative completion of another's utterance is given, and aspects of how such a proposed completion is received, vary with the "directionality" of the first part of the turn and of its candidate completion by another, where "directionality" refers to just such matters as are summarized by the "patterns" diagrammed in #2 above. Something robust is afoot here, something real for those who share a turn's space -- whether by competing for it or combining to produce the talk in it. And what is central or peripheral for studying simultaneous talk may have to be differently assessed for studying other joint occupations of a turn's space.[7]

## IV

I have touched on the bearing of numbers on two aspects of talk-in-interaction, two aspects of the organization of participation in that talk, two aspects of the turn-taking organization.

For inquiry into the general topic of turn-taking, it has seemed necessary to begin not where many efforts have begun, with the case of two persons, but rather with the case of "n" participants. But order is quickly introduced into this potentially chaotic circumstance by making turn-taking operate not on the participation of persons *per se*, but on the participation of parties. Turn-taking organizes the distribution of talk among *parties*, but not necessarily among the persons who compose a party.

When we come to investigate the "social star" of the turn-taking family, the one which excites wide popular interest, i.e., overlap, it turns out that just that starting point which can set us off in the *wrong* direction with respect to turn-taking in general is precisely where we must start. Not only is it empirically the case that more than one speaker at a time is almost always two speakers at a time; it is also the case which requires no more than two -- the case where the two speakers are speaking to each other -- which is the general case of overlap, the one with which inquiry must begin. Whereas for turn-taking in general "two" is precisely *not* the general case, for overlap it precisely *is*.

In these and other cases of the significance of numbers for interaction, that significance will not turn out to be merely geometric or logical or formal. It will require digging out from the details of conduct in interaction. For the significance of numbers is not in the first place a significance for academic social science; it is a significance discerned, and imposed, by the parties to interaction, whose conduct it is our calling to describe.

---

* This paper was first prepared for a session organized by Alessandro Duranti and Charles Goodwin on "Dyadic vs. Multiparty Participation Frameworks: A Crosscultural Perspective" at the 86th Annual Meeting of the American Anthropological Association, Chicago, Illinois, November, 1987; its topic reflects the theme of that occasion. In the context of my own ongoing writing, this paper presents two prolegomena to a larger scale treatment of overlap in talk-in-interaction. My thanks to John Heritage, George Psathas and Marja-Leena Sorjonen for comments which prompted clarification of the text.

1 This provides a neat demonstration of the general claim (requiring more elaboration than is appropriate here) that dispreferred responses are sequence-expansion relevant, whereas preferred responses are sequence-closure relevant.

2 Note also that in the case of each of these overlaps, neither speaker withdraws in favor of the other, but each speaks to completion. That is, the practices by which overlaps are regularly resolved are not adopted here (although the import of this observation is somewhat blunted by the brevity of the utterances involved, a brevity which is projectable from the start of each turn, and which has the overlaps resolving themselves within the span ordinarily achieved by quickly resolved overlaps.)

3 Cf. Jefferson and Schegloff, 1975 for an early partial formulation of such an account.

4 Of course, there may be much more to be said about the temporal and sequential organization of these activities than that they are done in concert. There is now ample documentation of the detailed orderliness of laughter (e.g., Jefferson, 1985, for example, among many others). And Alessandro Duranti has suggested (p.c.) that there may be a detailed orderliness in the apparent randomness of collective greetings. So also may there be normative obligations on who should lead in collective congratulations or condolences, and who should join in, and when.

5 Because of the complexity of the patterns of overlap here, I offer some guidance on the reading of the transcript. I presume familiarity with the convention that brackets mark co-incidence of the points on lines that they connect: left brackets marking the simultaneous onset or continuation of the utterances at the point of placement; right brackets simultaneous arrival of the preceding talk to that point. Equal signs (=) mark (in this excerpt) the no-break continuation of an utterance by a speaker which has been deployed over

two or more lines (e.g., Vic's talk at lines 05-07 or at lines 10-12; or James' talk at lines 11-13, or Mike's at lines 15-16). So:

At line 14, Mike comes in on the already overlapping talk of Vic and James on lines 12 and 13. After all three speakers have stopped, Mike starts "in the clear" at line 15, but has James come in on his talk at lines 16-17. In turn (so to speak), Mike comes in on James talk at lines 18 and 19, and Vic comes in on Mike's at lines 20 and 21.

Mike and Vic start together at lines 23 and 24, terminally overlapping James talk at line 22. And Mike then comes in on Vic's talk at lines 25 and 26, and then again at lines 27 and 28. At lines 29 and 30 James and Mike start simultaneously, Mike's turn then continuing at lines 32 and 34, with intermittent overlaps by James.

[6] Cf. Jefferson and Schegloff, 1975 and work in preparation.

[7] Also cf. Goodwin, 1980 and Schegloff, 1987[1973] for another use of a conversational device -- in this case, cut-off + identical restart -- for dealing with different, but related, contingencies of talking-in-interaction, namely "turn launching" contingencies.

# 3

# Laughing *at* and Laughing *with*: Negotiation of Participant Alignments Through Conversational Laughter*

Phillip J. Glenn

Through talk people continuously adjust their relative affiliation with or disaffiliation from each other. Conversational laughter contributes to displays of both alignment and distancing; which (if either) laughter helps accomplish at any particular moment may be displayed and redefined over several turns. How people interactively orient to variations in laughter's affiliative status is the focus of this analysis.

The phrases *laughing at* and *laughing with* suggest a long-recognized distinction between the power of laughter to promote distancing, disparagement, or feelings of superiority; or, conversely, to promote bonding and affiliation (for a review of theories concerning laughter, see Holland, 1982). Within conversation analytic research, Jefferson (1972) proposes (in passing) laughing *at* vs. laughing *with* as a conversational feature (see below). More recently, Clayman (1992) analyzes the affiliative status of audience laughter during televised American presidential debates. Out of a total of 174 audience responses in three different debates, Clayman codes 24 as "disaffiliative." Of these, 12 are "disaffiliative laughter" and 4 are "equivocal laughter." Affiliative laughter tends to follow (and refer to) criticisms of opponent which are marked as humorous through such devices as pre-warning that a joke is coming; using far-fetched, metaphorical descriptions; and employing fillers and hesitations after the laughable to allow turn space for anticipated audience response. Disaffiliative laughter occurs following positive self-talk by a candidate (description or assessment of own qualities and accomplishments), and in such a context laughter can be heard as treating positive self-praise as "not-serious." Clayman's study demonstrates that analysts (like participants) must look to features of the local sequential environment to disambiguate laughter's status as affiliative or disaffiliative.

The analysis below shows how participants utilize resources available over trajectories of several turns to negotiate laughter's affiliative status. Four keys, which may be present in any laugh-relevant sequential context, help distinguish laughing at from laughing with: laughable, first laugh, (possible) second laugh, and subsequent activities. After explaining each and showing how configurations of the four display laughings at, I will present cases where participants effect transformation from with to at or at to with.

## Keys to distinguishing laughing *at* from laughing *with*

1. ***Laughable.*** Of the broad class of conversational laughables (including any object which serves as a referent for laughter), certain types appear likely to make laughing at relevant. Specifically, in laughing at environments, *laughable appoints/nominates some co-present as a butt.* Participants may act as perpetrators of such laughables by ridiculing, teasing, or making fun of co-present others. The butt may collaborate in this alignment, even in the absence of perpetration, by producing overbuilt turns that make teasing relevant (Drew, 1987), errors (Hopper and Glenn, in press), unintentional double entendres, talk or actions revealing a naive or otherwise sanctionable state, etc. Thus the laughable which nominates some co-present as butt may be produced by that person or by someone else as perpetrator.

In such cases co-participant laughter likely will get treated as laughing at. In this face to face conversation between two American college students, Kate comments that something smells bad. After a long pause, she asserts that he may be the source of the smell. He willingly agrees with this probability. After a pause, he recounts a past activity -- he took a bath -- which would seem to rule out one reason why he might smell. In her next turn Kate praises him for this action and laughs:

(UTCL D6)

| | |
|---|---|
| Kate: | Shyoowee Brandon something rilly stinks. |
| | (10.0) ((movement sounds in leaves/grass)) |
| Kate: | 'S probly you. |
| Brandon: | °Hm° probly is, |
| | (1.6) |
| Brandon: | I took a shower this morning though? |
| Kate: | Good for you hah hah ↑huh |

Now the topic has shifted from what smells bad to Brandon's hygienic habits. By her mock praise she treats his self-disclosure as ludicrous or overdone, as inviting praise for an action which any adult ought to do by routine. Thus they collaboratively construct an interchange in which he is made the butt. Kate's laughter is at Brandon.

2. ***First laugh.*** *First laugh by someone other than the butt (especially by perpetrator) likely indicates laughing at.* Current speaker may invite laughter from other by adding laugh particles within or following the utterance in progress (Jefferson, 1979). In such cases, current speaker makes laughing with explicitly relevant. Other joining in ratifies the affiliation.

Following laughable which nominates a co-present as butt, first laugh by someone other than the nominated butt of the laughable provides additional confirmation that it is a laughing at environment. This first laugh may come from current speaker, especially if current speaker produces laughable which identifies someone else as butt. As two couples are beginning dinner together, Shawn comments on the chicken which Vicki has prepared. His hyperbolic suggestion that the chicken isn't sufficiently cooked gets followed by a silence and an other-initiated repair repeat by Vicki, the butt of this tease. Overlapping her repeat, Shawn himself laughs. Neither of the other participants join in laughing; for them to do so would be hearable as affiliating with Shawn in laughing at Vicki.

(CD II:3. Ts by Jefferson, modified. Face to face)

Shawn: 'Ts got there's still ice on it.
(1.3)
Vicki: I: ce:?
[
Shawn: °kheh-heh-heh-h eh
[
Vicki: They weren' even frozen.

First laugh from Shawn, who produced laughable tease nominating Vicki as butt, further confirms this as a laughing at environment.

3. ***(possible) Second laugh.*** *In multi-party interactions, (possible) second laugh by someone other than butt reinforces laughing at. In two-party situations, laughing at is not shared.* Thus two-party shared laughter will likely be a laughing with, while multi-party laughter may be laughing with or laughing at.

In the following two-party example, Cara has asserted that she will earn a top grade of A in a tennis class. Rick asks why and offers a candidate reason: that she knows the instructor (and thus that her high grade will be due to personal relationship rather than to in-class performance). Rick follows this with laughter. Cara gives a po-faced response (Drew, 1987), not sharing his laughter and rejecting a premise for his candidate reason:

(UTCL D8a. Phone)

161 Rick: Why. D'you know the instructor? hheh heh
162 Cara: ↑No. Th'instr↑uctor's a ↓lady.

His laughable nominates her as butt by suggesting an unethical basis to her assertion that she will earn a high grade. His first laugh is at her. Her not providing second laugh further confirms the laughing at status of this sequence.

Thus far we have looked at three clues to distinguish laughing at from laughing with: nature of the laughable, first laugh, and (possible) second. This may also be a matter of retroactive display: What people do *following* first laugh (and possible second) also helps negotiate these alignments.

**4.** ***Subsequent activities.*** *Subsequent talk on topic displays laughter as at.* Whether laughter is at or with may may depend on retroactive definition through subsequent activities. One such activity (Jefferson 1972: 300-301) involves extending the topic through word or phrase repetitions. Repetition of another speaker's prior talk plus laugh tokens can be a way of appreciating something just said:

(Jefferson, 1972, p. 299. Face to face)

| | | |
|---|---|---|
| | Al: | Then th'r gonna dismantle the frame 'n |
| | | see if the frame's still there. |
| | Louise: | hh//heh heh heh! |
| | Al: | Got *ter*mites. |
| | | (0.6) |
| -> | Ken: | "T(hh)er(h)mite(h)s" hhh |
| | Louise: | Well y'know wi-n-*fall*out. |
| | | Who knows what they'll eat now. |
| | | (0.6) |
| | Ken: | hhhh |
| | | (1.5) |
| | Ken: | hh hh |
| | | (1.0) |

Ken repeats "termites" and embeds laugh particles within it. This accomplishes appreciating the prior item. Whether this laughter is at or with Al (who produced the term in the first place) gets displayed in subsequent talk. Jefferson notes that repeats with laugh tokens regularly co-occur with shutting down talk about that topic. In the example above, Ken's repeat of the laughable with laugh particles is followed by another utterance from Louise which attempts to continue talk on that topic. But talk on this topic does not continue: there are several seconds of silences and small laughs from Ken. Finally, the group moves on to another topic (not shown on transcript).

In some cases repeat + laughter does get followed by attempts to continue topic talk. Here, laughter's ambiguity becomes relevant. If laughter is with, that is, appreciating, then it will function as a terminator. If the laughter is "at" -- disaffiliative -- it functions, like a questioning-repeat, to produce more talk, perhaps including a repair, of the trouble item. Delay then repeat may show participant uncertainty about which meaning of laughter is in operation. The attempt to continue the topic gives more chances to resolve that ambiguity.

In this next instance, Cara (line 33) retrieves and laughs at a word she seems to have *heard* Rick say a few turns earlier (line 24). The repeat plus laughter *at* Rick's word generates a lengthy sequence of talk devoted to resolving its meaning:

(UTCL D8a. Phone.)

```
21       Cara:   ↑Well-  uh we've been looking fer:: apartments all
22               ↑da:y  n' no::w (.) we're keuking.
23               (.)
24-->    Rick:   Ye:r (p) (.) yer punting.
25               (0.3)
26       Cara:   Keuking.
27               (0.5)
28       Rick:   Kicking.
29       Cara:   ↑Cooking.
30       Rick:   Cooking   hh hh    •eh hh
                                 [         ]
31       Cara:                   ↑Ye::s.h
32       Rick:   Uhh hhuh ho   °ho°
                                 [
33       Cara:                   Pumping. Wer pumping. (hh) ↑eh
                                                            [  ]
34       Rick:                                              (hh)
35       Cara:   ↑huh-huh-h       uh
                                  [
36       Rick:                     •ehhh  •uhh=
37       Cara:   =•h:hh  Hu:h what could that mean,
38       Rick:   u:h  I don' kn↑o::w  u:h-h.
39               (0.4)
40       Cara:   (t)Hu:h?
41               (0.2)
42       Rick:   °ih-° You got me: hheh-heh-↑he h •hhh
                                               [
43       Cara:                                  hhhh
44       Cara:   You' the one that s:aid the wo:rd.
```

This continues for some time. For these potential dating partners, the possible sexual innuendo of "pumping" may be relevant to Cara's relentless pursuit of its meaning here.

Jefferson (1972: 301) further suggests that these alternatives are not symmetrical -- rather, there exists a "uni-directionality" to them such that "laughing at" is unambiguously hearable as such, while laughing with may also be laughing at. Even when one speaker does something specifically to be funny, there is the possibility that hearers laugh, not for the reasons speaker wants, but for reasons carrying some degree of judgment or criticism of the speaker.

Subsequent activities can retroactively display laughter as at or with its object, and serve as a fourth key by which conversationalists negotiate this alignment. In summary, conversationalists key laughing *at* via these features:

1. Laughable which proposes some co-participant as butt;
2. First laugh by someone other than the butt, especially by the perpetrator;
3. In two-party settings, no shared laughter; in multi-party settings, possible second laugh by someone other than butt; and
4. Extended talk on the topic of the laughable utterance.

The following exemplifies how these features combine to display a clear instance of laughing at. Kate tells Brandon to forget about the tape recorder (which is recording them). After several exchanges during which he remains silent, she goes on to construct a tease:

(UTCL D6a. Face to face)

```
1→         Kate:    Betchyou sound really stupid on tape too.
                    (2.0)
2→         Kate:     Bhh hah ↑huh huh    °•hh°=
                    [[                    ]
(3→)    Brandon:      Do ↑I soun' stupid?
           Kate:    =I betcha do:.
4→      Brandon:    Yeah: ↑I've heard myself before ↑I sound
                    pretty °stupid.°
                    (.)
           Kate:    W'↑you sound pretty (.) stupid. . .
```

The #1 arrow marks the laughable which nominates Brandon as butt, providing an imagined assessment of how he sounds on tape recorder. After a silence, Kate provides first laugh (arrow #2). Simultaneously Brandon produces non-laughing talk; he does not share in Kate's laughter (arrow #3). This leads to subsequent talk on topic (arrow #4). The combination of cues -- laughable which nominates a butt, first laugh by someone else (the perpetrator), butt not sharing laughter, and subsequent talk on topic -- clearly displays this as a laughing at.

These features provide a starting point for understanding some of the ways people may disambiguate laughing at from with. In the following section some more complex instances are presented, in which conversationalists transform situations from laughing at to with or with to at. Explication of these instances displays how laughing at and with are alignments to which participants orient; such explication will also show that these alignments are not fixed but changeable, sometimes equivocal, and subject to moment-by-moment negotiation.

## Converting laughing *with* to laughing *at*

Joke-tellings would seem inherently to set up laughing *with* environments. The teller seeks recipient laughter, which one would expect to display affiliation among participants, appreciating the joke and the telling. However, joke-telling environments may be volatile. Tellers must deliver the joke successfully; hearers must "get" the joke and respond appropriately. Failure in either role may convert a laughing with context into a laughing at.

Six people representing three generations of an extended American family are gathered in a kitchen, telling jokes. Milt brings a narrative joke to completion. The joke itself seems appropriate for this gathering, for it concerns a granddaughter and grandmother, and its humor turns on the child's naivete and on declining sexual activity of older adults. Following the punch line Chris laughs (line 31) and Cecil adds an appreciative "oh no" with laugh particles (line 33). It is, at this point, a laughing *with* environment:

(NP, family joke telling. Face to face)

| | | |
|---|---|---|
| 27 | Milt: | Sh'aid (for-) a:bso↑lutely right. (0.7) She says I |
| 28 | | think I: know why you and grandpa sleep in separate |
| 29 | | rooms.=Sh'said ↑Why is that. |
| 29a | | Said you got an F in se:x. |
| 30 | | (0.8) |
| 31 | Chris: | Ohh HA HA HA HA HA HA •↑Hooo= |
| 33 | Cecil: | =↑Hoh ↓n:o. •↑huuh |

Overlapping Chris's laugh, Vaughn's repair initiator (line 32) asks for a repeat of the materials that follow "got a." The non-laughing question hearably displays that Vaughn does not get the joke. But Milt does not immediately provide the information Vaughn seeks, and Vaughn repeats the question (line 34).

| | | |
|---|---|---|
| 31 | Chris: | Ohh HA HA H [A HA HA HA •↑Hooo= |
| 32 | Vaughn: | [Ya gotta what? |
| 33 | Cecil: | =↑Hoh ↓n:o. •↑ [huuh |
| 34 | Vaughn: | [°Got a° what? |

Milt, the joke-teller, now laughs. But placement of Milt's laugh suggests that it orients not to his own joke, but to Vaughn's questioning repair initiator. Evidence for this includes Milt's use of Vaughn's name, with laugh particles embedded in it, and his subsequent turn calling for someone to explain the joke to Vaughn (lines 39-40). The joke punch line provides an opportunity for the participants to align and laugh with each other. Now the others are invited to laugh with Milt *at* Vaughn. Although it is not clear from talk at this point whether others in the group *also* didn't hear or get the joke, Vaughn's repair initiators make clear that *he* doesn't understand.[1] For this demonstrated naivete, Vaughn gets laughed at:

```
34  Vaughn:  °Got a° what?
35           (0.3)
36     (?):  ↑•hu uh-huh
                [
37    Milt:      Va (hh)ughn?  •hh yes ha ha ha h   uh
                     [           [                  [
38   Cecil:          ↑oh: ↑oh   ↑ohuh-hoo           ↑•uhhh-hoo
                                                       [
39    Milt:                                             Somebody
40    Milt:  expl_ai_n that to him.
```

Vaughn's repair initiators (lines 32 and 34) suggest that the problem lies in failure to hear part of the punch line, rather than hearing it but not understood its full meaning. Yet Milt, through his turn at lines 39-40, treats this as a failure to "get" the joke. Such a failure makes hearer subject to teasing and ridicule. Sacks (1967: 346) explains that

> Jokes, and dirty jokes in particular, are constructed as "understanding tests." Not everyone supposably "gets" each joke, the getting involving achievement of its understanding, a failure to get being supposable as involving a failure to understand. Asserting understanding failures can then reveal, e.g., recipients' lack of sophistication, a matter that an appropriately placed laugh can otherwise conceal.

By this last utterance, Milt singles Vaughn out for ridicule, suggesting that someone, indeed anyone else in the room could explain this joke to Vaughn. More laughs follow from Milt and others, but not from Vaughn. Vaughn accounts for his failure to laugh and repair initiators (line 49). This account invokes "not hearing" as the source of trouble rather than, for example, hearing but not "getting" the innuendo in the joke. It orients to his prior actions being sanctionable -- and in this case, sanctioned. It thereby provides confirmation of the isolating actions performed by Milt's laughing at him:

```
39-40   Milt:  Somebody expl_ai_n that to him.
41       (?):  °nh-h    uh°
                      [
42      Milt:          hu hah hah hah hah hah hah
                                  [
43     Cecil:                     ↑hu::h-  ↓huh
```

[
44 (?): °↑huh hih-hih°=
45 (?): =°↑uh-hunh!°
46 (?): °hhh ::::::°
[
47 Ethel: ↑O:h ↓no(h)o=
48 (?): (ehih uheh)
=[[ ]
49 Vaughn: I didn't hear the ↑first word.

At the punch line of a joke, especially a joke with dirty or naughty overtones, hearers have an opportunity to display their understanding by laughing in appreciation. In this example, the participants affiliate in appreciating the joke until one of them makes clear that he hasn't gotten it. Then the joke-teller makes this hearer's failure itself into a laughable, thus transforming the interactional environment from laughing with to laughing at.

## Transforming laughing *at* to laughing *with*

As the prior example shows, alignments displayed through laughing at or with are not static but changeable, dependent upon moment-to-moment ratification or re-negotiation. One sort of change involves the butt -- the person laughed at -- attempting to shift participant alignment to a laughing with via subsequent activities.

In the following example three American college students are talking on the telephone. After a prior topic winds down Stanley refers to an earlier conversation he had with the "fellas" at the dorm. Neither Jeffrey nor Rhonda speak during several transition-relevance places and gaps (not shown below). Stanley emphasizes the term "deeming" within his turn which refers to the co-present interactor, Rhonda, in the third person, in a playful-formal phrase, "a young lady."

(UTCL A30. Phone)

Stanley: But deeming that a young ↑lady's on the phone wu' we
woh' discuss none u'thet.

This turn proposes that Jeffrey and Stanley, as the "we" who won't discuss, align apart from Rhonda, the "young lady." As such it may make relevant Jeffrey and Stanley laughing with each other, at Rhonda. However, following a gap of 1.6 seconds, Jeffrey initiates a repair sequence by a repeat and first pair part question. Stanley's second pair part reveals that he doesn't know the meaning of the word he has just used, and that he employed it only because it is "catchy":

Jeffrey: Deeming. Now ↑wha' does ↓deeming mean ma::n).
[
Stanley: eh Deeming ↑I don't
know ma:n ↑is jus'as jus uh c:atchy wo:rd ma:n.

Overlapping this Jeffrey starts laughing. That this is a laughing at environment is hearable by the nature of the laughable (getting caught using a term one doesn't understand), by Jeffrey's other-initiation of laughter, by Stanley's withholding second laugh and Rhonda providing it, and by initiation of subsequent talk on topic:

Stanley: eh Deeming ↑I
don't know ma:n ↑is jus 'as jus uh c:atchy wo:rd ma:n.
[ ]
Jeffrey: ↑hih-huh hu↑AH! huh-hah!
Rhonda: °↑hih heh.°
[
Stanley: It don't fit shit.

This last turn by Stanley serves as a new laughable orienting to his prior word-error. This turn's laughability lies at least in part in its brevity, internal rhyme, and use of the expletive "shit." By this Stanley bids to transform the environment to laughing with. Rhonda laughs and Jeffrey provides appreciative talk. Stanley continues, with another laughable relevant to his use of "deeming":

Stanley: It don't fit shit.
Rhonda: ihh huh huh •h:::h
[ ]
Jeffrey: Wu'I tellyou what ma::::n.
[
Stanley: My English teachuh be exin
Stanley: my ass on that. ↑Ev'ry time.=

Stanley produces comic characterizations of an English teacher deleting an item from a paper as if it were to be banished or decapitated. Jeffrey and Rhonda laugh. Stanley has now successfully converted a laughing at environment into a laughing with, realigning from an accidental producer of a teasable error into an intentional producer of comic accounts and narration. The realignment achieved, he proceeds with non-laughing talk on the same subject.

Rhonda: =°Who deeming?°
[
Stanley: Deemin',
(0.2)
Stanley: Ooph! It don' fit.
(0.7)
Stanley: Off with it.
[[
Jeffrey: (t'sh) mh! hmhuhmhuh.
[
Rhonda: u-huh?=
Stanley: =I'm like right oh kay?
(1.8)
Stanley: See ↑I got that from this white guy ma:n,

Errors -- in this case misusing a word and not knowing what it means -- make relevant laughing at. The producer of an error can recover artfully, as does Stanley, and bring those laughing back into alignment with him.

The possibility of getting laughed at following an error may be oriented to even before the laughs begin. Thus, error-producer may pre-empt opportunities for others to laugh at and try to convert the environment to a laughing with by leading self-laughter. In the next example a young American married couple are at home, watching television and chatting about what's on. In response to Jay's question, Anna produces the wrong name for an actor. This wrong name belongs to another media celebrity of recent years, Karen Ann Quinlan, the unfortunate young woman who remained in a coma for years and became the focal point for national debate about the right to die. Jay initiates repair, and they produce a collaborative time out to hunt down the correct first name.

(AS 1, 7/89. Face-to-face)

Jay: Who's that girl.
(0.5)
Anna: That's u::h Karen Ann Quinlan.
(2.5)
Jay: I'dn she in a coma honey?
Jay: °hhh°
[[
Anna: No::. whatzit (.) what's her name?
Anna: Something Quinlan,
(1.2)
Anna: Elizabeth Quinlan?=
Jay: =Kathleen Quinlan?
Anna: ↑KAthleen.

Once they have arrived at the correct "Kathleen" Anna laughs and produces a next laughable relevant to the erroneous use of "Karen Ann":

Anna: ↑KAthleen.
(?) ((slapping sound))
(.)
Anna: Huh (h)'ve got the wo man •hhh
[ ]
Jay: She
Anna: I'VE GOT THE WOMAN. (.) IN A COMA DRIVIN' HER CA:R.=
Anna: =huh hih huh (0.8) •ihh
Anna: Duh EE::e-huh!
Jay: Amazing what they do with strings.

Anna leads the laughter in reference to her own error. By this she laughs at herself and invites Jay to align with her in appreciation of it. She transforms a laughing at sequential environment, keyed by her error, into a laughing with environment keyed by her laugh invitation and subsequent laughable.

Willingness to go along with, or even initiate, laughter at self provides potential payoffs in realigning towards affiliation. Once laughing at either is underway or relevant, willingness to laugh at self provides a resource for converting the environment to laughing with.

## Discussion

A prime domain of social negotiation involves moment-by-moment displays of alignment with co-participants. Laughter may accomplish affiliation or distancing, laughing with or at someone else. Conversationalists utilize features in the sequential environment to create, amend, or disambiguate the affiliative work laughter may be doing. These features include the nature of the laughable, first laugh, (possible) second laugh, and subsequent talk. Laughing at environments are recognizable as such by: laughable which nominates some co-participant as butt, first laugh by someone other than butt (especially by perpetrator), possible second laugh by someone other than butt, and continued talk on topic. These cues do not rigidly determine orientations, but are themselves subject to re-negotiation. If others laugh at us, we may try to convert that to a laughing with. We may provide opportunities for others to laugh at us. We may shift at a moment's notice from laughing with to laughing at another. The options are many.

By transforming laughing at to with (or vice versa), participants may accomplish a micro-transformation of social structure. In his autobiography, professional comedian Dick Gregory describes how he did this as a child:

> I got picked on a lot around the neighborhood ... I guess that's when I first began to learn about humor, the power of a joke ...
>
> At first ... I'd just get mad and run home and cry when the kids started. And then, I don't know just when, I started to figure it out. They were going to laugh anyway, but if I made the jokes they'd laugh *with* me instead of at me. I'd get the kids off my back, on my side. So I'd come off that porch talking about myself ...
>
> Before they could get going, I'd knock it out first, fast, knock out those jokes so they wouldn't have time to set and climb all over me ... And they started to come over and listen to me, they'd see me coming and crowd around me on the corner ...
>
> Everything began to change then ... The kids began to expect to hear funny things from me, and after a while I could say anything I wanted. I got a reputation as a funny man. And then I started to turn the jokes on them. (Gregory 1964: 54-55, cited in Bauman 1977: 44-45).

Gregory realigned his role from that of unwilling butt to willing creator of jokes, from others laughing at him to laughing with and, ultimately, to him laughing at others. From his description we can infer that the transformation from laughing at to with happened over a series of interactions. Yet the same process can occur within several seconds of a single interaction, as examples above show.

Laughing at makes the other into an object, distancing and disaffiliating laugher and victim. But such distancing is labile and subject to change. As examples shown here suggest, those being laughed at may attempt to transform the sequential environment into one in which affiliation becomes relevant. Examples above show this occurring following errors. It also can occur in the environment of teasing. Drew (1987) describes teasing sequences arrayed by a continuum of victim responses ranging from absolute seriousness and rejection of the tease to laughing and full participation. Those who laugh along when getting teased can be seen as attempting affiliation with the teaser(s), realigning a laughing at to a laughing with.

Knowledge of this possibility itself provides a resource for creating affiliation. Conversationalists can create situations in which laughing at them is relevant, as a means of inviting and promoting affiliation. One phrase in our common parlance for this is "playing the fool." The individual willing to regularly take on a role that entails pratfalls, mistakes, and embarrassments, for purposes of generating recipient laughter, may get laughed at, yet can provide for displays of group affiliation. Those who provide this role may begin as victims, like Dick Gregory, or begin by willingly producing items for others to laugh at. In ongoing relationships, who is to say which comes first. Does Stanley, in the example above, play the fool because his friends laughed at him? Or do his friends orient to the *possibility* of laughing at him because he has, at other times, willingly played the fool?

I do not intend the with/at distinction to be a too-limiting dualism, suggesting that all laughter must do one or the other. Rather, these can be seen as two possibilities that arise with laughter, which do seem to be opposites. Viewed in this way, the with/at possibilities stand as microcosms of, and ways of enacting, cybernetic adjustments common to all relationships. The development, maintenance, and termination of relationships involves continuous adjustments between movement towards greater intimacy and movement towards distancing and differentiation. We do this moment by moment, through such seemingly insignificant actions as laughables and laughter. Thus conversational laughter plays a fundamental role in the organization of human interactions.

---

* Earlier versions of this article were presented at the Performance Studies Festival, New York University, October 1990; the International Institute on Ethnomethodology and Conversation Analysis, Amsterdam, July 1991; and the International Communication Association Convention in Miami, May 1992. My analysis has profited from my discussions with Ron Pelias, Robert Hopper, Gail Jefferson, Paul Drew, Stephen Clayman, and others.

1 In fact, some evidence suggests that Vaughn isn't the only one who fails to get the joke on first telling. Only Chris and Cecil explicitly demonstrate understanding through laughter and appreciative comments. Display of one participant's understanding failure foregrounds the relevance for others to display that they *do* get it. In such an environment, an absence of positive understanding cues -- note, for example, Ethel's silence -- may serve as stronger evidence of failure to get. (My thanks to Gail Jefferson for this observation.)

4

# Episode Trajectory in Conversational Play*

Robert Hopper

Play episodes unfold as mutually improvised ensemble performances in which players sustain alignments around the question: Is this play? Players sustain alignments by orienting to a dialectic of ironic/playful versus literal/serious interpretations. The present essay describes some interactive accomplishments of trajectory in an episode of play-in-conversation.

The term *trajectory* encompasses episode-direction-setting accomplishments including, but not limited to, sequential relevance.[1] Trajectories are pathways through communicative episodes. Trajectory, like Goffman's (1974) term "strip," indicates a series of acts occurring in one time and experienced place. But the term trajectory also emphasizes the sense of being-on-a-path, of interactive thrown-ness along an emerging course. Trajectories reveal turning points, both abrupt zig-zags and subtler shadings of direction.

How do actors accomplish these turning-points in episode trajectory? Analysts have considered related issues[2] by depicting interacting humans as performance artists who toil at multi-task sites. Social actors structurate their activities, in part, by formulating them into trajectories.

The following descriptions depict: (1) how play-partners, especially at trajectory turning-points, orient to a dialectic[3] between playful and serious activities; (2) how actors use practices of conversation (e.g. adjacency slot-construction) to in-form turning-points for episode trajectories; (3) how actors align joint activities by building upon partners' immediate prior utterances to extend a trajectory-in-progress; (4) how actors invoke and sustain normal forms of social action within play activities, (e.g., flirting, racial stereotyping).

## Play Episodes

Mammals, in certain skeins of interactional time, interactively construct improvised episodes of full-tilt, flooded-out play. Critics and scholars have long examined play activities to describe how human interaction works.[4] Psychologist Robert Bales, (1969) described play episodes in group interaction using the category-label *fantasizes* to indicate that play displaces other activities (especially task activities) for a period of time characterized by laughter and other celebration. The experience is poetic, and achieves jointly-created fantasy.

Anthropologist Gregory Bateson described play in zoo animals' mock combat. Bateson wondered about the accomplishments of framing involved in constructing a joint performance of play.[5] Goffman (1974) followed Bateson's lead to argue that we construct a play episode by placing a framing *key* at its beginning. For instance an opening curtain keys audience members that a set of fictional activity has begun. Thereafter, each message unit in the play episode is transformed by this key, or opening-bracket meta-message. Each key indicates "when the transformation is to begin and when it is to end."[6] Likewise everyday fantasies in playful teasing are accomplished by keys placed at a opening bracket of the strip.

For over a decade my colleagues and I conduced futile searches for opening-bracket keys in play episodes. Rarely have we found clustering of play-keying at the very start of fantasizing episodes. Rather play gets re-accomplished and re-ratified throughout an episode, especially by shared laughter, speech errors, and repetition.[7]

UTCL D8

| | |
|---|---|
| Carol: | Have you ate t'day? |
| | (0.5) |
| Carol: | Eaten?= |
| Rick: | =eh heh heh= |
| Carol: | =day hay huh huh eated. ·hhhh= |
| Rick: | =No I- I- I- already eated heh heh heh |

In this segment Rick and Carol begin to play. But where is the front bracket to this activity: the key of the transformation "this is play?" Play-relevant keying is displayed throughout each utterance in this fragment. A speech error occurs in this segment's first line. The speaker self-corrects and the other laughs. The speaker repeats the error and does so "erroreonsly"! At the same time she laughs, accepting a pratfaller's role in the emerging play. This play frame gets created, sustained and changed through each of these interactive details-across-turns -- not just at play's opening moment. Each possible play-keying indicates the continuing relevance of the question: "Is this play?" (Bateson, 1972) Each such instance of interrogative-possible-keying thereby provides a slot for aligning activities that trace and project trajectory.

Drew (1987) describes one sort of playful episode trajectory in which teasing utterances are followed by serious, or "po-faced" responses. These instances display a three-turn path: a turn in which a speaker complains or brags to an "overbuilt" degree, followed by a tease, to which the teased party then responds as though the tease had been serious.

Cambell 4:5 (Drew, 1987: 224;236-7)

(1) B: I'm still gettin:g you know, hh ·hh stomach pains
I spewed last ni::ght, ... chronic diar we-e-ll,
just before Iwent to bed and.... I've been getting
funny things in front of my eye:s actually. ·hh A
bi:t, just slightly, Li:ght flashes. But uh,
(0.3) tsk (sti:ll.)
(2) A: Well you probably got a least a week.
(0.4)
(3) B: What of thi:s:.
(0.3)
A: No a week before you die:,
B: Ohh yhhh heh heh

By the end of this segment, a three-part trajectory becomes evident: (1) overbuilt turn, (2) tease, and (3) po-faced response. Drew suggests that the episode-construction of teasing trajectories resembles those in other kinds of strips (in press). Speakers project trajectories, and their partners may react by agreeing-with-and-or-resisting proffered projections.

Each of Drew's descriptions inscribes only a few paths among a number of trajectory-shapes that teasing episodes may take. To enhance description of episode trajectories-in-progress we describe the trajectory-making in one playful episode. We conceptualize this episode's construction as the making, deployment and alignment-with of items within a series of slots in which utterances in-form ongoing dialectic between the "playful" and the "serious."

As teases are patterned on the serious, "po-faced" responses occur proximate to traces of amusement such as laugh tokens. This may be observed in Drew's example above. Drew's analysis focuses on the "po-faced," or somewhat serious "What, of this?" Notice, however, that this utterance actually may occur before the butt of the tease has comprehended its drift.

A: Well you probably got a least a week.
(0.4)
=> B: What of thi:s:.
(0.3)
A: No a week before you die:,
B: Ohh yhhh heh heh

"What of this?" communicates failed comprehension as much as absence of irony (po-faced seriousness). Speaker A then produces a fuller statement of the tease, specifying that "before you die" had been the implied predicate -- not the literal best-guess, the course of the current non-grave disease. This clarification elicits a gasp of recognition from the butt of the tease -- a change-of-state token followed by laughter. The tease, and tease-responses, unfold across multiple speaking turns. And the unique zig-zag episodic character of this teasing episode is accomplished by speaker B's displaying (in successive turns) serious and playful interpretations.

We describe below some turning points in one play episode. We perform this exercise to illustrate players' displayed orientations to a playful-serious dialectic.

## A Televised Play Episode

This play episode occurred on a televised talk show, which renders its details available to inspection. Also, live audience members' vocal appreciations of the performed play, audible on the recording, assist our efforts to find the episode's turning points. The program was broadcast on the North American Univision Network. The show's bilingual host, comedian Paul Rodriguez, skillfully interviews guests who speak Spanish and guests who do not -- such as actress Dyan Cannon (DC), for a largely-bilingual audience. In her interview DC has displayed a number of partially-informed opinions about Hispanic language and culture, culminating in an assertion that Hispanic men are more sensitive than Anglos. Rodriguez (PR) disagrees, citing his own frustrations with *machismo* mythology. PR especially decries the "myth of the Latin lover," and this utterance sparks a play episode. I propose that, at the points marked by arrows in the transcription, play keying turns upon exploitation of a playful-serious dialectic:

```
       PR:  .hhh this uh machi:smo stuff we have to live up to uh
            (.) to- to an image that we- th'we just can:'t you like
1=>         for example you know thee- ·hh the myth of the
            la:tin lover how we're en:dlessly cra:ving for love,
            and- ·hh an you all night long,
            uh [ look,
2=>    DC:     Sounds good to me: huh [huh huh huh huh
       PR:                             uhyuh
       DC:  [huh huh huh huh  huh huh huh huh
3=>    PR:  Wul let me tell you Dyan, we're goo:d now,
       DC:  HAH [HAH  hah  hah   hah  hah  hah [hah hah
       PR:        don't get us wro::ng,          th`y'know-
      AUD:  [((Laughter, whistles -->            ))
       DC:  [ hah ·hh ha ha ha, ·hh hah hah hah hah hah hah
       PR:  _huh-    uh huh     you kno:w
       DC:  [·h h h  [I-              [oli(h)-
4=>    PR:  but but  ALL NIGHT  L O : N G, come o:n.
```

DC: Oh (.) oh [ho hoh hah huh huh huh huh huh huh huh
5=> PR: [Ohnl- three, four ho:urs, oka:y.
DC: huh huh huh huh huh huh huh huh
[huh huh huh [huh huh huh huh
PR: [you know [even I could do that
DC: hhuh huh hah hah huh- ·hhh O::h
6=> [I bet you could go all night lo[:ng, Pa:ul.
PR: [(lets)- hhuh- [·hhhhh
AUD: (( gasp, OO_OO:::::: [OO ->
DC: [nuh [uh hah hah hah hah
7=> PR: [Yeah I could,
AUD: [OO:::::::: -> ))
DC: [hah hah hah hah hah hah hah hah hah hah hah ·hhh
hawh huh [huh huh huh huh huh huh huh huh huh
PR: [lemme t- lemme tell you Dyan
DC: ·hh huh huh huh huh huh [huh huh huh huh
8=> PR: [I couldn't vacuum
carpet all night long,

Description of the turns marked by numbered arrows in this extract may shed light on how players establish and modify an episode's trajectory. At each arrow we observe actors working *both* serious material and playful material into utterances. The playing becomes patterned on serious activity as speakers show alignment at those places where the tease-serious status of the episode is called into question.

1=> PR offers a serious characterization of the burdens that *machismo* stereotypes place upon Latin males. His sociological seriousness is keyed in his choice of the words "image" and "myth." His statement includes uses of the first-person plural pronoun "we," by means of which he claims first-hand experience in these burdens. Yet in the latter portions of the utterance, PR shifts focus from *machismo* in general to one example: stereotypes about *Latino* sexual performance. He exaggerates his intonation of the cliché phrase "all night long," and keys the word "all" by rolling his eyes. That is, PR's extreme case formulation (Pomerantz, 1986) for male sexual adequacy goes over-the-top of overbuilt seriousness into deconstructive irony.

1=> PR: ... myth of the la:tin lover how we're
en:dlessly cra:ving for love, and- ·hh an you all
night long,
uh [look,
2=> DC: [Sounds good to me:

PR projects this activity to indicate that progress toward a punchline ("look"); but DC interrupts this gambit to project a surprising new trajectory.

2=> DC responds to PR's overbuilt characterization of "Latin lovers" who perform "all night long" with: "Sounds good to me," which assesses positively the very thing that had been proposed as problematic. "Sounds good to me" cuts across PR's serious discussion of a negative aspect of cultural stereotyping by responding as if PR had been bragging, or even pre-inviting DC to sexual activity. This response casts DC as a candidate sexual partner who might appreciate a man's extremely virile performance. First, any assessment at this moment entails that DC is knowledgeable about sexual activities. Second, DC uses a singular pronoun, "me," and thereby shifts PR's social-participation tone ("we") toward a more personal focus. Whereas PR has spoken on behalf of his ethnicity's males, DC speaks of and for herself.

DC's tease, like those studied by Drew, may be taken as responsive to PR's overbuilt characterization "all night long." DC's tease retrospectively reframes PR's sociological discussion as sexual bragging or inviting. DC casts herself in a sexpot role by displaying this willfully thick mishearing. DC's utterance presupposes that PR has pre-propositioned her, and that she is pre-accepting. That is the serious read of DC's tease.

DC orients to possible playfulness in her utterance as soon as it clears her lips. She laughs right afterwards, apparently marking the utterance as a laughable, and inviting responding laughter which PR provides.

DC: Sounds good to me: huh [huh huh huh huh
PR: [uhyuh

PR orients to DC's tease by laughing briefly in overlap with her. PR's laugh is a minimalist, compelled-sounding exhaltation, like the response-cry men utter when punched in the stomach: "uhyuh." So far, this episode resembles those Drew describes: an overbuilt turn by PR and a teasing response by DC. But we observe that PR embeds playful elements into his overbuilt sociology (rolling eyes, a vocally-emphasized cliché), and that DC embeds serious elements in the answering tease.

3=> PR builds on DC's tease, repeating her term "good" with a twist into positive self-assessment of *Latinos'* sexual prowess: "We're good now."

DC: [huh huh huh huh huh huh huh huh
3=> PR: [Wul let me tell you Dyan, we're goo:d now,
DC: HAH [HAH hah hah hah hah hah
PR: [don't get us wro::ng,

Shrouded in laughter, PR's utterance at 3=> affirms the very sex-role stereotype he recently had been at pains to deny. PR still resists DC's singular pronoun, which makes some his phrasing sound a bit odd: e.g., "don't get us wrong." This hedges PR's stance: he is not yet responding personally to DC's tease, but still speaking on behalf of his ethnicity. On behalf of Latin men, however, he brags, and thereby extends the play proposed in DC's tease.

DC, responds with her loudest laughter of the segment, showing alignment as an appreciator of PR's possible play at 3=>. DC's extreme laughter exhibits mock-arousal at PR's assessment of Latin virility. PR subsequently laughs briefly in overlap with DC, keying probable acceptance of her invitation to laugh. Meanwhile:

4=> PR offers a possible backdown from his sexual bragging: "But all night long, come on." Notice that PR talks, and not too fluently, in the moments leading up to that utterance.

DC: HAH [HAH hah hah hah hah hah [hah hah
PR: don't get us wro::ng, th`y'know-
AUD: [((Laughter, whistles --> ))
DC: [ hah ·hh ha ha ha, ·hh hah hah hah hah hah hah
PR: huh- uh huh you kno:w
DC: [.h h h [I- . [oli(h)-
4=> PR: but but ALL NIGHT L O : N G, come o:n.

PR's dysfluencies (leading up to 4=>) can be shown as artifacts of an emergent contention for a speaking turn. In overlap with turn 4=>, DC attempts to speak. DC has been laughing with her face averted from PR. Just as she begins an in-breath she turns her gaze abruptly toward PR and spreads her hands into a shrug that indicates readiness to speak. DC has perceived this moment as a transition-relevance-place. From a reciprocity standpoint, it is her turn to speak.

But as it happens, PR overrides her attempt, and his performance in this turn-contention sheds light on how players launch playful actions. PR performs considerable activity to maintain the floor in order to add the turn-unit at 4=> to his gambit-in-progress. PR's right hand is especially active in this work. As both DC and the audience laugh in response to "we're good, don't get us wrong," PR engages in a series of right-hand gestures, which accompany his possible re-starts, "you know-" and (a and b below) "but but" (item c):

a. PR raises the right hand, and gives it a lateral shake. This two-sided gesture establishes a ready-and-cocked position for subsequent gestures.
b. PR's right hand touches the arm of DC's chair, which, intrudes into her personal space and acts as a possible summons to continuing attention.

c. As DC signals incipient speakership PR raises the right hand, palm toward DC, in a "hold on" gesture. As the competition for the floor intensifies, he raises this hand higher.

DC has turned away during PR's re-starts and gestures. She seems not to see the first two sets of gestures, and the audience's vocal responsiveness may obscure PR's vocal projections of continuing. DC therefore senses an opportunity to speak, and she prepares to speak as she turns toward PR with her shrug and in-breath. PR responds in kind to maintain the floor:

a. PR repeats his previous "but," making it into a vocal restart: "but but," and thereby upgrading his summons to attentiveness.

```
        DC:  [·h h h  [I-              [oli(h)-
4=>     PR:   but but ALL NIGHT  L O : N G, come o:n.
```

b. PR mimes DC's two-hand gesture, (at "ALL") leading with his already raised-for-attention right hand, but moving into a symmetrical shrug -- as if to say I see your shrug and answer you with a bigger shrug. The right hand, raised in this shrug, moves a bit toward DC as if driving her visually from the contested field.
c. PR increases his spoken volume, shown on the transcription by capital letters (See Schegloff, 1990).

These actions document two parties competing to build a trajectory-turning-opportunity slot at the same moment. The contention here shows both parties orienting to the projection of this moment as a moment appropriate for the next trajectory-turning. PR wins the turn and completes the punchline of a gag:

```
        PR:  [but but     [ALL NIGHT    [L O : N G, come o:n.
        DC:  Oh (.) oh   [ho hoh hah huh huh huh huh huh huh huh
5=>     PR:               Ohnl-  three, four ho:urs, oka:y.
```

5=> PR now characterizes the Latin-lover capacity as "three, four hours" -- still a high estimate. Hence he puts a stinger on the line he's been constructing: We're good, we can't go all night, just three or four hours! This estimate continues the line of "we're good," and hence it re-introduces the theme of sexual bragging. Thereby PR once more actualizes a sexual stereotype of virile *machismo*.

The brag continues with "even I could do that," which shows self-deprecation ("Even I"), and also displays PR's first use of a singular pronoun. PR marks the "I" with a pronounced head-toss, as well as with vocal emphasis. He has finally come out from sociological detachment and made himself a candidate for sex-play by stating his own qualifications as a performer. He thereby further embodies and further embraces a *machismo* stereotype.

Is this play? Is irony accomplished; in part by a recipient's response?

6=> DC casts a counter-tease, framed as a wager over disputed time-estimate of PR's capacity for sexual activity: "I bet you could go all night long."

```
       PR:  [you know        [even I could do that
       DC:  hhuh huh hah hah huh- ·hhh O::h
6=>         [I bet you could go all night lo[:ng, Pa:ul.
       PR:  (lets)-    hhuh-                ·hhhhh
      AUD:  (( gasp, OO_OO::::::
```

Since PR used "I" in his last utterance, DC may now specifically address his skills. DC delivers this "bet" line with a demure deadpan face, turning slightly away from PR. DC had been laughing as though "out of control," yet she suddenly stops laughing to deliver this line.

DC's format here builds into the banter of sex-play a suggestion of mock-bargaining: he has offered three or four hours, she is holding out for an offer to go all night, since she believes his kind of man to be capable of such activity. She answers PR's head toss on "I" with a coy head-cant on her emphasized word "bet." As PR has traded on his ethnicity to critique DC's sociology, DC here acts within blonde-bombshell-actress stereotypes to critique PR's sexual performance -- and to insist that he be the best that he could be at actualizing her ethnic-sexual stereotype.

The audience gasps appreciatively after this DC utterance, then utters a high-pitched choral "OO::::," indicating that DC has scored in the tease-game. Spectators' responses are important play-keys (Alberts, 1992). Only after the audience has clearly certified the effectiveness of this play gambit does DC end her deadpan holdout to join in the audience laughter.

```
      AUD:  (( gasp, OO_OO::::::  [OO ->
       DC:                        nuh [uh hah hah hah hah
7=>    PR:                            Yeah I could,
```

7=> PR says: "Yeah I could," which literally accepts what he has denied so far. Is this flirting? Bragging? A serious response? This utterance displays PR embracing in the first person the sexual-performance estimate that he previously had denied on behalf of his ethnicity and gender. PR has actualized his own overbuilt stereotype. Teasing's pun-ishments get locally occasioned to fit proximate crimes.

8=> PR offers a final self-assessment, his most self-deprecating of all, and one that entails denial of all that has gone before: "I couldn't vacuum carpet all night long." This is a po-faced response to DC's teases. It retrospectively indicates that all the foregoing has been foolishness: foreplay perhaps, but still play. At this point, PR also adroitly shifts the focus of the interview, and addresses his audience in Spanish. This language switch ends a play segment.[8]

## Conclusions

These observations illustrate some ways that two players (and a live audience) construct a trajectory through this episode. This particular episode's agons include sexual flirtation, as well as the raising and filling of a social stereotype. These themes emerge through co-enacted turning points constructed to be interpreted as both playful-ironic and serious-consequential.

PR initiates a serious disagreeing discussion of experiential sociology. DC's feint at seduction derails this topic, and also induces PR to enact the sexual-prowess aspects of the stereotype he had sought to escape. PR eats his words. DC's sexual conquest helps her escape from a weak case in a possible argument. It is also the accomplishment of a slur on Hispanic men. Teasing does ideology.

The artful timing of play's turning-points, and the players' combining of play and seriousness, can be matters of considerable delicacy. Many years ago, when my brother-in-law enjoyed great success in teasing our mutual parents-in-law, I attempted to initiate some teasing trajectories at their expense. I did not achieve playful or celebratory uptake. When I asked my spouse why I had failed, she observed that my playful utterances had been "too true." The player's challenge is to achieve playfulness while casting actions that can bear serious interpretations -- but not too serious, not too close to the bone. "Too close" is measured by recipient response. All of this must be performed within constraints of timing and the other's probable options. And the performance must unfold as moment-to-moment improvisation. Too much planning, or rationality, may hinder play.

What are players doing, or trying to do, during such episodes? How should we treat the intentionality of playful give-and-take? Suppose you observe, when you look from an upstairs window, a person walking across a park, and entering a store on the other side of the park. You might describe the walker's action-path as relatively *purposeful* (she went to the store) or as relatively *emergent* (she crossed the park and entered the store). The first description entails that the walker engaged in planned strategic activity. The second account is comparatively agnostic about the walker's motives as the episode opens. Either account may describe the same observed activity, and neither accounting is in principle more patterned than the other. A walker's trajectory through a park, like play-partners' interactive path through an encounter, may be described as more or less constructed of actors' purposes.

Drew (in press) argues a distinction between trajectories undertaken in goal pursuit and those that emerge as found art. He exemplifies planned-pursuit trajectory using this instance of pre-invitation:

(NB:II:14) simplified

| | | |
|---|---|---|
| PRE | E: | Whadiyih doin. |
| | | . . . |
| REPORT | N: | I'm ironing . . . [it] leaves me cold |
| INVITE | E: | Yeah Wanna come down'n have a bite a lunch with me? |

These partners' three-part path shows evidence of E's purposeful pursuit of an invitation, and N's report of ironing activity shows compliance with that pursuit.[9]

Drew argues that, in a second kind of trajectory, the sequential relevance does not unfold in response to speakers' plans, but emerges in interaction. Drew's example of emergent trajectory is the teasing series described earlier: (1) overbuilt turn, (2) tease, and (3) po-faced response. Although this pattern is an interactive phenomenon relevant to the participants, no participant anticipates or plans its course. Rather, speakers generate it out of the normal turn-by-turn course of interaction.

Drew's cases are usefully described, but the present discussion blurs his distinction. The trajectories of DC and PR are neither clearly purposeful, nor only emergent. The present descriptions have emphasized emergent accidence in the episode. Yet much of the analysis would not change were we to learn that these actors had carefully rehearsed this episode's course. Furthermore, even the most emergent trajectories usually get constructed from relatively prefabricated subroutines -- especially in sexual banter.

Finally, we might observe members of a culture making judgments about whether, for instance, DC is a "flirt" or a "bigot" based on this episode. In what ways do these judgments (like court judgments of wrongdoing) turn on the (lay or scholarly) analyst's estimates of the extent of a player's premeditation? How do actors calculate and negotiate such estimates? May scholars advise citizens about such quasi-theoretical judgments?

Until we can offer such advice, analysts may wish to remain agnostic about speakers' purposes or conscious strategy during trajectory preliminaries (Heritage, 1991). This stance does not limit episode-description, but stresses the structuring interactive emergence of trajectory across turns. Speakers interact to create lines of action, and these lines continue to evolve functions and structures during enactment. Preliminary utterances leave some options open. Actors project possible paths with vague or ambiguous gestures -- gestures that entice other actors to answer in kind.

The emergent productivity of play grows from activity forms packaged into back-and-forth iteration across speaking turns. Play trajectories get built as speakers instantiate dialectic orientations to the playful and to the serious. Gadamer (1975) argues that play's back-and-forth motion is the ground of being from which all artistic action flows. Playful interaction seems to flow without effort, on its own momentum. The individual speaker recedes, and we hear Whitman's America singing.[10] Play episodes lift up a corner of the universe to reveal the great Poem, speaking us.

---

* Many colleagues worked these data with me including: Phil Glenn, Jess Alberts, Kent Drummond, Bud Morris, Sandra Ragan, Jenny Mandelbaum, Jurgen Streeck, Charlotte Jones, Ray Thomason, Duff Wrobbel, and Madeline Maxwell (who collected this tape of the Paul Rodriguez show). Paul ten Have, Gail Jefferson, and Paul Drew provided valuable criticism of earlier versions of this work.

1 Here are some reflections on the notion of "trajectory" and the notion of "sequence." The term *sequence* denotes organization of more than one utterance by more than one speaker, such that the utterances display conditional relevance to each other. That is, given the occurrence of one item in a sequence, a next item may be projected. If any utterance-part of a sequence is missing, interaction participants hear it as "officially absent." (Schegloff, 1972: p. 363) Adjacency pairs provide prototypes of conditional relevance.

Certain sequential analyses of lengthy strips of talk have concentrated on those utterances that show conditional relevance to one another, e.g., analyses of pre-sequences: (Terasaki, 1976; Schegloff, 1980; Drew, 1984; Heritage, 1984) sequential analyses of stories (Sacks, 1970, lecture 2; 1974; Jefferson, 1978), and analyses of topic initiations (Button and Casey, 1984).

Similarly, telephone openings display series of adjacency sequences (Schegloff, 1968, 1979, 1986; Hopper 1989a and b, 1992a and b). Telephone partners establish *slots*, (Sacks, 1975 p.,70; Hopper, 1992b, Chapter 3) or moments at which a first pair-part offers a range of respondent options. For example an initial inquiry like "how are you?" accomplishes a slot that may be filled by utterly routine responses like "fine," or by trouble-premonitory responses like "Oh, not too bad." (Jefferson,1980b). Options within each slot provide opportunities to steer emerging episode trajectory.

The Sacks et al. (1974) turn taking model is based in a kindred conditional relevance, that a next speaking turn should occur immediately upon the completion of the prior turn. Further, each next turn takes up an obligation to show some analysis of immediate prior activity.

Sequential analyses have shown some ways that conversational partners begin topics and stories. But we have only begun to illuminate the courses of story plot or topic development. These issues may not be resolved entirely by conditional relevance.

One proposal: *to reserve the term "sequence" to instances satisfying strong tests for conditional relevance. and use terms such as "series" to describe utterances connected in less lockstep ways.* This proposal is complicated by fuzzy boundaries of conditional relevance phenomena.

Pomerantz's notion of action chains (1984; 1980) describes weakly-bonded utterance sequences. The relationship between first and second assessments, for instance, may fail to satisfy tests for conditional relevance, but the actors constructing these utterances do show (thereby) relevance ties between utterances and actions. A first utterance in (what turns out to be) an action chain establishes a moment in interaction that is especially rich with somewhat specifiable possibilities for responsivity. A consequent turn in an action chain is any utterance that, upon analysis, displays itself to be responding to another part of a sequence-like activity.

In the current essay, we review some of Drew's descriptions of teasing episodes as action chains: If a tease does not elicit a po-faced response, has such a response been made officially absent? Probably not; there are to be numerous directions that could be taken in response to teases: counter-teasing, displays of amusement, showing anger, asking "are you kidding?" and so on.

One of the tasks of the current essay is to supplement what can be described as "sequential" with descriptions of other phenomena: that is, to integrate strong-sequential explanations, weak-sequential explanations, and other activity we can observe actors doing to build a path through a play episode.

2 The following are especially valuable to the present inquiry: Sacks on jokes and stories; (e.g., 1979; 1971 lectures) Jefferson on shared laughter, (1979; Jefferson *et al.* 1987), troubles-telling, (especially 1980a, 1988) and on the poetics of conversation, (1977) Drew on po-faced receipts of teases, (1987) invitation sequences (1984), and anticipatory interactive planning (in press); C. Goodwin (1984) and M. Goodwin (1991) on participation in stories.

3 This notion of dialectic owe's Jefferson's (1980a) description of troubles talk as orienting to a dialectic between telling the trouble and returning to business as usual. Are we justified in using this term, dialectic, to describe alternations in conversation? Abbagnano (1958) describes philosophical uses of the term dialectic, noting that each of these uses rests on presupposed dialogic interchange, e.g., of questions and answers.

4 See Huizinga's *Homo Ludens*, the first 70 sections of Wittgenstein's *Philosophical Investigations*, Gadamer's *Truth and Method*: 90ff.

5 Bateson labeled such framing "metacommunicative," a term that has baffled us ever since. Human play episodes commonly include commentary on form. Perhaps there are families of meta-speech objects (Schiffrin, 1980; Simons, 1990) that indicate and frame an utterance: e.g., "Isn't that what you said?" Simons (1990) refers to instances in political discourse in which parties are "going meta," or moving out the ordinary forward-moving focus of talk to raising awareness of previous talk. Simons' use of "going" shows speaker activities shifting partners' attention-state to discourse.

6 Goffman, 1974:45. He writes that, "like brackets in mathematics, keys establish the boundaries of a strip of any length, all items in which are to be transformed in the same way and at the same time, and a place next to and on the outside of the left-hand bracket, the operator slot, in which any mathematical expression there inserted determines what the transformation will be" (254). As the "a" in the expression a(x + y) transforms both items inside the bracket, the keying of a "drama" frame by a raised curtain transforms each actor's utterance during a theatrical performance.

7 Hopper and Glenn, in press; Hopper, 1992b: chapter 8; Glenn, 1989; this volume. These works may be summarized as follows:

> ***Speech errors:*** We play when we make speech errors -- and orient to these errors -- Play often gets begun after we say something (as Drew puts it) "overbuilt." Jefferson's treatment of poetics of conversation (1977) begins with a discussion of the poetic properties of speech errors, because they provide a break in the normal surface of speech, at which poetic phenomena can be observed. The performer of an error may experience a comic pratfall, a moment of broken surface, that may chain out into extended play episodes. Hence, certain speech errors operate, at least in retrospect, as opening brackets. Once play episodes are underway, there are uses for further errors, figurative language, and stretching of language's capabilities.
>
> ***Shared Laughter*** fuels speakers' alignments to play activities. When laughter occurs, it ties itself to the last thing said (Sacks, 1991, Volume 1, p. 746), and celebrates that prior event by inviting play-keying. Parties share laughter by marking actions as potentially laughable (Jefferson, 1979). Glenn, who defines shared laughter as occurring in overlapping or immediately adjacent turns, finds that most play episodes include rejuvenating bursts of laughter every few seconds (1989).
>
> ***Repetitions*** enfigure the structure of a trajectory. Gadamer writes, "Play... renews itself in constant repetition." Aristotle defined all poetic activity as imitation. Bateson writes that play emerges in imitation of combat. In conversation-play partners frequently repeat things said shortly before. Repetitions accomplish repair initiation, metacommunication, and play keying. Any repetition may do all of these at the same time (Hopper, 1992a).

8 This play segment is part of a cluster of such episodes, which had begun earlier, and would flare up again moments later. It seems characteristic of play, especially sex play, that its episodes cluster together in groups. Once partners have done a spate of such play, it is easier to go back into that play.

---

9 Alternatively, the recipient of such a pre-invitation may report non-trivial activities (such a typing up a course paper, see Hopper, 1992b: chapter 7), that may be used to justify refusing a possible invitation. A projected trajectory may be resisted as well as embraced.

10 Because the present formulation postulates a primacy of poetic activity over rhetorical activity, we must not presume that all utterance-skeins are meritorious literary artifacts. The DC-PR episode is, after all, a largely doggerel re-enactment of stereotyped formats in pursuit of retrograde ideological statements.

# 5

# "Mm hm" tokens as interactional devices in the psychotherapeutic in-take interview [1]

Marek Czyzewski

## I. Introduction

### *1. "Big issues" and "garbage"*

"In one of his lectures, Harvey Sacks proposes that the social sciences have tended to view a society as having 'relatively few orderly products, where then much of what else takes place is more or less random.'" Effectively, sociology "tends to focus on 'what are in the first instance known to be big issues, and not which is terribly mundane, occasional, local, and the like.'" The alternative approach offered by Sacks consists in the research presupposition "that there is order at all points." The alternative approach leads to the preoccupation with the "garbage," i.e., with the phenomena usually considered to be "terribly mundane" as well as "'too trivial to be one of society's orderly products'" (Jefferson 1984:97).

The main advantage of Sacks' recommendation "one may alternatively take it that there is order at all points" lies in the possibility for paying attention to those aspects of the interaction which are usually conceived to be irrelevant in terms of the interaction order. In this way, Sacks' recommendation appears to be a conversation-analytic application of Garfinkel's original recommendation to focus the ethnomethodological interests on the "ignored orderliness." Both ethnomethodology and conversation analysis are an operation on common-sense and sociological relevance structures (in Schütz's sense of the term) -- both ethnomethodology and conversation analysis tend to accord relevance to what "lay" as well as "professional" sociologists consider to be either simply irrelevant or so obvious that "there is no use even to talk about it."

Response tokens such as "mm hms" are a salient example in this context. From the common-sensical as well as from the sociological point of view, "big issues" refer to social structure, systems of values, macro-processes (for example, urbanization), and social problems (for example, alcoholism). Consequently, any interest in the structure of talk appears to be superfluous or "un-sociological." Generally, all interactional concerns seem to be "garbage," even if larger interaction objects (i.e., sequences) are to be taken into consideration, or even if the talk under investigation occurs in the social framework of "big issues." But to claim that small bits of talk such as "mm hms" can have vital importance for the construction of the interaction order is to take the double risk, because "mm hms" seem to be the very worst sort of "garbage" ever heard, the residual "garbage."

## 2. *The conversation-analytic approach to "response tokens"*

Some of the research in CA has dealt directly and explicitly with such "response tokens" as "mm hm," "uh huh," "yeah," etc. (Schegloff, 1982; Jefferson, 1984; Heritage, 1984; and others). The conversation-analytic approach to "response tokens" differs programmatically from that of linguistics and sociolinguistics. According to conversation analysis, both "lay" as well as "professional" linguists and sociolinguists tend to separate the "real talk" from the other "accompanying" conversational events. What is being separated and discarded can be picked up by the "professional" investigators for separate treatment under the rubric of "backchannel communication." The general characterization of the backchannel communication refers to signaling attention, interest or understanding.

Contrary to this research strategy, conversation analysis itself does not intend to extract bits of talk from their local embeddement in the ongoing interaction process. Instead, conversation analysis tries to show that (a) "response tokens" can be heard differently, depending on their sequential placement, and (b) that effectively, "response tokens" can have systematically different sequential implications. In general, conversation analysis is interested in the "job" which "response tokens" do in the interaction (Schegloff 1982; Heritage 1985).

It is worth noting that "response tokens" are in part non-lexical items (again, "mm hms" can serve as an example). Exactly with regard to these cases the controversy between the linguistic and conversation-analytic approaches becomes particularly visible.

According to the linguistic research of Konrad Ehlich (1979) on singular "hm" tokens in German, the pragmatic function of a token is constitutively connected with its phonetical profile. Ehlich claims that the pragmatic function of "hm" tokens amounts to the expression of the "convergence" (agreement) or "divergence" (disagreement) between the conversational partners. Four basic phonetical profiles of a "hm" token are said to express different versions of "convergence" and "divergence," respectively.

The approach of Ehlich can be described as an "atomistic" one. Contrary to the "atomistic" approach, conversation analysis enrolls in the "*Gestalt*-dynamic" tradition. According to conversation analysis, the meaning of the non-lexical items depends on their sequential location, and not the other way around. Moreover, in this context it may be claimed that "response tokens" might be considered to be the implicitly prototypical object of conversation-analytical research. In the tradition of speech act theory, Ehlich is interested in the perfomative function of "hm" tokens (i.e., the expression of the "convergence" or "divergence" between the conversational partners). As it will be explained, the conversation analytic interest refers to strictly interactional functions of "mm hm" tokens (i.e., to how "mm hm" tokens are interconnected with the ongoing process of talk).

From the conversation-analytical point of view, there are two main features of "response tokens" which deserve special attention: (a) presumably irrelevant, "residual" utterances can in fact be of significant interactional relevance; deployment of "response tokens" is an aspect of the construction of the interaction order; (b) response tokens are *interactional devices*, i.e., they should not be considered as isolated signals fulfilling some specific communicative function, but rather as locally situated components of the ongoing interaction organization.

### 3. *Gail Jefferson's study on the deployment of "mm hm" tokens -- an initial comparison with results of my research*

Gail Jefferson (1984:200) has suggested that the deployment of "mm hm" and "yeah" tokens differ systematically: "'Yeah' can exhibit a preparedness to shift from recipiency to speakership, while 'Mm hm' exhibits [...] 'Passive Recipiency.'" The latter means that "its user is proposing that his co-participant is still in the midst of some course of talk, and shall go on talking." The interactional job which is accomplished by "Passive Recipiency" is concurrent with what Emmanuel Schegloff (1982:81) has described as a "continuer" with regard to "uh huh," "mm hm," and other similar tokens: "perhaps the most common usage of 'uh huh,' etc. (in environments other than after yes/no questions) is to exhibit on the part of its producer an understanding that an extended unit of talk is underway by another, and that it is not yet, or may not yet be (even ought not yet be) complete."

In my research, I have located four different interactional devices based on a systematically different use of "mm hm" tokens:

- the *conversation-oriented* "mm hm,"
- the *analytical* "mm hm,"
- the *parallel* "mm hm," and
- the *starting* "mm hm."

The first three "mm hm" interactional devices can be treated as a further specification and internal differentiation of "Passive Recipiency" (Jefferson) or "continuer" (Schegloff). The fourth interactional device based on "mm hm" operates very much like "yeah" in Gail Jefferson's description ("shift from recipiency to speakership"). I shall present the four versions of "mm hm" interactional devices in the following.

## II. Research findings and some questions for further consideration

### *1. The conversation-oriented "mm hm" and the analytical "mm hm"*

(A) The *conversation-oriented* "mm hm"

"Mm hms" of this kind can occur at a transition-relevance place, especially when the patient has just come to the potential completion of his/her utterance. Sometimes it happens as well that the intonation of the patient is falling. Directly afterwards, or after a short pause the therapist makes use of a "mm hm" token in the following way:

- the intonation is slightly rising,
- the second sound of the "mm hm" is often stressed,
- the volume is as usual (i.e., performed neither discernably louder nor lower than in the surrounding talk).

The precise transcription of the *conversation-oriented* "mm hm" looks as follows: [ mm *hm*? ], or, according to the Polish spelling: [ m*hm*? ].

There are two alternative developments of this interactional device:

a) either the patient continues to speak after a relatively short pause (as in example 1), or
b) a longer pause occurs after which the therapist takes his/her turn in talk (as in example 2).

1. ((P=Patient, T=Therapist))[2]

| | | |
|---|---|---|
| 1 | P: | Well simply I can't get any air. |
| 2 | | (0,6) |
| 3 | T: | mm *hm*? |
| 4 | | (.) |
| 5 | P: | If if is (still) somewhat loose then yes but if there are more people then it seems to me that I just suffocate and, |

| | | |
|---|---|---|
| 1 | P: | No po prostu duszno mi sie robi. |
| 2 | | (0.6) |
| 3 | T: | m*hm*? |
| 4 | | (.) |
| 5 | P: | Jezeli jakies tam luzy (jeszcze) no to jeszcze ale jezeli wiecej osob no to juz wydaje mi sie ze sie calkiem dusze i, |

2. ((and later in the same interview))

53 P: In the hall I could barely sit there and wait.
54 (0,4)
55 T: mm *hm*?
56 (3,6)
1 T: Have you tried to do something about this during
these last five years ?

53 P: Ja juz tu nie moglam na tym korytarzu wysiedziec.
54 (0.4)
55 T: m*hm*?
56 (3,6)
1 P: Czy pani probowala cos z tym zrobic od tych
pieciu lat?

In other words, the *conversation-oriented* "mm hm" is an interactional device which operates as an "encouragement" (the patient is being "encouraged" by the therapist to continue his/her utterance).

The "encouragement" appears to be effective when the patient continues to speak after a short pause. In such cases the therapist manages to transform both "inter-turn" silences (the silence between the patient's first turn and the "mm hm," as well as the silence between the "mm hm" and the patient's second turn) into what can be effectively heard as one "intra-turn" silence on the part of the patient. The therapist steps back, so to speak. He/she makes room for the patient, as if the therapist had not said anything at all.

The "encouragement" proves to be ineffective when the therapist takes his/her turn in talk, preventing a possible longer pause which might have appeared to be problematic. In cases like that the silence between the patient's turn and the "mm hm" continues to be heard as the actual "inter-turn" silence, while the silence between the "mm hm" and the therapist's turn is being transformed into what can be heard as the therapist's "intra-turn" silence.

To recapitulate: I propose to call the first option an *effective continuer*, and the second one an *ineffective continuer*. The first option would be interchangeable with what G. Jefferson has identified as "Passive Recipiency," and what E. A. Schegloff has called "continuer." Within the other option the therapist becomes active -- he/she initiates the next turn. Both options accomplish the same "job" in the conversation -- they contribute to a minimization of pauses and, in this way, to the fluency of talk.

(B) The *analytical* "mm hm"

This kind of "mm hm" can not only occur when the patient has just come to the potential completion of his/her utterance and his/her intonation has been falling, but also when the patient interrupts his/her turn (e.g., an identifiable phrase has not been completed, the intonation is continuing). In both cases the silence after the patient's turn is usually short. After this pause the therapist makes use of a "mm hm" token in the following way:

- the intonation is continuing,
- the second sound of the "mm hm" is often prolonged,
- the "mm hm" is spoken discernably more quietly than the surrounding talk,

The precise transcription of the *analytical* "mm hm" looks as follows: [ °mm hm:°, ] or, according to the Polish spelling: [°mhm:°,].

The following instance may serve as an example:

3. (this example stems from an interview led by another therapist))

44 P: And right now,
45 (0.4)
46 T: °mm hm°,
47 (5,2)
48 P: And right now I already don't- don't feel afraid
when I'm with him anymore.

44 P: A w tej chwili,
45 (0,4)
46 T: °mhm°,
47 (5,2)
48 P: A w tej chwili juz nie- nie czuje przy nim
strachu.

The crucial sequential implication of this kind of "mm hm" is that after the subsequent pause (which can be quite long, up to several seconds) it is the patient who takes the floor again. The patient's second utterance may contain a continuation of the patient's previous utterance or an introduction of the new topic. In other words the analytical "mm hm" is a specific version of "Passive Recipiency" or the "continuer." Therefore I propose to call this interactional device the *passive continuer*.

From the formal point of view, the interactional function of the *passive continuer* is similar to that of *effective continuer*: in both cases the pauses before and after "mm hm" tokens are being retrospectively transformed into what can be heard as a longer "intra-turn" pause. The specific feature of the *passive continuer* is that relatively long pauses after the "mm hm" tokens are being regularly tolerated.

It is important to note that the *analytical* "mm hm" operates often in context of the patient's avowals concerning his/her personal situation or his/her family history. More specifically, the interactional implication of the analytical "mm hm" consists in the continuation or solicitation of the patient's personal avowal. This may be seen in the extended transcript of the instance quoted above:

3a. ((an extended transcript of example 3; begins directly after the sequence on the endocrinological tests))

| | | |
|---|---|---|
| 37 | | (2,4) |
| 38 | T: | u:hh. |
| 39 | | (1,6) |
| 40 | P: | hh Well in general I- I- I have always been so since I was child ((longer statement of the P. about her childhood and fear of her father - ca.1min.)). |
| 41 | | (0,4) |
| 42 | T: | °mm hm°, |
| 43 | | (5,2) |
| 44 | P: | And right now, |
| 45 | | (0,4) |
| 46 | T: | °mm hm°, |
| 47 | | (5,2) |
| 48 | P: | And right now I already don't- don't feel afraid when I'm with him anymore. |
| 49 | | (0,4) |
| 50 | P: | Not at all. |
| 51 | | (0,8) |
| 1 | P: | I can say that's- that's been gone for- for two- two years now. |

| | | |
|---|---|---|
| 37 | | (2,4) |
| 38 | T: | u:hh. |
| 39 | | (1,6) |
| 40 | P: | .hh Ja to juz w ogole od dziecka jes- jes- jestem taka ((longer statement of the P. about her childhood and fear of her father - ca. 1min.)). |
| 41 | | (0,4) |
| 42 | T: | °mhm°, |
| 43 | | (5,2) |
| 44 | P: | A w tej chwili, |
| 45 | | (0,4) |
| 46 | T: | °mhm°, |
| 47 | | (5,2) |
| 48 | P: | A w tej chwili juz nie- nie czuje przy nim strachu. |
| 49 | | (0,4) |
| 50 | P: | Absolutnie. |
| 51 | | (0,8) |
| 1 | P: | Moge powiedziec ze od- od dwoch- dwoch lat to- to mi przeszlo. |

Next to the sequence in which the therapist and the patient have reached an agreement that the patient should make the endicronological tests and present the results to the therapist, i.e., after closing a topic in conversation, it comes to a long pause (line 37) and the therapist's sigh (line 38). Thereafter the patient delivers a longer personal avowal dealing with her childhood, her problematic relationship with her father and her fear of him. For reasons of clarifying the formal structure of the whole sequence, only the introduction to this avowal is being rendered in this transcript (line 40). Next it comes to the series of the two analytical "mm hms" (first one in line 42 and another one in line 46) and then to the subsequent continuation of the patient's avowal.

Another option is illustrated in the following example:

4. ((following examples 3 and 3a, respectively, in the same interview))

10 P: Well generally you know there are (different-)
11 families .hh are very- very differently (
12 ) actually .hh not to create such
an atmosphere as uh for example I had at home.
13 (1,6)
14 T: °mm hm°,
15 (1,0)
16 P: We:ll my sister also: .hh ha:s (0,4) as the
mother of her child just a horrible really
*hor*rible attitude ((longer statement about the
P's sibling's -- ca.2min.).
17 (6,4)
18 P: And I am looking for an a*part*ment ((longer
statement about the P's family situation and
about her emotional state -- ca.2min.)).

10 P: Nie w ogole sa wie pan (rozne-) swoje zycie .hh
11 rodziny cal- calkiem inaczej naprawde (
12 ) .hh zeby nie stworzyc takiej atmosfery w
domu jak y przykladowo ja mialam.
13 (1,6)
14 T: °mhm°,
15 (1,0)
16 P: Moja siostra rowniez no: .hh ma: (0,4) podejscie
jako matka do dziecka no wrecz okropne no ok*rop*ne
((longer statement about the P's siblings -- ca.2min)).
17 (6,4)
18 P: I szukam mies*zka*nia ((longer statement about the
P's family situation and her emotional state --
ca.2min))

After the sequence on the patient's family problems and her own emotional state, the therapist proposes the generalized visual image of the patient's situation (lines 50-6). The patient accepts the proposed image (line 8) and starts to differentiate in general and very vague ways her family circumstances from other families (lines 10-12). The analytical "mm hm" in line 14 leads to the patient's interactional "explosion" consisting of her two subsequent longer personal avowals, specifying her family situation and her emotional state (lines 16 and 18; also in these cases, for reasons of clarifying the formal structure of the whole sequence, only the introductions to the longer utterances of the patient have been included in the present transcript).

As a preliminary recapitulation, it is worth mentioning that both the *conversation-oriented* as well as the *analytical* "mm hms" are interactional devices:

- they are systematically connected with the local construction, reduction, prolongation and/or tranformation of silences,
- they do not fully exclude each other although at least in part of the in-take interviews a clear preference for one or the other interactional device can be observed (examples 1 and 2 come from one interview, whereas examples 3, 3a and 4 are taken from an interview led by another therapist).

### 2. *Interconnection between the two "mm hm" devices and the overall organization of the therapeutic interview.*

(A) The *conversation-oriented* "mm hm" offers a specific formula of the therapist's control over the overall structure of talk, turn-taking and the length of pauses. The process of talk becomes fluent ("dialogical"), changes of "speaker" and "hearer" roles occur often, long pauses occur rarely or do not occur at all.

(B) The *analytical* "mm hm" offers a different formula of the therapist's control over the overall structure of talk, turn-taking and the length of pauses. The "dialogical" structure of talk is being often replaced by longer "monological" utterances of the patient (the "monological" utterances of the patient are obviously interactionally constructed as well, e.g., by the therapist's use of the *parallel* "mm hm," see below); these longer utterances often assume a character of personal avowals; longer pauses are tolerated by the therapist (in connection with the *analytical* "mm hm" or out of this connection as, e.g., in case of "inter-turn" pauses within the patient's longer utterances); questions put by the therapist are often spoken quietly.

If so, the following conjecture may be formulated: the two systematically organized ways of deployment of "mm hm" tokens (or, to put it in other words, the two interactional devices based on "mm hm" tokens), namely the *conversation-oriented* and the *analytical* "mm hms," respectively, are interconnected with the two varieties of the overall structure of the therapeutic interview. It is for this reason that I propose to understand both aforementioned "mm hm" interactional devices as *therapeutic* ones. The deployment of either the *conversation-oriented* or the *analytical* "mm hm" can be connected with the specifically different ways of therapeutic work.

### 3. *"Technical" therapeutic literature and conversation analysis.*

Apart from general and programmatic statements, therapeutic schools usually deliver more or less detailed "technical" recommendations as to how the conversation with the patient should proceed. The described *conversation-oriented* "mm hm" calls forth the principles of Rogerian therapy, while the *analytical* "mm hm" comes close to the principles of psychoanalytical therapy. For these reasons, I have retrospectively assigned the two categories to the described phenomena.

An important further research task might concern a comparison of two empirically describable "therapeutic styles" ("styles" of therapeutic conversation) with the "technical" recommendations offered in handbooks of therapeutic schools. The proposed research would relate to the relation between varieties of therapeutic "ideology" and varieties of therapeutic "practice."

### 4. The *parallel* "mm hm" and the *starting* "mm hm" as the two *ordinary* interactional devices in the therapeutic interview.

I have proposed to subsume the *conversation-oriented* "mm hm" as well as the *analytical* "mm hm" under the rubric of *therapeutic* "mm hms" because they both seem to be connected with the specificity of therapeutic work. Certainly, both the *conversation-oriented* as well as the *analytical* "mm hms" have their everyday prototypes. This is evident in the case of the conversation-oriented "mm hm" as a device contributing to the minimalization of the pauses in talk. In my transcripts of Polish everyday conversations, a similar interactional "job" is being accomplished with the use of Polish tokens "aha" and "no" (in English, "so," or "well"). The analytical "mm hm" as an interactional device does not seem to be self-evident in terms of everyday conversation competence as applied to ordinary situations in everyday talk. Instead, the everyday proto-version of the analytical "mm hm" appears to relate to what Gail Jefferson (1984:206-213) has called the "perverse" passive. Some uses of "mm hm" in everyday talk are "systematically 'perverse'" because -- according to the everyday conversation competence -- they appear to be "inappropriate," "misfitted," especially if they occur at points "where movement to speakership is appropriate." Gail Jefferson has observed that the "perverse" use of "mm hms" "can elicit further talk" and that this technique is "routinely used by interviewers." In addition to Jefferson's remarks, it seems to be plausible that the "perverse passive" performed in ordinary, "usual" circumstances of common-sensical talk can solicit the display of interactional uncertainty on the part of the conversational partner. Similarly, in one of the analyzed therapeutic in-take interviews the *analytical* "mm hm" has led to the following utterance of the patient: "I simply do not know what I should say."

In my data I have located two other varieties of "mm hm" interactional device: the *parallel* "mm hm" and the *starting* "mm hm." I propose to subsume these two varieties under the rubric of *ordinary* "mm hms" for the reason of their direct interconnection with the common-sensical mastery of ordinary everyday talk.

(A) The *parallel* "mm hm" occurs in overlap, i.e., when the patient's utterance is still on its way. The *parallel* "mm hm" can be heard as the therapist's understanding, acceptance or as an encouragement with regard to the patient's ongoing utterance. The intonation of the *parallel* "mm hm" can be either rising or continuing. I propose to call this kind of "mm hm" a *continuer in overlap*. The following example provides an illustration:

5. ((this example comes from the same interview as examples 1 and 2))

| | | |
|---|---|---|
| 19 | P: | lSimply l I can't get air alnymore l |
| 20 | T: | l°mm hm°,l l°mm hm°,l |

| | | |
|---|---|---|
| 19 | P: | Po l prostu l brakuje mi polwietrzal |
| 20 | T: | l°mhm°,l l°mhm°, l |

(B) The *starting* "mm hm" prepares the therapist's coming shift to speakership: it functions as a *shift operator*. Similarly to the *parallel* "mm hm," the intonation of the *starting* "mm hm" can be rising or continuing. The intonation of the *starting* "mm hm" can be locally differentiated from the *therapeutic* "mm hm" in a given conversational context, or it can keep an undifferentatied intonation profile. The local differentiation of the intonation profiles of the *therapeutic* and *starting* "mm hms" facilitates the patient's understanding of what the therapist is going to do next in the conversation: whether he/she is "encouraging" the patient to speak (as in the case of all varieties of the *therapeutic* "mm hm"), or is just beginning his/her own utterance (as in the case of the *starting* "mm hm"). The next two examples show the locally differentiated (example 6) and the locally undifferentiated (example 7) intonation profiles of the *starting* "mm hm":

6. ((this example comes from the same interview as examples 1 and 2))

| | | |
|---|---|---|
| 44 | P: | I *don't* know what is the matter with me anyway |
| 45 | | I know I can't get *air* anymore. |
| 46 | | (0,8) |
| 47 | T: | mm hm, I understand that- that there is also the fear yes? |

| | | |
|---|---|---|
| 44 | P: | *Nie* wiem co sie ze mna dzieje w kazdym razie |

45 wiem ze sie *dusze*.
46 (0,8)
47 T: mhm, Ja rozumiem ze- ze temu jakis lek
towarzyszy tak?

7. ((this example comes from the same interview as examples 3, 3a and 4 and appears in the interview directly before example 3a))

25 T: °And have you made these tests?°=
26 P: =Not yet (.) | not yet | (.) the next
27 T: |°not yet°. |
28 P: time.=
29 T: =°mm hm, If this matter should clear up somewhat
before our next meating then you'll bring the
results along ye:s?°

25 T: °A miala pani te testy zrobione°?=
26 P: =Jeszcze nie (.) | jeszcze nie | (.) za nastepnym
27 T: |°jeszcze nie°.|
28 P: razem.=
29 T: =°mhm, Jezeli do naszego nastepnego spotkania
ta sprawa bylaby jakos wyjasniona to niech pani
przyniesie ze soba wyniki dobrze:°?

It is possible that the use of *ordinary* "mm hms" (i.e., the *parallel* and/or the *starting* "mm hms") in the therapeutic context is systematically interconnected with the deployment of *therapeutic* "mm hms" (i.e., the *conversation-oriented* and the *analytical* "mm hms"). One of my initial conjectures is: the *parallel* "mm hm" as an interactional device can co-operate with the *conversation-oriented* "mm hm" as another interactional device. Both are close varieties of "continuer" (an *effective continuer* and a *continuer in overlap*, respectively). Both accomplish a similar common-sensically rooted "job" in a conversation. Moreover, in some local circumstances both devices appear to be sequentially coordinated: first the *parallel* "mm hm" "encourages" the patient to continue his/her utterance (still when it is on its way), then the *conversation-oriented* "mm hm" provides a further encouragement when the patients ceases to speak, as the following instance shows:

8. ((the example 8 is an extended transcript of the instance quoted above in example 5))

19 P: |Simply | I can't get air a|nymore | at this
20 T: |°mm hm°,| |°mm hm°,|
21 P: moment.=
22 T: =mm hm?
23 (1,0)

| | | |
|---|---|---|
| 24 | P: | And I just have to go out. |

| | | |
|---|---|---|
| 19 | P: | Po ⌊prostu⌋ brakuje mi po⌊wietrza⌋ w tym |
| 20 | T: | ⌊°mhm°,⌋ ⌊°mhm°,⌋ |
| 21 | P: | momencie.= |
| 22 | T: | =mhm? |
| 23 | | (1,0) |
| 24 | P: | I po prostu musze wyjsc. |

My other conjecture is that the use of the *analytical* "mm hm" seems to be connected with a substantially less frequent use of any other varieties of "mm hm." Besides, the analytical "mm hm" does not seem to be sequentially coordinated with the *parallel* "mm hm" the way the *conversation-oriented* "mm hm" appears to be.

### *5. The ambiguity of "mm hm" tokens.*

Given at least four functionally different varieties of "mm hm" interactional devices, the question arises whether a therapist is able to differentiate the production of the token so that the patient will be able to "hear" it appropriately. Especially when the therapist tends to use the same phonetical profile of the token in functionally different "mm hm" interactional devices within the same local context of conversation, one might expect that an ambiguity of a signal can lead to the temporary disorganization of talk. In fact, some therapists do not differentiate between the *conversation-oriented* and the *starting* "mm hm" phonetically. It happens as well that after a phonetically undifferentiated "mm hm" token both conversation partners (the therapist and the patient) begin to speak simultaneously. This can be treated as a formal feature of the therapist's lack of control over the local production of the interview.

However, two reservations should be made at this point. First, when I am talking about the phonetically differentiated or undifferentiated production of the "mm hm" token I mean neither an overall regularity nor a quantitative tendency throughout a single interview but only the *local* differentiation vs. undifferentiation of the token within a given interactional exchange. Secondly, it is doubtful whether the lack of local differentiation amounts to a sufficient condition for the patient's misunderstanding of what the therapist intends to do next in conversation. The decisive factor for the patient's clear and undisturbed "hearing" of the therapist's signals is the therapist's circumspection with regard to the sequential order of talk. Even if a therapist tends to use only one phonetically undifferentiated profile of the token throughout the whole interview in order to accomplish functionally different "jobs" in the conversation, he is still able to avoid the patient's confusion if, e.g., the *starting* "mm hm" occurs regularly after question-answer sequences and the *parallel* "mm hm" occurs very rarely (this example comes from my data -- from the interviews led by still another therapist than in the examples quoted above). Another important requirement for the patient's clear understanding of the "mm hms" produced by the therapist is also a cautious and limited use of tokens. For sure, the abundance of sometimes hardly discriminable signals cannot contribute to the patient's effective coping with the interview situation.

### 6. *On the "individual style" of a therapist.*

The conversation-analytic approach makes the question about the "individual style" of talking invalid. Social rules of talk are to be considered the only legitimate object of study. However, in the materials the individual differences between the therapists with regard to the use of "mm hm" tokens are easily discernable. Some therapists distinctively prefer the *conversation-oriented* "mm hm," while others prefer the *analytical* one. Some therapists visibly coordinate the use of "mm hms" with the sequencing order of talk; others fail to manage this. These presumably "individual differences" can be explained by reference to the social differences concerning at least two circumstances:

- the influence of a particular therapeutic school, and
- the different amount of one's own professional experience.

### 7. *What happens when the patient is crying?*

I was particularly interested in what happens (sequentially, with regard to "mm hm" devices) when the patient is ill at ease, visibly ashamed, when he/she is crying. Situations of this kind point to the double nature of the professional conduct: on the one hand the therapist is working on the case, using his/her techniques, exercising his/her interactional power over the patient (e.g., via "mm hm" devices as well as via numerous other therapeutic "tricks"); on the other hand, the therapist meets the Other who is suffering, vulnerable, and exposing himself to the therapist. According to the ethics of Emmanuel Levinas (1969), the first dimension is systematically organized as a totality and it is susceptible to analytical description, whereas the latter dimension relates to the moral responsibility for, and the unlimited subordination to the Other. Within the first dimension the therapist has to do with the client who should be processed in an appropriate and effective way; within the other dimension the notion of patient regains its original meaning relating to patience and suffering. Looking at my data conversation-analytically, I was interested in the reconstruction of some aspects of the systematically organized conversational "totality" more specifically: in the reconstruction of the "mm hm" interactional devices as components of the professional therapeutic competence. Another question which is relevant from the conversation-analytic point of view is how are the components of the professional therapeutic competence enrooted in the everyday interaction competence. Looking at the same data from an ethical point of view, I was interested in the moral responsibility of the therapist for the patient. Trying to benefit from both points of view, I was interested in whether it is possible to identify the observable features of responsibility -- such as, what happens when the patient is crying?

My observation is that therapists who usually apply the *conversation-oriented* "mm hm" tend to suspend this device when the patient gets tensed, visibly ashamed or starts to cry. The following instance provides an illustration:

9. ((this example comes from another part of the interview from which examples 1, 2, 5, 6 and 8 have been taken; crying is indicated with the & sign at either end of the passage))

| | | |
|---|---|---|
| 38 | P: | &And now I feel like crying because-&,= |
| 39 | T: | =What is it? |
| 40 | | (1,8) |
| 41 | T: | mm hm? |
| 42 | | (2,2) |
| 43 | P: | ((looks for the handkerchief)) &Simply when I tell it like that then- but .hh&, |
| 45 | | (1,4) |
| 46 | P: | &hh& |
| 47 | | (3,6) |
| 48 | P: | &Generally it is not at all easy for me u:h with °this°&, |
| 49 | | (1,6) |
| 50 | T: | °mm hm°, |
| 51 | | (14,8) |
| 52 | P: | &I try to explain this (to myself) and all but uh I can't .hh&, |
| 53 | | (0,6) |
| 54 | P: | &I don't know °why°&, |
| 55 | | (0,6) |
| 1 | T: | °mm hm°? |
| 2 | | (4,2) |
| 3 | P: | (Well) you can continue asking then hh. |

| | | |
|---|---|---|
| 38 | P: | &Teraz to mi sie plakac chce bo no-&,= |
| 39 | T: | =Co sie dzieje? |
| 40 | | (1,8) |
| 41 | T: | mhm? |
| 42 | | (2,2) |
| 43 | P: | ((looks for the handkerchief)) &Po prostu |
| 44 | | jak tak opowiadam to- ale .hh&, |
| 45 | | (1,4) |
| 46 | P: | &hh& |

| | | |
|---|---|---|
| 47 | | (3,6) |
| 48 | P: | &W sumie to mi nie jest tak latwo y: z °tym°&, |
| 49 | | (1,6) |
| 50 | T: | °mhm°, |
| 51 | | (14,8) |
| 52 | P: | &Staram (sobie) wytlumaczyc i wszystko ale y nie moge .hh&, |
| 53 | | (0,6) |
| 54 | P: | & nie wiem °dlaczego°&. |
| 55 | | (0,6) |
| 1 | T: | °mhm°? |
| 2 | | (4,2) |
| 3 | P: | (No) juz moze pani pytac hh. |

In the emotionally tense situation the therapist:

- is tolerating much longer pauses after the *conversation-oriented* "mm hm" than she usually does (lines 42 and 2), and
- she starts to use the *analytical* "mm hm," and tolerating long pauses afterwards (line 50).

Later in the interview, after the quoted emotionally tense episode the therapist returns to her usual deployment of the *conversation-oriented* "mm hm."

In accordance with Levinas, one might say that the therapist's responsibility for the patient is being displayed by her temporary renunciation of her own usual work procedure (suspension of the *conversation-oriented* "mm hm" device) for the sake of passive listening to the patient.

It might be interesting to observe what happens to the *analytical* "mm hm" device when the patient starts crying. Unfortunately I have no materials on situations of this kind. However, if listening is already enclosed in the analytical work procedure (within the *analytical* "mm hm" device) one could speculate that in this case the responsibility for the patient would require from the therapist that he/she does something "more" than mere listening, namely that he/she shows respect for and care about the patient in an active way.

Speaking more generally, my supposition is that responsibility for the Other in psychotherapy can be displayed by the therapist's temporary suspension of his/her work routine. More specifically, it might happen that the therapist transforms his/her usual, routine deployment of a therapeutic "mm hm" device if the patient gets visibly ashamed, tense or starts to cry.

## III. Analytical framework of the study: three dimensions of the therapeutic work.

Therapeutic work is a complex heterogenous activity. One can distinguish three dimensions of the therapeutic work:

- interaction work (everyday interaction competence),
- professional interaction work (professionally specific varieties of interaction competence), and
- responsible interaction work (display of responsibility for the Other).

Interaction work refers to rules of everyday talk as described in conversation analysis. Some orderly features of everyday ordinary talk re-occur in the context of professional conduct (e.g., the *parallel* and the *starting* "mm hms").

Professional interaction work includes interaction structures specific to therapeutic work, as e.g., the *conversation-oriented* and the *analytical* "mm hms." Further research should concern a possible comparison of therapeutic work with other professional (institutional, "system-specific") contexts as well as with its everyday prototypes.

Responsible interaction work refers to the work of the therapist under circumstances of the patient's visibly displayed tension. According to Levinas, "I" am responsible for the Other who suffers, who is exposed to me and ashamed, who needs help and concern. The question arises whether it is possible to identify the observable features of responsibility?

---

[1] This research has not been completed yet; all results are provisional. Twenty-nine recordings of psychotherapeutic intake interviews were at my disposal. The interviews were made by ten different psychotherapists at a mental health institution in Lodz, and have been recorded by myself. J. Stabno and I have transcribed 13 selected interviews from their beginning to their end. The research focus has developed during the research itself, that is to say that the research was not preceded by a formulation of hypotheses nor by a delineation of a more specific research interest.

[2] In each of examples, the English translation is followed by the original passage in Polish.

6

# Meeting Both Ends: Between Standardization and Recipient Design in Telephone Survey Interviews*

Hanneke Houtkoop-Steenstra

## Introduction

In modern societies, authorities and private companies frequently address citizens in order to obtain information on their beliefs, attitudes, needs, wishes and actions. For this purpose, researchers design a questionnaire and send it to a representative sample of the population that is requested to fill it out. In other cases the questionnaire is handed over to interviewers, who visit or telephone the intended respondents. The interviewers read out the questions, and fill out the respondents' answers.

To ensure reliability, the research instrument must be standardized. The instrument is reliable when it generates the same answers when the respondents are subjected to it again. All respondents must answer every question, and they must understand the questions in the same way. This means that the questions are to be formulated precisely and unambiguously, which easily leads to long and elaborate formulations (Boddendijk, 1991).

The research instrument must also ensure validity. Validity refers to the extent to which the questions are heard and responded to in the way that the researchers intended. The answers should not be influenced by the way in which the questions are formulated on the questionnaire or by the interviewer. The information provided by the respondents should match with their true beliefs, opinions, desires and actions. The questions, therefore, must not suggest that one response is more correct or desirable than another (e.g., Hyman, 1954; Kahn and Cannel, 1957).

It has been pointed out (e.g., Cicourel; 1964, Briggs, 1986) that reliability and validity are incompatible goals. Complete reliability implies complete standardization, though a completely standardized interview is not likely to obtain valid information on the respondents' real feelings and opinions. This knowledge has not decreased the extent to which survey interviews are being used.

In order to avoid bias in the interview, occasioned by interview errors, the interviewers must restrict themselves to the interviewing rules. These rules say, among other things, that no question should be dismissed, that the questions must be asked in the order in which they occur in the questionnaire, that every question must be worded as it is formulated, and that the interviewer must not provide the answer for the respondent (Kahn and Cannell, 1957).

These interviewing rules are contrary to the procedures that participants are normatively oriented to in ordinary conversation. Whereas questionnaires are designed for an unknown audience, talk in conversation is recipient designed. Speakers try to design their talk for their specific recipient (Sacks, Fall 1971, L15), and by reference to what the recipient knows (Sacks, Fall 1972, L5). This is possible since ordinary conversation is locally managed by the participants. They learn about their recipient in the process of the conversation, and they can adapt to this on an ad hoc basis.

There is also a tendency in ordinary conversation not to provide more information than seems necessary for the time being (Sacks and Schegloff, 1979, cf. Grice's (1975) maxime of quantity). This is contrary to the precise and elaborate way of formulating questions in standardized questionnaires. And since interviewers are not supposed to redesign the questions or to make inferences based on information given earlier by the respondent, respondents may be confronted with much more information than they need to answer a question.

Scholars in the tradition of survey research know that daily interviewing practice differs from how it is supposed to be done. Brenner's (1982) analysis of tape-recorded interviews showed that more than 30 percent of all questions were not asked as required. In a Dutch study, Dijkstra et al. (1985) found that interviewers altered the essential content or the meaning of the written questions, to the effect that 40 percent of all answers could not be trusted.

The survey researcher Schaeffer (1991: 368), states that "*locating where standardization fails and suggesting solutions require a closer look at interaction in the interview.*" She formulates a series of conversation analytical research questions. However, there are reasons to believe that this type of research will not provide suggestions on how to improve standardization (Mishler, 1986; Johnstone, 1991).

Suchman and Jordan (1990), for example, who studied five video-taped face-to-face interviews, recommend that the interviewer should be allowed to talk about the questions, and to engage in a limited form of recipient design and common sense inference. They state that the survey interview contains potential problems of validity because stories by the respondents and elaborations on their answers are disallowed. In the elaboration, respondents may contradict their initial response. However, "*as long as interviewers stop at the first acceptable response, the validity problem will never become apparent*" (ibid.: 236). Disallowing elaborations and stories prevents the interviewer from detecting possible problems in the understanding of the meaning of an utterance.

In this chapter I will concentrate on one particular phenomenon as it occurs in a series of Dutch computer assisted telephone survey interviews. One of the features of these interviews is that interviewers sometimes ask a question and provide the answer themselves. Let me give an example of this:

1 (CHRISTINE, question 74)

I: En (1.0) e:hm (1.0) kunt u mij
zeggen wat uw leeftijd is,=
=u had het al gezegd, éénenzeventig

I: And (1.0) u:h (1.0) could you
tell me your age,=
=you've already said that, seventy one

The interviewer may be seen as acting against the expectation that holds for ordinary conversation that one does not ask one's co-participant for information that he or she has already provided. At the same time the interviewer violates an interviewing rule that says that, in order to obtain valid research data one should not answer for the respondent.

This chapter shows that respondents in survey interviews are to a considerable extent normatively oriented to the conventions of ordinary conversation (Schegloff, 1990). It will be proposed that asking a question and providing the answer to it oneself, is a device that interviewers use to solve the interactional problem that their respondents' orientation to ordinary conversation constitutes. It will be further proposed that where the interviewers depart from the interviewing rules, they continue to manage their task of gathering valid information.

## The research data

The data presented here consist of Dutch survey interviews on adult education, as well as the written questionnaire on which these interviews are based. The questionnaire is designed by two sociologists who did the research. The interviews are carried out by trained interviewers employed by a marketing research company.

The population to be investigated exists of a random sample of Dutch people "*of 18 years or older, who went to Highschool or Lower Vocational School, but who have NOT completed it*," as it says on the questionnaire. The respondents are asked questions as: have you ever heard of the adult educational institution by the name of such-and-such, would you be interested in taking any courses, what do you consider good reasons to take any courses, how much time and money would you be prepared to spend on them, et cetera.

The questionnaire is designed for interactional use. This becomes clear from phrases like "*I would like to ask you*," and, as it is stated in the introduction, "*The conversation generally does not take very long.*"

## The analysis

Let us return to fragment 1, in which the interviewer asks a question and provides the answer himself.

1 (CHRISTINE, question 74)

I: En (1.0) e:hm (1.0) kunt u mij
zeggen wat uw leeftijd is,=
=u had het al gezegd, éénen[zeventig
R: [Eénenzeventig.
I: Eénenzeventig. Zei u hè?

I: And (1.0) u:h (1.0) could you tell me
your age,=
=You've already said that,
--> seventy [one
C: [Seventy one.
I: Seventy one. You said, right?
I: ((next question))

The next sequentially relevant action following the interviewer's age-question is the respondent's answer (Schegloff and Sacks, 1973). However, rather than allocating the turn to the respondent and awaiting an answer, the interviewer immediately takes the next turn and provides the requested information himself. In doing so, the interviewer may be seen as doing a self-correction (Schegloff et al., 1977) with respect to the type of action he performed in his turn of talk. What was a question during the time of the production of the utterance, is now redefined as a type of action that does not call for a respondent's answer, because she has "*already said that,*" as the interviewer indicates. The status of "*Could you tell me your age*" is retrospectively redefined by the interviewer as a case of reading a sentence on the questionnaire aloud.

This changes the co-participants' institutional identities (Heritage and Greatbatch, 1991) of interviewer and respondent. The normative procedure in research interviews is that the interviewer asks the questions and the respondent answers them (cf. Mazeland, 1992).[1] The interviewer then fills out the answer slots on his screen, which is an activity that falls outside the immediate scope of the interaction. Though hardly ever mentioned in the literature, interviewers have a double institutional task. Apart from being an interviewer as such, which implies asking questions to respondents, they have the task of filling out the form. And as item 73 of this questionnaire ("*Int.: note sex without asking*") makes clear, this second task does not always require asking questions.

Now, rather than being involved in questioning and answering, interviewer and respondent begin to fill out the form collaboratively. The respondent helps the interviewer do his institutional work by repeating what she has told him earlier: *"seventy one."* And the interviewer makes sure he got this right: *seventy one. You said, right?"*

Before mentioning the respondent's age, the interviewer gives the basis of his knowledge (Pomerantz, 1984): *"you've already said that."* Later on he requests the respondent to confirm the correctness of his assertion: *"seventy one. You said, right?"* This turns the interviewer's initial statement into a candidate answer confirmed by the respondent. The authorship of the information as it will be noted on the form, can be credited to the respondent in that way (Pomerantz, 1988). The interviewer has generated accountable information, that is, information that is taken as verifiable, objective, valid, and properly achieved.[2]

In generating accountable information in this way, the interviewer manages to do both institutional and conversational work. With the phrase *"you've already said that"* he shows his recipient that he is a competent conversationalist, who listens to her and who does not request information which he has already been given several times. In self-correcting his initial question, he prevents a possible other-correction by the respondent (Schegloff et al., 1977), who otherwise might have said: I have already told you.

This fragment is from the last section of the interview, which is devoted to demographic questions, one of them being the respondent's age.[3] The interviewer's situation is that the question and the answer slot show up on the screen one by one, and in a fixed order. At this point of the interview the age question appears, and the interviewer has to enter the respondent's age.

However, just asking this question and waiting for the answer, as the interviewer is supposed to do according to the interviewing rules, would occasion an interactional problem, because the respondent has already voluntarily mentioned her age earlier in the interview. Ordinary conversationalists design their talk for their recipients, which, among other things, means that they take the history of the conversation into account. From that perspective, the interviewer is not supposed to ask the age-question, and he shows that he is indeed oriented to this conversational principle.

The first question on the questionnaire is concerned with the respondents' highest level of education. This question comes right after the interviewer has made sure that the person who answered the telephone meets the research criteria. The question is worded on the questionnaire as following:

ITEM 12

Allereerst wil ik u vragen, wat de hoogste opleiding is, die u in het VOLLEDIG dagonderwijs heeft gevolgd? Onder volledig dagonderwijs verstaan wij een opleiding, die minimaal drie dagen per week wordt bezocht.

> First of all I would like to ask you, what is the highest level of education that you took in FULL-TIME daytime education. By full-time daytime education we mean any course or education that is taken at least three days a week.

In the following three fragments, in which this question is delivered to the respondents, we again find the interviewer providing the answer himself.

2 (DAME, question 12)

I: Eerst wil ik u vragen wat uw hoogste
opleiding is geweest, (.) die u in het
volledig dagonderwijs heeft gevolgd,=
=>dat was het lager onderwijs zei u hè?
R: 't Lager onderwijs, en dan heb ik nog
een eh k- een eh een jaar voor de zaak
een eh (1.0) ja, hoe heet dat nou eh (0.4)
dat diploma heb ik moeten halen.=
I: =Hoe heet dat diploma?
R: Vakkennis.
I: <VAK KEN NIS:> ((op dicteertoon))
R: Vak- eh ja van de winkel moest ik dat
allemaal kennen. .hh
I: Ja, en is dat een schoolopleiding geweest?=
R: =Dat was eh (1.2) een paar keer in de week.
moest ik da [ar
I: [MINIMAAL drie dagen in de week?
[Of
R: [Ja:, ja:.
(0.8)
R: Drie keer in de week.
I: Drie keer in de week.
R: En in Maastrich ben ik toen voor dat diploma gegaan.

I: First of all I'd like to ask you
what is your highest level of
education (.) that you took in full-
time daytime education,=
that was elementary school you
said, right?<
R: Elementary school, and then I also
took a uh c- a uh a year for the
store a uh (1.0) well, what's it
called uh (0.4) I had to get
this certificate.=

I: =What's the name of this certificate?
R: Professional knowledge.
I: <PRO FES SION AL KNOWL E:D GE>
R: Prof- eh yes because of the store I
had to know all this. .hh
I: Yes, and was this a school?=
R: =That was uh (1.2) a few times a week.
I had to go the[re
I: [AT LEAST three days a week?
[Or
R: [Ye:s, ye:s. Three times a week.
I: Three times a week.[4]
R: And in Maastricht I went for that certificate,

As in fragment 1, the interviewer reads out the question and rather than waiting for the respondent to answer, he immediately says: "*That was elementary school you said.*" Note that he explicitly refers to the respondent having provided this information. He adds the tag "*right?*" which turns his statement into a request for confirmation.

The response is built as a dispreferred turn (Sacks, 1987; Pomerantz, 1984). After the respondent initially confirms that elementary school is her highest level of education, she then adds a course she took later on.

This fragment also exemplifies the relevance of giving the respondents the opportunity to elaborate on their answers, with respect to the validity of the answers, as Suchman and Jordan (1990: 236) suggest. The respondents behave as ordinary conversationalists when they structure their disagreeing responses in a dispreferred turn-shape.[5]

When we compare the interviewer's questioning turn with the item on the questionnaire, it turns out that he has left out the specification "*By full-time daytime education we mean any course or education that is taken at least three days a week.*" This is an important specification, because the everyday meaning of full-time daytime education is a form of education that takes about five full days a week. In terms of recipient design the omission of this specification means that the question is not formulated by reference to what the respondent may be assumed to know (Sacks, Fall 1971, L4).[6]

After having dealt with question 12, the interviewer was supposed to ask:

ITEM 13

Heeft u deze opleiding wel of niet voltooid,
of bent u er nog mee bezig?

Have you, or have you not completed this
education, or are you still busy with it?

In fact, he says:

3 (DAME, question 13)

I: Deze opleiding heeft u voltooid,
(.)
en ((volgende vraag))

I: You've completed this education,
(.)
and ((next question))

The interviewer transforms the question into a statement that he assumes to be correct: *"You've completed this education,"* and when the respondent does not contradict this, the interviewer proceeds to the next question. In fact, it is not sure whether the respondent has really got her certificate. Her prior talk about this (Fragment 2) is rather vague: *"I also took a uh c- a uh a year for the store a uh (1.0) well, what's it called uh (0.4) I had to get this certificate."* and *"And in Maastricht I went for that certificate."* She had to have this certificate, and she "*went for it*," but she does not say whether she passed the exam.[7]

In the next fragment we see the interviewer using a similar procedure as in the prior ones:

4 (BERT question 12 and 13)

I: Allereerst wil ik u vragen wat is de
hoogste opleiding die u in het volledige
dagonderwijs heeft gevolgd.=
=Nou, dat was dus de l.t.s., hè?
R: Dat was l.t.s., ja.
I: En die heeft u niet voltooid,
R: Nee. Die heb ik dus eh, het laatste eh
proefjaar >examenjaar< heb ik maar een
half jaar eh afgemaakt.=
I: =Ja.

I: First of all I'd like to ask you what — QUESTION 12
is the highest level of education that
you took in full-time daytime education?=
=Well, so that was l.v.s., right?
R: That was l.v.s, yes.
I: And you have not completed it, — QUESTION 13
R: No. I have uh, the final uh test year
>graduation year< I have finished only
uh half a year.=
I: =Yes.

The interviewer reads out question 12, without specifying it, and immediately continues to state the requested information, adding a question tag to it. The respondent confirms the information. By saying *"so"* in "*Well, so that was l.v.s., right?*" the interviewer implicitly refers to earlier talk by the respondent.

After having dealt with this question, the interviewer was supposed to ask *"Have you, or have you not completed this education, or are you still busy with it?"* However, the interviewer transforms the question into a statement: "*And you have not completed it,*" which is confirmed by the respondent.

Ordinary conversationalists usually ask questions without explicitly saying that they are going to do so. In these interviews, however, many questions are preceded by a question projection (Schegloff, 1980), generally formulated on the questionnaire as *"I would like to ask you."* In the last two fragments, the question projection was followed by the projected question, in the next fragment it is not:

5 (ELLY, question 12 and 13)

I: E:hm, dan zou ik u allereerst willen vragen,
eh u heeft dus het eh de v.g.l.o gedaan,
R: Ja,
[((geluid van tikken)) ]
[ 0.9 sec. ]
I: En die heeft u helemaal doorlopen hè?
R: Ja.
I: Ja?
[ ((geluid van tikken))]
[ 1.0 sec. ]

I: U:hm, first of all I'd like to ask you,
I: uh you went to the uh v.g.l.o then, QUESTION 12
R: Yes,
[ ((sound of typing)) ]
[ 0.9 sec. ]
I: And you've completed it, right? QUESTION 13
R: Yes.
I: Yes?
[ ((sound of typing)) ]
[ 1.0 sec. ]

After having projected a question (*"I'd like to ask you"*), the interviewer does not produce this question to which he already knows the answer from the introduction of the interview. This enables him to produce the answer to the unstated question himself: *"Uh you went to the uh v.g.l.o then,"* which is confirmed by the respondent. The next question on the questionnaire whose answer is known by the interviewer as well, is reformulated as a request for confirmation: "*And you've completed it, right?*" And again, the respondent confirms it.

In these interviews it is clear that the respondents' highest school level is known to the interviewer by the time the question appears on the screen. This is due to the way in which the respondents are selected. The computer randomly selects telephone numbers, and the first thing that the interviewers do is to find out whether the person who answers the telephone meets the criteria for the research.[8] These criteria are that the person should be over eighteen years old, and should not have completed a certain level of education. By the time that it has been decided that a person is a candidate for this interview the interviewer already knows the answers to the first few questions which he must ask. This means that the selection procedure creates an interactional problem for the interviewers. Right from the start of the interview, they are supposed to request information which they have just acquired. They solve this problem by answering the questions themselves, for which they use the information provided by the respondents.

In the fragments shown earlier, the interviewers produce the question and then provide the answer. In other instances, they give a report that may serve as an account for a specific answer (Drew, 1984). This happens, for example, in the following fragment, when the interviewer asks a lady whether job security or promotion would be a possible reason for her to take any courses. The fragment is part of a series of questions that are all concerned with the question whether something would be a reason for the respondent to take courses.

6 (CHRISTINE, question 24)

I: <Om meer zekerheid of kans op promotie>
in mijn huidige baan te hebben.
hh Nou (.) u >bent éénenzeventig<,
R: Ja::.

I: <To better secure my present job or to
increase my chances for a promotion>
I: .hh Well (.) you >are seventy one<,
R: Ye::s.

This lady has already indicated several times that she is seventy-one years old. Now the interviewer mentions her age right after having produced the question. Being seventy-one years old is indeed a plausible reason for this respondent not to take any more education for job reasons. This can be inferred from what she said earlier in the interview:

7 (CHRISTINE, question 16)

I: Eh U heeft de laatste vijf jaar (.) niet aan
een cursus of opleiding deelgenomen,
R: [Nee:.
I: [kunt u zeggen waarom niet?
R: Ja:, omdat ik eh ik ik ben nou te oud.
(1.2)
R: Ik ben éénenzeventig.
I: Ja, u u zegt ik ben te oud.
°éénenzeventig°
[ <te:: (.) ou::d (1.2) éé:ne:nze:ve:ntig jaar,]
[ (( geluid van tikken )) ]

I: Uh for the last five years (.) you have not
taken any courses or education,
R: [No:
I: [Could you say why not?
R: We:ll, because I uh I I am too old now.
(1.2)
R: I'm seventy one.
I: Yes, you you are saying I'm too old.
°seventy one<°
[ <too:: (.) o::ld (1.2) se::ve::nty:: one> ]
[ (( sound of typing )) ]

When a person indicates that she is seventy-one, and that that is too old to take any further education, it stands to reason to assume that she will not be interested in further education for the sake of securing her present job, let alone for promotion. Apart from this, considering her age, it is most likely that this woman does not have a paid job anyway. In saying "*Well (.) you're seventy one*," the interviewer demonstrates his competence to listen, and to understand the social world in which he and his recipient live, and to make inferences.

At the same time, the interviewer acts out his role as an interviewer when he proceeds to read out question 12 as it is worded on the questionnaire. I will quote again the first part of the fragment:

8 (CHRISTINE, question 24)

I: <Om meer zekerheid of kans op promotie>
in mijn huidige baan te hebben.
.hh Nou (.) u >bent éénenzeventig<,
R: Ja::.

I: E:h (.) dat- is dit een zeer >belangrijke,
een belangrijke of een niet zo belangrijke
reden voor u om deel te nemen aan cursussen
of opleidingen<, .hh of (.) <is die reden (.)
niet (.) van toepassing op u?>
R: Nee:, dat is niet van toepassing.

I: <To better secure my present job> or to
increase my chances for a promotion.
I: .hh Well (.) you'>re seventy one<,
R: Ye::s.
I: U:h (.) that- is that a very >important,
an important or not such an important
reason for you to take any course or
education<, .hh or (.) <does this
reason not apply to you?>
R: No:, it does not apply.

At first glance it is surprising that the interviewer proceeds to read the questionnaire out loud after having already indicated that this specific reason to take any courses will not apply to the respondent. His action makes sense when we think of fragment 2, where the same participants were collaboratively doing the organizational work of filling out the form. Seen from this perspective, here the participants are "doing the interview." The interviewer reads the question, and makes it clear that he understands that this is an irrelevant question for his co-participant. The respondent's "*ye:s*" may be seen as in agreement with this. Having "discussed" the irrelevance of the question, the two of them go back to work and continue to do the interview. The interviewer reads out what he has to read out, and the respondent provides the information.

Note, however, the pace in which the interviewer continues to read out the questionnaire. He reads the first part, which is irrelevant for this respondent, relatively quick *(U:h (.) that- is that a very >important, an important or not such an important reason for you to take any course or education<,)*, and slows down when he comes to the last and relevant part*: or (.) <does this reason not apply to you?>*. Christine responds to this last part indeed: *"No:, it does not apply."* In changing his pace of reading, the interviewer is able to instruct the respondent that one part of the utterance is only to be heard as the interviewer's reading aloud, and the other part as a question to be answered. In terms of Goffman (1981), the respondent's *participation status* shifts from *overhearer* to *addressed participant*, during this short episode.

In the fragment below, the interviewer both answers the question and gives an account.

9 (DAME, question 42)

I: Is het belangrijk voor u dat er
kinderopvang bij de cursus is?
(1.7)
I: [Nee.
R: [Kinderopvang?
I: Nee::. Niet meer. N[ee.
R: [Nee::.
I: Nee, zo klein zijn uw kinderen niet meer.=
R: =Nee, die hebben al allemaal zakes.

I: Is it important to you that there are day
care facilities in the place of the course?
(1.7)
I: N[o
R: [Day care?
I: No::. Not anymore. N[o.
R: [No::.
I: No, your children aren't that small anymore.=
R: =No, they all have stores.

Rather than taking the turn and answering the question, the respondent keeps silent. The interviewer waits for 1.7 seconds (Jefferson, 1989), and then takes a next turn himself to make an educated guess: "*No*." Almost at the same time, the respondent displays her surprise about the question by her *questioning repeat* (Jefferson, 1972) "*Day care?*" after which the interviewer again gives the answer: "*No::. Not anymore. No.*"

One might wonder what is so troublesome about this question that the respondent does not answer it. Earlier she told the interviewer that she is an older woman with grown-up children. In the everyday world this implies that one has no personal interest in day care facilities, which consequently makes this question an irrelevant one in the context of ordinary conversation.

With the phrase "*Not anymore*" the interviewer shows to the respondent that, whatever irrelevant questions he seems to be asking, he is a competent listener and conversationalist who takes his co-participants' particulars into account. He has learned from the respondent that her "*children aren't that small anymore*," and demonstrates his knowledge that day care facilities are not of personal interest for people with grown-up children.

Earlier in this interview, the interviewer has indicated to the respondent why he sometimes asks questions that are irrelevant for her. On several occasions, the respondent displays her belief that the questions do not make sense. At one point the interviewer says: "*We ask these questions to everybody in the same way, you see,*" and later on, "*But, as I said, we ask these questions to everybody in the same way, right.*" Apparently, this did not instruct the respondent about the rules of the survey interview, according to which she is supposed to answer whatever question the interviewer will ask her.

## Conclusion

According to the theory of interviewing, interviewers should not give the answers themselves, should not lead the respondent into a certain direction, and should not rephrase any questions. In that respect, these interviewers do a poor job. However, since the questionnaire is designed for a large and heterogeneous group of people, it contains several questions which, when delivered to a particular person, turn out to be rather peculiar. In other cases they have become redundant in the process of the interaction. One may say that questionnaires are "*audience designed*," but not recipient designed.

If interviewers would stick to their role as a survey interviewer, they would present themselves to their co-participants as incompetent conversationalists who do not listen to what they have been told, who are unable to properly deal with this information, who ask the same thing twice, and who have no knowledge of the social world around them. For the main part, these interviewers indeed act out their role as a survey interviewer. And the respondents demonstrate on several occasions that strange things are going on indeed. In this respect, they rely on conventions from ordinary conversation. The consequence is a -- at least partial -- clash between two speech exchange systems.

The interviewers solve this problem by means of answering questions themselves when they already have obtained the information. At the same time, they structure the sequences in such a way that the respondents are invited to confirm the correctness of the interviewers' answers, or to correct them when they are wrong. The interviewers still follow the interviewing rule that says that they should not answer for the respondent. They just use a more conversationally adequate form to generate the information sought for. The effect of this procedure is that the interviewers are able to generate accountable survey data.

In this way the interviewers are able to meet both ends, that is, being a competent interviewer, as well as a competent conversationalist. As a few fragments made especially clear, this may be done by shifting frames. The co-participants may collaboratively shift from conversationalists, who implicitly comment on the irrelevance of a specific question, and then proceed to take up their institutional identities and do the work of asking questions and answering them in the prescribed way.

---

* Much of the work reported here was first drafted while I was a visitor at the Department of Speech Communication of the University of Austin at Texas in 1991. I am grateful to the Department and to Jürgen Streeck for allowing me to stay three months, and especially to Robert Hopper's patience to discuss the earliest drafts of this paper with me. I have benefited from Wayne Beach, Paul ten Have, Anita Pomerantz and George Psathas, who carefully read earlier versions of this paper to make comments on it.

1 As Schegloff (1988/89) points out, this is the most fundamental component of what is considered an "interview." For example employment interviews, cf., Button (1987), Komter (1991), medical interviews, cf., Frankel (1984), ten Have (1987), news interviews, cf., Clayman (1988), Heritage and Greatbatch (1991), and court proceedings, cf., Atkinson and Drew (1979).

2 Compare the work by Maynard and Marlaine (1987) and Marlaine and Maynard (1990) on the "interactional substrate" of educational testing. They refer to the interactional substrate of educational testing as consisting of those skills of the participants that allow them to arrive at accountable test scores.

3 Although on the questionnaire it says "*could you tell me how old you are?*" the interviewers say "*could you tell me your age.*" When I asked several people what they felt was the difference between the two formulations, it turned out that the one on the questionnaire was considered less polite than the interviewers' formulation.

4 Notice how the woman confirms the interviewer's "*three days a week?*" and then adds "*three times a week*" to it:

I. AT LEAST three days a week?
[Or
D. [Ye:s, ye:s. Three times a week.
I. Three times a week.

Although there is no hard evidence in the interview, it is likely that the answer is documented as *three days a week.* In that case, the answer may be invalid, because it is not clear that the course that the woman refers to takes at least three full days a week.

5 The production of dispreferred turn formats by respondents is part of the conversational style of the interview. Consequently, when interviewers should be allowed to be engaged in a limited form of recipient design, they should be prepared for the respondents to produce an agreement token, followed by disagreement.

6 In another paper (Houtkoop, 1992) the issue of omitting question specifications is addressed in more detail. It is demonstrated that omitting these specifications is partly due to the structure of the questioning turn. In the questionnaire, the specification frequently follows the question it specifies. The respondents, however, often start to talk as soon as the interviewer has produced talk that can be heard as a question.

7 As one of the designers of the questionnaire told me, by "having completed" school or a course, they meant having passed the examination. However, as becomes clear in one of the interviews, this is not necessarily how the respondents understand this term. Bert, for example, says in the introduction to the interview "*I am the only one* ((in the family)) *who finished this u::h Lower Vocational School, but I u:h did not pass the exam.*" And when the interviewer then checks: "*So you have not finished it?*" Bert says "*I have not passed the carpenters' exam. No.*" One reason why questionnaire designers should make a detailed analysis of the interviews, is to see to which extent the terms used on the questionnaire are also members' terms (Garfinkel and Sacks, 1970).

8 This means that the telephone conversation begins with talk about the interview and the possible respondentship of the answerer. Only when it has been decided that the interview will take place, the co-participants change their interactional status from caller and answerer into interviewer and respondent, and they begin to do the interview as such. When the last question has been dealt with, the interviewer markedly terminates the interview, e.g., by saying "*Well, that was it. I thank you very much for your cooperation.*" The co-participants may exchange some further talk that is not part of the interview, and terminate the conversation. The interview as a speech exchange system is thus embedded in an ordinary telephone conversation.

# 7

# The Distribution of Knowledge in Courtroom Interaction*

Martha L. Komter

## 1. Introduction

The distribution of knowledge has been mentioned as a powerful interactional resource. In interaction people design their utterances on the basis of what they think their conversational partners know (e.g., Goffman, 1970; Goodwin, 1981; Komter, 1991a; Labov and Fanshel, 1977; Pomerantz, 1980). A distinction has been made between first-hand knowledge of "the facts," and common sense knowledge of social structures (Benson and Drew, 1978). It has been shown that this distinction is a more general feature of storytelling, but that it is particularly relevant for the participants in the courtroom (Bogen and Lynch, 1989).

The Dutch laws of evidence make a similar distinction between the two kinds of knowledge that are consequential for the value of the evidence. That is, only those statements of defendants or witnesses are admissible as evidence that are based on direct observation or professional knowledge; evidence that is based on "facts of common knowledge" needs no further proof. "Direct observation" is considered to be the most straightforward link between an event and the report of it; "facts of common knowledge" reflect the body of knowledge that every competent member of society is assumed to have about social relations and structures. It is implied that these "facts of common knowledge" are essential for the interpretation of "the facts."[1] The laws of evidence assume a potential disputability of "the facts," and a consensus about "facts of common knowledge."

In this article I shall discuss the significance of the distribution of knowledge in the courtroom for the negotiations about "the facts" and for the credibility of the sources of the information. Beside first-hand knowledge and common knowledge, a third kind of knowledge will be distinguished: strategic knowledge. The argument is based on an analysis of observations of 48 courtroom trials of violent crimes such as murder, rape, assault, and armed robbery, in three regional courts in the Netherlands. Thirty-one of these trials have been audio-taped and transcribed. To begin with, the attention will be drawn to the strategic force of first-hand knowledge of "the facts" for the discovery of "what really happened." Next the strategic force of common knowledge in the courtroom will be discussed. And finally, strategic knowledge is discussed in relation to the credibility of the participants. It should be pointed out that although these topics are discussed separately, they cannot be strictly separated. "The facts" are only relevant when they are interpreted, and interpretations rest on common knowledge. And knowledge about what strategies contribute to, or detract from one's credibility is also shared, although it has to remain unspoken.

## 2. First-hand knowledge as a strategic resource

Defendants have an ambiguous position in the courtroom. As interested parties they have to defend themselves against an accusation; as objects of inquiry they are expected to assist the judges with their fact-finding.[2] The defendants' dilemma revolves around providing the required information without damaging their interests in the process (cf. Komter, 1990).

Someone who tells a story on the basis of first-hand knowledge can be held accountable for its truthfulness. And reversely, people cannot be held accountable for the veracity of a story they have on hearsay. The defendant is usually the only person present with first-hand knowledge of the events. This means in the first place that an important part of the information is provided by a probably unreliable source, as defendants are not expected to contribute to their own conviction, and secondly that ultimately the judges must act on information that they have on "hearsay," as they do not themselves have direct access to the "facts."

The main sources of knowledge of "the facts" for the judges are what they have been able to read beforehand in the dossier and what is told them on the spot by the defendant. It has often been pointed out that judges have an inordinate amount of power over the goings on in the courtroom and consequently over the fate of defendants (Bal, 1988; Bennett and Feldman, 1981; Carlen, 1976; Cody and McLaughlin, 1988). On the other hand, the distribution of first-hand knowledge can be a crucial source of power for defendants and reversely, a potential source of doubt for the judges. The defense knows what the judges know and what they don't know, so defendants basically know what they have to admit to and what they can deny with some kind of credibility. The judges know that it may be impossible to elicit information from the defendant when its "truth" cannot be checked.

Although judges lack first-hand knowledge of the case, they may make the most of the knowledge that they have from other sources. The judge who asked the defendant who were his accomplices in the robbery added: "You need not be mysterious about it because I already know who are involved." Defendants know that it is no use denying what is already known and held to be true. This knowledge can thus be a strategic device to be used by the judge as a direct check on the honesty of the defendant (Goffman, 1970).

Judges derive their strategic position from the fact that they are in a "first position," that is, they are the initiators of the interaction, they elicit the contributions of the defendants, and thereby they control the course of the interaction. Broadly speaking, the information available in the dossier provides the judge with two courses of action for the elicitation of defendants' responses: if the information is more or less consistent judges present the defendants with more or less indisputable facts; if the information in the dossier is inconsistent judges present defendants with the contrasting versions. Since cases are never wholly indisputable nor wholly inconsistent, judges make use of both these elicitation techniques, as will be shown in the following sections.

## The disputability of the facts

Dutch law requires that a verdict be based only on facts that have been mentioned in the trial. So judges must select and bring up those items from the dossier that they consider potentially relevant for their future judgment. They often start the hearing by recapitulating the facts as they are described in the dossier. The more consistent the statements in the dossier, the more likely it is that the judge gets the defendant to agree on them:

1 MK: 21: 1-2 ((J = judge; D = defendant))
J: And then the third fact is, that is that you have
allegedly stolen a bicycle on april the 28th,
→ D: yes.
J: that's right, and (1) the owner of the bike, with his
father, and his brother, they pursued you,
→ D: yes.
J: and they arrested you,
→ D: yes.
J: and then they say, that you took a knife, opened it, and
made threatening and swinging movements towards
those three people. (1)
Is that right?
→ D: Yes.[3]

J: En dan is het derde feit, dat is dat u op 28 april een
fiets zou hebben gestolen,
D: Ja.
J: dat klopt, en (1) de eigenaar van de fiets, met z'n
vader, en z'n broer, die zijn u achterna gekomen,
D: Ja.
J: en die hebben u aangehouden,
D: Ja.
J: en dan zeggen ze, dat u daar een mes heeft gepakt, dat
opengemaakt heeft, en dreigende en zwaaiende
bewegingen heeft gemaakt naar die drie mensen. (1)
Is dat zo?
D: Ja.

Judges thus apply their knowledge of the case to get the defendant's confirmation of the facts. The strategic consequence of this type of "questioning" is that the defendant is asked to confirm what the judge already knows (cf. Labov and Fanshel, 1977: 100). This kind of interaction is likely to occur in the beginnings of the trials. In this way the judges create a body of knowledge about those facts that everybody can agree on, and that can serve as a basis for their verdict. But it is not just a confirmation of "the facts" that is sought. As there is no strict division-line between giving information and giving evidence, or between giving information and defending oneself, agreeing with "the facts" can be heard as a confession. Because "the facts" are part of the accusation, a request for confirmation is in this context at the same time a request for an admission of guilt (Atkinson and Drew, 1979).

On the other hand the confirmation of the defendant may not be forthcoming, even if his earlier statements would indicate so. In the following fragment the judge reads to the defendant one of his earlier statements:

2 MK: 12:2

J: I grabbed that girl, and my accomplice snatched that money from her knickers,=
→ D: =no=
J: =after he had first undone her [jeans.
→ D: [I've done that my<u>self</u>.
J: You've done that yourself.
→ D: The accomplice missed.

J: Ik heb dat meisje vastgepakt, en mijn mededader heeft dat geld uit haar slipje weggegrist,=
D: =nee=
J: =nadat hij eerst haar spijkerbroek had openge [maakt.
D: [Dat heb ik <u>zelf</u> gedaan.
J: Dat heeft u zelf gedaan.
D: De mededader greep mis.

One interactional effect of statements made in the presence of a "knowing recipient" is that the statements are open for correction or amendation when the recipient finds inaccuracies or omissions (Goodwin, 1981: 156). The defendant in this example denies what the judge brings forward and adds an account to explain the reason for his greater involvement in the robbery than he admitted before.[4] The defendant is addressed in his capacity to confirm, disconfirm or correct the judge's statements, by virtue of his direct knowledge of the events. This involves at the same time an appeal to his capacity to deny or to confess.

## Contrasting versions

The inconsistencies in the dossier are powerful techniques for the judges for the elicitation of the reports and accounts of the defendant (Drew, 1990). For example judges may confront the defendant with depositions of witnesses that contradict the version of the defendant. In the following fragment the defendant has been accused among other things of trying to hit a man with his car:

3 MK: 14:9

|  | | |
|---|---|---|
| | J: | So you're saying that you haven't seen that Fongers at all, |
| | D: | No. |
| | J: | Let alone that you've seen him jump away or that you wanted to hit him with your car that's what you're really saying, |
| | D: | Well that's it yes. |
| → | | And if it was such a small distance, |
| → | | I simply must have seen that man. I think. (3) |
| | J: | Do you think he's lying or uh |
| → | D: | Well, that uh I don't say that. |
| → | | [But I haven't seen him so I |
| | J: | [No. |
| | D: | I assume that it isn't like that. |

|  | |
|---|---|
| J: | U zegt dus dat u die Fongers helemaal niet gezien hebt, |
| D: | Nee. |
| J: | Laat staan dat u hem hebt zien wegspringen of dat u op hem wou inrijden zegt u dus eigenlijk, |
| D: | Nou zo is dat. |
| | En als het zo'n kleine afstand was, |
| | dan had ik die man gewoon moeten zien. Lijkt mij. (3) |
| J: | Denkt u dat hij erom liegt of eh |
| D: | Nou, dat eh dat zeg ik niet. |
| | [Maar ik heb hem niet gezien dus ik |
| J: | [Nee. |
| D: | ik neem aan dat het niet zo is. |

In repeating the defendant's earlier statements, the judge first invites his confirmation. However, the implication of a confirmation in this instant is that the defendant then has to account for the discrepancy between the different versions, and to convince the judge that his version is the correct one. The defendant's point is, that if he had wanted to hit the man with his car, he must have come close enough to see him. And as he did not see the man at all, he cannot have tried to hit him with his car. By means of this line of reasoning the defendant demonstrates that he does not know more than an innocent man can reasonably be expected to know. He implies that he does not know why the alleged victim has told the police and the judge of instruction that he was almost overrun by the suspect. He only claims that, if the alleged victim is right, he must have seen him; as he did not see him the alleged victim cannot be right. His presentation of his version demonstrates his official position of innocence. He draws inferences of what would have been the case should the victim have been right in his accusation, without directly denying it. He talks from the perspective of a "theorist" who logically derives what might have transpired from the elements of the situation (Brannigan and Lynch, 1987). His argument is based on assumptions about what people can reasonably infer from the facts. Although he does not solve the puzzle of the contrasting versions, he shows his cooperation by offering to clear up the problem as far as his "knowledge" of the case allows him.

The attempts of the judges to engage the defendants in the solving of the problem of inconsistencies or contrasting versions constitute an important strategy in their fact-finding. Such a strategy generates not only a statement of the defendant's version of the events, but also an account to substantiate the veracity of the defendant's story. The idea behind this is, that there is only one "true" version possible of the events (Pollner, 1987). Thus the participants act on the assumption of a direct relationship between consistency and truth.

## Facts and inferences

In the Netherlands the law requires that a verdict must not only be based on legal evidence, but also on the judges' own conviction. Whether "the facts" are consistent or not, it must be possible for them to be pieced together to form a plausible sequence of events:

> In a rape case the defense counsel underlined the fact that the alleged victim had provided the defendant with a condom. This fact was interpreted by him as an indication of her active participation in what he described as an act of mutual consent. The position of the victim was, that as she was going to be raped anyway, she might as well minimize the risks.

The fact of the alleged victim's handing over the condom is not contested, but the interpretation of it is. The example illustrates that, however important the "facts," it is the interpretation of them that illuminates the guilt and responsibility of the defendant.

It is noticeable that what seems to be a factual question often generates an account:

4 MK: 26:5

J: Were you clean when you left prison.
D: Yes I felt fine.
But yes uh all my problems at home,
I uh I I thought well I'm sure to get welfare.
U::h yes I'd gotten uh fatter,
my clothes didn't fit me any more,
so I asked for a clothing allowance
well they were standing there laughing at me.
J: Hm.
D: At the welfare agency.
I got 100 guilders in advance, to eat,
for my girl-friend and me, (2)
and uh well that that's impossible.

J: Was u clean toen u uit de gevangenis kwam.
D: Ja ik voelde me goed.
Maar ja eh al m'n problemen thuis,
ik eh ik ik dacht nou ik krijg wel 'n uitkering.
E::h ja ik was eh dikker geworden,
ik was uit m'n kleding gegroeid,
dus ik vroeg om kledinggeld
nou stonden ze me daar uit te lachen.
J: Hm.
D: Bij de sociale dienst.
Ik kreeg 100 gulden voorschot, om daarvan te eten,
voor m'n vriendin en ik, (2)
en eh nou dat dat kan niet.

What can be seen in this fragment, is that the defendant does not only respond to the question, but also to its implications. The defendant's answer shows that he does not interpret the judge's question as an interest in his health, but as a question after the reason why he has committed the robbery following his release from prison. Everybody knows that a drug addiction is an expensive habit, and this is often brought forward to account for robberies. The judge's question then implies that, if this account is no longer valid, the defendant must provide other reasons for his need of money.

What we see here is another kind of contrast. This time the contrast is not spelled out but implied in the question. The defendant understands that the judge's question is geared to probe into his motives to steal. Implied is the contrast between being a responsible person who is not dependent on drugs, and being someone who must have had a reason for stealing. So by providing another motive for his robbery, the defendant both solves the problem of the contrast, and accounts for his actions.

Another way in which facts and inferences are interrelated is shown in the manner in which the motives of the defendant can be deduced from the facts (Komter, 1993). A distinction can be made between "observed facts" and "internal states." A defendant may share first-hand knowledge of observed facts, the knowledge of his internal states is his exclusive domain. The accuracy of his reports on observed facts can be checked by comparing these with other reports or with forensic evidence, whereas the reports of his internal states, such as accounts of his intentions and feelings, have to be taken on trust:

5 MK: 17:6

→ J: You knew that your that your brother was going to
→ steal it,
you pointed out to him that those those keys were in the boot,
→ D: No I've only told him uh that those keys was in the boot.
→ J: Yes. Yes.

J: U wist dat uw dat uw broer hem ging stelen,
u hebt hem erop gewezen dat die die sleuteltjes in de kofferbak zaten,
D: Nee ik heb alleen gezegd eh dat die sleutels in de kofferbak zat.
J: Ja. Ja.

The defendant in this fragment displays a keen sense of what is deniable. The judge already knows from other sources that the defendant had pointed out to his brother where the keys of the car were. The defendant also knows that. But he denies the suggestion that he also knew his brother was going to steal the car. This inference would reveal a deeper involvement of the defendant in criminal actions than he cares to admit. As we have indicated earlier, a confirmation of the facts can be heard as an admission of guilt. The defendant then, in denying the judge's inference, denies his guilt as an accomplice.

All the same, the "facts" may impose an interpretation of the events that overrides the intentions of the defendant, at least according to the public prosecutor:

6 MK: O7 ((P = public prosecutor; I = interpreter))

P: The knife has in any case penetrated her chest quite deeply. That must be intentional.
((interpreter translates for defendant, who responds))
I: But he didn't mean to do it.
→ P: Yes, but the objective facts move his intentions to the
→ second place.

P: Het mes is in ieder geval vrij diep in haar borst doorgedrongen. Dat moet opzettelijk zijn.
((tolk vertaalt voor verdachte, die reageert))
I: Maar zijn bedoeling was het niet.
P: Ja, maar de objectieve gegevens doen zijn bedoelingen naar de tweede plaats verhuizen.

At first sight motive seems to be the most "private" kind of first-hand knowledge, and thus the least accessible for external inspection. Yet motives are so inextricably built into the description of an action, that they also explain the action (Watson, 1983). This example shows that the reverse can also be true in that the action explains the motive. In this way accounts may be invalidated by what are taken to be the "objective facts."

In sum the strategic positions of the participants in the courtroom depend both on the distribution of the initiative, and on the distribution of first-hand knowledge. The main strategic resource for the judges is their initiative, and for the defendants their possible first-hand knowledge of the events. That is to say, the judges have the initiative in the asking of questions, while the defendants are in a second position; the defendants presumably have first-hand knowledge of "the facts," while the judges only have "the facts" on hearsay. This affects the ways in which "the facts" are brought up and responded to in the courtroom. The judges' presentation of facts that are assumed to be indisputable invites a confirmation, disconfirmation or correction of the defendant; their presentation of contrasting versions anticipates attempts of the defendants to account for the inconsistencies.

First-hand knowledge is treated as a straightforward link between the alleged crime and the report of it. Moreover, the teller can be held accountable for the truth of his report. The assumption is that there is only one "true" report possible, and the defendant is invited to provide an accurate "replay" of the original events. The ambiguous position of the defendant in the courtroom accounts for the fact that a confirmation of "the facts" can also be heard as a confession. A feature of trials is that people negotiate about "what really happened," not only by denials or admissions of "the facts," but especially by way of the scope there is for drawing different inferences from those "facts." This blurs the distinction between first-hand knowledge and common knowledge.

## 3. Common knowledge as a strategic resource

The significance of common sense knowledge resides in the fact that people hold one another accountable on the basis of a socially shared stock of knowledge which enables them to produce and recognize ordinary social events (Garfinkel, 1967). This kind of knowledge also includes knowledge about what types of individuals can be expected to have what types of knowledge (Berger and Luckman, 1967), what kinds of information one can hide from whom (Goffman, 1970), and what kinds of information one can reasonably claim to have forgotten (Bogen and Lynch, 1989). The social distribution of knowledge is usually taken for granted, and used as a tacit resource for the interpretation of social phenomena. The participants in the courtroom draw from basically the same stock of knowledge to negotiate the plausibility of their claims as to what happened: "If an interpretation makes good sense, then that's what happened" (Garfinkel, 1967: 106). Yet competing interpretations may make equally good sense, and that is the substance of negotiations about "what really happened."

The cogency of the defendants' accounts depends to a large extent on the consistency of their stories with what is known generally about how people normally behave. This also includes knowledge about what kinds of activities are disapproved of, and about the availability of innocent stories as alternatives to the accusations, for example:

- alleged rape is typically described by the defense as a sexual act by mutual consent;
- alleged child-abuse is described as a strict upbringing;
- attempted manslaughter is described as an attempt to scare the victim off, etc.

Besides, the participants share a body of common knowledge about what people can reasonably know or remember. Defendants are not expected to know or to remember everything. The events may be forgotten because they happened such a long time ago, because the defendant was drunk, or because "it all happened so quickly." What is more, the details of the events may not have been noticed because they were not thought to be of any consequence at the time:

> In a homicide case the driver of the bus that the defendant was supposed to have taken knew the exact time of departure: 27 minutes past 11. According to the defendant the time the bus left was "after a quarter past 11."

An exact knowledge of a "non-professional" of the time of departure of the bus might arouse suspicion, as innocent people are not supposed to take notice of these details. For a defendant who claims to have had no criminal intentions at the time, the events have acquired their significance only in retrospect.

An essential element of common knowledge about what people usually do is the negotiability of that knowledge. In the following fragments the defense counsel and the public prosecutor disagree about the question how a rape victim usually behaves:

7 MK: 10:30 ((C = defence counsel))

C: When a rape takes place, and one thinks it is a rape I say
then one must go to the police immediately. And not

afterwards, over a period of time, to go and say well actually that was a rape. It doesn't work like that that detracts from the credibility, of the complaint, that is filed by someone like that.

C: Als er een verkrachting plaats vindt, en men vindt dat een verkrachting zeg ik dan moet men daar direct naar de politie gaan. En niet achteraf, over een periode beschouwd, aan gaan aanwijzen nou toch eigenlijk was dat toch wel een verkrachting. Zo werkt het niet dat dat tast de geloofwaardigheid aan, van de aangifte die dan, door zo iemand wordt gedaan.

8 MK: 10:33

P: Uhm that the the victim has not filed a complaint right away, brought forward by the defence counsel as the uhm (1) argument to say that her statement is untrustworthy, uhm it's absolutely not uncommon that after a sexual offence people don't go to the police at once.
When I think of uh incest victims, then it sometimes takes years before the people have uh freed themselves from the situation of terror under which they have lived, (1) to such an extent that they feel free to come forward with it to the police.

P: Ehm dat het 't slachtoffer niet meteen aangifte heeft gedaan, door de raadsman naar voren gebracht als 't ehm (1) argument om te zeggen dat haar verklaring ongeloofwaardig zou zijn, ehm 't is volstrekt niet ongewoon dat mensen na een zedendelict niet meteen naar de politie gaan.
Als ik denk aan eh incestslachtoffers, dan duurt 't soms jaren voordat de mensen zich hebben eh vrijgemaakt van de terreurtoestand waar ze onder leefden, (1) in zodanige mate dat ze zich vrij voelen om daarmee bij de politie voor de dag te komen.

The fact that the victim did not report the rape at once can thus be taken at the same time as an indication of the unseriousness of her complaint, and as a sign of the severity of her trauma. The significance of these two examples is not that the defense counsel and the public prosecutor know different things about the behavior of rape victims, but that different ideas about how people usually behave exist side by side. Thus common knowledge also includes a knowledge of competing perspectives on reality (cf. Pollner, 1987).

## The "normal" innocent

Reference to common knowledge is a strategic resource available to all the parties. An incongruence between how "normal" innocent people would conduct themselves, and what is known about the criminal events, is often a source of questions to the defendant. For example a judge asked the defendant: "When you take a woman on an evening out, why do you carry a sawn-off double-barrelled shotgun?" The strategic position of the judge derives from the circumstance that transgressions of "normal appearances" are clearly in need of an explanation (Goffman, 1971). Apparently, in committing a felony people break more norms than only the legal ones.

For the defendant the appeal to common knowledge may serve to get everyone to agree on something that is obvious. Defendants often substantiate their -more innocent- versions of the events by pointing at what is evident:

9 MK: 15:3

J: But did she undress her<u>self</u>, or (1) she undressed right?=
D: =Yes, she [undressed herself
J: [yes.
D: in order to lie down on the bed.=
J: =or had you told her that uh or <u>asked</u> her to do that? (2)
→ D: Well when you lie down on a bed,
→ you surely don't keep on all your clothes on the bed,
→ under the blankets?

J: maar heeft ze zich uit zich<u>zelf</u> uitgekleed, of (1) ze heeft zich uitgekleed hè?=
D: =Ja, ze heeft [zich zelf uitgekleed
J: [Ja.
D: om te gaan liggen op bed.=
J: =of had u gezegd dat eh of ge<u>vraagd</u> dat te doen? (2)
D: Nou als je op een bed gaat liggen,
dan ga je toch niet met je hele kleren op het bed liggen,
onder de dekens?

The claim of this defendant is that the alleged rape victim went to bed with him of her own free will. The point of his story is that people don't keep their clothes on when they go to bed. It is noticeable that he changes his description from his original: "on a bed," to: "on the bed, under the blankets." His description progressively corresponds with common expectations about how people normally go to bed.

This device of corroborating one's version of the events by pointing out discrepancies between the accusation and what is generally held to be true is very common in the courtroom. This is often presented by way of conditional clauses:

- If I had wanted to rob her, I would have been able to just take the money then.
- If I had wanted to kill him, I wouldn't have asked everybody where he lived.
- If I had needed the money, I would have asked my mother.

Thus the presentation of "contrasting versions" can also be used by defendants to discredit the plausibility of the claims implied in the accusation. This allows defendants to bring forward a "negative" substantiation of their version of events: if they had committed the offense of which they stand accused, they would not have behaved the way they did.

## The "normal" criminal

The public prosecutor and the defense counsel often rely on common knowledge as a strategic resource to aggravate and mitigate the defendant's guilt and responsibility. These negotiations may be based on what is professionally known about "normal" criminal behavior (Sudnow, 1965):

10 MK: 22:78-79

P: What's also telling is the behavior uh of van Vuren that he displays before and after the act.
He is totally uh (1) emotionless if I may put it uh like that, he has no emotions, beforehand or shortly before he just sleeps and shortly after he just goes back to sleep again.
And uh that is one of the characteristics as it has been presented by Demeersseman in his well-known book uh (2) about criminal intent, that that uh the offender does not worry that is to say feels little or no excitement about the perpetration of the offence.

P: Illustratief is ook het gedrag eh van van Vuren wat ie voor en na de daad vertoont.
Hij is totaal eh (1) gevoelloos als ik het zo mag eh uitdrukken, hij heeft geen emoties, van te voren of kort tevoren ligt ie gewoon te slapen en kort daarna gaat ie ook gewoon weer slapen.
En eh dat is één van de karakteristieken zoals door Demeersseman in zijn bekende boek inmiddels eh (2) wordt opgevoerd over de voorbedachte rade namelijk, dat dat eh de dader zich niet druk maakt bij de uitvoering dat wil zeggen niet of nauwelijks aan opwinding onderhevig is geweest.

In this instance the public prosecutor takes the occurrence of the -denying-defendant's sleeping on the night of the murder both as an aggravating circumstance and as an indication of his guilt. That is, as an aggravating circumstance it testifies to the defendant's exceptional immorality, which is then interpreted as a "normal" characteristic of this kind of murderer. The argument of the public prosecutor illustrates the ubiquitous nature of the strategic use of facts of common knowledge. What is damaging in the case of the defendant's guilt (his sleeping on the night of the murder), is a normal way of conduct if he is innocent. The circularity of this kind of reasoning is shown in that the argument holds only when it is assumed that the defendant is guilty, yet it is also meant to serve to convince the judges of his guilt. Common knowledge can thus be invoked to underline what everybody knows already but at the same time it serves to corroborate what is not known: the guilt or the innocence of the defendant, depending on one's "party position."

A point often made by the defense counsel is to emphasize the clumsy and amateurish "modus operandi" in the crime. This can serve either to mitigate the guilt and responsibility of the defendant, or to exonerate him altogether. His "getting himself caught" may serve as the most telling demonstration of his criminal unprofessionality. In the following fragment the defense counsel displays his knowledge of how a criminal would typically organize a hold-up, in response to the point made by the public prosecutor that it was a very well planned hold-up:

11 MK: 20:15

C: If you (1) prepare such a <u>well</u> planned hold-up, then it is very strange, that one of the alleged offenders starts using his own car for that. For that is not something that you'd over<u>look</u> during the preparations...
Well I <u>think</u> if I'd be <u>some</u>thing of a robber, that I'd surely think of <u>that</u>, and then I'd <u>rent</u> a car under a false name, or I'd <u>steal</u> a car. That seems to me to fit better in a in a perfect uh plan (1) than to go and commit a robbery with your own bright canary yellow car.

C: Als je (1) een dergelijk <u>goed</u> geplande overval eh op touw zet, dan is het toch heel vreemd, dat één van de vermeende daders daarbij zijn eigen auto gaat gebruiken. Want dat is toch iets wat je niet over 't <u>hoofd</u> ziet bij de voorbereiding. ...
Nou ik <u>denk</u> toch als ik een <u>bee</u>tje overvaller zou zijn, dat ik <u>daar</u> wel aan zou denken, en dan <u>huur</u> ik op een valse naam een auto, of ik <u>steel</u> een auto. Dat dat lijkt mij in een in een perfect eh plan beter (1) thuishoren dan met je eigen felgele kanarie auto daar een overval plegen.

This argument again points to the versatility of the strategic use of common knowledge. A well planned hold-up includes making provisions for avoiding detection and arrest. However, the public prosecutor also knows that success is never guaranteed, and regards the arrest as one of the normal risks of the trade:

12 MK: 20:18

P: I can only give one reaction to this and that is that uh the perfect crime apparently still has to be invented and offenders uh will keep on making mistakes, and (1) a good thing too I'd say.

P: Ik kan alleen maar één reactie hierop geven is dat eh de perfecte misdaad kennelijk toch nog uitgevonden moet worden en daders eh toch nog wel fouten blijven maken, en (1) gelukkig maar zou ik zeggen.

Thus facts of common knowledge are brought forward by both parties to substantiate the inferences that can be made from the "modus operandi" of the offenders. In this way facts of common knowledge serve the public prosecutor to point to the professionality and immorality of the defendant, or are used by the defense counsel to underline the fact that the defendant is not guilty, or just a clumsy opportunist who happened to get involved in something of which he could not oversee the consequences.

## 4. Strategic knowledge and credibility

People share knowledge both about "normal" behavior, and about the ways in which to invoke this knowledge strategically. The difference is, that the first kind of knowledge can be explicated, whereas the second kind has to remain implicit. Strategies work only when the actor is supposed to be ingenuous. At the same time, the strategic uses of knowledge that I have described above are brought into play on assumptions of the defendant's self-interests. The nature of these interests cannot be revealed because that would interfere with a convincing performance.

People act on the assumption that the less someone has to gain by a statement the more it can be credited (Goffman, 1970: 111). And as defendants are not expected to provide information that will damage their interests, confessions are more likely to be interpreted as "honest" than denials. In the last resort the interests of innocent and guilty defendants are the same: to escape or to minimize punishment. This makes it difficult to distinguish between a denial as straightforward statement of one's innocence, and a denial made to disguise one's guilt. This means that behind the negotiations about the guilt and responsibility of the defendants, there is always the question of their credibility.

In our culture there is not much scope for claiming credibility through dramatizations of innocence. Some Turkish or Moroccan defendants demonstratively invoke god as witness to their innocence, or swear on the bodies of their mothers, fathers, or children that they have committed no crimes (Komter, 1991b). The reactions of the judges reveal that they are not convinced. In our courts of law truthfulness needs to be demonstrated to others, so that these can draw their own conclusions.

## The extension of truthfulness

In an armed robbery case the defendant claimed his accomplice played the main role and he just tagged along. The accomplice however, has earlier told the same story with respect to the defendant. The defense counsel points to a difference between the two offenders: his client, Marco Zegers, has given himself up to the police when there was no other evidence against him, whereas his accomplice, Mr. Lommel, initially denied his involvement, and only confessed at the trial when he apparently thought that there was too much evidence against him:

13 MK: 16:23

C: I must tell you if I consider all that, that mr. Lommel who has actually uh denied everything uh straightout, apparently till or up to the trial, and then at the trial uh apparently confessed because he thought I won't be able to get away with it after all, and uh then points in the uh in in in the direction of uh Marco Zegers, that that he uh that he should have dragged him along, that he should have been the leader, uhm then I don't think that is very credible.
Uh all the more, because Marco Zegers has volunteered his confession to the police. While there was no evidence against him.

C: Ik moet u zeggen als ik dat nou zo tegen elkaar afzet, die meneer van Lommel die toch eh alles eh knalhard heeft ontkend, kennelijk tot en met of tot aan de zitting, en dan op de zitting eh kennelijk heeft bekend omdat ie gedacht heeft verder kom ik toch verder niet onderuit, en eh dan in de eh als in in de in de richting van eh Marco Zegers wijst, dat dat die eh dat die hem meegenomen zou hebben, dat die de leiding zou hebben, ehm dan vind ik dat niet erg geloofwaardig.
Eh temeer niet, omdat Marco Zegers bij de politie zelf spontaan bekend heeft. Geen aanwijzing tegen hem waren.

The credibility of a defendant then depends not only on his confession, but also on the way in which this confession has come about. A confession under the pressure of overwhelming evidence is seen as plain common sense. On the other hand a confession that is volunteered in the early stages of the investigations can be seen as a sign of cooperation, and as an indication of the defendant's essential decency and trustworthiness.

A defendant may make the best of a bad bargain by confessing to what to his mind cannot be denied. The idea is that once the defendant has demonstrated his truthfulness by his confession, this is then to be extended to strengthen his claims to truth for his denial:

14 MK: 21:8

C: Uh mister Sahil does find it important to stress one more time that it wasn't 800 guilders that he took from mrs. Soetendaal, and that he has not broken that window. He also says uh yes I want to come clean, and uhm (1) if I'd done it I would have (said so), but it is somehow also (1) the principle that counts.

C: Ehm meneer Sahil hecht er wel veel waarde aan om nogmaals te benadrukken dat het niet 800 gulden maar 600 gulden was die die bij mevrouw Soetendaal heeft meegenomen, en dat hij dat raam, zeker niet verbroken heeft. Hij zegt ook van ja ik wil schoon schip maken, en het ehm (1) als ik het gedaan had had ik het ook (erbij gezegd), maar het gaat nu toch een beetje (1) ook om het principe.

In this case the defendant has confessed to having stolen 600 guilders instead of the 800 that have disappeared according to the victim.[5] The defense counsel's point is that the defendant wants to "come clean," but that he does not want to take the blame for things that he has not done. The confession is brought forward as a demonstration of his truthfulness, and consequently as evidence for the credibility of his denials.

The strategic sophistication of defendants is demonstrated by their selection of confessions and denials. When there is not much counter-evidence, the more "innocuous" aspects of their behavior are often readily admitted to, whereas the more serious aspects tend to be denied or forgotten. Defendants often confess to theft, but deny the violence that they have allegedly used. In the next example the defendant has admitted to indecent assault, but he denies having shouted: "I'm going to jump you, and if you shout once more I'll strangle you." The defense counsel elaborates on this position:

15 MK: 19:5

C: My client has no reasonable interest whatsoever, I think, (1) in uh (2) confessing on crucial points, and now precisely in the case of an offence that is indicted separately, a threat, to say about that no that just isn't true. (2)
I've also asked mr. Steenbergen who says yes what I've done I've done, and there uh justice will have to run its course, and what I haven't done, I won't go into it uh any further, he says yes it just isn't true the way mrs. Hartman describes that.

C: Mijn cliënt heeft geen enkel redelijk belang, denk ik, (1) om eh (2) op cruciale punten een bekentenis af te leggen, en nu juist voor wat betreft een apart telaste gelegd feit een bedreiging, daarover te zeggen nee 't klopt gewoon niet. (2)
Ik heb dat ook aan meneer Steenbergen gevraagd die zegt ja wat ik gedaan heb heb ik gedaan, en daar zal eh het recht zijn loop wel moeten nemen, en wat ik niet gedaan heb, daar zal ik dan eh ook niet verder op ingaan, hij zegt ja 't klopt gewoon niet zoals mevrouw Hartman dat naar voren brengt.

The defense counsel's point is made from the strategic position that there is no evidence to corroborate either claim: it is her word against his. The honesty of the defendant is to be inferred from his confessing to a part of the charge. However, his claims as to the honesty of the defendant show a curious disattendance of the defendant's interests. It is easy to imagine that the admission of the threat to strangle the victim will aggravate the defendant's guilt. It appears that the advantage of the demonstration of honesty by partial admissions works best when the defendant's self-interest is ignored.

## The disattendance of self-interest

The overt blindness to the strategic consequences of the interests of the defendant for his position in court may then in itself be employed as a strategic device for the demonstration of credibility. Some defendants tell the judges that if they had committed the crime they are accused of, they would have said so:

16 MK: 11:11

D: Look if I had done it I'd be the last to say I have not
done it.

D: Kijk als ik het gedaan zou hebben dan ben ik de laatste
die zegt van ik heb het niet gedaan.

17 MK: 18:39

D: I know that I have nothing to do with this.
For if I had done it I would have told it long ago.

D: Ik weet dat ik hier helemaal niets mee te maken heb.
Want als ik het gedaan had had ik het allang verteld.

The paradox of the situation is that everybody knows that denials may serve the interests of the guilty. Yet an open recognition of these interests apparently undermines the defendants' claims to credibility. The defendants claim that even if they had been guilty, they would have been so honest as to confess. The innocence of these defendants is to be inferred from the circumstance that it is much more convincing for a guilty man to confess to his guilt than for an innocent man to state his innocence, as a guilty man invites punishment, while an innocent man just describes the actual state of affairs. The display of ingenuity of these defendants is perhaps the closest they can come to an on the spot demonstration of innocence. Of course if one assumes they are guilty it is not ingenuity they are demonstrating but sophistication.

The ambiguous strategic force of the defendants' interests can also be brought into play by the prosecution:

18 MK: 20:13

P: and I also take into account the to my mind uh aggravating
circumstance that (1) while he should know better to my
mind, he continues to deny the charge.

P: en ik hou eveneens rekening met de naar mijn idee eh
verzwarende omstandigheid dat meneer (1) naar mijn
mening tegen beter weten in, blijft ontkennen.

19 MK: 22:81

P: Finally uh mister president I take into account the mendacity, the insincerity of all the defendants present here.
They persist in denying while they should know better.

P: Tot slot eh meneer de president hou ik rekening met de leugenachtigheid, de draaierijen van alle verdachten hier aanwezig.
Ze blijven ontkennen tegen beter weten in.

In these fragments the defendants' denials are firstly taken as indications of their mendacity, and secondly as aggravating circumstances to be taken into account for the amount of punishment. It appears that, as the defendants' guilt cannot be directly concluded from their statements, it must be derived from the discreditability of those whose self-interests are served by denials. Yet these interests are officially disregarded when the denials are adduced as evidence for the aggravation of their guilt and responsibility.

The examples exhibit the dilemmas of the participants in a situation where the assumed interests of the defendants weaken their credibility, while this credibility is negotiated by way of a disattendance of their interests. Apparently the substantiation of the accusation works best on the assumption of guilt, and the substantiation of the defense works best on the assumption of innocence. Both work best on the strategic ignoring of the obvious interests of the defendant.

## 5. Conclusion

The distribution of knowledge is both the topic and the resource of negotiations about the guilt and responsibility of the defendant in the courtroom. It concerns three broad categories of knowledge: first-hand knowledge of "the facts," common knowledge of social relations and social structures, and strategic knowledge. The strategic positions of the participants depend both on the distribution of knowledge and on the distribution of the initiative. That is to say, the judges make use of their "first position" in the interaction by asking their questions, whereas the defendants are addressed in their capacity of "owner" of first-hand knowledge of "the facts."

The presentation of "the facts" by the judges may seem a straightforward matter as long as they are undisputed. "The facts" as they are known by the judges from the dossier are brought forward for the defendant's confirmation, disconfirmation, or amendation. In this way a body of knowledge of the facts is built up that everyone can agree on. The consistency of statements about "the facts" is taken as an indication of them being true. Inconsistent statements on the other hand require an explanation. Inconsistencies are taken up by the judges as elicitation techniques that invite the defendants to solve these "puzzles." The underlying idea is that the exact details of the criminal events can be verbally "replayed" in the courtroom, and that there can only be one true report of what has happened.

However, inconsistencies may not be presented directly as contrasting versions, but they may be assumed by the implications of guilt and responsibility in the judges' questions. Although the judges' questions may at first sight seem to be geared to the establishment of "the facts," the nature of the answers shows that facts and interpretations are inextricably interwoven. The simultaneous concern for facts and inferences reflects the double involvement of the defendant in the courtroom. As a provider of the information for the fact-finding of the judges, the defendant is asked to report on the events; as someone who has to defend himself against an accusation, he is expected to account for his actions. Of course these two identities are inseparable. Thus a request for confirmation of the facts may at the same time be heard as a request for an admission of guilt; and a request for information may be taken as a request for an explanation.

Because the interpretations of the facts are based on common knowledge about how people usually behave, the distinction between first-hand knowledge and common knowledge is blurred. Common knowledge is an important resource for the establishment of the plausibility of one's version of events. It is invoked time and again to corroborate or question claims that a particular event has happened. Moreover it appears that the knowledge shared by the participants also includes knowledge about competing perceptions of reality. Common knowledge contains controversies and contradictions. This makes for its negotiability, which is the mechanism by which "the facts" may acquire their meaning, and the participants their credibility.

Next to the strategic application of different kinds of knowledge, the knowledge about strategy itself provides an orientation to what kinds of information can be hidden and what has to be owned up. This knowledge cannot be explicated at the risk of its interfering with a convincing performance. Strategic knowledge can only operate by virtue of its being implicit. The credibility of the participants in the courtroom depends on their disattending the strategic implications of their position in the courtroom. This makes it impossible to distinguish between strategic sophistication and ingenuity. It is not only the defendants' alleged criminal involvement that is on trial, but also the credibility of their performance in the courtroom.

---

* An earlier version of this paper (Komter, 1991c) appeared in Recht der Werkelijkheid 12(2): 3-19.

---

[1] I shall use the term "the facts" in the same way it is used in the courtroom. It refers to the alleged events in which the defendant is allegedly involved.

[2] In the Netherlands we have a combination of an inquisitorial and an adversarial criminal justice system. The inquisitorial aspects are shown in the importance of the "preliminary investigations." Prior to the trial, defendants and witnesses have been heard by the police and the judge of instruction, and their depositions have been recorded in the defendant's dossier. In court this dossier is an important source of information for the judges, next to the statements of the defendants themselves. Witnesses are only summoned to appear in court when it is expected that their direct testimony is indispensible. A substantial part of the interaction in the courtroom is the "hearing" of the defendant by the judges. Defendants have the right to remain silent, and they swear no oath that they will speak the truth.

[3] The translations of these fragments have been made so as to capture the conversational style of the original Dutch text. The names have been changed.

[4] In jail the alleged accomplice (who denied his involvement in the robbery) had threatened to kill this defendant if he'd tell on him.

[5] Even innocent victims may have something to gain from their involvement in the events (when they are insured). In robbery cases there is usually no agreement between the defendant and the victim about the amount of money that has been stolen. The profits for both sides are easy to imagine.

8

# Seeing Conversations: Analyzing Sign Language Talk*

Paul McIlvenny

## Introduction

The study of the organization of conversation, discourse or language use in general is firmly based on the analysis of the speech and writing of dominant hearing communities. In contrast, I will discuss the preliminary results of an attempt to analyze the talk-in-interaction of the Finnish Deaf[1] community from the perspective of conversation analysis (CA). The premise of this research is that it is essential to study how sign language talk is socially constituted, maintained and used in real practical settings that the Deaf encounter and actively construct in their community. Some of the analyses will be illustrated with written transcripts of fragments of natural multi-party sign language talk activity and line drawings of pertinent moments in the stream of interaction.

## Background

In the 1960s, the so called "gestures" of the Deaf community in America were established in the academic world as a natural language that complied with all the requirements set for spoken languages (Stokoe 1960). Following this breakthrough, Finnish sign language (FiSL) became the object of linguistic attention. Sign language picture dictionaries (glossaries) have been produced and specific linguistic features of FiSL have been studied, e.g., manual gestures using the hands; grammatical modifications of the sign; and the non-manual use of the face, body and eyes (See Rissanen 1985; Pimiä and Rissanen 1987). It is now clear that sign language in Finland is a natural language used by the Deaf community (estimated at approximately 5000 members), which is passed down from generation to generation as an intrinsic element of Deaf culture.

However, since the academic "discovery" of sign language, very little work has been conducted on the interactive organization of the talk of native signers. Discourse analytic studies of sign language have been reported in Hall (1983), Wilbur (1983), Prinz and Prinz (1985), Roy (1989) and Nowell (1989). Also, an initial analysis of features of dyadic turn-taking in sign language has been reported in Baker (1977), and this analysis forms the backbone of almost all of the later analyses of sign language discourse. However, this work was based on the signal theory of turn-taking and the data was drawn from recordings of experimental dyadic conversations. In the sign language literature it is often admitted that turn-taking and talk are interesting phenomena, but accounts of their social organization tend to assume that "rules of behavior" govern conversational interactions between Deaf people, as codes of dress might be said to govern appearances (see Kyle 1991 for such a view). A recent and more promising study of turn-taking and overlap in interpreter-mediated interactions between a lecturer and a Deaf student are reported in Roy (1992). Roy examines how the competing attentions of the two modalities of spoken English and ASL (American sign language) affect the construction of turns-at-talk between a Deaf student and a hearing lecturer when mediated by a qualified interpreter.

Rather than adopt a linguistic or discourse analytic approach, I will draw upon the empirical methods of conversation analysis (CA). Thus, it is a fundamental principle of the research reported here that the object of study is natural everyday talk between Deaf people, and therefore it is not a study of the failure or incompetence of Deaf people in settings in which they are constructed as a dominated and handicapped minority.

When we consider CA, most of the foundational work on natural conversation has focused on British or American spoken culture, though research is in progress on Indo-European and Asian spoken languages, and the Finnish spoken language has recently been subjected to analysis using these techniques. But, CA methods have not so far been applied to sign language conversation and at first glance this does raise some distinctive problems because of the difference in modality as well as culture. One problem is that the techniques developed for collecting, rendering and analyzing spoken talk may not be appropriate for sign language or may be problematic in their routine application. These issues are discussed separately in McIlvenny (1991) and will not be mentioned further.

It is important to note at this point that I use the words "talk," "say," etc. to refer to the signing activities that Deaf people engage in together because those are the terms that they themselves use to describe and refer to their own use of sign language. Unfortunately, some researchers (even within CA) are actively constructing an analytic discourse in which the Deaf community does not talk. For example:

> Conversation is not talk's sole form, but it does seem to be its most general one, composing many social scenes, leaking into others, and probably providing the source from which other forms of speech and writing derive. There is no doubt that some societies are more silent, some more terse, some more formal than others. Some communities

> -- *the deaf, for example -- do not talk at all.* (Moerman 1988: 3, my italics)

Rather than reserve these terms for spoken language interaction, I will use them in the broad sense of language-rich interaction in practical everyday contexts. If Moerman really wants to suggest that Deaf people do not talk simply because they do not vocalize then he is being blatantly unfair and audiocentric. There is no need for the talk activities of Deaf people to be described as different from those of certain privileged spoken language communities. Deaf people do converse and have a rich set of social talk activities as this paper documents.

## The Preliminary Study

The analyses presented here are based on video recordings made over a period of a year or so in a weekly Deaf club[2] in a small city in northern Finland. Wednesday evening is a regular time for Deaf people to congregate and chat, or to attend a meeting or watch a talk given by an official from outside the community. Some other data was gathered from the Deaf youth club which also meets once a week and from a meeting of Deaf youth in Finland which takes place once a year. Two cameras were used to film most of these events and both camera operators worked together to obtain complementary perspectives on the events if this was possible. However, none of the recordings were pre-planned or set-up; they were all recorded discretely as they developed *in situ* without interference from the researcher. Initially, the analyses were conducted with the aid of one hearing interpreter[3], who is a native signer born to Deaf parents, but later the contributions of a Deaf informant and a second interpreter were crucial, both instrumentally in doing analysis and politically in that a Deaf representative shaped not only the methods adopted but also the reporting of results back to the Deaf community. In addition, the Deaf informant worked as a camera operator to obtain video data.

In the remainder of the paper I will discuss evidence for the social organization of talk-in-interaction in a Finnish Deaf sign language community. First, the distributed and local nature of much sign language talk activity is demonstrated. We must clearly understand that participation frameworks, group dynamics, applause and laughter, for example, are accomplished within the visual-spatial modality of sign language. Second, examples of explicit attention-getting are presented in order to spotlight the pervasive and embodied work of creating and maintaining mutual orientation and of reorganizing participation frameworks; also, an example is given in which the spatial orientation of participants is shown to be crucial for tracking the conversation. Third, I will look at turn transition, which is the space in which one signer stops and another signer gains the floor. The working conjecture is that in the sign language community, studied signers in a group routinely orient to "one signer -- one floor -- no gap" just as spoken conversationalists in some cultures have been shown to do, but in turn transitions a different systematics is locally operable than in spoken conversations because of the visual-spatial modality. In addition it is shown that competitive self-selections are themselves accomplished through an ongoing process of interaction between signers and recipient(s).

With regard to the examples used in this paper, I have provided a line drawing[4] to illustrate the relative gaze, body and hand positionings at a crucial moment in a fragment of talk activity. Transcripts are provided for some of the turn-taking examples. The transcript notation system is based upon that used in Boden and Zimmerman (1991), but there are some special symbols necessarily included because of the visual-spatial modality in which sign language talk is accomplished.[5] The system is still undergoing development because it is difficult to represent sign language activity in a way that is amenable to interactional rather than phonological or morphological linguistic concerns and also given the present lack of an established written form that is indigenous to the community. One worry is that standardized conventions for use with spoken language data may bias the transcription of sign language data. Features of sign language, such as visual movements or facial expressions that are linguistically, as well as interactionally, meaningful, may be inadequately represented or lost from the record. Consequently, there is a real danger of ethnocentrism (see the discussion of "audism" in Lane 1992) penetrating the analyses, which may lead for example to a premature claim for conversational universals. The special transcription conventions can be found in Appendix A.

## Distributed Activities: A Preliminary to the Analysis of Turn-Taking

The aim of the next section is to show how bodies in space are organized in the construction of locales for talk-in-interaction given that sound is not a resource for the Deaf community. Many of the activities of the Deaf community in gatherings are conducted through the distributed work of members of the group. It is essential to understand this before looking at turn-taking in talk, for we may assume that sign language talk is managed using the same resources and within the same constraints as those found in spoken languages. *The visual-spatial modality shapes the social organization of interaction and of talk-in-interaction specifically in that it must be accomplished in situ with hands, eyes, faces and bodies, but not with ears.*

A fundamental constraint on interaction and participation is that each member has only restricted and *local access* through gaze to all the activities of other members in a group. An individual cannot help but have a blind region[6] (normally about 170 degrees) at any one moment, and this may be the reason for the repeated scanning and side-to-side head movements that many hearing people tend to call "distracted" or "disinterested" when they first try to converse with Deaf people. However, these behaviors do not obviate the constraint of the *mutual-exclusivity* of focal regions, such that if one focuses on one visual field then one automatically excludes another visual field because one cannot focus on both simultaneously. I will show that this individual property is compensated for by the phenomenon of *social reflection*, i.e., seeing relevant activities that one cannot directly see by monitoring the actions of others who are currently visible. I also intend to illustrate the phenomenon of *cascading*, i.e., activities that propagate or chain-react in transitions between one focused group activity and another.

## Local Access, Reflection and Cascades

I will now illustrate with some examples how local access constraints are linked to the phenomena of reflection and cascading. In Example 1, the propagation of a look through reflection is displayed. The three men A, B, and C are watching an interpreted lecture from the periphery of the group (in the middle of the long hall) when the lights at the back of the hall were switched off accidentally. In the Deaf community, flashing the lights is a common signal for group attention as it is simultaneously visible by all. Maybe because of this convention, B turns to scan the back of the hall; C then turns, followed by A after he happens to glance at C. At this moment (see Figure 1) the three men are thus attending to a potentially relevant activity behind them and their collective attentiveness is triggered in turn first by B and then C, such that through reflection A, B and C come to "see together" what may be relevant behind them. This phenomenon occurs on many occasions in Deaf gatherings and conversations (see Example 3). In this case, they find nothing to attend to and indulge in new scans.

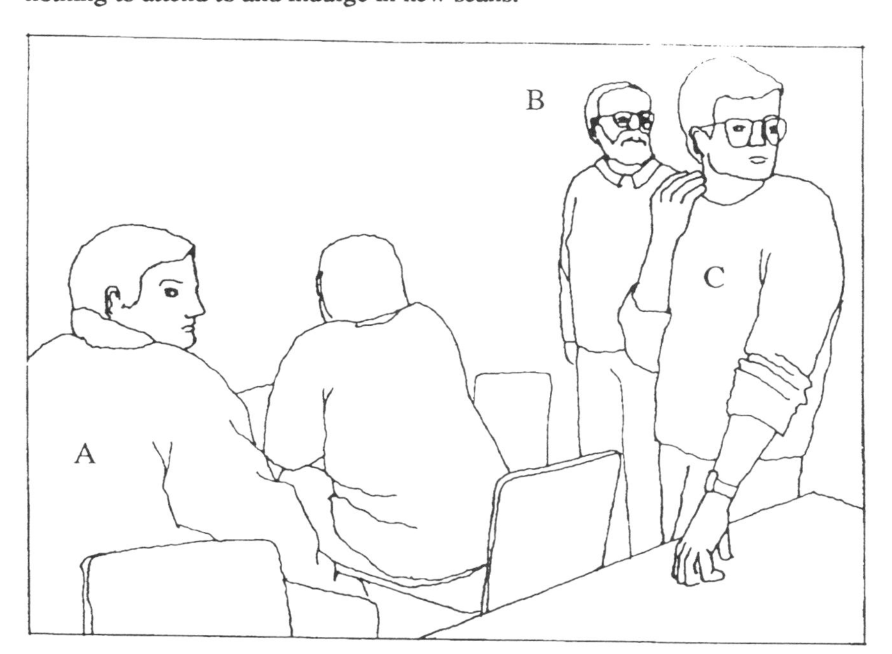


Figure 1

In Example 2, the Deaf leader (DL) has just apparently finished a topic in a closing piece at the end of a lecture. One section of the audience on the left begins to distribute leaflets and thus the audience as a focused group starts to dissolve. However, the Deaf leader calls for attention again with a sweep of the arm during which he notices the distracted section to the left. He waves several times, first side-to-side then up-and-down, upon which other members of the group start waving and signing to the distracted parties, too. The *cascade* of attention-getting works to the back of the room as different attentive members (marked A on Figure 2) work at different times on particular inattentive or otherwise engaged people who are only locally accessible, i.e., those who are not-yet-attentive move into new positions which are differentially accessible to members of the attentive audience. Much supportive and distributed work is required to reorient the people in the room to focus on the Deaf leader. He then signs that there is one more thing to inform them about; he reopens the address and thus orients to the prior activity as a distraction to a not-yet-finished address which has one more item to complete before closure.

Figure 2

Further examples of distributed and group activities can easily be found in the Deaf community. For example, applause and laughter are two activities that further illustrate the particular embodied work that Deaf members do. Atkinson (1984) has shown that applause and group appreciation displays are interesting phenomena in hearing communities, but in the Deaf community sound is no carrier of meaning. In the Finnish Deaf community an appropriate means of displaying appreciation is with a two handed handwave with the hands high above the head. From video fragments it is noticeable that audience members as well as those on the "stage" are monitoring closely the behavior of others. But certain dynamics occur because of local access and mutual-exclusivity. The audience cannot necessarily see all the other members nor the appropriate behavior at the same time, i.e., those at the front cannot see those at the back without turning around, while those on the periphery are otherwise engaged and may not see the response begin out of their visual field. What is clear is that movement into applause is swift as the behavior *cascades* through the audience, though those members on the periphery of the audience who are engaged in conversations or incipient talk are commonly late starters and late finishers. This demonstrates that the main audience must be attentive to each other and this group display is built quickly as a publicly visible phenomenon from the distributed work of its members. Equally, we could ask how signers engage in laugh activity when, in contrast, hearing communities systematically orient to the sound of laughter (see Jefferson 1985). From video fragments of laughter in multi-party talk it appears that certain distinctive movements of the upper body -- bending and swaying -- and a teeth-smile are carefully coordinated. Also, orientation to the accomplishment of mutual gaze by all parties is often present through the laugh sequence.

## Seeing Conversations: Aspects of Turn-taking

### Attention-getting

Explicit attention-getting by means of hand and arm waves (*G) and actual body contact taps (*T) is pervasive in sign language talk-in-interaction, and it is often supported by third party members. Indeed, attention-getting clearly influences the situated management of turn-taking as signers can only gain a right to a "turn" if others are looking at them. Thus attention-getting and self-selection often go hand in hand. For example, self-selections are often prefaced with an attention-getter and are initially directed to the current signer, but from video data it appears that a turn does not necessarily have to be directed to the previous signer in multi-party talk once the turn has been relinquished. Also, repeatedly we find that after the onset of the first sign(s) by a potential next signer the attention of another participant or of all parties is not attained. Attention-getting activity is then resumed and the sign(s) recycled until mutual attention is achieved (see Example 7).

In Example 3, attention-getting behavior is illustrated in the context of seeing another conversation. Displays are thus exposed on the video of appropriate transition relevance places, indicated for example by a return to rest position, mutual eye gaze, etc. C attempts to gain the attention of A, who is conversing with B, by waving her left hand up and down quickly (see Figure 3). Her attempts are structured around possible completion points at which transition is relevant. She fails repeatedly as the conversation between A and B continues, though A is in a position to see C. Finally, just after she disattends their conversation for a moment she returns to find B and A looking away to the same neutral space (as in Example 1, B had looked first, then A tracked the look). She tracks the same space and returns her gaze to A as she begins to wave again. Unfortunately, A has just turned back to the front of the hall and thus is looking in the opposite direction. Her actions and those of A (and B) demonstrate that neither found talk relevant activity in the neutral space that they all scanned, but, during the scan, monitoring of each other was not possible because of the local access and mutual exclusivity constraints. Thus social reflection was both the resource for her gaining entry to a possible transition space, but also the undoing of a successful transition because A could not be monitored while she scanned the neutral space. Luckily B looks to C and C asks for him to contact A, whereupon he moves the chair in front of him to knock A's chair (third party messengers, vibration (*V) and air flow are other less common resources for attention-getting). A turns around and C asks a question on a different topic from the conversation between A and B.

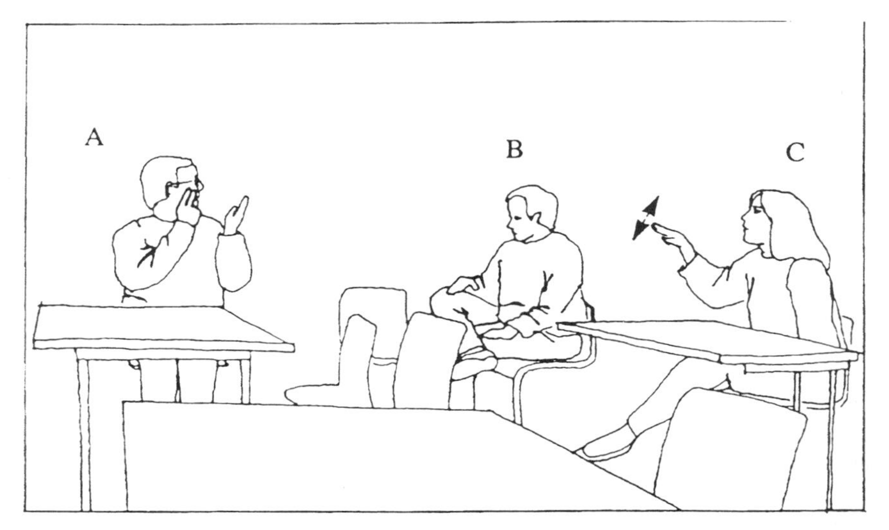


Figure 3

## Not Seeing Conversations?

As participants commonly have only local access to the disparate activities of the group it is interesting to ask how signers monitor and take part in conversations in particular spatial configurations. In the next case (Example 4), the conversation is possibly problematic for signer A because of the group's spatial configuration. Small talk results when participant C drops her orange and thus becomes accessible to A and B who are standing behind her. A initiates a conversation about the dirty orange, C responds and then B continues the conversation. At this point their participation forms an obtuse triangle (greater than 90 degrees) with A at the apex. A turns to look at B sign, but, at what seems like an appropriate transition relevance space, she returns her gaze to C at the moment B continues (see Figure 4a). C responds and A monitors, but A cannot possibly see directly the three minimal responses that B uses during C's signing. A returns gaze to B, who glances at her; meanwhile, C begins signing again. B notices (see Figure 4b) and shortly afterward A (through reflection) returns to look with expectancy at C, who has just finished and is now looking away. A appears to use the talk in progress and the gaze of the other participants to accomplish her "seeing the conversation," but the spatial positions and orientation of the three participants are not irrelevant in this conversation, thus we could argue that the participants (especially C) have only local (and inferior) access to the conversation. However, can it be so if social reflection operates as described earlier? Ultimately we may have to agree that C does take part fully in the conversation if we grant that ideal participation and mutual intersubjectivity are themselves problematic notions empirically and theoretically. Thus, through the talk-in-progress participants routinely provide mutual support for multiple interpretations and participations such that understandings are displayed and circulated *in situ* out of the materials at hand.

Figure 4a Figure 4b

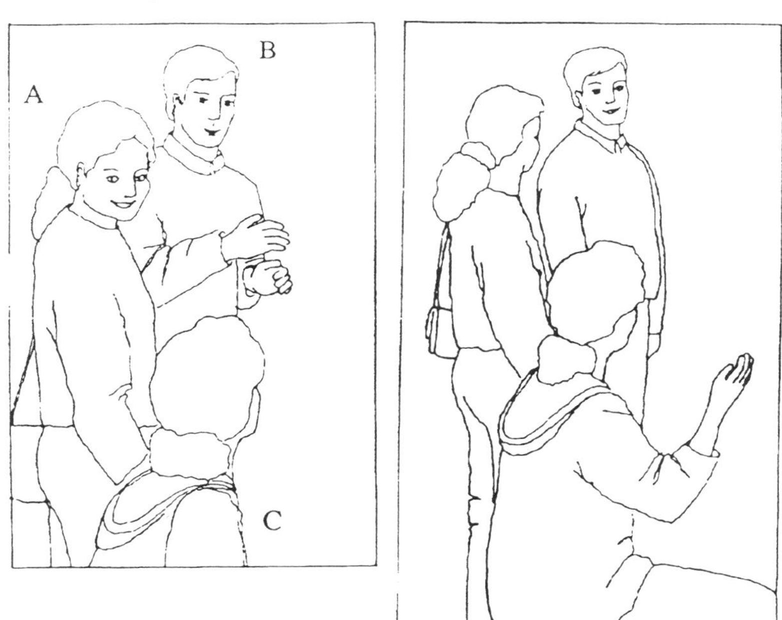


Turn Transitions: Onsets and Glances

It is routinely evident in sign language talk that signers orient to a "floor" on which signers take turns to sign and others as recipients attend to them.[7]

Sequential organization is also apparent and it is unlikely to be affected much by the modality as it is a serial phenomenon. When turn transition has been accomplished and another signer has gained the floor then sequence time has been built. Cicourel has expressed doubt.

> We do not know if the deaf are constrained by sequential ordering or chaining rules, because several signers can allow their signing to *overlap continuously* and several types of information can be communicated simultaneously which fall under the general notion of kinesic-visual communication (Cicourel 1973: 168, my italics).

However, the observation that several signers can allow their signing to overlap continuously is just not true for FiSL talk -- it just appears that way to the naive eye. In addition, it is dangerous to conflate sign languages with non-verbal gestures under the term kinesic-visual communication. Indeed, the manual and non-manual features are major elements of complex natural sign languages with distinctive characteristics of their own; "non-verbal" gestures are also used by signers but as a complement to sign language in social talk activities.

In order to uncover some particular features of FiSL talk, let us consider turns-at-talk and turn transitions in multi-party sign language conversation.[8] The turn-taking systematics (Sacks et al. 1978) describes a powerful context-free, context-sensitive mechanism that accounts for how speakers construct "next speaker" in conversation. As mentioned above, signers in FiSL clearly orient to a "floor" on which signers take "turns-at-signing," but it is at transition relevance places (TRPs) that we find interesting phenomena. In the turn-taking systematics, self-selection is an option available at a TRP that is ordered after the first option, viz. current speaker selects next. The two options are given in full below:

> a) If the turn-so-far is so constructed as to involve the use of "current speaker selects next" technique, then the party so selected has rights, and is obliged, to take next turn to speak, and no others have such rights or obligations, transfer occurring at that place.
> b) If the turn-so-far is so constructed as not to involve the use of a "current speaker selects next" technique, self selection for next speaker may, but need not, be instituted, with *first starter acquiring rights to a turn,* transfer occurring at that place. (Sacks et al: 13, my italics)

The first option is definitely found in FiSL talk: it can be accomplished by a question, a shift in current speaker's gaze to a particular participant, etc. However, a realization of the second option in speech turn exchange is assumed to be simultaneously hearable by all and thus simultaneous overlaps, when two participants self-select in a TRP, are possible and orientable to moment by moment by those involved in a mutually addressable fashion. Self-selection for next speaker becomes operable by simply speaking at a

TRP. Equally, a first starter is routinely hearable as first at the moment of uttering. The assumption of mutual addressability is built into the rule set so to speak. But for sign language talk this cannot be assumed. Unlike in spoken talk, sign onsets are not always available to all participants and this is a fundamental feature of FiSL talk. Thus, just because two people start signing does not entail that they or any of the other participants will automatically see both or even one of these onsets. In effect we must challenge the assumption that self-selections by two or more participants will be received simultaneously by everyone. And so in general it cannot be assumed as a matter of course that there is a single channel "airspace" into which all contributions are placed in immediate equal competition with others. Because of the *distributed* nature of sign language activities, the *mutual exclusivity* of gaze regions, and the *local access* of participants to the activities of the group, *self-selections can occur concurrently in time but without simultaneous visibility*. Thus, the construction of a mutually ratified "floor" is an endemic problem in FiSL talk because of the modality, and consequently co-occurrence in time can be discovered later or remain unseen by a participant. Constructing a next signer is shaped by fundamental constraints and so for FiSL talk we find that self-selection is itself contingent and "first starter," "acquiring rights," and "transfer" are more problematic than they appear in the systematics for spoken (American) conversation.

Now let us consider the social organization of turn transition and competition itself. It was a major result of the foundational work in CA that turns-at-talk were shown to be a locally managed, interactive accomplishment, i.e., that speaker and recipient were mutually involved and that a speaker-centered analysis of utterances in isolation was missing something important. Later it was argued in Goodwin and Goodwin (1987) that "individual utterances and single turns at talk are themselves constituted through an ongoing process of interaction between speaker and recipient" (p. 3). That is, a speaker-centered analysis of turn construction itself is inadequate. What I would also like to demonstrate is that a further step is required: we can no longer focus simply on a signer-centered analysis of turn competition. Of course, CA has addressed the local resolution of overlap in TRPs but it is usually examined from the point of view of two speakers who find themselves competing for a turn-at-talk. For FiSL talk I will show that *competitive turn transitions are themselves accomplished through an ongoing process of interaction between signers and recipient(s).*

In the following I present some examples of how turn transitions are managed in FiSL within this distinctive modality. In a similar scenario to that of a spoken conversation, Example 5 illustrates how two competitive self-selections are resolved quickly through an interaction between signers and a recipient which leads to one signer dropping out. Signer B finishes her turn (returns to rest position) and looks with a particular "would you believe it" expression at D. C signs REALLY low on the table, self-selects by starting an attention-getting table tap which is then followed by the sign SUNDAY, but mutual gaze has not been achieved. At this point several things happen in quick succession but without the global attention of all concerned, i.e., it is locally managed through the constraints of local access. D glances to C (a flick of the head) and in that glance finds C's hand moving to the table. Note that glances are restricted windows onto potentially relevant other-activity in which one must find evidence of a projected or expected activity (cf. Sudnow 1972), otherwise gaze returns or moves to another focal point/participant. D's gaze returns to B and she begins signing FIRST to the same recipient. C concurrently finishes another attention wave and B begins to glance at C (tracking the just prior glance of D). However, C glances to D, maybe tracking the continued gaze, up until this moment and during her attention-getting attempts, of B towards D. She then discovers a competitive onset by D (see Figure 5: in the transcript the exact moment at which this image is representative of the camera's viewpoint is marked with a "#"). During this glance, B has glanced to C and thus finds her attending to D (still Figure 5); B's gaze returns to D. Significantly, C upon finding a competitive onset returns gaze to B, the directed recipient of both signers, and recycles SUNDAY. But she is too late and finds B apparently still gazing at D. She drops the sign, returns to rest position and looks back to D, who is still signing. Thus the resolution is achieved through the recipient's behavior in the context of finding the next signer, i.e., the behavior of C displays an orientation to recipient gaze in resolving competitive onsets.

```
EXAMPLE 5 - [3-19,2]

Initial gaze:  [a>?; b>d; c>b; d>b?]
---------------
      B:  couldn't give birth head first it was a difficult situation so it
          was born feet first and it went okay.
---------------
      C:  REALLY+
          oh really!
---------------
- > C:    *G(V) SUNDAY       *G  +         SUNDAY ((rest))
          hey    on sunday-   hey           on sunday-
- > D:           [{hs}        [(FIRST
                              (was it the first?)
Gaze:                   d>c=d>b
                              b>c=b>d
                                c>d=c>b         c>d
Fig:                               #5
---------------
      D:       (FIRSTGIRL)
          the first was a girl
      B:   [(                    )
            (                    )
Gaze:      c>b
---------------
```

From this and other examples we can conclude that each participant in talk is actively engaged -- through scans, glances or noticings -- in discovering current or next sign language activity. But, in so doing they *reorganize the possibilities for other signers and shift their own focal regions thus excluding the possibility of attentiveness to other regions at that moment*, e.g., if I turn my gaze (call this a focal region or a field of visual awareness) from one participant to another behind me I cannot then directly see the first.

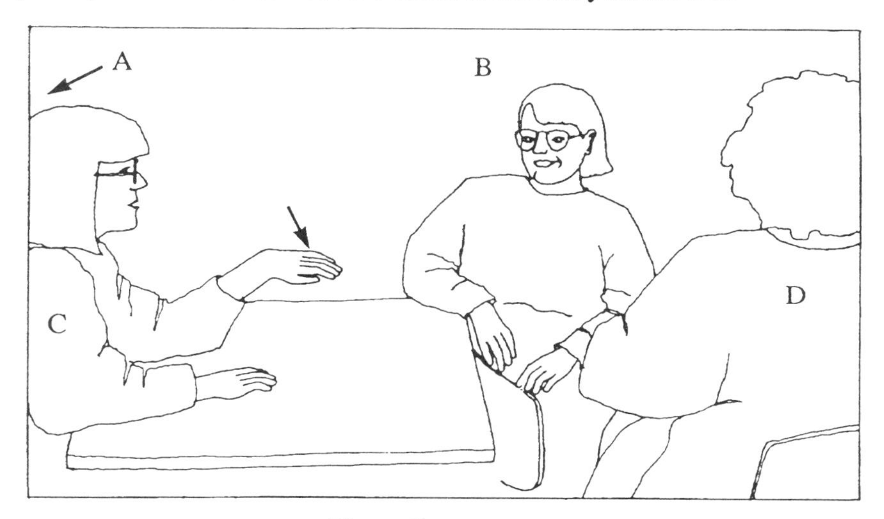


Figure 5

Example 6 illustrates both the importance of gaze monitoring and the local and distributed nature of sign language talk in transitions. One participant D, who is signing, reaches a transition relevance place. This is demonstrated in the immediate gaze shifts of B, A and C who reorient to a potential next signer. But the continued shifts of gaze suggest that a transition is not accomplished: B and A look to D again and C looks to the vicinity of her coffee cup. Here we have a "lapse" in the conversation. After a short period, A begins signing and B glances to A; as B's gaze settles on A, A's hand is falling low. Immediately, B returns gaze to D and starts an attention wave to D (Figure 6), having discovered no activity in the vicinity of D's apparent gaze (in which nothing has happened during B's glance). B does hesitate and double check halfway through the return of her gaze to D, but continues with the wave. However, A's signing continues, C notices B's attention waves, but, for B, D still does not attend to B. After a short period B returns to check what is attracting D's gaze and discovers after the onset of self-selection that somebody else (A) is currently signing. B monitors the signing while still waving, gets mutual gaze from A who returns to rest position, and nods and returns to D. She discovers D is attending to her and immediately starts signing.

EXAMPLE 6 - [3-19]

Initial gaze: [a>d; b>d; c>d; d>?]

--------------

D: ( BOOK TEACH NOTHING)
( the book teaches nothing)

--------------

Gaze: b>a b>ø=b>d
c>a c>ø
a>b a>d

--------------

A: ( ) ( )
--> B: [*G + + + + {mth} +
hey yeah? hey
Gaze: b>a (b>d)=b>d b>a b>d
c>d
a>b
d>b
Fig: #6

--------------

B: YOUNG-LAST BROTHER SECOND WAIT
the youngest brother was waiting for the second baby

--------------

B: BORN BOY HAVE
a boy was born.

--------------

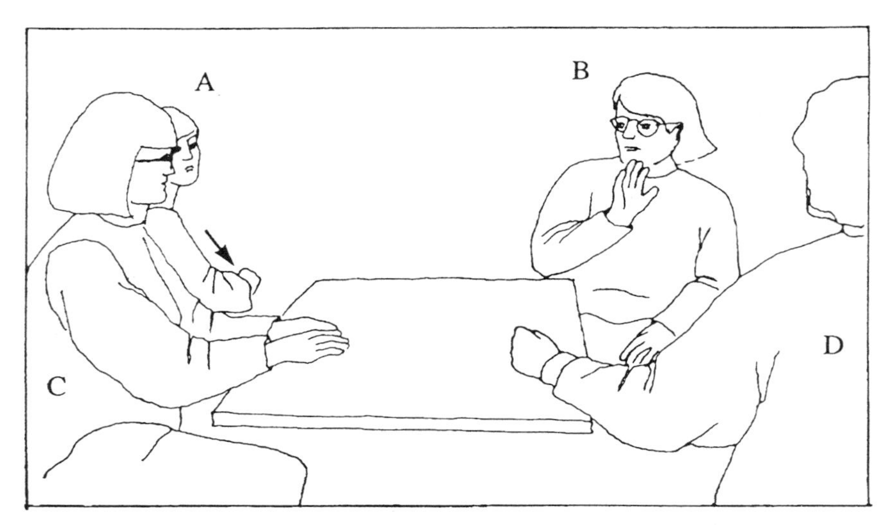


Figure 6

In this case, double onset self-selection is resolved and a group focus is re-operable, but this does not have to happen because accomplishing transition could result in a temporary dissolution of a group focus. However, in two and three party talk, resolution must result in a group focus because signing normally requires a recipient and so in a triad the third participant cannot sign to either of the two otherwise occupied participants. In the next example this situation is illustrated.

I will consider next what happens when more than two participants self select in multi-party talk. In Example 7[9], we have an instance of tripartite directed self-selection in which F is at the apex of an obtuse triangle participation space. After some turn exchanges W signs and returns to the rest position with F and M gazing at W and W gazing at M. In this transition relevance space, all three participants self-select but without all necessarily being immediately aware of their simultaneity. M signs a question to W, F turns from W to M and signs to M (Figure 7), and W turns from M to F and waves and taps for attention (and discovers F signing in Figure 8). M resolves the triad of competitive onsets by shifting his gaze to F, to whom W is looking. It could be that M has already seen F signing or that he discovers that F is already signing in overlap; either way, by orienting to F at this moment a successful resolution is accomplished. F recycles CONFLICT upon M's gaze, M becomes a recipient and F continues signing having gained the floor. That F wants to sign to the triad is demonstrated when W looks away after she fails to get F's attention; consequently, F waves while persevering with a one handed sign and recycles upon receipt of W's gaze once again. Finally, F stops and W takes over the floor. An important finding here is that *recipients' activities and the timing of glances, gaze transitions and mutual gaze are systematically relevant to the resolution of signer transition*; it is not simply up to the competing signers to resolve a potentially troublesome overlap.

EXAMPLE 7 - [3-13]

Initial gaze: [f>w; w>m; m>w]

---------------

W: ( )DEAF HOLIDAY (*G) ((point)) (HOTEL) NO
( ) a deaf holiday thing hey not that (hotel)
M: [ahh [NO?
ahh no?

---------------

W: DEAF HOLIDAY (ps-7) {hn}
a deaf holiday thing [yes
M: [I-SEE HOLIDAY I-SEE
i see you mean a holiday thing

---------------

M: MEAN?
what does it mean?
Gaze: f>m

---------------
W: (marketing) NOW
marketing should start now
Gaze: f>w
---------------
M: MARKETING?
what is marketing?
---------------
F: MARKETING + ]
marketing
W: [ASSOCIATION: *G + +
the association, hey
Gaze: f>m f>w
m>f m>w
w>f w>m
---------------
W: ASSOCIATION NEED SELF MARKETING NOW (ps-7) {so}
the association needs self marketing now, so
---------------
-> M: WHAT MEAN MARKETING?
what does marketing mean?
-> F: [MARKETING/CONFLICT
there was a conflict
-> W: [ *T +
hey
Gaze: f>m w>f m>f
Figs: #7 #8
---------------
F: CONFLICT ONE- TWO-YEARS-AGO: *T:TWO-YEARS-AGO:*T:
a conflict one- two years ago: hey two years ago hey
W: + + +]
Gaze: f>ø f>w
w>Ω w>f
m>w
---------------
F: TWO-YEARS-AGO CONFLICT {bad}
two years ago there was a conflict it was bad
W: [ *T +
hey hey
Gaze: f>ø f>w
m>f m>w
---------------
W: I ( ) BOARD
---------------

Figure 7

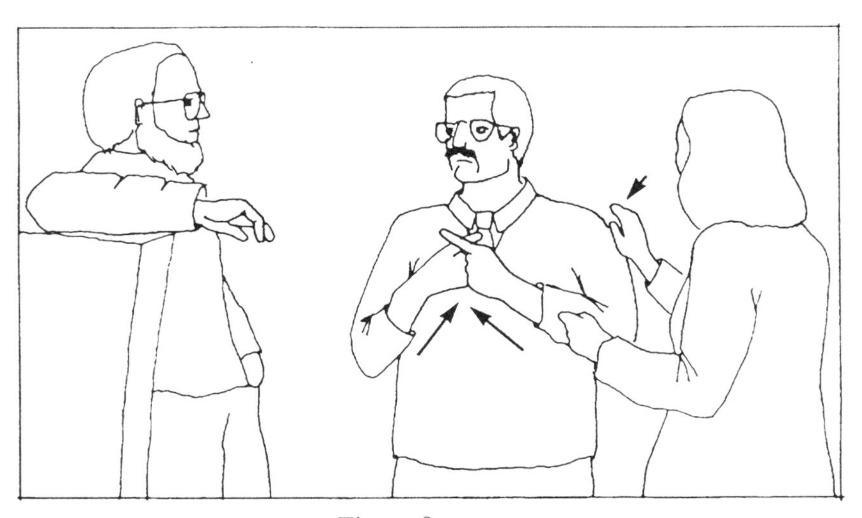

Figure 8

## Discussion

The main finding of this paper is that in turn transitions and group activities Deaf signers display a heightened and distinctive use of visual space and the body in the accomplishment of these activities. Indeed, the modality of sign language provides many materials out of which participants construct their talk and their lives, and these embodied constraints and resources clearly influence the organization of situated talk. But, we must recognize that much further work on the organization and accomplishment of talk and interaction in a sign language community is required. In particular, it has yet to be determined to what extent the participation space itself influences talk and turn-taking (Examples 4 and 7), particularly in the context of gatherings. Also, it is not yet clear that the phenomenon of multiple directed self-selection onsets that we found in Example 7 are a common occurrence and what other trajectories they may have. This is a preliminary study, but it has suggested that sign language talk is worthy of analytic interest.

However, we should be cautious if we conclude that the organization of the talk of sign language communities is qualitatively different from or the same as that of spoken talk. We should be cautious because this research is based on a study of the Finnish sign language community and the findings are compared in part to the work on Anglo-American communities in which spoken talk is predominant. One should not generalize from the work of one sign language to all, as one should not generalize from one spoken language to all, or from spoken language to all possible languages. But it is true that some of the phenomena and mechanisms described here do occur in certain contexts in spoken language communities, as they also can see and they often organize their social activities without sound as a relevant resource.

If we consider this issue further, some researchers in CA have recently suggested that general or fundamental or primordial mechanisms or phenomena can now be postulated. For example, Boden and Zimmerman (1991) in their introduction to their edited collection suggest that some researchers might claim that the organization of turn-taking proposed by conversation analysis is a primordial mechanism of social organization, invariant to historical progress or cultural variation. Also, Schegloff (1991) mentions in a footnote to his paper that no reference to "context" was made in certain early papers in CA and thus the results were not tied to a sociologist's or anthropologist's notion of the "American cultural context." Thus, he hints that the turn-taking mechanism may be thought of as an underlying resource for constructing social organization. If we look to the empirical studies of conversation in different cultures we find that, surprisingly, early indications suggest that some notion of "implicational universal" may be useful for comparing conversations across cultures. For example, Moerman (1987) finds agreement between certain features of turn-taking found in "American" spoken conversation and those discovered by him in Thai conversations.

However, I feel it is premature to make a claim for a universal mechanism. Early work in CA persisted with the principle that empirical research in a certain manner will reveal interesting orders of detail. Has such a principle been discarded? It seems far more interesting to view the organization of turn-taking as an endemic problem for any community whose members must organize and coordinate their embodied activities. The subtle differences between communities in how a "turn-at-talk" is accomplished *in situ* and just what is a "turn" are more pertinent than the apparent similarities seen from an ethnocentric point of view. To remove "turns" from their embodied production within particular communities and then to posit a context-free mechanism for their production may hide specific and interesting differences between the way the problem of next actor in conversation is locally accomplished. We should say that finding a next speaker in talk is a primordial *issue* for talkers in all cultures.

A further issue that is implicitly raised in this paper is whether or not the turn-taking systematics should be rewritten to account for sign languages. I have argued that turn transitions are managed in particular and novel ways in and through the lived-in visual-spatial modality. Thus at TRPs transition to a next signer may occur through the operation of self-selection procedures for example, but the resolution of multiple self-selections that are predicted by the systematics is locally accomplished with the resources and constraints of talking with hands, eyes and bodies. But I also argued that the turn-taking systematics contains an implicit assumption that cannot hold for FiSL talk. It would seem that the distributed nature of Deaf activities (and of many hearing activities) -- which I have attempted to explain as a consequence of the modality -- leaks into the organization of sign language talk and of turn-taking in ways that are precluded in spoken talk because of the lived-in features of an aural modality. Of course, finding a next signer is a fundamental issue for signers in conversation as finding a next speaker is in spoken conversation. In that way, we could say that the problem is endemic across cultures. Whether the mechanism is "invariant" is a matter that I feel requires further empirical work and care with cross-cultural comparisons given the attendant dangers that are involved.

Lastly I would like to say that it is my hope that this research will be of benefit to the Deaf community. An analysis of the Deaf community that starts to focus on the construction of identity and membership in natural everyday talk is preferable to a study of failure or incompetence. Future studies can then revert to studying language and social contacts between powerful hearing institutions who have wielded an audist ideology and Deaf people who draw upon their services and constantly live in the shadow of the hearing world. What we need now is for more studies to be undertaken by Deaf researchers who are trained in the study of conversation, language and social organization.

## Appendix A: Special Transcription Conventions

|  |  |
| --- | --- |
| *G | Attention gesture, e.g., wave |
| *T | Attention tap (to the body) |
| *V | Attention through vibration |
| {hs} | Head shake. |
| {hn} | Head nod. |
| {mth} | Special mouth shape. |
| + | Repetition of sign. |

Gaze shifts are marked in the following way. Only transitions are explicitly marked.

|  |  |
| --- | --- |
| > | Gaze shift, e.g., x>y means x shifted gaze to y. |
| Ω | Gaze outside group. |
| ø | Gaze to neutral space. |
| = | Glance, e.g., x>y=x>z means x glances to y and then gazes at z. |

---

* Acknowledgments: I would like to thank Pirkko Raudaskoski for her collaborative research and interpreting, Anne Hämäläinen for her native insights into sign language and the Deaf community, Sirpa Suomela for her native insights and sign language interpretation, Ulla Hiironen for sign language interpretation, and the Deaf community in Finland for their kind assistance. Marjo-Liisa Moilanen had the difficult task of drawing the figures from the video frame-grabs. I thank my colleagues for their incisive comments offered in the Current Work in Ethnomethodology and CA Conference in Amsterdam, July 1991, and also Paul ten Have who kindly commented on the draft manuscript. The Department of English of Oulu University generously supplied technical facilities to support the study.

1 The convention of using "Deaf" to denote the deaf community is adopted in this paper. I will use it as a standard way of pointing to a difference between the audist view of the hearing disadvantaged as "defective" and the positive view of Deaf people themselves that they are a self-determined cultural and ethnic minority.

2 Ethnographies of Deaf clubs in Britain and the U.S. can be found in Kyle (1990) and Carmel and Monaghan (1991). Kyle notes that "the social club can be seen as the heart of Community life though it would be wrong to see it as the only locus of that life. Nevertheless, it is the area with which

hearing people have had very little contact and in which the pressures of the hearing society are least obvious" (p. 178).

3 The author of this paper is not a native signer, but has studied FiSL in Finland for a few years and has contacts with the community. Thus, an interpreter was required in order to fully appreciate and discuss the subtleties of the sign language activity. However, it soon became clear that a Deaf person should be involved as well in the transcription and analysis and luckily someone was found from the Deaf community early on in the project.

4 The line drawings are taken from the video data, which were shown at the talk I gave at the Current Work in Ethnomethodology and CA Conference in Amsterdam, July 1991, from which this paper has been compiled. Of course, I would have been more appropriate to include short-interval sequences of video frame-grabs, or even better, that the video fragments themselves could be distributed. Alas, this was not feasible. It should be pointed out that all analyses have proceeded with the videos as the primary record of the phenomena under investigation.

5 Besides the special symbols, it is important to note that capitalization of a word is a gloss for a sign in Finnish sign language. This is not a happy state of affairs -- being an imposition of a foreign language onto the structure of FiSL -- but will have to suffice for this paper. English language translations of sign language utterances are presented in lowercase underneath the glosses. Overlap markers and double parentheses apply to both sign language stream and the translation. Prolongation of a sign is marked with the standard ":" but in sign language a sign may be held while the other hand continues with a further sign or signs. Often, a sign is held statically while the other hand attracts attention from a recipient. Repetitions of a sign are common and are marked with a "+" for every occasion. Curly brackets, e.g., {lowercase}, indicate a mime or non-manual feature of a sign, e.g., a mouth shape may be grammatically important. A "/" between glosses indicates that two signs are assimilated to each other. Conventional markers of functional intonation also apply to sign language utterances, though questions for example are commonly indicated by non-manual features, e.g., by raising or lowering the eyebrows and/or a tilting of the head.

6 Sighted people can normally notice things in their peripheral vision with a range of just over 90 degrees to the left and right when focusing straight ahead. However, peripheral movements or features are distinguished with much less clarity than when present in the focal region, cf. Swisher et al. (1989).

7 Clare Lowing (personal communication) reports that signers in British sign language (BSL) orient to turn-constructional units and transition relevance places, and this is exhibited through features such as latched utterances and unmarked next position. Also reports suggest that the findings described here echo with the organization of American sign language (ASL) talk.

8 The interaction between deaf-blind people who sign and between deaf-blind and Deaf people are interesting special cases. In the data corpus, a fragment illustrates how a deaf-blind woman, who became blind after acquiring sign language, interacts with two Deaf signers. All are members of the Deaf community. Participation is asymmetric in that she can sign freely but obviously without being able to see her own signs or her participants'; however, only one person can sign to her at a time, except for simple touches to the body. Her hands (and head orientation) are the mechanism for turn taking -- she can offer her hands to someone or they can grab them and start to sign-trace with them. It is through her hands that turns-at-talk are systematically accomplished. Of course, not all deaf-blind people have such a means of interacting, nor do all interact with a language (see Goode 1979).

9 In sign languages, space in front of the signer is grammatically structured into zones that can be used to construct reference and grammatical case, for example. Early on in the transcript of Example 7, signer W points to the far right and thus indicates a pronominal reference to a prior referent set up in that position earlier in the interaction. A little later another point to the near left of the signer refers to a second referent.

# 9

# Multiple Mode, Single Activity: "Telenegotiating" as a Social Accomplishment*

Alan Firth

An increasingly common feature of present-day business transactions is that deals are done, items bought and sold, and commodities exchanged, *exclusively* via telecommunications. Where previously transactions were conducted in and as face-to-face encounters, the widespread availability of cellular telephones, telefacsimiles, telexes, video-conferencing, computer on-line, and electronic-mail facilities now makes a growing number of such encounters superfluous. Organizations, observes Williams (1982: 154), are becoming more critically aware of the "communication-transportation" trade-off, and, as a result, the traditional marketplace is being gradually superseded by a "virtual marketplace" of "tele-encounters."[1] Accordingly, lattices of "electronic networks" span the globe, resulting in an upsurge of activities such as "telemarketing," "teleconferencing," "telecommuting," and "telenegotiating" [see, e.g., Mulgan (1991), and Williams (1987)].[2]

This paper focuses on the latter of the above-mentioned "tele-activities": telenegotiating. Defined simply as a form of conflict-resolution/aversion and joint decision-making via telecommunications, the instance of telenegotiating examined below occurred within one particular organizational (work) setting.[3] Within this setting, the parties concerned are engaged in the exchange of resources (specifically, dairy products for money). In order that the exchange may take place, the parties must overcome or avert potential or real work-related disagreements and decide jointly upon the details of the exchange (cf. Hodgson 1988: 174). This they do by engaging in "telenegotiating." Telenegotiating, then, may be viewed as a socially- and institutionally-sanctioned mechanism which provides for the situationally efficient exchange of resources. As we shall observe, "telenegotiating" in this particular context entails the utilization of multiple modes of telecommunications (most commonly, telephone, telefacsimile, and telex). In this way, the activity of telenegotiating is not conducted as a "one-off" or "one-encounter" undertaking, but as an interrelated *series* of spatio-temporally distinct actions. What this paper seeks to do is address the question of how parties to the telenegotiations are able to conduct their joint actions in orderly, meaningful ways. We ask: How is the particular "virtual marketplace," and the telenegotiating occurring within that "marketplace," *socially* constructed? And further: What is it about the social context that enables the parties to recognize and make sense of their organizationally joint (though commonly spatio-temporally disjoined) actions?

In order to answer these questions, it is necessary to consider the negotiations not as socially or organizationally isolated undertakings [as is often the case in negotiation research (see Firth 1991: chap. 2)], but as activities integral to the work practices they reflexively serve and instantiate.[4] Naturally-occurring negotiations -- whether conducted via telecommunications or not -- are thus fundamentally embedded in context. The embedded nature of negotiations is not organizationally given or preordained, however, but locally accomplished in and through communicative action. As I shall attempt to demonstrate in this paper, by attending to the sequentially-organized "interactional work" through which the parties demonstrate and accomplish the contextual embeddedness of their actions, insight can be gained into how those same actions, though spatio-temporally disjoined and performed via multiple communicative modes, cumulatively evince a recognizable, coherent, and indeed, "single" activity.

## The Data

Our point of departure is the two following data extracts, reproduced from the same international telephone communication. The following telephone call, as well as the series of written documents also reproduced below, is typical of a data corpus comprising twenty-eight telephone calls and over one hundred written documents.[5] The protagonists in this particular call are a Dane, Michael Hansen, and an Indian, Asif Guptah. Hansen (H) is the Export Sales Manager of a large Danish Dairy company ("Melko Dairies"), and Guptah (G) is the Commodity Buyer for a Saudi Arabian importation company ("Saudi Royal Import-Export Co."). Both are engaged in attempting to complete an outstanding commodity transaction. In the first extract (1), Hansen has called Guptah's company in Saudi Arabia; Hansen's call is first answered by "A," an unknown employee within the Saudi Arabian company:

(1)

| | | |
|---|---|---|
| 1 | A: | ello:? |
| 2 | H: | yes hello? er saudi royal import export company:? |
| 3 | A: | ye:s? |
| 4 | H: | it's er michael hansen er melko dairies speaking. |
| 5 | | (0.8) could I speak to mister guptah please? |
| 6 | A: | moment |
| 7 | | (17.0) |
| 8 | B: | allo:? |
| 9 | H: | yes hello er michael hansen melko dairies speaking |
| 10 | B: | one minute |
| 11 | | (4.0) |
| 12 | G: | hello? |

| | | |
|---|---|---|
| 13 | H: | hello mister guptah (.) how are you? |
| 14 | G: | fine? (.) how're you? |
| 15 | H: | fine than' you (0.6) you know now the summer time |
| 16 | | has come to denmark uz well |
| 17 | G: | ((laughing)) huh hh:eh heh heh heh ::hh |
| 18 | H: | so for:: the:- us here in denmark it's hot (.) it's er |
| 19 | | twenty five degree, but for you it will be- it would |
| 20 | | be cold (.) I think |
| 21 | G: | NO, here in this er: forty- forty two |
| 22 | H: | yes? |
| 23 | | (1.0) |
| 24 | G: | yes |
| 25 | H: | well I prefer twenty five (.) it's better to me |
| 26 | | (0.9) |
| 27 | G: | yeah |
| 28 | | (1.1) |
| 29 | → H: | GOOD er (.) I got a telex for er- from you |
| 30 | | (1.3) |
| 31 | G: | yeah |
| 32 | H: | you don' er: (.) accept our prices. |
| 33 | | (1.2) |
| 34 | G: | for this er cheddar |

((continues))

Consider now the second extract (2), occurring approximately three minutes after the juncture marked in the above extract:

(2)

| | | |
|---|---|---|
| 1 | H: | I'm not (0.8) able to reduce my price er with more |
| 2 | | than hundred dollars (1.0) but then I will accept to: |
| 3 | | reduce it er: (1.3) hun- er:: yes (.) hundred dollars |
| 4 | | off all items (.) except the feta cheese. |
| 5 | | (3.4) |
| 6 | G: | huh hmm |
| 7 | | (5.1) |
| 8 | H: | er I have- I have been er |
| 9 | | calculating= |
| 10 | G: | =okay [can- |
| 11 | H: | [on the: er: (.) the feta cheese. |
| 12 | G: | yeah= |
| 13 | H: | =an' er the maximum I can give on the feta cheese |
| 14 | | (0.6) is twenty dollar less than er your first offer |
| 15 | | (1.0) |

16 G: huh hmm
17 (2.1)
18 --> then can you- can you send us a: telex an'
19 we will confirm this?
20 --> H: yes (.) I will send you a telex
21 G: okay
22 H: er just one other question
23 G: yes

((continues))

My immediate concern with these two extracts is with the interactants' explicit references to preceding actions [in (1)], and subsequent actions [in (2)] (both references are arrowed in the extracts). In (1) Hansen makes explicit reference to a telex he has received from Guptah regarding non-acceptability of prices of cheese (lines 29-32). In this way, Hansen is demonstrating that the current call is a "response" to that particular telex. In extract (2) Guptah requests telex confirmation of Hansen's proposed price reduction of one hundred dollars (line 3) and twenty dollars (line 14). Here, although Guptah is explicitly occasioning a "next action" from Hansen, the action itself is to be performed at a juncture temporally distinct from the present interaction, and in a different (written) mode of communication. Just as Sacks et al. (1974) discovered in their work on the "latching" characteristics in the design of (some) turns-at-talk, here it is the telephone call *per se* that is afforded "latching" features, thereby displaying "gross organizational features that reflect [its] occurrence in a series" (Sacks et al. op cit.: 722). Hence the observation I want to make and discuss initially is that the participants clearly demonstrate that they are engaged in an activity which is properly performed *as a series of separate (tele)communications*. From the perspective of the telephone call reproduced in part above, we see that it is occasioned by a prior written communication, while the call itself implicates a "next" written communication. The above telephone communication is thus embedded in a particular sequential organization; it is, then, but one in an *interconnected* series of communications involving both written and spoken modes of interaction. I hope to show that the implications of this observation are important not only for an understanding of how "telenegotiating" is undertaken within a particular work-setting, but also for an understanding of how the displayed order is a situated, contingent achievement, accomplished via actions performed in a variety of communicative modes.

What I shall specifically propose is that, despite the spatio-temporal separation and diversification of communications exchanged, the participants' joint actions cumulatively evince a unitary, coherent activity. This unity and coherence is accomplished and recognized in the way that the participants orient to a particular sequential configuration of actions. The sequence is undertaken via exchanges of written telecommunications and shall be referred to as the *"purchasing sequence"* of actions. Participants' orientations to the purchasing sequence can be seen to exert constraints on actions and provide an interpretive structural framework within which complex elaborations can be meaningfully engaged in and made relevant for the purposes at hand. It is within elaborations to the purchasing sequence that *telenegotiating* is seen to take place as an institutionally rational and coherent activity.

In order to demonstrate the locally-achieved structure and the sequentially ordered character of these features, I shall draw upon the findings and methodologies provided by Conversation Analysis (hereafter, "CA").[6]

## CA and Structural Organization

The notion of structure is central to CA, though researchers' awareness of its importance in the organization of social behavior pre-dates the discipline. Kenneth Pike (1954), for example, noted that social activity is understandable when it can be seen to be *structurally* organized. In adopting such an observation as a fundamental assumption in its research practices (see Heritage 1984: 241), the enduring concern of CA has been to identify structural features underlying the orderly construction of talk. With an emphasis on the way *participants* orient to structures in talk, a range of features have been uncovered and described. At the most basic level, talk is seen to be organized sequentially and thus to be structured on a turn-by-turn basis; this provides members with a recursive "proof procedure" (Sacks et al. 1974: 728) for the in-situ analysis of speaking turns. In this way, mutual understanding is collaboratively and locally achieved in the sequential structure of talk. A structural relationship between turns has also been identified in the way that some utterances exert "conditional relevance" (Schegloff 1972) on subsequent utterances.[7] The strictest and perhaps most fertile formulation of this feature is the concept of "adjacency pair" (Schegloff and Sacks 1973: 295-8), and the related notions of "pre-" and "insertion-sequences" (Schegloff 1972). In each case, talk is seen to be organized and made meaningful in terms of participants' orientations to the constraints and resources which sequential structures impose and contain.

With the aim of identifying and formalizing structural patterns in talk, researchers have uncovered how particular conversational *units* are recognized, organized, and made meaningful by members. Thus telephone openings (Schegloff op cit.) and closings (Schegloff and Sacks op cit.) are not haphazardly arranged, but have been seen to follow iterative and structurally-organized patterns. Additionally, the orderly management of interactional phenomena such as the acceptance or rejection of proposals in conversation has also been accounted for in terms of members' orientations to particularized structural patterns. Houtkoop (1987), for example, noted members' orientations to a three-part or a five-part sequence of actions, the shape of the sequence being dependent upon perceptions of the "immediacy" of the proposal. Similarly, the supposition of a particular "underlying" structural pattern enabled Jefferson and Schenkein (1978) to account for the orderly way in which members were able to "parry" acceptance or rejection of "appeals." The "parrying" was accomplished via the use of either "conference-" or "processing passes," thus evincing "expansions" of a putative underlying (three-part) sequence of actions. A central finding in their work was the interpretive force and constraining effect of the underlying "unexpanded" sequence; thus Jefferson and Schenkein (op cit.: 161): "It is this unexpanded sequence that exerts a constraint upon, and provides resources for, the building of an appeal sequence successively 'expanded' by the passes we observed initially."

Recently, a growing amount of work in CA has attended to the structure and organization of talk in ostensibly non-conversational, or "institutionalized" settings, included in which are courtrooms (e.g., Atkinson 1982; Atkinson and Drew 1979), classrooms (McHoul 1978), emergency services (Whalen, Zimmerman, and Whalen 1988; Whalen and Zimmerman 1990), news interviews (Greatbatch 1988; Heritage and Greatbatch 1991), doctor-patient consultations (Frankel 1990), and jury deliberations (Maynard and Manzo 1992).[8] Here focus has been given to the way interactional practices differ from or equate with interaction in "mundane" conversation, as well as to the way setting-related tasks are accomplished in and through talk.[9] The tasks themselves shape the structural configurations of interaction. Whalen and Zimmerman (1990: 468-9), for example, observed how telephone calls to the police could be seen to be structured in terms of five ordered components. Similar to Jefferson and Schenkein's (op cit.) findings, the authors proposed that participants orient to a structural "framework" which informs the production and interpretation of discourse, thereby rendering interaction meaningful. Also Maynard (1984: 78-100), in his work on the discourse of plea bargaining, noted how talk was structured in terms of two "basic" actions: the first where a "position" or "proposal" is forwarded by one party, the second where the recipient displays alignment or nonalignment with the initial position. Maynard (op cit.) then showed how the basic two-part "bargaining sequence" could be subjected to complex elaborations. It was the setting-related task -- what was referred to as the participants' "institutional mandate to process cases" (op cit.: 12) -- which enabled the parties to recognize the rationality behind and the coherence of the "bargaining sequence's" elaborations.

## The Accomplishment of Structural Regularity

In order to corroborate and extend the findings on the structurally-organized accomplishment of work-related tasks, let us return now to the two data extracts reproduced above. My original interest in these data centered on telephone interaction between parties ostensibly engaged in commodity trading. Specifically, I was interested in observing how the participants themselves, as part of their working practices, defined and managed activity recognizable and characterizable as "negotiating." Analysis revealed that although the telephone communications could be examined as self-contained "units" of interaction, complete with sequentially-organized "openings" (e.g., Schegloff 1972, 1979), "argument sequences" (e.g., Coulter 1990), "closings" (e.g., Button 1987; Schegloff and Sacks 1973), etc., the "negotiating" activities undertaken during telephone encounters were oriented to by the participants as *part of* a series of work related tasks. Moreover, it was this serial orientation that enabled the parties to undertake recognizably relevant and meaningful action. Negotiating activity, then, where it was seen to occur, was not an isolated phenomenon, but was *embedded* within a sequentially-constructed context of work routines. This was most immediately apparent in the way that references were made by participants to both preceding and projected communications. Through such references, the parties were not only able to underscore the unitary appearance and ongoing nature of their activity, but were able to display an orientation to preceding and subsequent communications as interactional "signposts" which inform "what is happening" as their joint activity unfolded. For example, note how, in extract (1), the reference to the preceding telex (arrowed), occupies "first topic" slot (following interchanges on the weather).[10] In this position, both parties confirm their recognition of the preceding telex [note Guptah's syntactically felicitous completion of Hansen's utterance (lines 32-4)] and orient to its "first topic positioning" as the "reason for the call"; its mentioning thus curtails further "conversational" interchanges, and demonstrably occasions a "down-to-business" phase in the talk by providing a recognizable "working agenda" for subsequent action. The reference to the preceding telex is thus a resource which allows for the demarcation of a particular body of talk. This is achieved in the way that the reference retrospectively defines the talk preceding its mentioning as falling outside the confines of the current work-related concerns, while simultaneously inviting the recipient of the reference to engage in work-related talk. By so doing, both parties are able to "get to work" and establish their "working agenda" in an orderly manner. In a very streamlined fashion, then, the telephone interaction is demonstrably "called to order" with the initial reference to a preceding written communication.

In extract (2), Guptah's request that the revised offer be put in writing is oriented to by Hansen as indicative of Guptah's acceptance of the (revised) offer. Thus, in uttering "just one other question" (line 22), Hansen displays his orientation to Guptah's request *not only as topic-closing-implicative but also as acceptance-implicative*. In broader terms, what appears to be happening here is that, once an "offer" to reduce prices is made by the seller, the buyer's request that the "offer" be put in writing is hearable as "acceptance" of the offer. And Guptah's (at least provisional) acceptance of the revised offer is clearly recognized by Hansen in the way that Hansen shifts topic, moving the talk on to "one other question." The request that the offer be put in writing thus effectively concludes the outstanding business of the call. This is certainly a common occurrence in the data corpus as a whole, where requests for offers to be put in writing (and the sequentially next-positioned affirmation of the request) either give rise to topic shifts or initiate the call's "closing section" (see Schegloff and Sacks 1973: 100ff.). In the latter case the requests for offers to be put in writing serve to place the calls "on a closing track" (compare Button 1991: 251), while in both cases the "one-in-a-series-of-interrelated-activities" feature of the calls is displayed.[11]

Based then on the participants' explicit references during telephone interaction, it becomes clear that the *activity of commodity trading* is fundamentally structured and organized in terms of exchanges of *written* communications between the implicated parties.

In an attempt to locate structural regularities of the "single activity" of commodity trading, the necessity now arises to consider data of naturally-occurring written materials exchanged between the implicated parties. The written data reveal that, in the majority of cases, the proper initiation of an order can be seen to occur once the buyer requests information pertaining to the current prices of commodities. The subsequent disclosure of commodity prices is interpretable and hence treated as a specific type of information: an "offer." Upon receipt of the producer's "offer," a particular response type is due, the response type being consequential for the trajectory of the subsequent discourse. That is, briefly, when the buyer's response to the offer is "positive," the offer is "accepted," and the requisite goods are dispatched. In this case we can state that the positions of the two parties are (organizationally/institutionally) "aligned." However, when the buyer's response is "negative," the positions of the implicated parties are "misaligned," and subsequent discourse is structured in such a way that the parties attempt to "align" their positions, resulting in "acceptance" of the (often revised) "offer." In this case, "(tele)negotiating activity" emerges, as the parties exchange "offers," "counter-offers," and "accounts" (Firth 1993) until agreement is reached and the offer is accepted.

As data attest, and as we shall witness forthwith, the buyer's (i.e., Guptah's) response to the producer's (i.e., Hansen's) first offer is a rejection. The (adjacent) actions of the two parties are thus "misaligned." Guptah's response is consequential for the trajectory of subsequent interaction. To see this, consider first Guptah's written (telex) communication, sent to Hansen on 14.3.90:

[Telex (3)]

---

TO: MELKO DAIRIES, DENMARK
FROM: SAUDI ROYAL IMPORT CO.
DATED: 14.3.90

ATT. MR. MICHAEL HANSEN

PLS QUOTE YR VERY COMPETITIVE C+F PRICE FOR
ALL CHEESE ITEMS

BEST REGARDS
4936 GUPTAH

---

Hansen's response to the above telex is as follows:

[Telex (4)]

---

OUTGOING TELEX REF: PA077
TO: ROYAL SAUDI IMPORT COMPANY
FROM: MELKO DAIRIES, DENMARK

WITH REFERENCE TO YOUR TLX DTD. 14.03.90 WE ARE PLEASED TO QUOTE YOU AS FOLLOWS:

| CTNS | DANISH CHEESE | USD/MT |
|---|---|---|
| 200 CTNS | FETA 40+, BRIK | 1425 |
| 300 - | FETA 40+, DUMYATI | 1620 |
| 35 - | FYNBO 45+, 12 X 500 GR. | 3255 |
| 25 - | FYNBO 45+, 12 X 1 KG | 3175 |
| 35 - | FYNBO 45+, 12 X 225 GR. | 3455 |
| 40 - | CHEDDAR 50+, 20 X 450 GR., WHITE | 3245 |
| 40 - | CHEDDAR 50+, 20 X 450 GR., YELLOW | 3245 |
| 40 - | CHEDDAR 50+, 40 X 225 GR. WHITE | 3405 |
| 40 - | CHEDDAR 50+, 40 X 225 GR., YELLOW | 3405 |
| 150 - | PR. CREAM CHEESE 70+, 36 X 2 X 50 GR. | 2665 |
| 150 - | PR. CREAM CHEESE 70+, 32 X 200 GR. | 2665 |
| 300 - | FETA 40+, 1 X 16 KG | 1510 |

TERMS OF DELIVERY: C AND F RIYADH BY REEFER CONTAINER
TERMS OF PAYMENT: CASH AGAINST DOCUMENTS

HOPE YOU FIND OUR OFFER COMPETITIVE AND LOOK FORWARD TO HEARING FROM YOU.

KIND REGARDS
MELKO DAIRIES AMBA
MICHAEL HANSEN

TELEX SENT 15:34:28 16/03/90

---

Note that this telex (4), which is characterized as an "offer" by the sender, Hansen (n.b. the sentence immediately preceding the salutation: "Hope you find our offer competitive ..."), opens with a reference to Guptah's preceding telex message ("With reference to your tlx dtd ...") and closes with a further reference to a projected response ("look forward to hearing from you").

Situated between these references is information on commodity quantities, types of cheeses, and prices in U.S. dollar per metric tonne.

On the basis of Hansen's response (4), then, we see that Guptah's telex (3) is understood as both a request for information regarding prices (a "quotation"), and as a solicitation of an "offer." This can be seen in the way Hansen initially responds to Guptah's request for a "quote" (Hansen writes: "we are pleased to quote you as follows:"), provides Guptah with the requested information ("very competitive prices for all cheese items" -- telex (3)), and then, immediately preceding the salutation, recharacterizes his (Hansen's) telex message as an "offer" ("Hope you find our offer competitive ..."). Note further that Guptah's telex message (3) does not make references to preceding communications. For present purposes, then, and for the participants, telex (3) may be seen as an initiatory action, neither solicited by the other party nor conditionally relevant vis-a-vis a preceding action. Hence, if it can indeed be shown that an interactionally-relevant sequence is being jointly produced and oriented to, the sequence (at least in this particular case) may properly be seen to commence upon receipt of telex (3).

Guptah's response to Hansen's above "offer" is as follows:

[Telex (5)]

---

TO: MELKO DAIRIES, DENMARK
FROM: ROYAL SAUDI, JEDDAH

DATED 20.3.90
MSG. NO. 976/90

ATT: MR. MICHAEL HANSEN

WE REFER TO YOUR TLX NO. PA077 DTD 16.3.90 AND VERY SORRY TO INFORM YOU THAT CHEDDAR WHITE/YELLOW PRICES QUOTED BY YOU ARE HIGHER THAN SELLING PRICES OF OTHER LOCAL IMPORTERS. WE THEREFORE REQUEST YOU TO PLS RECHECK ALL YOUR PRICES AND INFORM US BY RTN TLX SO THAT WE CAN CONFIRM OUR ORDER.

BEST REGARDS
4936 GUPTAH

---

As I shall concentrate on the form of this message presently, note first message content: Guptah informs Hansen that competitors' prices are lower, and explicitly requests Hansen to "recheck all ... prices." Interestingly, the way in which Guptah's request for price revision is readable as a request for price *reduction* here [see extract (2)], is predicated on the assumption of shared organizational knowledge of factors seen to impinge upon price acceptability (i.e., competitors' lower price levels). And once again, as with the telex and telephone extracts, there are explicit references to both preceding and impending (or projected) written communications.

A focus on the form of the message provides valuable insight into the participants' orientations to, and the structural organization of, an encompassing "single" activity. In addition, it allows us to witness structural similarities between the organization of disagreement or "rejection" in these written communications and the performance of "rejections" in conversation (cf. Mulkay 1985, 1986). What we are privy to here, I suggest, is Guptah and Hansen working collaboratively toward the production of an aligned, or "preferred," response. To begin with, note that the message can be seen to be composed of three constituent components. The first is an *apology* for the buyer's particular response to the seller's "offer"; to this end, the telex opens with the wording "we are ... very sorry to inform you that ...." The second component provides an *account*[12] (Scott and Lyman 1968) for the unacceptability of the prices offered ("prices quoted by you are higher than selling prices of local importers"). Both components have been noted in spoken interaction where "rejection" of "invitations" are performed as "dispreferred" responses (see, e.g., Heritage 1988: 132). The "account" mitigates the effectual rejection of the offer by referring to relevant causal factors (i.e., "local importers' prices"); as well, it provides mutually accessible resources for the accomplishment of eventual agreement (see Firth 1993). The apology and account components evidence that the relationship between the preceding and the present communication is seen by the participants in terms of a "preference" for "acceptance" of the offer (see, e.g., Pomerantz 1984). This is both confirmed and actively pursued in the third component of the telex, which is occupied with the account-giver (here, the buyer) proposing an action to effect the *transformation* of the presently "dispreferred" response. This he does by requesting that the seller "recheck all ... prices." In other words, the "dispreferred" status of the present response is not to be seen as a *de facto* rejection of the offer, but as a temporary and provisional hindrance to eventual acceptance, and hence a "preferred" response.

Guptah's telex (5) thus represents a multifaceted action in that, when he writes "we ... request you to please recheck all your prices," he is (a) accounting for and responding to the relevance of the previous action (i.e., the "offer"), (b) retrospectively confirming the preceding action as an "offer" (and not, say, a request, ultimatum, or demand), (c) characterizing that offer as provisional and negotiable (by virtue of the fact that he is requesting an unspecified revision of the offer), and (d) projecting both the relevance and the mode of an accountably due next action; that is, he is holding the order placement in abeyance by projecting for a next action (performed via telex) wherein "price revision" is conditionally relevant.

On a related note, observe how, throughout these written messages, the parties work to preserve and confirm their cordial relations. This is visible most prominently in the use of various politeness markers. In (3), for example, Guptah asks Hansen to "please" quote prices, closing his message with "best regards." Similarly, in (4), Hansen is "pleased" to quote, "looks forward" to hearing from Guptah, and closes with "kind regards." Even when Guptah rejects Hansen's offer in (5) he is "very sorry" to do so, and requests Hansen to "please" recheck all prices before closing with his "best regards." These politeness markers, as reflexive components of the preference structuring of the parties' joint actions, give the appearance of personalness, cooperation and cordiality, aspects of the (sometimes antagonistic) trading relationship which are clearly valued by both parties.

Hansen's next actions are not performed in writing, but in talk, as extracts (1) and (2) (above) attest. For reasons of space, I cannot describe the character or progression of this particular talk [though see Firth 1993], suffice to say that the parties, in their telephone interaction, manage to "transform" the offer, and thereby ultimately align their positions. What is important to note here is that though the parties display agreement in the talk, the agreement itself does not accomplish definitive acceptance of the offer. Rather, the agreement achieved via telephone is "provisional" pending Guptah's receipt of written "confirmation" of the details agreed upon in the talk. What is required, then, is that Hansen formulates his revised offer (a price reduction of $100) in writing, whereupon Guptah will "confirm" their oral agreement. Hence Guptah's words in extract (2): "can you send us a telex and we will confirm this?" (lines 18-19). Hansen's subsequent telex -- a revised offer of a $100 reduction in price -- is reproduced below:

[Telex (6)]

OUTGOING TELEX REFERENCE: MH852
TO: SAUDI ROYAL IMPORT CO.
FROM: MELKO DAIRIES, DENMARK

WITH REFERENCE TO OUR TELECON TODAY WE ARE PLEASED TO QUOTE YOU AS FOLLOWS:

| CTNS | DANISH CHEESE | USD/MT |
|---|---|---|
| 200 CTNS | FETA 40+ BRIK | 1405 |
| 300 - | FETA 40+, DUMYATI | 1600 |
| 35 - | FYNBO 45+, 12 X 500 GR. | 3155 |
| 25 - | FYNBO 45+, 12 X 1 KG. | 3075 |
| 35 - | FYNBO 45+, 12 X 225 GR. | 3355 |
| 40 - | CHEDDAR 50+, 20 X 450 GR. WHITE | 3145 |
| 40 - | CHEDDAR 50+, 20 X 450 GR. YELLOW | 3145 |
| 40 - | CHEDDAR 50+, 40 X 225 GR. WHITE | 3305 |
| 40 - | CHEDDAR 50+, 40 X 225 GR. YELLOW | 3305 |
| 150 - | PR. CREAM CHEESE 70+, 36 X 2 X 50 GR. | 2565 |
| 150 - | PR. CREAM CHEESE 70+, 32 X 200GR. | 2565 |
| 300 - | FETA 40+, 1 X 16KG. | 1490 |

TERMS OF DELIVERY: C AND F RIYADH BY REEFER CONTAINER

TERMS OF PAYMENTS: CASH AGAINST DOCUMENTS

HOPE YOU FIND OUR OFFER COMPETITIVE AND LOOK FORWARD TO HEARING FROM YOU

KIND REGARDS
MELKO DAIRIES AMBA
MICHAEL HANSEN

TELEX SENT 11:44:40 20/03/90

---

Like telex (4), the telex (6) (immediately) above is explicitly characterized (by its sender) as an "offer," and provides information on quantity, commodity (cheese) type, and price in U.S. dollars per metric tonne. Contrasted with (4), the prices of commodities in (6) are lower (n.b.: "hundred dollars off all items, except the feta cheese" - extract (2), lines 3-4). And again the message makes references to preceding actions ("our telecon today") and projects for a conditionally relevant response ("Hope you find our offer competitive and look forward to hearing from you").

The following telex is Guptah's response to the above:

[Telex (7)]

---

DATED 21.3.90
MSG. NO. 174/90

ATT: MR. MICHAEL HANSEN

WE REFER TO YOUR TLX NO. MH852 DTD 20.3.90 AND PLEASED TO INFORM YOU THAT ALL CHEESE PRICES QUOTED BY YOU ARE ACCEPTABLE AND REQUEST YOU TO PLS ARRANGE TO SHIP ASAP. THANK YOU VERY MUCH FOR YOUR NICE COOPERATION.

BEST REGARDS
4936 GUPTAH

---

This message "accepts" the "offer" communicated in (6) and, unlike the preceding message, does not explicitly solicit a response. By not doing so, the message can be seen to implicitly propose termination (for the time being)

of further communication between the parties. In organizational terms, the telex represents the successful culmination of a particular series of communications. "Success" can be judged in relation to the task which occupies and informs the preceding communications, that being the achievement of mutual agreement on the details concerning the exchange of resources.

It is clear that these telex communications are sequentially interrelated. Telex (6), for example, in being characterized as an "offer," can be seen to exert conditional relevance on a projected (and therefore accountably due) response. In explicitly "accepting" the "offer," telex (7) both attends to the conditional relevance established by the preceding communication while confirming the status of (6) as an "offer" (rather than, say, an ultimatum). Taken together, (6) and (7) dislay the characteristics of an "offer-acceptance" (or "proposal-aligned response") adjacency pair, identified widely in mundane conversation (see, e.g., Davidson 1984, 1990) and noted by Maynard (1984) to be a central constituent of plea bargaining discourse. Although performed here in the written rather than the spoken mode, the structural, adjacent relationship between the spatio-temporally disjoined telex messages is preserved. Contrasted with adjacency pair sequences in spoken interaction, however, the major distinguishing feature of the written communications is that explicit reference is made to the preceding "pair part." In spoken interaction, of course, because of the immediacy of utterance exchange and the relative ease of inter-turn "checking," such explicit references are redundant. In written communications, then, interactants would appear to rely on implicit conversational mechanisms in order to effect coherent message exchange, while at the same time utilizing explicit text-linking mechanisms to accomplish and ensure orderly patterns of activity.

## The "Purchasing Sequence"

By tracing the parties' interactional steps both backwards and forwards from the telephone interaction, we are now in a position to propose that a "seen but unnoticed" sequence of actions, jointly constructed and oriented to, is apparent in the data.[13] In the particular instance examined in this paper, the initiation of the sequence takes effect through telex (3), and is completed in telex (7). I shall propose that the participants' orientations to the sequence can be seen to configure the content and trajectory of the above communications, telephone communication included. This is not to say, of course, that the sequence "accounts for" or "explains" the orderliness of the observed actions. On each occasion, whether performed in writing or in telephone-talk, the sense and import of actions is locally achieved, demanding in-situ "interactional work" on the part of the implicated members. What we are witness to here is the way that such work is configured by and sensitive to a particular sequential pattern of written documents. The patterned sequence is minimally composed of three relatively ordered and discriminatively related parts: Part 1 is initiated by the buyer, and requests commodity price information; Part 2 is the seller's provision of prices, and Part 3 is the buyer's acceptance of the prices. Part 3's acceptance occasions the expedition of the requisite commodities. Referred to as the "purchasing sequence," the three actions minimally constituting the sequence can be displayed as followed:

| | |
|---|---|
| Part 1 | buyer requests price information; |
| Part 2 | seller provides requested information; |
| Part 3 | buyer accepts prices and confirms the order. |

This sequence bears similarities to Jefferson and Schenkein's (op cit.) "unexpanded sequence" and Whalen and Zimmerman's (op cit.) "structural framework" in that it (i) exerts a constraint upon actions, and (ii) provides an interpretive framework upon which elaboration sequences can be meaningfully built. Combined, the actions of the purchasing sequence establish the mutually acceptable conditions for the placement of an "order." In effect, then, it is through and in this sequence of actions that the trading work is undertaken. Elaborations to the purchasing sequence can be recognized as rational in the sense that they are demonstrably goal-oriented, and coherent in relation to the encompassing activity of commodity trading.

In the present series of actions, Part 1 is represented by telex (3), Part 2 by telexes (4) and (6), and Part 3 by telex (7). The sequence is elaborated between Parts 2 and 3, the elaboration being initiated by telex (5), and concluded in the telephone interaction [(1) and (2)]. (Elsewhere [Firth 1994], I have described how elaborations to the purchasing sequence occur in "positions" both internal and external to the sequence.) The constraints exerted by the purchasing sequence are of both an institutional and an interactional character. The institutional constraints relate to the organizationally-sanctioned "way of doing things," where prices are quoted once the seller is in possession of the buyer's request for a quotation. For the buyer, an order is placed on the basis of the acceptability of the details provided in the quotation, and the commodities are dispatched by the seller on the basis of a written document confirming the acceptability of those details. So the discourse actions performed by the parties are both sensitive to and informed by these organizational contingencies.

Interactional constraints are apparent firstly in the way that the parties jointly orient to Part 1 as both a request for information and as an "offer" solicit, and secondly in the way that Part 3 (i.e., "acceptance" of the "offer" in Part 2) is made ongoingly relevant. This explains how telex (5) and the ensuing telephone interaction [(1) and (2)] can be interpreted as actions which do not nullify the relevance of Part 3, but rather hold that relevance in abeyance until agreement has been reached. "Agreement" thus revolves around the details in Part 2, and it is seen that both parties are willing to transform and thereby negotiate the details of Part 2 in order to attempt to complete the sequence of actions. And of course, completion of the sequence is concomitant with an organizationally-defined goal recognizable to both participants, that goal being the exchange of one scarce resource (commodities) for another (money); in other words, to trade. It is the ongoing relevance of this goal, its practical achievement represented by Part 3, which gives telex (5) and the following telephone interaction their character as provisional "insertions" in the three-part purchasing sequence. Psathas (1990a: 232) has observed that "insertion sequences can do considerable work and nevertheless not modify the sequential structure of an adjacency pair within which they are embedded." This observation is apposite here, as the inserted actions -- recognizable and understandable to the parties as instances of (tele)negotiating activity -- allow the parties to accomplish the "work" involved in commodity trading. Telenegotiating thus contains two characterizing features: first it is a social accomplishment in that its recognizability and meaningfulness is transparent as a result of its "achieved organization" (Zimmerman 1984) within the jointly-constituted purchasing sequence; second it is an "enabling" activity which allows the currently misaligned parties to achieve alignment and ultimate agreement over the details of Part 2 of the purchasing sequence.

Let us now momentarily consider the structural characteristics of the three-part "purchasing sequence" in more detail. What, for example, is the structural nature of this sequence? Certainly the three parts are sequentially related: Part 1 is a "request" which exerts conditional relevance on the succeeding action (Part 2), while the relevance of Part 3 -- as an "acceptance" -- is shaped by Part 2's oriented-to and explicitly labelled function as an "offer." What seems clear is that the sequence is oriented to as a unitary, bounded interchange, where each part is a necessary, rather than an optional, constituent. Thus no one part is accorded structural dominance over the other (for example in the way a question-answer pair is accorded structural dominance over an intervening "insertion sequence"). A notable feature is that, though an elaboration sequence arises between Parts 2 and 3, the adjacency of the written communications -- Parts 2 and 3 -- is nevertheless preserved; this can be seen in the way that Guptah requests that the "revised offer" agreed upon in telephone interaction [see (2)] be formulated in writing [see (6)]. While such requests attend to organizational exigencies in that printed materials, unlike spoken "materials," can (amongst other things) be disseminated within the receiving institution, they are nevertheless consequential for the trajectory of the interaction.

And the purchasing sequence itself, as a bounded unit, is perhaps rather more common, and hence more culturally pervasive, than one might first suspect; it underlies the following three-part exchange between customer and trader:

| | | |
|---|---|---|
| 1. | Customer: | How much are the bananas? |
| 2. | Trader: | One pound fifty a bunch, sir. |
| 3. | Customer: | Okay. Two bunches please. [14] |

In this exchange, the customer's first utterance equates with Part 1 in the purchasing sequence, the trader's response with Part 2, and the customer's acceptance and "order" with Part 3. Such a sequence of actions -- at least in its underlying form -- is likely to be encountered across a range of settings wherein "traders" successfully sell their wares -- whatever description or form those "wares" might take. The ubiquity of the three interconnected actions may thus account for the projectability and comprehensibilty of the purchasing sequence once it is initiated by "Part 1."

The unitary and bounded character of the sequence is doubtless accounted for by the pivotal, interlocking (see Schegloff 1986: 131ff.) role played by the actions in Part 2. Actions occurring in this interactional "slot" can be seen as *both* a second pair part of a "request-grant" adjacency pair, and as a first pair part of an "offer-acceptance/rejection" sequence or, (to borrow Maynard's (1984) terminology) a "proposal-align/misalign" sequence. This produces the following sequentially-ordered structure:

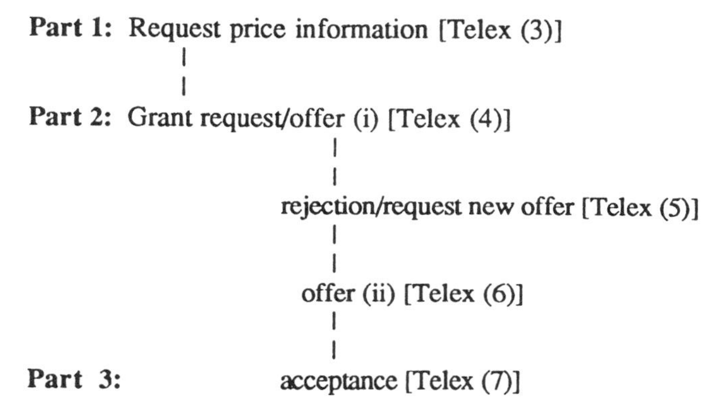


In this case, Guptah's rejection [Telex (5)] of Hansen's first offer occasions Hansen's telephone call. It is in this mode that the parties "transform" the details of the initial offer in such a way that both parties are able and willing to align their positions. Thus what transpires to be the "last offer" [Telex (6)] (and its acceptance, [Telex (7)]) has been mediated by the telephone call.

## Concluding Remarks

By way of closure, let me briefly summarize the main points made in the paper and relate these to more general considerations. To begin with, we have seen how underlying mechanisms of conversation (i.e., structural organization, sequential implicativeness, conditional relevance, and "preference") can be applied in the description and accomplishment of a work-related activity. Moreover, we have seen how such mechanisms are apparent in a context involving multiple modes of (tele) communication.

The result is that, despite the multiplicity of modes employed, the spatio-temporally disjoined communications transcend the separation of modes, space, and time, to evince coherent, orderly discourse activity. In this light, we may be justified in referring to the observed configurations of communication not as a particularized "speech exchange system" (Sacks et al. 1974: 730) per se, but as a particularized "activity system" (Goffman 1961;

Anderson 1989). This latter notion is more encompassing than the former in that it emphasizes incorporation of a broader range of interactional phenomena (e.g., written and spoken materials) made relevant by the participants. Thus the context wherein the commodity trading we are here witness to may be viewed as a particular "activity system" in its own right, where the "system" itself is informed by institutionally-sanctioned "ways of doing things." Importantly, though, the "activity system" focused upon is not an *a priori* "system" or "structure," but ongoingly and incrementally constituted, its form and trajectory "negotiated" in and through exchanges of spatio-temporally separated communications. Yet despite the separations, the exchanges display the parties' orientations to a regularized pattern of actions, basic to which is a three-part sequence composed of written communications. The sequence itself, while emergent in and through action on each and every occasion, is rendered meaningful and coherent firstly by locally-managed discourse actions, and secondly by the parties' ongoing orientations to who they relevantly are and what they are doing together (cf. Wilson 1991: 24-5). This explains, for example, how disclosures of commodity prices are interpretable as "offers," and how requests for a transmutation of an "offer" into a different mode are interpretable as provisional "acceptances."

Referred to as the "purchasing sequence," the actions within the sequence cumulatively represent the "work routines" of the implicated parties (cf. Collins 1981: 995), an embedded component of which is "telenegotiating activity." Such activity, I have argued, is made meaningful and rendered understandable through its orientation to and accomplished placement within the interpretive framework provided by the "purchasing sequence."

Work and negotiations are, of course, pervasive aspects of everyday living. Yet knowledge is lacking of the most fundamental details of how members routinely construct organized events in work settings as well as of how "negotiations" are procedurally made recognizable and accomplished. Whilst work settings and "negotiations" have long attracted the attention of social scientists, few studies have described these phenomena in procedural terms by accounting for the way in which settings and activities are reflexively constituted and managed in orderly, methodic ways through and in discourse activity. To this extent, an imbalance of research perspectives currently prevails. Workplaces and concomitant embedded activities (such as negotiations) tend to be described either on the basis of participants' questionnaire responses or analysts' coding matrices. Thus the "seen but unnoticed" features of workplaces -- i.e., the orderly, recognizable, unremarkable, appearance of social activities -- are taken for granted and often exempt from description (see the discussion in Heritage 1984: chap. 9). With its commitment to the finely detailed description of *participant*-relevant features and structures of talk-in-interaction, and informed by ethnomethodology's emphasis on the "occasioned" and contingent character of social order, Conversation Analysis is perhaps uniquely placed to provide insight into the socially-accomplished nature not only of *talk*, but also, where relevant, *discourse activity* "at work." By attending to the procedural bases of communication between trading parties, and by incorporating situationally and interactionally relevant data into the analyses, the present paper has attempted such an undertaking.

---

* This paper was originally presented at the conference on "Current Work in Ethnomethodology and Conversation Analysis," University of Amsterdam, July, 1991. The data presented in the paper is extracted from a corpus collected in Firth (1991). I am particularly grateful to Douglas Maynard and Jack Whalen for detailed comments on an earlier draft. I alone take responsibility for the paper's remaining shortcomings.

1 For an insightful overview and treatment of the notion of "market" from the perspectives of economic theory and political science, see Hodgson (1988:chap. 8) and Rangarajan (1985), respectively.

2 A great deal has been written recently on the way information and communication technologies impact upon social and economic behaviour in modern societies. For a thorough and lucid account of research and recent developments in this area, see Mulgan (1991).

3 It is important to point out that though the term "telenegotiating" is an analyst construct, one of the parties [those (Danish) personnel undertaking the recording] offered a vernacular characterization of the series of communications examined in this paper as an instance of "negotiating" with a client; in this particular case, as we shall discover, the "negotiating" was restricted to a series of telecommunications.

4 A bibliography of studies on the subject of negotiation would fill volumes. For an indication of the extent and breadth of such studies, see the overviews provided by Bacharach and Lawler (1981:chap. 1), Firth (1991:chap. 2), Gulliver (1979:chap. 2), Putnam and Jones (1982), and Putnam and Poole (1987). For an indication of the volume and diversity of studies of negotiation and bargaining undertaken in social psychology alone, see Druckman (1977), Morley and Stephenson (1977:chap. 3) and Zartman (1989).

5 The data reproduced in this paper were collected over a four-month period in 1989-90. The source of the data is "Melko Dairies," one of the largest dairy conglomerates in Denmark. As a matter of policy, the company audio-records all international telephone calls made to and received from foreign clients. Invariably, international calls within the company are conducted in English. These calls were informally characterized by the personnel concerned as "negotiations." In order to protect the anonymity of the parties concerned, all personal names, company names and place names have been changed.

6 Limitations of space preclude a detailed account of CA's theoretical perspectives and analytical method. Interested readers may profitably consult the expositions available in Atkinson and Drew (1979: chap. 2), Goodwin and

Heritage (1990), Heritage (1984: chap. 8), Levinson (1983: chap. 6), Psathas (1990b), and Zimmerman (1988). Examples of CA's working methods are collected in Atkinson and Heritage (1984), Boden and Zimmerman (1991), Button and Lee (1987), Psathas (1979, 1990), and Schenkein (1978).

7 "Conditional relevance" means that the production of one item (utterance, action, activity) establishes expectations and therefore a "relevance" upon anything that occurs in the "slot" that follows. Thus whatever comes to be said (or done) in the slot will be inspected for its relevance to the preceding item. If a second item fails to occur, it is "noticeably absent"; if some other (first) part occurs it will be heard where appropriate as a preliminary to the doing of the impending second part, the relevance of which is not lifted until it is directly attended to or aborted by the announced failure to provide some preliminary item [see, e.g., Schegloff (1972: 363-5), and Levinson (1983: 306)].

8 See, e.g., the overviews of this type of work in Heritage (1989), and Heritage and Drew (1992).

9 Although, as Heritage (1989: 35) points out, recent CA "research has involved explicit analyses of the ways in which particular institutional contexts are recursively evoked and maintained in and through the talk of interactants," it is arguable that the primary motivation behind a great deal of such "institutional-setting" research is to describe how interactional practices differ from or equate with interaction in "mundane" conversation. In viewing different interactional practices as "modifications" of mundane conversation, such work confirms "the supposition that mundane conversation represents a broad and flexible domain of primary interactional practices" (Heritage op cit.: 34). Accordingly, "institutional practices" evinced in the organization of talk are seen as adaptions of the basic mechanisms, the adaptions serving the purposes of the particular setting or social occasion. This view also confirms CA's central concern with the sequential organization of talk; thus Zimmerman (1988: 425): "whatever the speech exchange system in question, once it is configured the principle that sequential organization furnishes the primary framework for interaction still pertains."

These emphases have had at least two consequences for work undertaken under the CA rubric. First, as Drew (1990) has observed, the turn-taking systems within the "institutionalized" settings investigated have often been highly constrained, for instance where turns at talk are pre-allocated. What is required, Drew (op cit.: 31) contends, is for

> CA's perspective [to be] brought to bear on the very much wider range of settings in which there is no ... formal constraint on turn-taking, and therefore in which the distinctiveness of the discourse, as compared with conversation, is not to be found in stylized sequential patterns.

Second, due to CA's concern with talk-in-situ, context is restricted to what is made demonstrably relevant in (and only in) the actual talk itself -- despite the fact that members routinely orient to (sequential) relevancies external to the immediate sequential/social context. For it is clear that in some contexts the relevancies may be forms of communication other than talk (e.g., sequentially implicative actions conveyed via written documents; see, e.g., Firth 1991). But, as yet, very few studies within CA have incorporated such "non-talk" data. Schegloff (1991: 57), for example, maintains that "We have to find those terms for formulating context which are both demonstrably relevant to the participants and are procedurally consequential for the conduct being treated, *on any given occasion*" (original emphasis). Though to what extent, one may ask, does such a precept cover "non-talk" materials? Not surprisingly, there is some disagreement amongst CA practitioners as to how context should be viewed and invoked vis-a-vis sequentially analyzed data; compare, e.g., Schegloff's (1991) position with the positions taken by Wilson (1991) and Mehan (1991).

[10] Harvey Sacks (1970, Winter Lecture 5) argued that talk on the topic of "the weather" may be seen and treated as a "false first topic" in conversation, the "real" topic commonly arising after "weather-talk." This observation would certainly seem to be pertinent here, particularly if the "real" topic is equated with ostensibly work-related matters.

[11] Similar to the data examined in this paper, Button (1991) considers data wherein parties display an orientation to what he calls their "standing relationship," i.e., that the (telephone) conversations undertaken are demonstrably "one-in-a-series." Button's aims are somewhat different from my own, however, in that he does not attend to the way such orientations are contingent upon and configured by the context-related tasks at hand; nor does he trace or analyze the "series" of conversations oriented to by the participants in the data.

[12] In their influential paper, Scott and Lyman (1968: 46) define an "account" as "a linguistic device employed whenever an action is subjected to valuative inquiry. Such devices are a crucial element in the social order since they prevent conflicts from arising by verbally bridging the gap between action and expectation ... [B]y an account, then, we mean a statement made by a social actor to explain unanticipated or untoward behavior." The authors contend that there are, in general, two types of accounts: excuses and justifications. Either or both are likely to be invoked when a person is accused of having done something that is "bad, wrong, inept, unwelcome, or in some other of the numerous possible ways untoward" [Austin (1979(1961): 176)]

[13] The identification of what I am calling the "purchasing sequence" as a regular, iterative sequence of actions, performed via the exchange of written documents and minimally composed of three sequentially-related actions, is based on analyses of over forty transactions between Melko Dairies and their international customers (see Firth 1991).

[14] The initiation of this sequence presupposes, of course, that the customer knows, or can actually see, that the goods (in this case, bananas) are for sale. In this case the very fact that the goods are physically "displayed" might be construed as "initiation" of the sequence. In other cases, the seller may initiate a sequence of actions by drawing attention to the fact that his goods are for sale in other ways, as in the following (invented) case:

| | | |
|---|---|---|
| 1. | Trader: | We've got some very nice and cheap bananas today, madam. |
| 2. | Customer: | How much are they? |
| 3. | Trader: | One pound fifty a bunch. |
| 4. | Customer: | Okay. Two bunches please. |

While I have some instances of this type of sequence in my own data corpus, what is clear in each instance in the corpus is that the equivalent of "Part 1" (above) is oriented to as a "preliminary," or "pre" (see, e.g., Heritage 1984: 278-9), to the buyer's subsequent request for a quotation (i.e., telex (3) in this paper). That is, the trader's Part 1 in the invented exchange above is "transparently prefatory to something [and] plainly ... understood as such" (Heritage op cit.: 278). In this case, Part 1 is not understood as a mere qualitative description of the items on display, but as announcing that the goods are "for sale" or "on offer." Further talk is then projected and necessary (e.g., inquiry into price, placing of an order, rejection of presupposed interest in purchasing) in order to effect the transaction.

In my own data corpus, there are some isolated instances where the seller (Hansen) informs (via telex) the buyer of impending price rises, whereupon the buyer's request for a quotation is dispatched. In these instances, however, participants indicate their understanding of Hansen's inform as a "pre," or "preliminary," to a structurally dominant "next" action: the buyer's request for a quotation. One factor influencing the interactants' orientations to the request for a quotation as a dominant action (in that it initiates the "purchasing sequence") is the volatility of the purchasing currency, namely the U.S. dollar. That is, the prices offered in the quotation are based on the (Danish Kroner-U.S. dollar) exchange rate for that particular day. The content of Part 3 -- and any intervening "telenegotiating" -- is thus sensitive to the information imparted in Part 2.

# 10

# Assembling a Response: Setting and Collaboratively Constructed Work Talk*

Marjorie Harness Goodwin

This paper examines the ways in which participants in work settings make use of multiple resources in formulating responses during routine work encounters. It draws on materials from a three-year research project conducted by members of the Workplace Project (a team of anthropologists brought together by Lucy Suchman at Xerox Palo Alto Research Center) at a mid-sized American airport. Two different settings -- an airlines Operations room where ground operations are coordinated and an airline's gate where passengers check in and depart for planes -- are selected for analysis because they provide two contrasting types of social spaces for the conduct of work.

Comparing types of social space Goffman (1959: 134) has stated that while "front regions" can be described as areas "where a particular performance is or may be in progress," "back regions" are "where action occurs that is related to the performance but inconsistent with the appearance fostered by the performance." According to Goffman (1959: 128):

> In general, then backstage conduct is one which allows minor acts which might easily be taken as symbolic of intimacy and disrespect for others present and for the region, while front region conduct is one which disallows such potentially offensive behavior.

While the airlines Operations room provides a "backstage" (Goffman 1959: 106-140) airport work space, the area where gate agents deal with departing passengers is by contrast quite public. The differences between these public and more backstage spaces influence the ways in which co-workers manage their talk and their bodies.

Quite crucial to each setting is what Goffman (1963: 16) has called the "mutuality of immediate social interaction"; individuals who are copresent to one another constantly monitor one another's action, such that "an adaptive line of action attempted by one will be either insightfully facilitated by the other or insightfully countered, or both" (ibid.). In describing *situated activity systems* Goffman (1961: 96) proposed that a basic unit of study should be a "somewhat closed, self-compensating, self-terminating circuit of interdependent actions." Goffman's notion of encounters captured nicely the nature of interaction within situations involving a *single* focus of attention. However, in more complex work settings participants are linked not only with immediately copresent workers, but also with co-workers with whom they can communicate at a distance (C. Goodwin 1990). Though physically absent, they may well be "culturally present through various other agents and technologies" (Duranti, Goodwin, Goodwin 1991: 2); thus Operations personnel participate in more than one focus of attention (or participation framework[1]) simultaneously. Workers make use of a heterogeneous array of paper and electronic documents as well as the collaboration of co-workers in the mundane activity of "assembling a response" amidst ongoing work.

While Goffman's notion of encounters allows a framework for investigating mutual social activity, the methodology within conversation analysis provides rigorous procedures for analyzing the structure of talk as emergent situated practice within activity. As Sacks (1984: 24-25) has argued

> It is possible that detailed study of small phenomena may give an enormous understanding of the way humans do things and the kinds of objects they use to construct and order their affairs. We would want to name those objects and see how they work, as we know how verbs and adjectives and sentences work. Thereby we can come to see how an activity is assembled, as we see a sentence assembled with a verb, a predicate and so on. Ideally of course we would have a formally describable method as the assembling of a sentence is formally describable.

Talk in a work setting such as the San Tomás airport is assembled or stitched together from moment to moment while simultaneously being embedded within situated activity systems which have their own routinized structure and sequence. Talk shapes an expanding horizon of possibilities, making relevant the articulation and deployment of tools in the setting as well as the invocation of collaboration from co-workers.

## Collaboration in Assembling a Response in the Operations Room

The Operations room of an airline provides a center for coordination (Suchman 1992, in press) of work-relevant activity pertaining to ground operations. Information about the operation of the airline enters these centers via a variety of modalities -- radio and phone calls as well as electronically transmitted messages on computer monitors, hard copy print-outs, etc. In conducting routine service encounters -- for example providing a response to an incoming radio call -- participants both make use of the material and electronic documents in their work space and rely on their co-workers' assistance. Responses to incoming service requests are thus the achievement of collaboration between an Ops worker and the material artifacts at her disposal in the setting, copresent coworkers who continuously monitor others' talk for its work-relevance, as well as co-workers who are linked electronically.

The following provides a diagram of the Operations room, showing the major positions in the room as well as the arrangement of artifacts. These include a schedule or "complex" board (at the right side of the room) and at the front of the room a bank of monitors connected to video cameras at each gate. These monitors provide a picture allowing those in the Operations room to see the activities in the area where each plane is parked.

**Atlantic Operations Room, New Terminal**

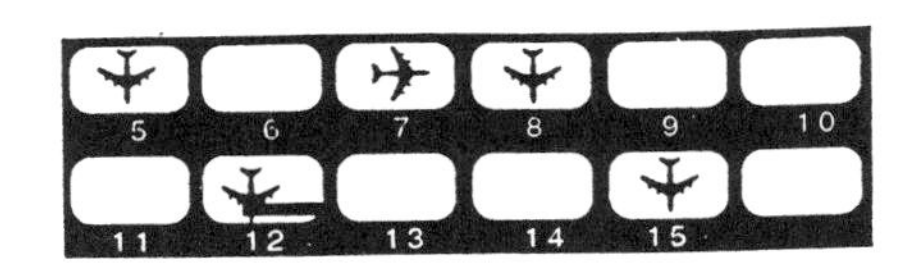


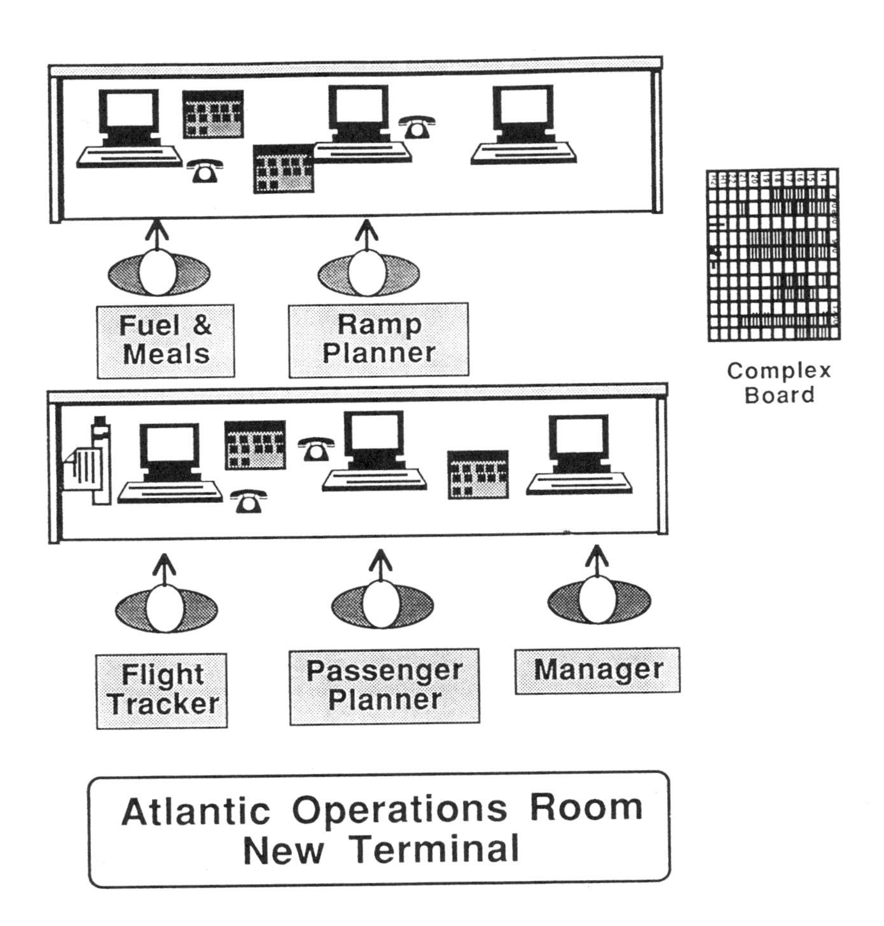

In this space, removed from public view, workers need not always be "on stage." In the Operations room people eat, read the newspaper, flirt, gossip, and engage in a number of different activities unrelated to work. On some occasions even the airline regulation dress code may be relaxed.

Participants in service encounters over the radio are located within different participation frameworks -- one entailing the caller/called and the other the framework of co-workers in their work center. In that the radio medium permits only one person to transmit at a time, each party can control what the other participant to the call can hear, so that conversations among copresent co-workers are unavailable to parties on the other end of the line. In essence participants can construct a "back stage" merely by not releasing the radio call button. Other activities in the room are inaccessible to those on the other end of the service encounter.

One routine service encounter in the Operations room involves announcements from pilots that their plane has arrived; in calling Operations pilots make inquiries about the status of the gate they are headed for, asking whether or not it is ready for the incoming aircraft. The announcement thus serves as a request for confirmation by the party receiving the call, the Flight Tracker (FT).

(1)
89.11.03
1:26:06

Pilot: Uh nine forty one's on the ground.
Confirm Charlie nineteen.

FT: Confirm.
Charlie nineteen.
Awaiting your arrival.

Pilot: Roger.

Given the predictability with which such sequences are routinely played out in this setting, it is not surprising that the mere announcement of a plane's arrival by a pilot should be *immediately* followed by observations about the readiness of a particular gate for the arriving plane (or indications of problems) by a Flight Tracker:

(2)
89.11.03
01:13:52

| | | |
|---|---|---|
| | Pilot: | Ramp Atlantic?<br>Three seventy two is<br>on the ground?<br>for gate fourteen. |
| Æ | FT: | Three seventy two.<br>Charlie fourteen's aircraft<br>Should be ready to push<br>in just a few minutes. |
| | Pilot: | Roger. |

The following service encounter differs from the two previous in that when the pilot calls in announcing his arrival, the Flight Tracker (FT) does not immediately confirm the readiness of the gate (Alpha seven) for the arriving plane. Conversation hearable over the radio is marked with a radio icon in the following transcript and RP is Ramp Planner. A bracket ( [ ) or double slashes (//) indicate onset of simultaneous action.

(3) 1.01.18 HP 17:01:581:12:08

| | | |
|---|---|---|
| 1 | Pilot: | Operations.<br>Atlantic ten ninety one's **on** the ground to gate seven.<br>[ |
| 2 | RP: | *((turns gaze towards monitor bank))*<br>(2.5) |
| 3 | FT | *((looking at monitors))*<br>Roger ten ninety one.<br>Charlie- Alpha: **se**ven:? uh:::, (0.2) °Shoo::. (0.9)<br><br>*((creaky voice quality))* Hold on one second,<br>Ten ninety one. |
| 4 | FT: | Alpha **se**ven, *((quizzical look as he gazes first towards monitor bank, and then to the complex board))* |
| 5 | RP: | That plane should be pushin. |

| | | |
|---|---|---|
| 6 | FT: | That aircraft should be // off the gate shortly. Stand by until seven clears. Ten ninety one. |
| 7 | RP | *((starts to put on glasses and engage in another activity, then gazes towards documents on his desk))* |
| 8 | Pilot: | Roger. Could you tell them we're gonna need ground power please. |
| 9 | FT: | That's affirm. |
| 10 | | Did you catch that Ed? |
| 11 | RP: | Yeah. |
| 12 | FT: | Okay. |

Within the Ops room the standard situation for Operations workers is that they participate in multiple participation frameworks (C. Goodwin 1990) in multi-activity settings simultaneously, rather than one single focus of attention. Therefore, co-workers' primary orientation is not exclusively talk among co-present participants situated in a classic "F formation" (Kendon 1977) where a single focus of visual and cognitive attention is maintained. Seated back-to-back or front-to-back they frequently rely on auditory rather than visual cues from co-workers for updatings regarding the status of ongoing activity. In delivering announcements to co-workers situated back-to-back, for example, Ops workers can make use of formulaic intonation patterns which distinguish their talk from the hub of other activity in the room (M.H. Goodwin in press), in effect singing their announcements of arriving planes to coworkers. In the present instance others in the room, on hearing the pilot call in, can recognize that a habitual sequence is in progress and begin to operate upon it.

While workers do not generally have visual access to each other they do have visual access to information of another sort -- a bank of monitors which display the current state of affairs on various gates and a "complex" or schedule board. Here another Ops worker in the room (the Ramp Planner) makes use of the monitor bank in helping Fred to assemble his response. Seeing the activity in progress and the problems with it, he can begin to interrogate resources in the room. When the gaze direction of the Ramp Planner is plotted (line 2), it can be seen that just after the opening term of address -- "Operations"-- (and even before the word "gate" is uttered) he is orienting towards the monitor display. As argued above, pilot call-ins routinely request information about the status of a gate they are headed for. Ramp Planners have considerable experience outside on the ramp and indeed their major job inside Operations is monitoring activities in that locale; they thus constitute particularly appropriate parties for interpreting events in that site.

Presenting a view of the current state of affairs from a particular perspective is a crucial feature of Ops work (as it is in the work of other institutional settings, such as the police (Whalen and Zimmerman 1990: 474-479) as well. Others in the room are alerted via auditory cues as to the epistemic stance (Chafe 1986) their coworkers are taking up towards ongoing talk; that is, they can monitor the voice quality of coworkers for indications of uncertainty or hesitation. In the present case the call-taker indicates in several ways he is encountering trouble in responding: 1) during the phone conversation through his repetition of the trouble source, first with *rising* intonation, an intonation contour associated with marking uncertainty in repair sequences (Schegloff, Jefferson and Sacks 1977), and 2) when off the phone through his repeat of the trouble source as an "outloud" with *falling* (Gunter 1974) intonation. In the present case the intonation contour is treated as indicating that speaker is having problems resolving the issue at hand, and solicits the coparticipation of the Ramp Planner. The look on the Flight Tracker's face (line 4) towards the complex board (an updated schedule board), while not visible to RP, displays a facial gesture recognizable to those so positioned to see it as "puzzlement."

Work on the construction of repairs in conversation has argued that there is a preference for self-correction over other-correction (Schegloff, Jefferson and Sacks 1977). Analysis of the interactive construction of word searches (Goodwin and Goodwin 1986) shows that the precise nature of coparticipation in such events is something negotiated by participants. Experienced Operations workers are expected to be able to complete their work without hitches, to have ready access to electronic and paper documents which can assist them in responding to incoming calls. When experienced Ops workers explicitly ask for help in routine service encounters their actions are open to chiding by co-workers.

In the present instance, though Ramp Planner is positioned to potentially help Flight Tracker in his quandary, he holds off offering his reading of the scene until after FT has turned off his radio channel and indicates through the production of his utterance "Alpha **se**ven." (line 3) that he indeed is in need of help. In response to the Flight Tracker's "Alpha **se**ven." the Ramp Planner offers an observation regarding the current status of the gate, a statement which will be helpful in figuring out what to tell the pilot. By stating "That plane should be pushin" (line 5) RP indicates that the gate should be ready to receive a plane in the near future. FT's next action is to open the radio channel and communicate with the pilot. This time (line 6) his utterance displays none of the uncertainty of his prior talk; hesitation, sound stretch, and creaky voice are eliminated and talk is delivered without hitches -- smoothly and authoritatively[2] in what is recognizable as an "airline register."

If we inspect the gaze direction of RP during this talk, we see that in the course of Fred's delivering his message to the pilot, after the word "be" in "That aircraft should be off the gate," RP (line 7) begins to disengage from his orientation towards the monitor display, puts on his glasses, and initiates activity unrelated to the prior activity, gazing towards his work surface. His actions thus provide a member's reading/ratification of the activity in progress as one no longer requiring his attention.

As the call continues with pilot's request that Ops contact relevant parties who can provide ground power (ramp workers) we see that the message was intendedly relevant in more than one participation framework; specifically, it implicates Ramp Planner. At the close of the exchange with the pilot, the Flight Tracker (line 10) explicitly asks if Ramp Planner has "caught" the message to be relayed -- that ground power is needed at a particular gate. Monitoring the incoming call, in fact, had occurred from the very onset of the pilot's call, even prior to the pilot's announcement.

Tools such as gate monitors allow workers to inspect a location situated at some distance. Response to a caller's question is achieved in part through linguistic resources which display called party's alignment towards the unfolding event: in the present case, for example, uncertainty about what is happening at the gate. The intonational cues in the Flight Tracker's talk secure the Ramp Planner's participation, which allows the call to be brought to a close. The assemblage of a response is therefore the product of both an interrogation of the material resources in the setting as well as the deployment of linguistic resources for invoking the backstage assistance of a co-worker. The particular shape of that invocation, and the context in which it emerges, have a bearing on how the request gets treated by co-workers.

## The Co-Construction of Collaboration at the Gate

The first example we looked at was from an Operations room, an area hidden from public view. Here while conducting service encounters with other divisions of the airline, a type of backstage is easily constructed through putting the radio caller on hold. Talk among co-workers which assists in assembling a response to the party on the other end of the line is not audible or visible to the caller. Activities such as eating or drinking also take place without problem, and participants are free to manage their bodies as they wish.

In another area of the airport, the gate, where passengers check in and depart for their flight, the principal type of service encounter is a public event. Here there are few private areas and the spatial constraints of the work setting affect how participants talk and manage their bodies. For example, workers in this public space must distort their bodies in order to be hidden from view to attend body cares; for example, gate agents duck beneath the ticket counter to take a drink of soda.

Emerging from such a position to conduct business with a passenger (as the following frame several seconds later shows) requires special attention to the reassembling of one's physical alignment to assume the appropriate "in play" facial expression and posture for greeting passengers.

At the gate as in the Operations room of the airport, monitoring of work-relevant activity is ongoing. Here talk among coworkers is, however, accessible to the public, especially to those standing at the ticket counter. If a worker requires prompting, then gate workers must find ways of designing talk which is in some fashion hidden from the public despite its being audible. One solution is for gate agents to make use of an elliptical code in order to coordinate activity at the gate.

The particular example of such code use to be analyzed involves a routine type of activity: an oversold flight. At the beginning of each new "complex" (a bank of planes that come in during an hour's time slot) the lead gate agent has the job of determining which flights are oversold (flights for which there are more passengers than seats available). In the commuter airline of Atlantic Airlines this is particularly important, in that no more than nineteen passengers can travel on any given flight. Once the lead agent has been informed of the "payload" (the number of persons who will be permitted to fly-- computed in terms of flight destination, weather, fuel, and amount of bags and mail on board by a co-worker whose job it is to coordinate communication between the various commuter divisions), she begins to trace incoming passengers' planes to see if they will in fact meet their scheduled arrival times (and therefore be available to board the flight in question).

The lead agent thus makes use of the work of colleagues at many distant locales who are connected through the nation-wide computer system as well as a local colleague who computes the payload and then radios to the gate the precise the number of people who can fly given baggage, weather and flight destination. After checking to see how many passengers can actually be expected to arrive for the problematic flight, she then figures out alternative later flights for incoming passengers (the ideal solution unless they themselves are oversold) and determines how much travel voucher money the airline should offer to a volunteer for forfeiting his seat to take a later flight. If time between complexes permits, the lead agent will verbally inform each of the other three gate agents and scotch-tape a slip of paper with instructions near each agent's workstation. For example, one note read:

SAIF
put on 5118
@ 7pm-7:49
offer $200 vocr

Oversold flights thus have their own predictable courses of activity. Repetitive features of oversold flights involve 1) indicating the alternative means of transportation available, usually a later flight (though occasionally ground transportation) and 2) offering a cash amount to someone for volunteering to give up his seat. The larger activity of "oversold flights" provides a grid against which a sequence of conversational activity is made relevant. Knowing the routine, co-workers can refer to features of it in a short-hand manner, especially useful for preventing passengers from knowing what's going on while providing co-workers information in as concise a manner as possible.

In the following example we will see gate agents collaborating in the production of a response to the initiation of a service encounter by a passenger who is scheduled to fly on an oversold flight. In this particular instance the lead gate agent, Linda, is stationed adjacent to Sally, the agent involved in the service encounter; on this occasion Linda has not had the opportunity to inform her colleague (Sally) of anything other than that the Monterey flight she is in charge of is overbooked. As Sally begins to help a passenger who approaches the counter, Linda carefully monitors her coworker's interaction, cueing her into the details of the oversold flight. The service encounter begins as Linda emerges from beneath the counter where she has been taking a drink of soda.

(5)
90.9.7Y2:6:02:02

| | | |
|---|---|---|
| 1 | Sally: | °Hit the bottle. *((as Linda is drinking a soda underneath the counter))* |
| 2 | Linda: | Well, (.) This has gotta be on the list of (.) jobs that drive you to it. *((said from underneath the counter))* |

| | | |
|---|---|---|
| 3 | Passenger: | *((presents ticket to Sally))* |
| 4 | Sally: | Monterey this evening? |
| 5 | Passenger: | Yep. |
| 6 | Linda: | Two hundred. Cab. |
| 7 | Sally: | *((nodding to passenger))* **Okay.** [3] |
| 8 | | *((turning to Linda))* Not an eight o'clock? |
| 9 | Linda: | Over. |
| 10 | Sally: | O:**kay**,<br>Mr. B at um (if) you're going to Monterey<br>we're offering a two hundred dollar travel<br>voucher and a cab ride, as an alternative,<br>cuz the flight is oversold. |

As Sally attempts to solicit a volunteer for an oversold flight she gets assistance from her co-worker, Linda, who (line 6) cues her as to 1) what amount of money ("two hundred") is being offered in a travel voucher for being a volunteer and 2) what the alternative mode of transportation to one's destination will be ("cab.") This triggers a query by Sally; turning to her right towards Linda she questions whether the passenger could possibly fly on the eight o'clock flight as she asks (line 8) "Not an eight o'clock?" The following frame grab captures Sally's position in the midst of turning towards Linda:

In response Linda (line 9) replies "Over," a short hand way of indicating that the eight o'clock flight generally used as "protection" for earlier flights that are oversold is itself overbooked and therefore does not constitute a viable alternative for the passenger. After getting help from Linda, Sally is able to continue with her solicitation of volunteer status from the passenger (line 10).

For gate agents work is conducted in a public arena, face-to-face with passengers and there exists little backstage room for coordinating a response. Gate agents can, however, make use of an elliptical language to build a back stage to update one another, here about information regarding oversold flights. The public setting thus influences not only how one's body may be displayed, but also the ways in which co-workers assist each other. Though the talk of gate agents can be heard by passengers, it is disguised through the use of an elliptical code.

## Conclusion

While it is common to analyze texts and speech acts outside of the local situations in which they occur, in this paper I have examined several ways in which speech is embedded in specific activity systems, each with its own "circuit of interdependent actions" (Goffman 1961: 96). As talk is unfolding, participants make use of their local settings, interrogating the tools and resources in their environment to build appropriate, improvised responses. Given the predictable structure of work activity, co-workers can anticipate next moves and assist during the course of ongoing activity in the assemblage of responses to opening moves in service encounters, whether a radio call or the presentation of a ticket on the counter. Speech acts are thus not the product of isolated individuals; they are rather assembled achievements emerging from the collaborative work-web of copresent workers who constantly monitor ongoing interaction for their possible involvement in it, nonpresent participants whose work is made relevant through electronically transmitted messages and documents, as well as the tools in their work spaces (such as video monitors positioned at gates) which provide access to information of various sorts.

The setting in which talk occurs constrains both how the body is presented and how collaboration among co-workers is managed. In the nonpublic Operations room participants need not concern themselves with issues of dress or routine body cares; by way of contrast, in the gate area where workers meet the public, different demands are placed on one's presentation of self. Participants cannot turn on and off a back stage with the push of a button; though they collaborate in the co-production of service encounters, they disguise their interaction by using an elliptical code and hide private activities by distorting their bodies under the counter.

This analysis has obvious relevance for theories about human cognition. The notion that understanding the world is a situated practice that relies on collaboration among one's fellows as well as artifacts in one's environment has been a recent theme in the study of everyday cognition (cf. Hutchins 1989; Lave 1988; Lave and Wenger 1991; Rogoff and Lave 1984; Scribner 1984; Siefert and Hutchins 1989.) This perspective, building on work in the Soviet socio-historical school of psychology (Vygotsky 1978, 1981; Leont'ev 1981) argues that cognition involved in the accomplishment of everyday activity is not located within the mind of a single individual, but instead distributed across actors and their artifactual environment (Wertsch 1981: 11). The integrated study of how talk, the body, artifacts, and action with one's fellows are coordinated thus offers new perspectives on how moment-to-moment social order is shaped and reshaped in the workplace.

---

* Versions of this paper have been presented at the Conference on Current Work in Ethnomethodology and Conversation Analysis, University of Amsterdam , July 19, 1991, the Conference on The Body and Language in Interaction, Stockholm, August 22, 1991, and the Invited Session on Communicative Acts as Socially Distributed Phenomena, American Anthropological Association Annual Meetings, Chicago, November 24, 1991.

1 Goffman (1981: 137) defines the notion of participation framework. As he states "The relation of any one such member to this utterance can be called his "participation status" relative to it, and that of all the persons in the gathering the "participation framework" for that moment of speech. See also Erickson (1990) and Erickson and Shultz (1977).

2 Note that the modal "should be" is used. Such expressions are characteristic of more formal radio talk to pilots and constitute a routine way of presenting information where lack of access to complete information is generally the case (C. Goodwin and M.H. Goodwin in press).

3 On the multiple uses of "okay" see Beach (1991). In this sequence the first "okay" signals "state of readiness" for actions to follow and acceptance of prior talk. The "O:**ka**y" in line 10 is produced with falling rising intonation and has an additional affective loading; it assesses prior talk as something which presents a problem for matters to follow, while also cueing recipient of receipt of prior talk.

# 11

# A Technology of Order Production: Computer-Aided Dispatch in Public Safety Communications*

Jack Whalen

This chapter reports on an investigation into the ordered, *in situ* production of "calls for service" in public safety communications centers. These centers are responsible for dispatching police, fire, and paramedic assistance in response to citizen reports, complaints, and requests that are phoned in on both 9-1-1 emergency and seven digit nonemergency lines. I will be concerned with the question of how such reports, complaints, and requests are locally constituted as "calls," as nameable and countable organizational events that warrant some form of official response. The analysis centers on how certain computer tools and artifacts utilized by communications center staff enter into this production in a fundamental way, serving as a "technology of order production" (Suchman, in press a), and on the embodied courses of practical action and practical reasoning involved in the competent use of that technology.

My resources for developing this analysis include extensive field observations undertaken while working as a call-taker and dispatcher at a police and fire communications facility - Central Lane Communications Center in Eugene, Oregon - for fifteen months, as well as video recordings of call-takers at work that were collected at Central Lane. The discussion is also informed by field work at other public safety dispatch facilities.[1]

The analysis is for the most part built around the examination of a single case. Because the production of any "call" is an essentially situated activity, an examination of how this is actually accomplished for and in some singular set of circumstances, over the course of a specific occasion, should prove to be a profitable way to explicate some of its orderly features. At the same time, however, because this line of investigation is in its early stages, the comparative examination of numerous cases that would be necessary for elucidating and describing, with a high degree of confidence, the full range of this orderliness or the collection of practices by which it is produced is just beginning. Consequently, the analysis that follows is necessarily preliminary and suggestive, in both its form and content.

## Some Initial Observations

Although they are initiated by a citizen phoning the communications center, a good deal more is involved in the regular execution and production of "calls" than that conversational exchange; consequently, "calls" are best described as ongoing and developing sequences of action, actions that get formed up into organizational events. It is still the case, however, that the conversational encounter between citizen callers and public safety call-takers is a (perhaps *the*) crucial locus for much of this action, and I will begin the analysis there. The encounter with which we will be primarily concerned is the following (here, as elsewhere, CT designates the communications center call-taker, and C designates the citizen caller):

[1] CLV/1-18-91/2:09

| | | |
|---|---|---|
| 1 | CT: | >Nine one↓one whatiz yur |
| 2 | | emergency?< |
| 3 | C: | Weah::, I've confernted two guys in |
| 4 | | a:: uh, blue Toyota (0.5) car (0.6) |
| 5 | | fastback= |
| 6 | CT: | =what('r) they doing? |
| 7 | C: | Well they had uh (.) concealed |
| 8 | | weapon (.) they had a pistol and |
| 9 | | wuz shootin' |
| 10 | | (1.0) |
| 11 | CT: | [[How long ago?] |
| 12 | C: | [[and what I: con- ] (0.5) wha:at?= |
| 13 | CT: | =ho:w-= |
| 14 | C: | =just 'bout ten minutes ago |
| 15 | CT: | And where- (.) [di- you see ] |
| 16 | C: | [Willow Crick Road] |
| 17 | CT: | Whe:re? |
| 18 | C: | On Willow Crick Roa[d |
| 19 | CT: | [Did you see the |
| 20 | | ↑gun? |
| 21 | | (0.3) |
| 22 | C: | Yes I ^did hhh [(they-) ] |
| 23 | CT: | [wher- ] |
| 24 | | w-wha'were they shooting at? |
| 25 | C: | Ah::: well I'dunno, I've got |
| 26 | | livestock in the area= |
| 27 | CT: | =w'r'they closer to Eleventh or |

28 Eighte[enth?]
29 C: [ah:: ]they were closer to
30 Eighteenth about a- (0.3) block
31 south of- (.) two blocks south of
32 (k-) Eigh[teenth]
33 CT: [the:y ]were shooting
34 at li:vestock?
35 (0.5)
36 C: We::ll I'dunno what they were
37 shootin' at, the[y had sum stuff out in- ]
38 CT: [what's the liCENSE NUMBER OF ]
39 this ca:r?
((conversation continues for approximately six minutes))

Note first that this beginning segment of a Central Lane 9-1-1 telephone call exhibits an erratic topical course. The subject of the talk shifts from what the two men who were confronted by the caller were doing to how long ago this incident occurred, and then to where it occurred, whether the caller actually saw a gun, and what the men were shooting at; this is followed by more talk about where this all occurred, by another exchange about what they may have been shooting at, and then by talk dealing with the license number of the men's car.

Note also that the conversation assumes the shape of an interrogation of the caller by the call-taker, and that the often abrupt changes in its topical course are brought about by the shifting focus of the call-taker's questions. That is to say, over the series of questions that follow the caller's initial remarks (lines 3-5) about the confrontation and the blue Toyota, remarks that seem to foretell a story that never does (at least not at this point in the conversation) achieve a telling, the kind of information requested by the call-taker changes from one question to the next. Even those questions that are predicated on or seek to confirm an understanding of information elicited by a prior query are not produced as an immediate "follow up" to that query and its answer but rather occur later in the talk.

These initial observations suggest that some sort of organizational "agenda" - an agenda that in one sense is anterior and "external" to the conversational encounter even as it surely must be accomplished in and through it - is operating here (see Heritage and Sorjonen 1992), is deflecting the topical course of the talk recurrently through its shaping of both the choice of questions and the interrogation's ordering or trajectory.[2] With respect to the nature of this "agenda," prior research on telephone encounters between citizens and police or fire departments (Sharrock and Turner, 1978; Zimmerman, 1984, 1992a, 1992b; Shearing, 1984; Meehan, 1986, 1989; Gilsinan, 1989; Whalen and Zimmerman, 1987; Manning, 1988; Whalen, Zimmerman, and Whalen, 1988; Whalen and Zimmerman, 1990; Mellinger, forthcoming) has identified a distinct set of issues faced by those whose work is dedicated to managing such encounters, to organizationally processing and servicing people's troubles, crises, emergencies and the like. Perhaps the first and foremost of these "practitioners' problems" is to determine the exact nature of the caller's trouble or complaint, and to then assess whether this is something that should be the business of the police or fire department, something that warrants the generation of a "call." Then, if the trouble is determined to be organizationally relevant, there is the closely related problem of assessing its severity or seriousness, of deciding if it is a *bona fide* emergency or a trouble that can be handle is a less urgent fashion. Taken together, these are typically defined by practitioners as "call screening" and "call prioritizing" problems.[3]

In addition to screening and prioritizing the phoned-in troubles, communications center staff also face the problem of obtaining information about the location of the trouble. This location has to be formulated in such a way that it can be quickly and precisely recognized by the responding police and fire units, and formulating location in this manner may involve some special, technical (that is, peculiar to that organizational environment) considerations. Finally, there is the problem of determining just how to respond to the trouble or emergency, of specifying exactly what action the communications center and the police or fire department ought to take. This problem will necessarily require call-takers to obtain certain kinds of detailed, additional information about the trouble, its location, the involved parties, and so on.

Plainly, the management and resolution of these problems, and thus the forming up of reported troubles and complaints as "calls," depends on obtaining specific kinds of information from callers.[4] To guide call-takers in acquiring information during their telephone interactions with callers and to provide a means of recording and sharing that information with other communications center personnel, Central Lane and most modern public safety dispatch facilities make use of a computer-aided dispatch system and electronic data-entry forms. Computer-aided dispatch, or "CAD," is built around serially ordered steps.[5] A call-taker receives the phone call and, while engaged in interaction with the caller, enters information into a form on their computer screen, assembling a textual record - what is, in effect, a documentary representation - of the reported trouble or event. This form is then electronically transmitted to another communications center staff member serving in the role of dispatcher. The dispatcher reads the transmitted form and assesses the information, determines when and what organizational response is warranted, and then, via radio, dispatches fire and/or police units to the scene and coordinates their response.[6]

Together with the computer tools and writing practices involved in their use, the CAD forms play a pivotal role in the execution of public safety 9-1-1 operations. Indeed, it is through the use of CAD that the work of constituting citizen complaints or reports as organizational events, as "calls for service," is accomplished. That is to say, a phoned request for help, a complaint or report of trouble - *none of these exist as "calls" until they are entered into CAD and processed in this manner.*[7] We cannot speak with any assurance, then, of the ordered organizational processing of the "I've confronted two guys" report through the agenda-oriented character of the questioning, or account for our observations on the erratic topical course of the talk, without first investigating how the call-taker's use of CAD - the assembling of the text on the CAD form - may have entered into the nature and ordering of that questioning and the turn-by-turn unfolding of the encounter. Before undertaking an investigation of the *in situ* employment of this technology, however, it will be necessary to examine the distinct "organizational features" of the CAD form, including its structural properties and its rules or procedures for recording information. We will then be in a position to document how those features both constrain and enable its situated use.

## Data-Entry Procedures in Computer-Aided Dispatch

At Central Lane Communications, the information recording/data entry form used for processing "calls" is called a CAD face sheet. It is referred to as a face sheet because it is the primary and first information recording form used; there is another, ancillary "additional details" form (consisting only of a heading identifying the associated face sheet record followed by eight blank lines) for adding information to this initial record. The actual organization of data-entry forms of course varies from facility to facility; the Central Lane face sheet form is shown in Figure 1:

```
INC: ____________________ ___   TY: _   FD/CTY: ___/___   ID: ____
LOC: _________________________   EUG  PR: _   TY/NM: ___________
PHO: ____________   X: ___   PH ADR: __________________ ___   FL: __
SRC: ____   XST: __ _________________ ____   MAP: _____   DIST:____
BREATH:_ CONSC:_ AGE:__ SEX:_  AGYS: ___ ___ ___ ___   INI: ___
CALLER: ______________________________   CONT: ___   REF: _
ADR: _____________________________   EUG   DISP: ____   CSN: _________
DTL: _____________________________________________________________
     _____________________________________________________________
```

**Figure 1**

The form is arranged into different fields or information slots, each with an abbreviated heading. Five of the fields - INC (incident-type), LOC (location), PR (priority ranking of the incident), PHO (phone number at the location), and SRC (the 9-1-1 trunk line number) - are "required," which means there must be an entry there, and in each case an entry of a certain kind that conforms to certain rules (for example, a code selected from an enumerated list) or the face sheet cannot be transmitted by the CAD system from the call-taker to the dispatcher.[8] Other fields, such as DTL (for recording details concerning the incident, the location, the persons involved, and so on), are "optional" and thus do not have to be filled in before CAD will accept the form and transmit it to the dispatcher. Most of the optional fields do not set restrictions with respect to the type or form of text that can be entered, although call-takers are expected to follow certain organizational conventions with respect to syntax and the use of abbreviations in the DTL field.[9] The remaining fields are filled in by the CAD system itself, usually on the basis of information recorded in the INC and LOC fields (for example, both X and MAP, which stand for "cross street" and "map page" respectively, are determined by the location entry).

The CAD data entry form, along with the other types of electronic and paper forms that bureaucratic organizations use to document (and in many cases, execute) virtually every facet of their operations, is designed to function as an indifferent or "neutral" instrument; that is to say, as intendedly neutral with respect to who is filling it in and the circumstances of any particular call, with its organizational features thus indifferent and external to the actual work of filling it in on any occasion. It is therefore quite intentionally set up to standardize and routinize the recording of information and the processing of emergencies and other troubles, to provide a system for translating singular worldly events into standard and expected calls for service, and to thus serve as a resource for solving the numerous practitioners' problems identified above. From this view, the call-taker's task is merely a matter of filling in the standard slots for incident type, location, priority, details, and perhaps a few other things that are based on the public safety organization's distinct informational needs.

But the call-taking face sheet is clearly more than "just a form" for recording information; because it serves as a kind of methodological scheme for doing the work of call-taking - specifying just what information is to be obtained from the caller, what decisions are to be made, what must be done and what is optional, how information is to be processed, ordered and sorted - it cannot function purely as a neutral device, a standardized instrument whose organizational and structural details are for the most part materially external to the conditions and demands confronting call-takers and the problems they must resolve under those conditions during any particular call. Of course, this is not to say that CAD should be regarded as a technology that determines or dictates, in a global and direct way, the specific actions of call-takers. On the contrary; this kind of technological determinism would rule out any analytic consideration of the practical, fundamentally situated actions and reasoning involved in its use that should in fact be our principal concern. Instead, this technology in general and this form in particular (with its specific organization) should be characterized as a kind of ubiquitous and obligatory work instrument that call-takers must therefore manage and come to terms with over the course of each and every phone call. Bear in mind, too, that call-takers must do this while they are simultaneously engaged in interaction with citizen callers. The importance of this fact should not be underestimated, for it is this concurrent talking and typing that in large part presents the form to the call-taker *as* something to manage and come to terms with, to fit not just to the particulars of any call but to the highly contingent, turn-by-turn progression of conversational interaction.

This still leaves us with the question of precisely how the CAD form presents itself as an obligatory work instrument with specific, ineluctable properties over the course of some actual call processing encounter, and how it then comes to have a bearing on the action in that encounter. I want to propose in this regard that there are at least three aspects or properties of CAD that can have procedural consequences (Schegloff, 1991) for both the performance of the call-taker's work tasks and the progression of the interaction.

First, there is the matter of the form's *specification of information* through its arrangement into various fields or slots, each with its own purpose. As suggested above, the form's designation of informational fields - incident type, location, priority, and so forth - acts to select, out a large number of possibilities, certain dimensions of the world and certain types of knowledge as important for the successful performance of call-taking work. It therefore attempts to translate the underlying nature and needs of the work into a formal structure of standard tasks: give the caller's problem or incident a name, find out where the incident is occurring, determine how serious this problem is (whether or not it is a *bona fide* emergency), and so on. Put another way, even before the form is filled in, its formatting into various slots projects an indefinite *a priori* sense of what the work *could* involve. In this sense, the form functions as a electronic textual idealization of the organizational agenda sketched out above while simultaneously providing a convenient framework for the specific practical actions by which that agenda can be more or less realized (see Lynch, 1988). But if it is not merely a matter of the call-taker "filling in the standard slots," then we need to investigate just what might be involved in making sense of these specific tasks, of the "agenda," in local contexts - that is to say, in understanding and managing them as things to be "solved" not in the abstract, but rather during the activity of speaking to a caller, and thus during the actual performance of the work. Accordingly: Do call-takers orient to the specification of information, to this selection of certain types of knowledge as especially important? Does this seem to have some determinate consequences for their actions and the trajectory of the encounter?

A second and closely related aspect of CAD is the *geography of the face sheet* - the configuration of its various fields. That is to say, as the fields are arranged in a particular way, with some placed at the top and others below, some to the left and others to the right, call-takers are presented with the problem of how to move about or navigate the terrain while they are engaged in conversation with callers. Can we identify any procedural consequentiality for this geography? For example, do call-takers orient to the form's arrangement of fields from top to bottom and left to right, together with certain organizational policies, as ordering the processing of calls as a series of sequential steps?

Third, there is the CAD system's *rules* and the public safety organization's *conventions* about entering information into different fields. I have noted how information must be entered into the required fields in a certain fashion; an example of this would be the INC field, where, as we shall see below, a distinct code must be entered. As another example, the CAD software requires information entered in the LOC field to conform to certain formats, as we shall also see below. In both these cases, the call-taker is faced with the problem of converting the caller's description or formulation into a formulation and format acceptable to CAD. This problem may be implicated in the call-taker's questioning of the caller, as they try to facilitate the conversion.[10] We should therefore want to investigate how call-takers exhibit, in their conduct, an orientation to this problem. What consequences might this have for the way their interactions with callers unfold, and for the specific actions call-takers take in these exchanges?

These three sets of questions can only be addressed through detailed study of such encounters, tracing the "action in interaction" - both the moment-by-moment, turn-by-turn unfolding of the vocal exchange between the call-taker and citizen caller and the concurrent actions by the call-taker at the keyboard in CAD.[11] The remainder of this chapter will be devoted to addressing these questions through a close examination of the encounter presented above, concentrating now on the interrelationship between the talk and the call-taker's data-entry actions - on call-taking work as embodied action, as practical body conduct (cf. Sudnow, 1978).

## CAD in Use: Embodied Action in the Processing of 9-1-1 Calls

Consider once again the transcript of the opening sequence in the "confronted two guys" phone call, this time with the call-taker's keyboard actions and/or the results on her computer screen included directly below the line of talk in which they occur:[12]

1 CT: >Nine one↓one whatiz yur
**(("change screen" key, to switch to new screen))**
2 emergency?<

3 C: Weah::, I've confernted two guys in
**((display switches to other screen))**
4 a:: uh, blue Toyota (0.5) car

When this call came in on a 9-1-1 line, the call-taker was engaged in processing another call, one that had been phoned in on a nonemergency, seven digit line and involved the theft of property from a car sometime during the previous night. Consequently, the call-taker had a CAD face sheet up on her screen and had been entering information related to that theft report. Because 9-1-1 lines have priority and call-takers at Central Lane are expected to answer them immediately, even if it means putting a caller who does not have an emergency on hold, the call-taker does just that: she tells the theft report-caller to hold and quickly answers the 9-1-1 line. Notice that as she says "nine one one," the call-taker uses a special key, the "change screen" key, to switch to a new screen on her display, leaving the partially completed CAD face sheet for the theft report still active on the prior screen and thus available to be completed at a later time.[13] In making this switching action, then, the call-taker exhibits a gearing up for a new call, even before she finishes her opening turn at talk. She has not yet used the command that will bring up a blank face sheet on this new screen (the new screen display shows instead a list of active "calls" the center is currently handling), but can now choose to do so while still preserving the record she was working on prior to the shift. The call-taker's actions here evidence what we could term an anticipatory stance, one that recognizes the essential relevance of CAD as a means by and through which the work of call-taking gets done and anticipates its necessary employment.

I should now like to make several observations on the formatting of the call-taker's first turn at talk - "Nine one one, what is your emergency?" - and the organizational features of the CAD face sheet. Recall that the very first or top field on the CAD form is INC, for incident-type, and that this field is required - it must be filled in, or the system will not accept the form for transmission to the dispatcher. The incident type must be entered in code; some 100 codes are regularly used at Central Lane, and approximately 350 are available. These codes, which range from two to eight letters in length, are intended to exhaustively cover all the kind of things that can happen out there in the world, or at least provide a way of clarifying all those things. Some codes are more specific, such as GSW for gunshot wound, or DSPUTFAM for family dispute, or FIRHOU for house fire; others are more general, like SUSPCOND for suspicious conditions or EMNON for emergency medical non-specific. While putting an incident-type field first on a call recording/processing instrument may seem "natural" or self-evident, the design of the call-taker's first turn (what they say when they answer the line and how they say it) is definitely not a simple or obvious matter. Plainly, Central Lane's policy on how 9-1-1 lines are to be answered - call-takers are *instructed* to use "Nine one one, what is your emergency?" as their first turn - provides an opening turn format that is closely fitted to the format of the Central Lane CAD face sheet.

Determining whether or not a call exhibits an emergency problem is a basic task for call-takers; the nature of organizational response turns on it (see also Shearing, 1984:124-128). This particular turn format - specifically, the following of a categorical self-identification by a question - is designed to determine both (1) if the caller has an emergency and (2) what kind of emergency it is, and to do this as early as possible in the call. That is to say, a definite first action is selected for the caller to perform, namely, an answer to the call-taker's question that should be hearable as a report or description of some type of emergency (Zimmerman, 1992a). This *may* permit, *if* such an answer is forthcoming (there is certainly no guarantee that this will happen), the filling in of the first field on the CAD form (the selection of an incident code) and, possibly, the assigning of a priority ranking, at the very start of the call. This will, in turn, provide the basis for establishing what kind of response is needed. Finally, by immediately (in the very first turn at talk) requesting an account of the caller's emergency, the call-taker is indicating to the caller what sorts of business - emergencies and only emergencies - are appropriate to a 9-1-1 line, which may allow for early screening of nonemergency requests and complaints.[14]

These several observations point toward the possibility of a close interrelationship between the formatting/design and sequential placement of the call-taker's turns at talk, the problems and tasks that make up the call-taker's work, and the character and formatting of the CAD face sheet as an instrument employed in the performance of those tasks. Still, whatever tasks or procedures a call-taker might be oriented to, the trajectory of the encounter cannot be treated as the straightforward realization of some standardized agenda, technology, or policy; instead, because contributions to interaction are subject to the independent actions of others, the actual course of a call (or any other social encounter) will be a fundamentally interactional achievement (see especially Whalen, Zimmerman, and Whalen, 1988; Clayman and Whalen, 1989). Let us therefore turn our attention to the caller's response to the call-taker's opening action, and to the series of actions occasioned by that response.

1 CT: >Nine one↓one whatiz yur
**(("change screen" key, to switch to other screen))**
2 emergency?<

3 C: Weah::, I've confernted two guys in
**((view switches to other screen))**
4 a:: uh, blue Toyota (0.5) car (0.6)
**A A #**
5 fastback=

6 CT: =what('r) they doing?

7 C: Well they had uh (.) concealed

8 weapon (.) they had a pistol and
**((CAD face sheet appears))**
9 wuz shootin'

The caller's answer (lines 3-5) to the call-taker's "what is your emergency?" question has a great deal of material packed into it. He begins with a drawn-out, slightly drawled "weah::". This preface-type action serves to delay, however minimally, the production of an answer, and in doing so projects that the answer-to-come is something other than what might be normally expected - than what might be, in structural terms, "preferred" (see Pomerantz, 1984), which is an immediate and relatively concise answer to "what is your emergency?"[15] That is to say, what the use of "weah::" projects is that a simple or straightforward answer may not, in the speaker's view, be possible, and that a more extended explication, even a story, might be needed. Accordingly, following his "weah::," the caller then goes on produce what sounds very much like the start of an account or story about him confronting "two guys in a blue Toyota" (with some additional descriptive information then provided about the car). Indeed, by using "I've...," which focuses attention on his personal involvement in and knowledge of some incident, and "...confronted," which hints at an antagonistic involvement and some degree of conflict (after all, he has been asked to provide evidence of an emergency), the caller can be heard as indicating "I do in fact have a problem here, and I'll get to it eventually." What we find in the caller's first turn, then, is an incipient story.

Note that while the caller was speaking the call-taker had already changed to a new screen, gearing up for the processing of a new call, but had not yet typed the CAD software system command to bring up a blank face sheet on that display. Just after the caller says "confernted two guys," however, the call-taker types that command - **AA** (line 4). As suggested just above, the caller's use of the verb form "confronted" is designed to do certain interactional work, and it is evident from the call-taker's action at the keyboard (particularly the timing of that action) that she regards it as indicating the *possibility* of an incident that warrants an organizational response.[16] This conduct - changing to a new screen while answering the phone line and thus immediately putting oneself in a position to process a new call, but waiting until the caller has provided some evidence of a "legitimate" problem or incident before accessing the CAD data entry form necessary for that processing - can be said to embody some initial elements of "call screening" as a course of practical reasoning.

The fact that the caller, after his "confronted two guys" remark, goes on to produce a description of the vehicle these men are driving is also a matter of some analytic interest, as are the call-taker's actions with respect to that description. By mentioning a vehicle, at that place in his account and in that way (with that kind of descriptive detail), the caller exhibits his understanding of that information as particularly relevant for the 9-1-1 call-taker (and thus for the police). Indeed, the attention he gives the vehicle conveys a sense of "you're going to want to find these guys, and to do that you'll need to know the kind of car they're in."[17] However, in doing this, the caller is not offering the call-taker any more details concerning the nature of the incident, particularly what the two men were up to that precipitated his confronting them; again, it is the men's vehicle that is being singled out as somehow specially important. This presents a task problem for the call-taker: although there is some evidence, however minimal, of an actionable incident, there is still considerable uncertainty about its true nature, and thus about its classification, a classification that will figure in the ultimate determination of the incident's organizational relevance.

The evidence for the orientation of the call-taker to this issue can be found in her conduct. Notice that as the caller is producing his description of the car, he pauses twice. The first pause comes right after his reference to the "blue Toyota" and is followed by his specifying what type of Toyota (possibilities here being things like car, pickup, minivan, Corolla, etc.). The second pause follows that, after which the caller adds a further specification to the description. These pauses were opportunities for speaking that the call-taker did not take up; instead, she waits to "hear more," giving the caller the opportunity to present more information - information that will perhaps allow her to resolve this "nature of incident/reasons for the confrontation" issue.[18]

Moreover, and most important, when the caller goes on to provide even more vehicle description, the call-taker responds by asking for exactly that sort of incident information, jumping in very quickly (note the latching of her turn to his): "what('r) they doing?"[19]

## Classifying worldly troubles and events

In response to the call-taker's query, the caller provides a report that vividly exhibits, in its recipient design features, a recognition of what the call-taker's prior turn was oriented to. The men "had uh (.) concealed weapon," he says - not simply *a* weapon, which would probably not be a criminal offense (at least not in the United States), but a *concealed* one, which would be - "a pistol"; moreover, the men "wuz shooting."[20] Observe that the CAD face sheet is now available to the call-taker - it appears just as caller says "weapon" - and, as Figure 2 indicates, her cursor (here, as elsewhere, indicated by the ♦ symbol) is located at the beginning of the INC field; when a blank face sheet is brought up on the screen, the cursor is automatically placed in that position.

```
INC: ♦_______________ _____     TY: _   FD/CTY: ___/___   ID: ______
LOC:  ________________________  EUG  PR: _   TY/NM: ________________
PHO: ____________    X: ____    PH ADR:_______________ ____  FL: ___
SRC: _____    XST: __ ________________ _____   MAP: ______  DIST: ___
```

**Figure 2**

Given that the call-taker was pursuing the question of what the two men were doing, seeking information that would allow, among other things, for some classification of the problem and thus secure a basis for assessing whether the situation truly warranted an organizational response, does the kind of information she has now elicited about a "concealed weapon" and "shooting" provide for that? If so, might this still pose additional problems for performing tasks like incident classifying and coding? To address these issues, let us examine the call-taker's subsequent actions, and consider the trajectory the interaction then takes. (In this transcript fragment and elsewhere, when keys other than the letter and number keys were used, the following symbols are employed: space bar #; tab > ; back-tab < ; return ¶ ; cursor (arrow) keys ⇐ ⇑ ⇒ ⇓ ; back-space ⇐ . In some cases, it is necessary to describe what is visible or what is happening on the call-taker's computer screen, and these descriptions are presented in double parentheses.)

7 C: Well they had uh (.) concealed

8 weapon (.) they had a pistol and
**((CAD face sheet appears))**
9 wuz shootin'

10 (1.0)

11 CT: [[How long ago?]

12 C: [[and what I: con- ] (0.5) wha:at?=
**S H O**
13 CT: =ho:w-=
<
14 C: =just bout ten minutes ago
**A R M E D S H O**
15 CT: And where- (.) [di- you see ]
⇐ ⇐ ⇐ ⇐ ⇐
16 C: [Willow Crick Road]
**D U S B J #** ⇐
17 CT: Whe:re?
⇐ ⇐ ⇐ ⇐
18 C: On Willow Crick Road
**S U B J #** >

Notice the period of silence after the caller's "was shooting." During that interval, the call-taker does not engage in any action at the keyboard. After one second elapses, the call-taker and caller both begin talking. The call-taker asks (line 11) about the amount of time that has elapsed since the reported behavior occurred, while the caller (line 12) simultaneously starts to produce what sounds very much like a continuation of his story, perhaps an explanation of, or further details about, his reasons for confronting these men. It is only when the caller cuts off his account-in-progress and, after a brief pause, makes an effort to repair the overlap by asking the call-taker "what?", that the call-taker begins typing an entry in the INC field of the CAD form: **SHO**. Those initial keystrokes are soon corrected, however. The call-taker "back-tabs" to the beginning of the INC field (that is, returns the cursor to its starting point) as she starts to answer the caller - "how-" - and then, as the caller produces the requested time lapse information (line 14), types over her **SHO** and replaces it with **ARMEDSHO**.

The fact that the call-taker delayed (or waited) before beginning the incident code entry, began typing the entry just after asking the caller a question about time lapse, and then quickly modified/changed her entry suggests the following. First, while the caller's report may have provided the call-taker with details about the incident that will justify a call-for-service, his description of what the men were doing had two dimensions to it, and the incident could therefore be classified in two, somewhat different ways: (1) the men were armed, with a "concealed weapon"; (2) they were shooting a weapon. Thus, while there was now a great likelihood of some sort of police-relevant problem existing, the issue of how to code the incident remained, for the call-taker, unresolved. To reiterate: the choice of coding has considerable consequences for the treatment of a call by other communication center staff, especially (in this case) the police dispatcher. The nature of the organizational response - when (with what urgency) to respond, and what number and kinds of units to dispatch - depends in large part on the code selected. To be actionable, a worldly trouble or event has to be *representable* in organizational terms or categories; the categories become a means of summoning the organization into action. Thus, it is in and through the selection of an incident code that central aspects of call screening and prioritizing are embodied as courses of action. Of course, there will typically be opportunities to elaborate on or clarify the classification through the adding of "details" to the CAD record (and the INC entry can also be easily changed at some later point, as we shall observe below).[21] At the same time, to process a call a single incident code must be selected, and the practitioner's problem here is to choose the one that best fits the described circumstances at hand. When that description involves more than one dimension and suggests more than one possible classification, we should therefore not be surprised to find evidence of possible delay, uncertainty, or equivocality in making a selection.

Second, the call-taker's entry of **SHO** and subsequent correction to **ARMEDSHO** is additional evidence for "equivocality" and for her orientation to this incident as having different (even if closely related) dimensions. What the call-taker has done here is *combine* parts of two different Central Lane incident codes, codes that nicely represent the two dimensions exhibited by the caller's description of the trouble. **SHO** is the first part of the code **SHOTFIRD**, for "shots fired"; recall that the caller reported that "they was shooting." **ARMED** is a slightly erroneous (one spelling error) rendering of the first part of the code for "armed subjects," **ARMDSUBJ**; recall that the men were also described as having a concealed weapon. Thus, the equivocality is visibly embodied in her erroneous "mixed" entry; again, she started to type the code for "shots fired," went back to the beginning of the field and typed **ARMED** over those characters, and then appended **SHO** to that.

And what of the call-taker's "How long ago?" inquiry that precedes all of those CAD actions? Although the caller's remarks have not provided thoroughly unequivocal indications as to whether the incident (or at least the confrontation aspect of it) is still ongoing or no longer in-progress, recall that he did use the past tense (*had* a weapon, *had* a pistol, *was* shooting) in his prior turn, in response to a query from the call-taker that employed the present tense (what *are* they doing?). In this way, the caller's phrasing in his answer has occasioned what could be heard as a follow up question from the call-taker, one oriented to the issue of time lapse. At the same time, however, we can observe that there is in fact a slot for entering information about "time lapse since incident occurred" on the CAD form that is positioned just to the right of the INC field (in this sense, it is the next field on the CAD form, if moving from left to right); it does not have an abbreviated heading and is considered part of the INC field, although call-taker's do not have to fill it in (it is not "required" for CAD transmission). The placement of this slot, which is called the "incident-modifier field," is indicated in Figure 3:

```
INC: ________________ ____  TY: _  FD/CTY: ___/___  ID: _____
                       ↑
```

*slot for entering time lapse*

**Figure 3**

The positioning of the time lapse/incident-modifier slot on the CAD form reflects the fact that in 9-1-1 operations, and police work more generally, practitioners take it that the time-lapse between when certain kinds of incidents occurred and when the call was actually made is an essential piece of information, necessary for determining the appropriate police response, ensuring officer safety, and evaluating the possibility of apprehending any suspects. For example, an answer of "Oh, about an hour ago" to a time lapse question would, for most types of incidents, almost certainly lead to a very different treatment of the complaint by the call-taker and other public safety personnel than would "A few minutes ago." Thus, with respect to this case, ascertaining "how long ago" the shooting activity occurred would assist the call-taker's determination of the urgency of the situation, and would then have consequences for how she (and the police dispatcher) might proceed to process the call. The one second gap between the caller's "had a pistol...was shooting" turn and her "How long ago?" question might therefore have been occasioned by momentary uncertainty on the call-taker's part over whether the incident was in any way urgent, given the caller's use of the past tense, with her question thus directed at clearing this up.

More important, the sequential placement and timing of "How long ago?" - with the call-taker asking this question *before* she has even begun to type the entry for the INC field - points to some of the technical competencies involved with processing citizen calls for help in and through CAD technology. As a practical matter, if a call-taker is at some point ready to fill in, say, field X (in this case, it is the INC field), because prior questioning on their part has just elicited the necessary information, using their current turn at talk (the floor having returned to them upon completion of the other party's answer) to ask a question that is topically focused on the "next" field on the form will give them the opportunity (and time) to fill in field X while simultaneously eliciting data for completing that "next" field. This will keep the conversation going without having to pause (to not speak) until their typing is "caught up" or to employ minimal turn holders like "okay...okay" while completing the data entry.

This is not to say this kind of alternative "practical methodology" is rarely employed at Central Lane. Consider, for example, the following transcript fragment, which is taken from a different 9-1-1 call. In this transcript, because no video record exists of the information recording activity on the CAD form, we will have to rely upon the traces of this activity - keyboard sounds - that are available from the audio recording. Because the clicking sound produced as the keys are struck is often fairly loud and can usually be heard on the audio tape, it is presumably quite audible to the caller and may thus have implications for the organization of the interaction. On the transcript, the periods of time during which these keyboard sounds can be heard are marked by xxxxxxxxx below the line of talk or silence in which they occur.[22]

**[2] CL07B2**

```
1    CT:  Nine one one what is your emergency?

2     C:  Uh, yeah there's a girl getting beat up (.)

3         in my apartment complex

4         (0.4)

5    CT:  Okay (0.2) what's the address?
                xxxxxxxxxxxx
6     C:  Eighteen ten Harris

7         (1.5)
          xxxxxxxxxxxxxxxxxxxx
8    CT:  Do you know what apartment number::?
          xxxx
9     C:  Yes (.) one eleven   (0.4)  they're out- right
                                xxxxxxxx
10        out front
               xxxxx
11   CT:  Oka:y
          xxxxxxx
12    C:  He's hit her a couple of times that I'v no-
          xxxx
13        I've watched   (0.4)    just now
            xxxxxxxxxxxxxxxxxxxxxxxx
14   CT:  Does he have any weapons::?

15    C:  No: I don't think so (.) I don't know=

16   CT:  =>°okay°<
            xxxx
17        (1.6)
          xxxxxxxxxxxxxxxxxxx
```

18 CT: What's the name of the apartment?

19 C: Woodside Manor (0.2) on the corner of
xxxxxxxxxxxxxxxxxxx
20 eighteenth and Harris
xx
21 (0.9)
xxxxxxxxxxxx
22 it's getting
xxx
23 more radical now

24 CT: °Okay° <can I have your name?

25 C: Vicki (0.4) Lobagh (.) l. o. u. b. o. u. g. h.

26 (2.5)
xxxxxxxxxxxxxxxxxxxxxxxxxxxxxxxx
27 CT: And your apartment number?
xxx
28 (0.4)

29 C: Uh:, one thirty nine

30 (1.5)
xxxxxxxxxxxxxxxxxxxxxxxxxxxxxx
31 I'm right
xxxx
32 across from'um

In this conversation, the call-taker's typing in lines 7-8, 16-17, and 26 is treated by the caller as a proper or adequate response or next action to her just-completed utterance, one that indicates that what she just said is being recorded in some fashion, and that some responsive action is thus in progress; consequently, the absence of speech from the call-taker - or, in line 15, minimal acknowledgment in the form of a quickly and very softly spoken "okay" followed by an extended period of silence - was not regarded by the caller as a "no response" or "interactional breakdown" situation that called for repair. In instances such as these, then, the caller waited, while the call-taker was engaged in the typing, for the next question to be directed to her.

In other instances, in both this call and others I have examined, callers use the opportunity made available by the call-taker's typing activity to add to or elaborate on the information they just provided (see, for example, lines 30-31 above). This extends their turn at talk in a manner that exhibits a recognition that the call-taker's audible in-progress typing is dedicated, at that moment, to recording precisely that type of information. This can also create task performance problems for call-takers, however. If they are fully absorbed in their information entry activity, they may find it difficult to follow and comprehend the caller's additional remarks. One related practical methodology for dealing with this problem can be observed in the following exchange (from a second call, by a different caller to a different call-taker, to Central Lane on the same incident reported just above):

**[3] CL07B2/CALL #2**

((The call-taker has put the caller on hold to answer another 9-1-1 line; at last report, the male who was assaulting the female left the involved apartment and was walking toward his vehicle; the transcript begins as the call-taker returns to this 9-1-1 line.))

92 CT: You still there?

93 (1.5)

94 CT: Hello?

95 (3.9) ((voices can be heard in background))<br>xxxxx xxxxxxxxxxx xxxxxxxx

96 CT: He:llo:?

97 C2: Hello=he's got a gun and he's comin' back

98 CT: He's got a gu::n?

99 C2: And he's coming back

100 (1.2)<br>xxxxxxxxxxxxxxxxxxxxxxxxxxxxxxxxxxxxxxxxxxx

101 CT: Okay=stay on the phone with me<br>xxxxxxxxxxxxxxx

102 C2: 'kay<br>xxxxxxxxxx

103 (6.4)<br>xxxxxxxxxxxxxxxxxxxxxxxxxxx xxxxxx xxxx<br>xxxxxxxxxxxxxxxxxxxxxxxxx xxxx

104 CT: What kind of gun is it?

Having been informed about the gun, the call-taker immediately starts typing this information into CAD, as an "additional details" form entry (the text reads **MALE NOW HAS A GUN - IS HEADED BACK TO INV APT ***EXPEDITE****). After completing the first portion of that entry, he acknowledges receipt of the information and tells the caller to "stay on the phone with me," then resumes typing until completing the entry and transmitting it to the dispatcher, whereupon he picks up the interrogation again with a follow-up question about the gun. The vocal action inserted into what was a very extended period of "no talk, just typing" works both to indicate that the just received report is being recorded and to temporarily suspend the conversation so as to provide an opportunity for an *uninterrupted* recording of that vital information.

While these various pragmatic choices by call-takers are responsive to the same, rather generic practitioner's problem, each choice has certain implications for call processing and call-taking work (cf. Jefferson, 1972:328-330), given that the trajectory of any conversational encounter is a fundamentally collaborative, interactional achievement. For instance, a call-taker's following of a caller's answer to their question with typing alone, rather than talk (in the form of another question) or typing-with-talk, could have the consequence, contrary to what we observed in the first call reporting the assault, of a caller taking advantage of this "no vocal response by co-participant" situation - this failure of a potential next speaker to self-select as a speaker - by starting to talk about matters completely unrelated to the topic or problem the prior question or series of questions was designed to address. The call-taker would then have to engage in certain interactional work to regain the relative control of topical focus that their ongoing interrogation is designed to sustain. In addition, because this interrogative control of topical focus may be geared in large part to information entry on the CAD form, and thus to the organizational features of that form as described above, the caller's shift of focus may have interesting implications for that information entry. For example, the caller's talk that accomplishes the abrupt shift of that focus may nevertheless include information important to the processing of the call and the dispatch of assistance. If this is so, then this sort of information should of course be recorded in CAD; however, there may be some difficulty in recording it immediately if the cursor is positioned in a field that cannot be used for that kind of information (the call-taker would have to quickly stop typing in their current field, move the cursor to the other field, and then begin information entry there). We will have cause to return to these and other, closely related problems below.

## Managing Typing/Text Corrections in a Conversational Environment

Returning now to the analysis of the "I've confronted two guys" transcript, the preceding observations concerning the call-taker's conduct over the period of time represented by lines 7 to 14 in that transcript direct our attention to the multiple and overlapping relevancies that can figure in the performance of this work, as well as some of the "organized artful practices" (Garfinkel, 1967:11) involved in coming to terms with those relevancies. We can continue this line of analysis by examining the series of actions that followed the caller's "ten minutes ago" answer.

```
14     C:   =just bout ten minutes ago
                         A  R  M  E     D   S  H  O
15    CT:   And where- (.)  [di- you see          ]
            ⇐ ⇐ ⇐ ⇐ ⇐
16     C:                     [Willow Crick Road]
                                 D  U  S  B  J  #  ⇐
17    CT:   Whe:re?
            ⇐ ⇐ ⇐ ⇐
18     C:   On Willow Crick Roa[d
            S  U   B  J  #   >
19    CT:                           [Did you see the

20          ↑gun?
             1
21          (0.3)
            0  #   #   ⇐
22     C:   Yes I ↑did hhh[(they-)]
              A  G  O
23    CT:                  [w h e ]r-
            ((¶ to next line, then > to PR field))
24          w-wha'were they shooting at?
            ((types "3" in PR field; then +, to PHO field))
25     C:   Ah:::: well I=dunno, I've got livestock
            ⇑  WIL  L OW  #         C  R  E
26          in the area=
              EK    #
```

Recall that while the caller is answering the time lapse question, the call-taker is engaged in typing the incident code, and that she is typing an incorrect entry, **ARMEDSHO**. The actual completion of the typing of this entry takes place in the brief micro-second "space" after the caller finishes speaking and before the call-taker starts up with the next turn. In this turn, the call-taker starts to ask what sounds every bit like a location question of some sort (...*where*) but then cuts herself off and starts up again, this time with an utterance whose shape projects a different kind of question: whether the caller *saw* something. However, the caller has also started to speak; in fact, he produces an answer (line 16) to the call-taker's cut-off location inquiry, one that completely overlaps her "did you see-".

In analyzing the call-taker's talk in this turn (line 15), especially her self-repair and subsequent shift of focus from "where" to "did you see," we can first make note of the arrangement of the CAD face sheet form and its possible consequentiality for this talk. Here is the status of the form (again, only the top portion is shown here) and the position of the call-taker's cursor on that form just prior to her "And where-" remark:

```
INC: ARMEDSHO♦_________ ___     TY:_   FD/CTY:___/___   ID: _____
LOC: _____________________       EUG   PR: _    TY/NM:  __________
PHO: __________       X: ___    PH ADR: ______________ ___  FL: ___
SRC: _____      XST: __ ____________ _____     MAP: _____  DIST: ____
```

**Figure 4**

Since the TY, FD/CTY and ID fields are filled in by the CAD system rather than by the call-taker, the slot for location - LOC - is the "next" field on face sheet after (again, moving from left to right and top to bottom) the time lapse/incident-modifier slot. As the call-taker has just obtained time lapse information, determining the location where the incident occurred is thus the "next task" with respect to the form's projected ordering of tasks. But there is still the problem of the incorrect incident code, and it is at this point, as she starts to ask "where," that the call-taker apparently recognizes her error: she begins to back up the cursor, moving from the right side of the screen to the left over O, H, S, D, and E. These keyboard actions are visibly involved with correcting the incident code entry, and leave her with **ARM** as the only remaining letters in the code; given that the incident code for "armed subjects" begins **ARMD** (recall that the E initially inserted by the call-taker represented a spelling mistake, one she has now fixed), this projects **ARMDSUBJ** as the (correct) code that is now being selected. And this is precisely the code the call-taker immediately attempts to complete, typing **D U S B J**. I say "attempts" because she makes a typographical error, reversing the S and the U.

Further, the call-taker's action in cutting off her "where" utterance and then starting to ask "did you see" merits some scrutiny in terms of its possible relationship to this correcting activity at the keyboard. Consider in this regard the caller's initial claim about a "concealed weapon." Was the call-taker about to ask if he actually saw this weapon? Note that four turns later in the call (line 19), the call-taker does indeed ask, "Did you see the gun?" Without any definite knowledge of how the call-taker might have completed the unfinished turn in line 15 had the caller not overlapped her talk, the wording and sequential placement of that later "did you see..." inquiry suggests that "the gun" was the object on which that incomplete utterance was about to focus. Moreover, a question that certainly could be raised about a concealed weapon claim is, How could a person know this was the case? A person would have to *see* it being concealed or have some other convincing evidence of its (hidden) presence. Someone can hear shooting, though, or think they heard shooting, without a gun having ever been seen. Because a claim about the presence of a gun, particularly a concealed gun, is a very serious matter, one that may turn out to have considerable implications for the police response, certainty about its presence would be greatly preferred by public safety practitioners to inferences or speculation.

Of course, it is possible that the call-taker may have been about to ask instead, "Did you see them shooting?" Nevertheless, the cutting-off of the "where" inquiry and the initiation of a "did you see" question seems directed at eliciting information with respect to the completing of the "armed subjects" entry in the INC field, for it just as the call-taker finishes back spacing and starts to complete that coding, to type the remaining five characters, that she cuts off the location question and suddenly shifts the focus. Put another way, if **ARMDSUBJ** is the code being selected, then the "did you see" query is perhaps directed at verifying, as the code is being entered, the grounds for that same selection while at the same time terminating (however temporarily) any inquiry into location or other matters.

It remains the case, however, that the process of assembling this CAD record, and thus the constituting of this event as a "call," is taking place in what is fundamentally an interactional context. As was emphasized earlier in this chapter, the call-taker's keyboard work in the computer-aided dispatch system has to not only be responsive to the particulars of a call (to the circumstances or event being reported) but must be performed in and coordinated with the contingent, turn-by-turn progression of conversational interaction in that call. Keeping this essential point in mind, recall that it is the call-taker's truncated location-oriented utterance ("And where-") that the caller in fact responds to, and his answer thoroughly overlaps her effort to then shift the focus to, presumably, whether he saw the gun. This presents the call-taker with the choice, so to speak, of attempting to either re-introduce (and to now complete) her "did you see" question, and to therefore take no interactional notice of the caller's response to her abandoned "And where-" remark, or to treat that response as in fact an attempt to answer, and to do work to retrieve it from the overlap. It is this latter course that she pursues with her "where?" (line 17).

The importance of location information for the conduct of 9-1-1 operations perhaps figures in, and is exhibited by, the call-taker's initiation of this particular course of action. However, note that when the caller then repeats the location of the incident - "On Willow Crick Road" - the call-taker does not enter any information into the LOC field; rather, she uses the opportunity (that is to say, the span of time) provided by this exchange to correct the typographical error (the reversal of the U and S) in her incident code entry. Moreover, upon completion of that correction, she immediately (overlapping the final syllable of the caller's answer) re-introduces the question that she started to ask earlier, "Did you see the gun?" We have already discussed the significance of that question, given its placement and the accompanying keyboard actions at that point in the interaction, for selecting an appropriate incident code. Its re-introduction at *this* moment, when viewed in terms of its precise timing and in the context of the CAD actions that now accompany and closely follow it, directs our attention once again to the issue of how vocal actions might exhibit a marked orientation to the organizational features of CAD. Observe in this regard that the call-taker's overlapping question-turn is initiated just after she advances her cursor, using the tab key, to the incident-modifier/time lapse field and that she uses the time provided by brief silence and then the caller's answer - "Yes I did" (line 22) - that follows it to type **10 AGO** in that slot (recall that the caller had previously advised her that the incident took place some ten minutes earlier). Thus, while re-introducing a question can still serve what would have been that question's original purpose - in this case, obtaining information relevant to clarifying or verifying the incident coding - it can also (and simultaneously) serve, by requesting information specific to a CAD field that has already been filled in rather than new information, the purpose of giving the call-taker enough time, while the caller is speaking, to fill in the field on the form where their cursor is currently located and for which the necessary information has previously been elicited or offered but not yet typed/entered. That is to say, such a question makes it likely that what the caller says next will not be concerned with anything new, and thus will not deal with information that might be relevant for some other field further down the form - a field other than the one in which the cursor is currently located.

Further, notice that the call-taker completes typing this time lapse entry just as the caller finishes his answer, and that when he starts to say more - once again, to produce a what sounds like it could very well be the beginning of some narrative account or additional description about what the two men ("they-") were up to - she cuts off that incipient account with a question. This sort of call-taker conduct, which is plainly interruptive, can be employed to exhibit a position that the caller is producing talk or offering information deemed "not especially relevant" for what is, to the call-taker, some immediate task or issue at hand; most often, this task is obtaining and typing other, quite specific information for completing some field on the CAD face sheet, and this field is usually the one where the call-taker's cursor is currently located. Here, it is more a case of the call-taker starting up her turn at the same time the caller, having produced what can be heard as a complete turn, continues talking. However, when we take note of the nature of the call-taker's question, "w-wha'were they shooting at?", which is produced from a re-start after an initial (and abruptly halted) "wher-", it seems clear that *the timing of its initiation is closely fitted to, and coordinated with, her position on the CAD form*: she has just completed the time lapse entry, and thus the full incident/incident-modifier portion of the form, and appears ready to move on to other matters, to a next task. I say "ready" because her immediate subsequent actions involve doing just that. As the call-taker asks the caller what the men were shooting at, she (simultaneous with her talk) moves the cursor via the return key to the next line down on the form, to the LOC field (the return key always advances the cursor to the first or left hand side field on the following line), uses the tab key to move the cursor to the PR (priority ranking) field, and then types the number 3 there (incidents are ranked 1-5 according to their seriousness or urgency). At the conclusion of this PR entry, the status of the CAD form (including the position of the cursor, which has automatically been "jumped" by the system after the PR slot was filled in to the next field on that same line, TY/NM) is as follows:

```
INC: ARMDSUBJ______  10 AGO    TY:___    FD/CTY:__/__  ID:______
LOC:  ________________________  EUG  PR: 3   TY/NM: ♦____________
PHO: ___________   X: ____  PH ADR: _______________ ___    FL: __
SRC: ___   XST: __ ______________ ____    MAP: ______   DIST: ____
```

**Figure 5**

In reviewing this last series of actions (transcript lines 23-26) for how they exhibit an orientation to the organizational features of the CAD form, we can notice once again that after the incident and incident modifier fields ("after" in the sense of moving over the form from top to bottom, from the first line to the second line and so on), the next required fields are LOC and PR. We previously observed that when the caller, having reported that he did see the gun, began to continue talking, the call-taker overlapped his talk (actually, started simultaneously) with "wher-"; as was the case with her talk in line 15, the call-taker has started to ask a location-oriented question and then cut it off in mid-stream. Interestingly enough, almost precisely at the moment when call-taker is saying "wher-" she is moving the cursor, via the return key, to the field dedicated to recording location information. However, the caller has already (line 16 and line 18) told her that the incident took place on Willow Creek Road. Minimal or partial location information has therefore been provided in an earlier turn, and the call-taker's self-repair - the cut off and re-start - may in some fashion be occasioned by or related to this prior event. In fact, although the call-taker did not record "Willow Creek" when it was first mentioned, she is able, as the caller is answering (in line 25) her "what were they shooting at?" question, to quickly type in this street name without having to first confirm that earlier mentioning or to ask for the street name again.

Directing attention now to that "what were they shooting at?" query, two observations can be made. First, this is the kind of question that could elicit important information for processing this type of incident, and this information could possibly upgrade or downgrade the urgency of response to the situation; consequently, a query of this sort is plainly relevant for competent call-taking. At the same time, however, the fact that the "shooting" occurred over ten minutes ago pretty much precludes, by practitioners' own standards, anything higher than a priority ranking of 3; in fact, we can notice that the call-taker is entering a 3 in the PR field while she is asking the question, and thus *before* the caller can provide any additional information. Second, and related to this observation, the question is asked just as the call-taker advances her cursor to the PR field, raising the issue of its relationship to that particular keyboard/CAD action and the positioning of the cursor at this particular moment (and thus to the organizational features of CAD more generally). With respect to this issue, I would like to suggest that when a call-taker is faced with the task of making an entry in a CAD field where that entry is rarely a matter of directly eliciting some piece of information from the caller - and this is typically the case with entries in the PR field that are based on a call-taker's assessment of how to fit the organization's priority ranking rules and procedures with the circumstances of a particular call as they have been reported to that point (although there may well be situations where those circumstances occasion a specific question whose answer is then decisive in the ranking decision) - they face a timing-coordination problem similar to those identified at several points above. That is to say, they confront the recurrent practitioner's problem of coordinating their conduct on the phone with actions at the keyboard and positioning on the

CAD form in such a way that data entry can be facilitated - at that moment, given that positioning - through conversational actions. Here, the call-taker's question is aimed at eliciting information about a matter that could have some bearing on the dispatcher's reading of the incident, and is therefore information she might be expected to obtain, while simultaneously serving to (1) take the floor back from the caller, even if this has the consequence of suppressing his attempt to say more about the incident; and (2) provide her with the opportunity, during the time she has the floor, to complete an entry for one of the required fields, an entry that is normally based on the appraisal of previously acquired information.

As it happens, however, the caller in the transcript we have been examining professes to not know what the two men were shooting at, although he adds that he has "livestock in the area," an announcement that could be heard (and, as we shall, is heard by the call-taker) as a suggestion that these animals might be the target. As noted above, during the period of time when the caller is producing this answer, the call-taker, making use of information provided by the caller earlier in the conversation, is busy recording **WILLOW CREEK** in the LOC (location) field. Her movement in CAD to that field was initiated even before she finished her "...shooting at?" question: with the cursor positioned in the PR (priority) field, and thus to the left of (or, in another sense, "behind") the LOC field, the call-taker first used the return key to bring the cursor down one line to the PHO (phone) field as she was completing her turn at talk and then, as the caller began his turn, used the "up arrow" cursor key to move back up to LOC.

## Facilitating Location Formulation in CAD

When considered in sequence, the timing of this movement across the terrain of the face sheet, from the incident-modifier field to the PR field to the LOC field, points once again to the possibility of a very close coordination between the call-taker's questions, the organizational features of the CAD form, the caller's responses, and her keyboard actions. This is further evidenced by the fact that just as the caller completes his "I've got livestock in the area" remark, the call-taker immediately (that is, precisely as she finishes typing **WILLOW CREEK** and almost overlapping the last syllable of the caller's turn) asks a question regarding whether the two men (and presumably the shooting) "were closer to 11th or 18th?" (line 27). This is how the top portion of the face sheet appeared to the call-taker on her CRT at the beginning of that question:

```
INC: ARMDSUBJ ________  10 AGO   TY:_  FD/CTY:___/___   ID: _____
LOC: WILLOW CREEK ♦__________   EUG   PR:3   TY/NM: ______________
PHO: ___________  X:___  PH ADR: ____________________ ___  FL: ___
SRC: ____    XST: __ ______________ ____   MAP: _____   DIST: ____
```

**Figure 6**

In addition, here is the transcription of the vocal and CAD actions for that turn and several that follow it:

```
27  CT:  =w'r'they closer to eleventh or
28       eighte [enth?]
29   C:         [ah::  ]they were closer to
30       eighteenth about a- (0.3) block
                           &  #  1  8    #
31       south of- (.) two blocks south of
                      ¶
32       (k-) eigh[teenth]
         0  ¶
33  CT:           [the:y ]were shooting
                                6  1     ¶
34       at li:vestock?
            ¶
```

The format of the "...closer to eleventh or eighteenth" question warrants close inspection, as it is a format closely oriented to the CAD system's restrictions on how LOC formulations are to entered: Locations must be entered as either an exact address; a street "hundred block"; a landmark (preceded by a landmark-type designator, as in PARK/AMAZON or SCHOOL/EDISON) that the CAD system recognizes and will then replace, as the form is transmitted to the dispatcher, with the landmark's official address; or an intersection.[23] Having been informed that the incident took place (somewhere) on Willow Creek Road, the call-taker has already typed **WILLOW CREEK** when she asks that question and, by typing/recording it in the manner that she did, has now committed herself to an intersection-type formulation. That is to say, the prior recording of **WILLOW CREEK** in the LOC field now precludes an exact address, "street hundred block," or landmark formulation, unless the call-taker were to go back to the beginning of the field and retype the entry, and calls instead for the addition of a cross street - a street that intersects with Willow Creek Road - to complete a proper intersection formulation. This is exactly what the call-taker's "were they closer to eleventh or eighteenth?" question is designed to elicit.

One final point on this matter: there is the question of how a practitioner's knowledge of local geography (and their assumptions about a caller's knowledge) might occasion and be exhibited by the format/design of a question directed at obtaining location information. In this case, the call-taker's posing of the question as a choice between two specific cross streets rather than simply asking, for example, "Where on Willow Creek?", is sensitive - if someone has a knowledge of local geography, which the design of her question presumes the caller has (indeed, it exhibits this presumption) -

to the fact that these are the streets that intersect with the two ends of the largest segment of the road (there is one other segment within the city limits). As 11th and 18th thus "bound off" a good portion of the road and are in fact the *only* streets that intersect with or cross that segment, the posing of a choice between them therefore provides an efficient procedure for attempting a specification of approximately where on Willow Creek the incident occurred. Moreover, the selection of both an intersection formulation and this particular "locating procedure" is also sensitive to the distinct character of Willow Creek Road: it is a road in a rural area, with few if any distinguishing landmarks or buildings that could serve as approximate addresses for an incident that occurred nearby.

Turning now to the vocal and keyboard actions that follow the call-taker's typing of **& 18th**, observe that here, in contrast with earlier occasions, the caller is able to say more after first indicating "they were closer to eighteenth," by briefly elaborating on and clarifying this placement of the incident:

```
30    C:   eighteenth about a- (0.3) block
                         &  #  1   8   #
31         south of- (.) two blocks south of
                   ¶
32         (k-) eigh [teenth]
           0  ¶
33    CT:            [the:y ]were shooting
                                   6  1    ¶
34         at li:vestock?
             ¶
35         (0.5)

36    C:   We::ll I=dunno what they were
            M  A   L  E  #  ¶  ¶
37         shootin'at, the[y had sum stuff out in-          ]

38    CT:                 [what's the liCENSE NUMBER OF]
                           L  V  /  # U  N K  #  P  A  L
39         this ca:r?
           T  E #
```

The call-taker does not make any use of this more specific location information. That is to say, she does not record it on the CAD form (it is the kind of information that could only be included in the DTL or "details" field) or focus on it through subsequent talk. The call-taker does engage in keyboard and vocal activity during this latter portion of the caller's turn, however: she uses the return key to advance the cursor to the PHO (phone number) field, which is on the next line down and the left hand side of the form, types **0** there, and then strikes the return key again, advancing the cursor to the SRC (trunk line number) field, which is on the left hand side of the succeeding line.

Further, just after she records the zero and strikes return, which consequently positions her cursor at the beginning of the SRC field, the call-taker overlaps the concluding syllable of the caller's elaborating remarks with a question referring back to the his prior "I've got livestock in the area" statement: "they were shooting at livestock?" Finally, note that as she is asking this clarification query (lines 33-34) - it is directed at "clarifying" in the sense that she has taken that prior statement to indicate that, from his view, the livestock were the likely target for the shooting - she types **61** for the SRC entry and then strikes the return key two times in succession, advancing the cursor through/over the BREATH field (a slot used only with medical emergency calls) and down to the CALLER field (this latter slot is an optional field used for recording the caller's name or a similar identifying appellation).

Thus, at the conclusion of those keyboard actions, the screen display of the CAD form is as follows:

```
INC: ARMDSUBJ _____  10 AGO   TY:_   FD/CTY:___/___   ID: ______
LOC: WILLOW CREEK & 18TH___  EUG   PR: 3   TY/NM:  _________
PHO: 0_________     X:___   PH ADR: ______________ ___     FL: ___
SRC: 0___    XST: __ _____________ ____    MAP: _____   DIST: ____
BREATH:_ CONSC:_ AGE:__ SEX:_  AGYS: ___ ___ ___ ___     INI: ___
CALLER: ♦____________________   CONT: ___               REF: _
ADR: _________________________  EUG    DISP: ____   CSN: ______
DTL: __________________________________________________________
________________________________________________________________
```

**Figure 7**

With respect to the advancing of the cursor from the LOC to PHO field during the caller's elaborating remarks, recall that in the ordering of the CAD form, *if* its geography is taken to abet, over the course of entering a call-for-service, a top to bottom trajectory of navigation, PHO is after three of the other required fields - INC, PR, and LOC - and before the last such field (again, "last" only in terms of this ordering), which is SRC. Having completed the LOC entry, the call-taker is following this ordered route over the form's terrain, and the elaborating remarks by the caller therefore do not have, given this orientation, any data entry relevance at the present time: the formatting restrictions for LOC do not permit any such elaborations or additions (for example, "ON WILLOW CREEK, CLOSER TO 18TH THAN TO 11TH") in that field, and the next required field, PHO, calls for a completely different kind of information. While the call-taker obviously could have asked the caller for that information - his phone number - at this time, she does not; instead, she types a zero as a "placeholder" for that number in PHO. The software rules for CAD simply require a numerical entry in that field, but do not specify or limit what those numbers have to be. Accordingly, zeros are frequently used by call-takers, particularly in calls they take to be relatively urgent, to complete that entry and hold that place, allowing the form to be transmitted without having to take the time to ask for phone number information. As the call-taker was employing this technique, and was not going to ask for a phone number, allowing the caller to continue, to elaborate on his location information, this gave her the time and (interactional) opportunity to carry it out.

The initiation of the "shooting at livestock" question just at the point when the call-taker does complete the PHO entry is also of some analytic interest, as are the actions in CAD that are performed during that turn. The actions here appear to evidence a fitting of talking with typing similar to that previously observed in lines 19-20 and especially 23-24, where the initiation of a question is timed to accompany a movement from one field to another in CAD and where the type of question asked appears coordinated with the type of action projected by (required for) the field to which the cursor is being advanced or has just been advanced. Here, in a situation where the cursor is positioned in a field requiring information that cannot be obtained from the caller (it can only be obtained by glancing at the phone console display and noticing what trunk number this particular phone call is on, or by a call-taker recalling what trunk number they punched in on the console to answer the call), and where there is thus no questioning that would be relevant for that field, the call-taker's question "reaches back" to verify a hearing of (for practitioners) potentially important information; moreover, it also serves (as was the case with her question in lines 23-24) to take the floor back from the caller and give her an opportunity, during the time she has the floor, to complete that information entry and advance the cursor to another field.

At this point in the conversation, with the call-taker having positioned the cursor in the CALLER field even before she finished her "shooting at livestock" question, she is able to both type **MALE** in that field and advance the cursor two lines down to the DTL field during the time the caller is responding that in fact he does not know just what the men were shooting at. The recording of **MALE** here, in a field reserved for the caller's name, can be compared with the use of a zero in the phone number field. Although the call-taker could have asked the caller what his name was, she does not, selecting instead a categorical identifier.[24] As was the case with the recording of **0** for PHO, this points toward the intertwined practitioners' problems of assembling a complete face sheet record while also being responsive to the call's urgency and to how "completeness" might be defined, given these circumstances. Thus, while a sense of urgency can be certainly exhibited by and through the pace and nature of questioning in the conversation (or, for that matter, by the pace and tenor of the caller's speech), it can be displayed (as well as searched for) in the CAD textual record of that conversation, a record that will be read by others with an interest in how its "completeness" is "adequate" and "makes sense," particularly "at this point in the processing of the call," given "this kind of incident" or "this type of caller," with "this type..." also having to be exhibited and understood by and through that same text. In this case, the entry **MALE** could be read by the dispatcher and other practitioners as an indication that the call-taker recognizes the significance of getting that kind of information and completing that field, but that, for now, for the purposes at hand - getting the face sheet completed in such a way that it can be quickly transmitted to the dispatcher and will provide adequate information for making certain dispatch decisions - is treating it as not of crucial importance.

More important for our analytic concerns, however, is what happens next, after the completion of the entry in the CALLER field: with the cursor then advanced to DTL, the call-taker once again, as she did in line 23, cuts off the caller's attempt to tell more of the story, "...they had some stuff out in-", which is perhaps the same material he started to introduce in line 22 ("they-"). It is precisely at the point where the caller completes his "I dunno" answer to the call-taker's question and continues speaking with "they..." that she overlaps his talk, asking a question that is directed at obtaining the license number of the previously mentioned vehicle. Note that although the caller now produces a good deal more of his "story" - more details on what actually happened and what *really* concerns him about these two guys, which has something to do with "some stuff" - the call-taker increases the volume of her talk as he tries to do so, vigorously working at taking control of the floor until the caller drops out. In sum, the possibility of these details, this incipient story, getting told - a story/telling that was projected, however weakly, in caller's very first turn in this conversation - has again been precluded by the call taker's interrogative actions.[25]

## A Telling Untold

Does it seem reasonable, then, to speak of a dispreference in these kinds of conversational environments for any caller narrative concerning the details of an incident once the classification of that incident in CAD has been made? Consider in this regard the following exchange from later in the same call:

73 CT: And they=were shooting at ↑co:ws?
**T H # ⇑ ⇑ ⇑ ⇑ ⇑ ⇑ ⇑ ⇑ ((to INC field))**
74 in the fee:ld there?
**< ((to beginning of INC field)) S H**
75 C: Well I dunno what they uz shootin
**O T F I R D #**
76 at=they had some stuff hid out in
**¶ ¶ ¶ ¶ ¶ ¶ ¶ ¶ ((to 2nd line of DTL field))**
77 the brush and they took off
**((right cursor to 1 space after "11th"))**
78 run↓nin' (0.6) I didn't wanna
*** * * * #**

79 confront 'em any more after I
2 W # S U B
80 [found they had a wea↓pon ]

81 CT: [there=were TWO GUYS ]there
⇐ ⇐ ⇐ ⇐ ⇐ # S U
82 were two guys in the car?
B J ' S # I
83 C: Yah. (0.4) They wuz out in the
N # V E H , S H O T
84 brush (.) in the field, in the
⇐ O T I N G # I N
85 pasture (0.6) and uh after I
T O # B R U S H #
86 confronted and found they had a

87 gun I backed off from 'em=

88 CT: =okay (.) well I'm notifying the

89 p'lice=dispatchers just stay on
((CAD record sent to dispatcher))
90 the line with me he:re=

And consider as well the state of the CAD face sheet, including the position of the cursor (it is in the second line of the DTL field), at the beginning of this exchange:

```
INC: ARMDSUBJ __________ 10 AGO  TY:_ FD/CTY:___/___  ID: ____
LOC: WILLOW CREEK & 18TH _____ EUG  PR:3  TY/NM:____________
PHO: 0__________ X:___  PH ADR: ______________________ ___ FL: __
SRC: 61__  XST: __ _______________ ____  MAP: ______  DIST: ____
BREATH:_ CONSC:_ AGE:__ SEX:_ AGYS: ___ ___ ___ ___  INI: ___
CALLER: MALE__________________________ CONT: ___       REF: _
ADR: _____________________________ EUG  DISP: ____  CSN: _______
DTL: LV/HLV661.OR OLDER TOYOTA, 2H, BABY BLU  DOT/NBND
     ON WILLOW CREEK TOWARDS W 11♦_____________________________
```

**Figure 8**

Observe that at this juncture in the conversation the caller does complete a relatively detailed although still brief narrative account in lines 76-80, and that it appears to be the very same account he started to produce in line 37. Moreover, we can notice that the question from the call-taker that occasioned this account is virtually the same question she asked back in lines 33-34, one aimed at confirming her understanding that the two guys were shooting at livestock (only in this instance she refers to a specific species of livestock, "cows," and a more specific location, "in the field there?"). Further, this question receives virtually the same answer from the caller here that it did earlier: "I dunno". Finally, the segue from this claim by the caller into the remarks about "some stuff" takes place in almost exactly the same manner as it did in line 37. How can we account, then, for the caller being able to produce these details at this point in the call, after several failed/aborted attempts, including an attempt that was extraordinarily similar, in its initial sequential and syntactical features, to this one? What of the suggestion about a dispreference for any narrative detail by the caller about their trouble once an incident code had been selected?

To address these questions, we need to examine the keyboard actions the call-taker takes during this exchange and consider how these actions appear to be coordinated with or related, in a practical fashion, to the organization of the talk. As the exchange begins, the call-taker has recorded slightly more than one line of detail in the DTL field, including the vehicle license plate number, state, year, make, model, and color. She is completing her entry of information on the vehicle's direction of travel (**ON WILLOW CREEK TOWARDS W 11TH**), information that was elicited through some immediately prior questioning, when she asks yet another time about the target of the shooting. However, after recording the final component of that direction information, the call-taker - as she asks her question about the cows - uses the "up arrow" cursor key to leave the DTL field and move the cursor straight up the form, all the way to the INC field, and then back-tabs to the beginning of that information slot as she adds "in the field there?" Before the caller begins to answer the question, she starts to change the incident code from **ARMDSUBJ** to **SHOTFIRD**, which was the code she initially and incorrectly combined with the one for "armed subjects" but then rejected in favor of the latter at the very beginning of the data entry on this call (see lines 12-18). Whatever the reason for the call-taker's decision to change the incident code, her "...shooting at cows?" question appears to serve the same function as it did in its earlier incarnations with respect to managing the ordered terrain and format restrictions of the CAD form. Its delivery on this occasion coincides with the movement of the cursor to and the correction of an entry in an already completed field (and one that is at the other end of the form), while also working at addressing an issue (the target of the shooting) that has implications for what should be recorded in the DTL field but apparently still remains, for the call-taker, unresolved.

The substitution of **SHOTFIRD** for **ARMDSUBJ** is completed just before the caller finishes his "I dunno" response. As he continues, much as he started to do earlier, with some remarks about these men having "some stuff hid out in the brush," the call-taker is busy advancing the cursor, via the return key and "right arrow" cursor key, back down to its previous position on the second line of the DTL field. Further, as the caller goes on, after a brief pause, to describe how the two guys "took off runnin'" and how he "didn't wanna confront'em any more," the call-taker types ****** 2W SUB** on that second line, which is how a Central Lane practitioner would start to abbreviate the person description "two white sub[jects]" (the abbreviation still needs a J and a S after SUB) and textually demarcate (through the use of devices like a string of asterisks, dashes, or spaces) that description from other details. Finally, and precisely as she reaches the letter B, she simultaneously interrupts her both own recording of that description and the caller's ongoing turn-at-talk, just at the point where the caller begins to explain why he didn't want to confront them anymore (he discovered they had a weapon). That is to say, the call-taker abruptly starts to back-space over most of the person description and then types **SUBJ'S** in its place, thus eliminating the W (for "white") from the details, *exactly* at the moment when she overlaps the caller with a question aimed at confirming a key feature of that description, which is whether there were indeed "*two* guys in the car" (notice that although the caller has spoken of two "guys," he has not said anything about their race). This interruptive confirmation/verification query is therefore timed with the call-taker's "correcting" actions at the keyboard.

We can summarize these observations by stating that as a result of the call-taker having to use a number of keystrokes and two different keys to move the cursor from one end of the form to the other and then retype the INC entry, and next having to advance the cursor back to the place where it had first been positioned, the caller has been able to finally produce, given that the call-taker was so engaged, some of the details about what happened and why, details that he had unsuccessfully attempted to report at earlier junctures. Moreover, we can add that although this most recent and much more successful effort was eventually overlapped by the call-taker's resumption of the interrogation (a resumption plainly related, as before, to her positioning and activity at that very moment on the CAD form), when the caller answers that interruptive query, he is then able to continue on and recycle and elaborate upon these details at some length, without any interruption. Here too, then, the call-taker's engagement with CAD provides the interactional "space" for the caller's narrative: she is busy recording - and at one point, correcting an error in her typing - a somewhat extended account concerning the topic of her last question, what the men were shooting at (note that having failed on several occasions to resolve the question of what the specific target of the shooting was, she now extrapolates from the caller's immediately prior reference to "...out in the brush" to finish assembling this account before transmitting the form to the dispatcher).

Thus, while it may make some sense to speak of a dispreference for narrative accounts from callers following the entry of an incident code as call-takers then work at obtaining information for the remaining fields on the CAD form, this is certainly an interactionally achieved matter, and is in no way predetermined by the organizational features of the form or the technology, even as those features set certain parameters on that work. As I have sought to demonstrate throughout this paper, in the example presented just above, in instances taken from prior segments of that same call, and in examples from other calls, the organizational features of CAD, together with the practical methods call-takers employ for dealing with them and the responses from callers to those actions, stand in a complex interrelationship.

Of course, we should be equally appreciative of the extreme generality of this phenomenon: In all sorts of conversations, for all sorts of reasons, one or more co-participants may find themselves caught up in various physical, social and cognitive activities that distract them or require their close attention, or call for attention and engagement of a distinct type, and the consequences of this engagement will necessarily be something that must be managed locally, then and there, by those same co-participants, and in presumably systematic ways. Hence, this is hardly a phenomenon that is confined to or determined by features of the physical setting occupied by one party to this call - a work site that is, for them, a 9-1-1 operations center - or the "institutional" and "technological" character (in terms of the incorporation of computer-aided dispatch technology) of much of the business at hand.

Still, the local and interactional management of these matters will necessarily be embedded in and sensitive to that business, whatever it may be. In the "confronted two guys" call, the caller's incipient story remained incipient for some time in large part because what he took to be interesting and suspicious features of the behavior of the two men resisted any simple and straightforward summarizing or classification of the sort called for by the call-taker's "what is your emergency?" inquiry, and perhaps the incident coding requirement of CAD as well. Asked to provide some evidence that an emergency existed, he focused instead, after a brief reference to a confrontation, on what kind of car the police need to be on the lookout for if they were going to locate the "two guys" he confronted, a statement that presupposed rather than demonstrated the existence of a reason for the police to be concerned. Then, when immediately pressed to describe what these men were doing, in a manner that identified precisely what was inadequate about that initial statement, he offered an account that very nicely addressed that inadequacy, one that was therefore quite sensitive to what was now the *immediate* business at hand: describing what the men were up to in such a way that it would warrant police action. And his account occasioned just that kind of action: the conversion, through an organizational classifying/categorizing procedure, of that described event into an actionable "incident," thus providing the grounds for further organizational courses of action. However, once this incident classification had been made, the caller's reference to "concealed weapon" that had been incorporated into it, and to "shooting" (later incorporated into a classification that was substituted for the first), became the focus of much of the call-taker's interrogation, along with the topics and issues associated with the remaining fields on the CAD form. The call-taker's conduct in this regard exhibited an orientation to *assembling a textual record that was built around and, through its ordered production across the terrain of the form, "progressed" from that classification and those references*. The erratic topical course of the talk, a course driven by the ordering of the call-taker's questions, resulted to a large degree from her orientation to assembling that record in that form-ordered fashion. Consequently, the telling of any account of what made caller suspicious about these two men and warranted a police investigation, which turned out to be not so much the gun and the shooting, or not that alone, but rather "some stuff" that they had hidden in the brush, met with considerable difficulty. The CAD system, as a distinct kind of tool employed by one of the co-participants during and for this exchange, and the organization of its face sheet screen display, certainly entered into the achievement of this outcome, but it did not ordain it. Rather, as we have seen, the organizational features of the system and the face sheet repeatedly presented themselves to the call-taker - or, more accurately, were repeatedly encountered - as both enabling and constraining properties over the course of the conversation as she sought to assemble a textual record in CAD that successfully, for all practical purposes, represented worldly matters that were reported on or topicalized in that conversation, an assembling to which the caller was thus necessarily an active party.

## Concluding Remarks

This chapter has presented an analysis of embodied courses of practical action and practical reasoning involved in the ordered production of "calls" as organizational events, focusing on the utilization of a technology of order production: computer-aided dispatch tools. The analysis demonstrated the thoroughly endogenous nature of this tool use: CAD technology, which is designed to standardize the work and to be materially indifferent to local circumstances, must nevertheless always be employed in and through the actuality, the local circumstances, of unique and highly variable events. Thus, the progression of a call, or of any activity in a call (like "determining what the problem is") from one constituent task to another, when examined in its local production, will certainly be much more than a matter of enacting some standard technologically-mandated scheme. Further, the issues, problems, and choices for practitioners with respect to the CAD system and its data-entry form, while describable in general terms, will only and always arise in and through the immediate, local, sequential progression of some actual occasion. And things will become evident as an issue or choice for the practitioner in that manner, at that moment, for that interaction. It is in this fashion, then, that computational technology built to serve as an independent resource for the performance of work tasks fundamentally enters into the situated concerting and coordinating of those tasks.

---

* This research was supported by a grant from U.S. West Advanced Technologies. Several colleagues made detailed criticisms and suggestions on earlier versions of this paper. My thanks to Steve Clayman, Chuck Goodwin, Candy Goodwin, Michael Lynch, Doug Maynard, Manny Schegloff, Dorothy Smith, and Lucy Suchman. I have also benefitted over the course of this project from the advice of Francoise Brun-Cottan, Marilyn Carter, Gene Lerner, Marilyn Whalen, and Don Zimmerman. Finally, I would like to

express my deep gratitude to the Eugene, Oregon Department of Public Safety - especially the staff of the Central Lane Communications Center - for giving me the opportunity to work as a communications specialist in their department and permitting complete access to Central Lane's activities and records.

1 The research project from which this chapter is derived is but one of several ongoing ethnomethodological investigations into the relations between work tasks, social interaction, and technology in multi-activity, technology-intensive work sites: air traffic control centers (Hughes, Randall and Shapiro, 1992; Hughes, Shapiro, Sharrock, Harper, and Randall, in press), airline ground operations rooms (Brun-Cotton, 1991; Goodwin and Goodwin, in press; Suchman, in press a, in press b), subway line control centers (Heath and Luff, in press), and dealing rooms for trading stocks and bonds (Jirotka, Luff, and Heath, 1992). Studies of a similar nature are also being carried out on human-computer interaction (Frolich, Drew, and Monk, 1992; Luff and Heath, in press). In both their approach and findings, these investigations are respecifying the sociological project concerning the study of technology and the social world. As Shapiro, Hughes, Harper, Ackroyd, and Soothill (1991:3; emphasis in original) have pointed out, the task of that project should be not so much to discover *whether* technology is social as "to show *how* it is social"; accordingly, studies of the "social life of technology" must consider "not only the material objects but the collage of activities involved in making technology into an *instrument* which is incorporated into a weave of working tasks."

2 These observations concerning the conversation's erratic topical course are not meant to suggest that the talk lacks coherence. As Schegloff (1990:72) points out, "the structure of sequences in talk-in-interaction is a source of coherence in its own right," and "disparate topics can occur coherently within the framework of a single, expanded sequence and achieve coherence by being framed by it." In the conversation we are examining, it has been noted that the series of question-answer exchanges is recognizably an "interrogation," which can be thought of as an often extended, sequentially organized activity geared - in this case - to determining if the caller's account of trouble warrants a police response and, if so, what the nature of that response should be. As such, it is accessible to understanding as a coherent and sequentially "linked" series of turns by the participants. For an analysis of how participants in conversation construct their questions so as to propose their "expectable," standardized or agenda-based character, and to thus exhibit this understanding of the business at hand, see Heritage and Sorjonen (1992).

3 It should be clear from this account that not all citizen phone calls to police and fire departments result in actual "calls for service"; that is to say, lead to an organizational response. In 1991, for example, Central Lane Communications received close to 620,000 phone calls (on both 9-1-1 and seven digit lines) that generated 133,000 calls for service. While it is true that many of these calls, especially those received on weekdays and on

nonemergency lines, involve requests to speak to another department staff person, such as a police detective or patrol officer (with the call-taker playing a role similar to that of a switchboard operator), or are simple requests for information (concerning things like local or state laws and the state traffic code, backyard burning regulations, local and regional road conditions, or police department policies), the majority do involve complaints, direct requests for assistance, reports of trouble, and so forth.

4 As Meehan (1989) and Whalen and Zimmerman (1987) have noted, the fundamental predicament for call-takers is that their *only* access to an event is through the caller; consequently, they are almost completely dependent, in terms of doing their work, on what the caller tells them and what they are able to elicit.

5 While the abbreviation "CAD" is used by programmers, architects, and engineers to refer to "computer-aided design" software, people in the field of public safety communications -- both practitioners and designers of computer-aided dispatch systems -- use this same abbreviation to refer to their technology and its associated software.

6 I have used the term "information" at several points in this discussion, in what is admittedly a very loose fashion. By "information" I simply mean knowledge acquired in any manner. I certainly do not intend to suggest by this term that what is being said in 9-1-1 phone calls, or what is being recorded/typed by call-takers and what is then read from that textual record by dispatchers has some stable, self-sufficient, independent status, and can thus be removed from the immediate interactional activities within which such sayings, recordings and readings take place.

7 It is important to emphasize in this regard that the process of constructing the kind of objectified social knowledge that a "call-for-service" certainly exemplifies does not involve going from a definite initial event or object, such as a worldly trouble or problem, to an objective record of the event or description of the object, such as a "call"; instead, it is best understood as *constitutional work* that accomplishes an event or object in the very process of its textual inscription (Smith, 1990:216-217; see also Latour and Woolgar, 1979; Lynch, 1985). It is thus through the assembling of the CAD text that both events in the world (in public safety parlance, "incidents") and "calls" concerning those events achieve their organizational facticity, a facticity that then permits these textual records to be entered into further organizational courses of action.

8 On the computer screen, the headings and data entry slots/lines for the required fields are displayed in red (on a black background) - simulated in Figure 1 by boldface print - while the remainder of the form's text is in green. This "highlighted" display of specific text is similar to that achieved on paper forms by the use of bold or italic type face, upper case letters, or fonts that are larger in size than that used for the other text. In some organizations that make extensive use of paper forms, the workers use markers that produce transparent and fluorescent ink to *manually* highlight text. An insightful

analysis of "highlighting" that focuses on this type of manual inking of text on a form, showing how it transforms a "domain of scrutiny" into a "field of relevance," can be found in Goodwin and Goodwin (1992).

9 For instance, call-takers are expected to enter vehicle descriptions with a two-letter abbreviation (followed by a slash) that indicates whether the vehicle is a moving, possibly suspect vehicle that needs to be located (LV/); a stationary vehicle involved in the incident (IV/); the victim's vehicle (VV/); or a confirmed stolen vehicle (SV/); and to then enter the vehicle's license number and state, year, make, model, and color (in that order, including as many of these identifying details as possible, with commas separating each item). If a direction of travel is known, that should be entered next. For example: LV/KWK464.OR, 88, FORD, MUSTANG, 2D, LT BLU, DOT/EB ON 11TH. These conventions are designed to produce text descriptions that can be read by dispatchers off the CAD screen in precisely the same way they are to be broadcast over the radio. That is to say, the Eugene Department of Public Safety's policies on broadcasting vehicle descriptions require dispatchers to read out such descriptions over the radio in just that syntactical order - beginning with license plate and state, then year, make and model, then color (most departments adhere to these same policies) - and it was felt that the text entered by the call-taker should therefore follow this same order. The recording of vehicle information in the CAD form for the "confronted two guys" call is very briefly noted below.

It is assumed by practitioners that recording information in the "proper" way, and obtaining the "right" and "necessary" information to begin with, will reveal and demonstrate competence not only in data entry but in "doing the job." It should be clear, then, that CAD is not only a tool or means for recording information to do the work, to process calls, it is equally and simultaneously a means of *documenting and accounting* for that work - for showing what work was done, and how competently it was done.

10 In addition, recall that for the DTL field there are agency conventions and policies that govern how call-takers should enter the textual information (using certain abbreviations and syntax). For call-takers, this presents a problem: How to obtain this information in such a way that the text can be typed in the "proper" order/syntax? Space limitations prevent any examination of this particular problem here; a preliminary analysis of the textually mediated, interactionally accomplished character of person description in calls to the police is presented in Smith, Whalen, Whalen, and Carter (1992).

11 From this view, a CAD text has all the features of what Garfinkel, Lynch, and Livingston (1981; see also Garfinkel, 1967) term a "docile record." By this is meant documentary records in the form of writing, tape-recordings, photographs, charts, maps, and the like, all of which are "significant more for what they hide about their practical genealogies that for what they reveal about them" (Lynch, 1985:64). If we are to discover their practical genealogy, docile records need to be analyzed as "renderings" of the embodied real-time work that produced them (Lynch, 1985:64).

I should emphasize here that while other studies of police communications work have pointed to the construction of a call record (on either a paper or electronic form) as central for the performance of that work and have also, in some cases, examined the relationship between the telephone interaction and the textual record that is then produced, these studies did not subject the situated assembling those records - their practical genealogies - to any kind of detailed investigation. For example, Manning's (1988) intriguing field study of police communications facilities in Britain and the United States examines "message processing" - "the transformation of events in the everyday world into objects and organizational communication units" - as *conceptual work*, requiring a semiotic analysis of symbolic and interpretive practices. Consequently, while Manning emphasizes the role of computer-aided dispatch technology, the ethnographic description of this technology and its incorporation into call-takers' work is divorced from important details - the organizational features of the CAD form and the embodied real-time assembly of the textual record - of the phenomena described.

Related to this, several ethnographic and conversation analytic studies of "institutional" interactions between health care professionals and their clients have called attention to the significance of filling out a form for the ordering and progression of the talk (Heritage and Sorjonen, 1992; Engestrom, 1992). Although these studies have made important contributions to our understanding of textually mediated social organization (see also Heath, 1982), they were not able to systematically address the properties of those form(ed) texts or the complex, temporally developing, intertwining between such properties (such as the arrangement of fields) and the order in the conversation.

12 Whenever possible, the letter or number typed by the call-taker is aligned with the speech particle or span of silence that occurred simultaneously with the moment the keystroke registered on the CAD screen (the video camera was focused on the screen; there is of course an extremely slight, micro-second delay between when a key is depressed and when the keystroke registers on the display). In a few of the cases where what is happening on the call-taker's computer screen is described in the transcript, specific keystrokes were used to produce that screen result, and these prior keystrokes are also included in the transcript at the point at which they registered on the display. In other cases, a special key was needed to produce the result and, unlike letter and number keys, no record of the keystroke registers on the display when this key is depressed.

Note that both the "left arrow" cursor key and the back-space key produce the same cursor movement on the CAD screen, and that back-spacing does not delete any characters from the screen display; accordingly, because the camera was focused on the screen, we cannot determine whether a back-space or left cursor key was used to move the cursor to the left, "backing over" characters that were already typed.

13 Central Lane's CAD system allows users to have two screens for entering calls for service active at one time. These screens can themselves be broken into several windows, but few call-takers make use of this windowing

feature because of the considerable reduction in character size (and thus readability) that would then be required to keep an entire face sheet visible on the display (even in a window that was half the size of the screen) and the complex series of operations needed to execute these windowing features. Consequently, when call-takers have to manage two calls at once, they typically do what this call-taker did: preserve the partially-completed record by switching to another screen for the second call.

14 The non-obvious character of such a turn format can be demonstrated by considering how call-takers at other public safety communication centers answer emergency lines; Central Lane's procedurally mandated turn format is just one of many possibilities, and these different formats project, select, or provide opportunities for a variety of next actions by callers. Consider, for example, the opening turns employed by call-takers when answering these two 9-1-1 calls:

**MID-CITY/17-8**
1 CT: Mid-City Police and Fire
**DALLAS/CLAIRBOURNE**
1 CT: Fire=department

In these examples, the turn consists only of a categorical self-identification. It thus identifies who the caller has reached, but does not select a particular next action for the caller to perform, such as providing an account of what the emergency is, or indicating immediately that they do have a "real emergency." This is most definitely not to say that the caller could not or would not produce, in their very next turn, such an account or indication. Rather, my point is that the turn format used by these call-takers at two different communications facilities is not *designed* to obtain that action or make it more likely. In fact, in these calls the caller produced a direct request for help in the next turn, but did not give any reason or account of why help was needed, that is, did not say what the emergency consisted of, and were subsequently asked to do so:

**MID-CITY/17-8**
1 CT: Mid-City Police and Fire
2 C: Uh: yeah can you send the police tuh twenty six
3 fifteen North Brogan? Avenue .hh hh
4 CT: Twunty six fifteen Brogan North?
5 C: Yeah
6 CT: What's thuh matter?

**DALLAS/CLAIRBOURNE**
1 CT: Fire=department
2 (1.1)
3 CT: Fire department?
4 C: Hi:hhh we need an am:bulance (0.5) at ( )
5 (0.4)
6 CT: What's thuh problem ma'am

7 (1.1)
8 C: A h:eart pa- he's been a heart patient?

In these cases, then, the presentation of information that could be inspected by the call-taker to determine what kind of incident the caller was reporting, and if this constituted an emergency, is deferred, by talk dealing with other matters, until later (if only a few seconds) in the conversation. Again, I am not arguing that it must be deferred, only that "call-taker first-turn" formats like these do not specifically *select* the action of giving that information as something that should be performed next.

Finally, none of this should be taken to mean that in response to the opening turn format employed at Central Lane callers rarely or never fail to provide just the kind of information that is requested. Although it does appear to be the case, based on my observations at Central Lane and my review of numerous Central Lane tapes, that the request for an account of the emergency does very frequently produce that account (or a next turn that displays an orientation to that request, such as "Well, this isn't an emergency, but..." or "Oh! I'm sorry, I don't really have an emergency, but..."), this is a simple distributional observation. To reiterate my position, I am not intending in any way to suggest that such a pattern is predetermined or "caused" (in the conventional social scientific sense of this term) by the call-taker's opening turn format. Quite to the contrary: the observable outcomes - whatever the caller does in response to the call-taker's opening turn - for Central Lane calls (or any calls by anyone to anywhere) are locally and interactionally achieved outcomes; that is to say, they are accomplished on a case-by-case basis (see especially Whalen, Zimmerman, and Whalen, 1988).

15 Here are some examples of such immediate (several even overlap the call-taker's opening turn) and relatively concise answers:

**CL41A1**
1 CT: Nine one one what is [yer emer-
2 C: [My baby's dead hhhh

**CL08A1**
1 CT: Nine one one what is [yur emerge-
2 C: [yahh hh there's a fire
3 in my house(hh) .hh hh

**CL01A2**
1 CT: Nine one one what is yur emergency?
2 C: It's my brother he had a bomb an' it blew up in=
3 h-hand=hh .hh hh

**CL01A5**
1 CT: Nine one one what is yur emer [gency?
2 C: [.hhh OH MY GOD I JUST
3 GOT HOME AND MY WIFE SHOT HERSELF

**CL02A1**

| | | |
|---|---|---|
| 1 | CT: | Nine one one what is your emergency?= |
| 2 | C: | =uh yeah we have a little boy who can't breathe at |
| 3 | | ninety six thousand Malcolm Lane. |

16 We cannot know for sure when the call-taker hits her "enter" key and actually sends this command to the computer system, but the face sheet appears on her display some five seconds later. Usually, there is at most a two or three second time lapse between depressing the enter key and a command or action being carried out by the computer; here, the delay between when the call-taker types **AA** and when the face sheet appears is longer. Possibly, she was waiting to hear more from the caller before issuing the command. If so, she did not wait very long.

17 My observations on the caller's opening turn owe much to suggestions offered by Manny Schegloff and Gene Lerner during seminar and colloquia presentations of this material at UCLA and UC Santa Barbara.

18 These pauses, together with the intonational contour of the caller's first turn, also suggest that the caller was trying to produce a story that would "work" or be received as an acceptable (for the police) report; that is to say, the story's halting (with pauses) progress exhibits an effort to obtain the call-taker's alignment as a recipient of that story and/or its telling.

19 Note the call-taker's use of the present tense here: "What are they doing?" rather than "What were they doing?" There is some ambiguity as to whether the event is still in progress. This issue is addressed below.

20 Although having a concealed weapon is possibly a criminal offense, it is not an "emergency" to the degree that *shooting* a weapon is. We might then want to ask why the caller's description came to be formatted or ordered in this particular way, with first the concealed weapon and then the nature of that weapon - a pistol - reported before the shooting is even mentioned. Notice in this regard that the call-taker's query prompting that description uses the present tense: What *are* they doing? At the moment that question was asked, however, the men (apparently) *are not* shooting the gun. In contrast, the response "they *had* a concealed weapon" is a "natural" past tense, since if the caller can report it, the weapon is no longer concealed. It is then consistent, when next specifying the weapon as a pistol, for the caller to use the past tense (*had* a pistol), even though the men almost certainly still have the pistol. The past-ness of the shooting is now in keeping with the tense of the previous parts of the description and does not stand in marked contrast with the question. I am grateful to Manny Schegloff for providing this analysis. The caller's use of the past tense and its consequences for the call-taker's subsequent actions are discussed in detail below.

21 Of course, the selection of an incident code can be postponed while the call-taker pursues other issues (like location, caller's phone number, suspect information, etc.), and then returns to filling in the code later in the call. The entry of a code as the first business of the call-taker is thus not in

any way "sequentially required" or inevitable. As suggested in an earlier footnote, the actual delivery of information by a caller may not start with a description or account of an incident, even though the call-taker's first turn is designed to elicit it. For example, callers may start with a plea for help and then provide their location. In these cases, although the call-taker is still faced with the task of acquiring incident-type information and then categorizing/coding it, a degree of opportunism may prevail, in that the location information, given that it is available *now*, is entered first (in the LOC field), with the call-taker then going on to pursue the issue of "what's going on." The following Central Lane call fragment, taken from a tape recording and my associated field notes, illustrates this kind of pragmatic choice. The places where the call-taker was typing information in, and what field(s) he was filling at that moment, are indicated in double parentheses.

**CL20B3/field notes**

1 CT: Nine one one, what is your emergency?
2 C: I need an ambulance at thirty five thirty Z street,
3 immediately.
**((call taker advances the cursor to the LOC field and starts typing the address into that field; he is still typing it when he begins his next turn))**
4 CT: What's the problem there?
5 C: My husband is having a respiratory failure.
6 (0.7)
7 He has to get to the hospital.
**((call-taker moves the cursor to the INC field and types the incident code, RESPDI, for "respiratory distress"))**

Nevertheless, the formatting of the CAD form is oriented toward the organizational primacy of incident code selection. Moreover, dispatch decision-making is oriented to its primacy as well; that is, the work of the next staff person, in terms of the serial ordering of work tasks, relies on it to a large degree. (In addition, it is largely through incident coding that organizational work will be exhibited, recorded for posterity, counted, assessed, summarized, and so on.) Thus, it is not surprising that during the period of my employment at Central Lane a strong preference for recording INC first was evident among call-takers. Another factor here may be the number of keystrokes that would be needed to move down to other fields, and then move back up to INC; the more "fluid" a practitioner treats the form, rather than as sequentially ordered, the more keyboard actions they will generally need to perform.

[22] A preliminary treatment of the interrelationship between typing or keyboard sounds, the emergency service organization's "contingencies of response" and information-recording procedures, and the progression of the interaction can be found in Zimmerman (1992a).

23 Requiring either exact address, street intersection, or street hundred block for the LOC entry reflects a general organizational preference for formulations of place that are "map based" or, when describing or reporting a location whose exact address is not known or that cannot be formulated with this precision, "compass-based" in reference to some precisely-known address or landmark (e.g., "two houses east of 890 West Sixteenth," "north of O'Hara School," "the west side of the highway"). In Schegloff's (1972) terms, these preferred *geographical* formulations can be contrasted to *member-relevant* ones like "next to my house," "down the road from me," "on the left side of the store," "up the hill from Joe's Bar and Grill," and "behind the old Baptist Church."

24 She does ask for his name several minutes later in the conversation, just before the call is terminated and long after the face sheet form and several "additional details" forms have been transmitted to the dispatcher. This name is then recorded in the CALLER field of the face sheet, replacing the **MALE** identifier and updating the record.

25 The call-taker begins typing an entry for the vehicle's plate even before she asks the question, exhibiting the anticipatory or "forward looking" stance described earlier in this chapter. Notice that this anticipation extends beyond simply starting to type an entry: the call-taker types the abbreviation for "unknown license plate" (UNK) in expectation that the caller will not be able to provide that information. When he does provide the plate number, she has to correct her entry.

12

# The Mundane Work of Writing and Reading Computer Programs*

Graham Button and Wes Sharrock

## 1. INTRODUCTION

Although the program of *Ethnomethodological Studies of Work*[1] has concerned itself with a variety of occupations, it is studies of the work of natural scientists[2] and mathematicians[3] that have been both more widely recognized outside of ethnomethodology and most ardently pursued within it. One reason for this is undoubtedly the appeal that the natural sciences have to a sociology often obsessed with the idea of "scientific enquiry." Another reason is that studies of natural scientists and mathematicians appear to have a close connection to questions about the nature of "knowledge" and may therefore realize ethnomethodology's interests in foundational enquiries. Thus Coulter (1989) describes ethnomethodology as an epistemic sociology and Lynch (1993) proposes it become the study of epistopics. Yet a further reason may be that part of the work of scientists and mathematicians is the production of documentary evidence of their work. On some occasions this provides ethnomethodologists with artifacts from which to recover work practices through which those were produced and on others as a docile contrast to the animated activities that produced them.

The accountable practices of the work of science and mathematics that have been explicated in ethnomethodological studies have, however, their counterparts within the work of other occupations less endowed with the grandeur and prestige of the natural sciences. In this paper we are concerned with aspects of the mundane work of *computer programming* as that is organized within both software engineering and computer science. Unsurprisingly, we find that the ordering practices that have been described within ethnomethodological studies of the work of natural science and mathematics have their counterparts within the routine work of computer programming.

Ethnomethodological studies of the work of scientists and of mathematicians have emphasized the extent to which the formal representations of scientific and mathematical practice do not fully elucidate the practices themselves as they are displayed in the actual work of a scientist or mathematician, or in the work of collaborating scientists or mathematicians. This is because the formal representations do not recognize that the accountability of the work of science or mathematics resides in the contingent, situated nature of what Livingston (1986) calls the "lived-work" of doing professional science or mathematics. An example of this "lived-work" within the work of mathematicians is that mathematical rigor is achieved in the local work of producing what to mathematicians is a "followable" line of argumentation (Livingston 1986). Within the work of natural scientists an example of "lived work" is that extended scientific enquiry is done in the "temporalization" of shop practices (Lynch 1985). Both of these examples underscore the fact that the recognizability of professional work practices resides in the details of the organization and ordering of the actions and interactions of scientists and mathematicians in the situations and occasions of their display.[4]

Ethnomethodological studies of scientists' and mathematicians' work also emphasize the extent to which the practices of this "lived work" can be recovered from the production of the "organizational objects" of that work, be they mathematical proofs on the page and blackboard or documentary evidences of scientific phenomena. Thus, both can be examined for their exhibition, or concealment, of the work of mathematicians and the work of laboratory scientists.

An interest in both the relationship between formal representations of work practice and the actualities of the contingent and situated nature of that practice, and in the production of organizational objects of work is relevant for this present paper which is concerned with details of the screen-based work of computer programmers writing computer programs, and the document-based work of computer programmers reading computer programs.[5] This is because there are formal representations of programmers' work which take the form of programming methodologies but these only partially illuminate the actual practices of programming as they are encountered in the actual course of writing a program at the computer terminal and on the computer screen. Also, computer programs are "organizational objects" that exhibit the work of programming. We are concerned with two issues here. First, how the intelligibility of a computer program is achieved for and by programmers in the situated and contingent work of structuring the program on the screen, and second, with how computer programs are used by programmers operating under the auspices of working within a professional community, as artifacts that display that structuring screen-based work.

## 2. THE MUTUAL INTELLIGIBILITY OF STRUCTURE

Methodologies for writing computer code exhibit an obsession with the structure of the written program.[6] This obsession orients to a distinction between *writing a computer program* and *writing a computer program professionally*.[7] Within computer science textbooks, writing a computer program is portrayed as a *professional activity* to be distinguished from just doing a *hack*. An identifying criteria of writing a computer program professionally is the extent to which its writing orients to the fact that individual computer programmers are working as part of a community of practitioners and are, as professionals, under obligations to take the interests of those others into account, as for example and importantly, in writing a program that other programmers can read. For example, the recommended text book for the entry-level subject in computer science at the Massachusetts Institute of Technology enshrines the concept of a community of professionals in the following: "...programs must be written for people to read, and only incidentally for machines to execute" (Abelson, Sussman and Sussman, 1985: xv).

Writing a computer program so that it is intelligible to other programmers is a concept that has led to the development of *Literate Programming* by Knuth (1992), one of the doyens of the computer science community. Like Abelson, Sussman and Sussman, Knuth argues: "Instead of imagining that our main task is to instruct a *computer* what to do, let us concentrate rather on explaining to *human beings* what we want a computer to do" (1992: 99, italics in original). In this vein, Knuth compares the programmer to the essayist, not the mathematician.

Thus Knuth, and also Abelson, Sussman and Sussman recognize and orient to a divide between what we might describe as a computer programmer and a *professional* computer programmer.[8] In this respect, learning how to write computer programs is to not so much learning how to write a program that will, in engineering terms, process information in optimal and efficient ways, but to learn to write them so that the way in which information is to be processed and the reasons for processing it in that way can be easily seen from reading the program. In other words, learning to write a computer program is learning to write it in such a way that it is intelligible to a community of practitioners.

There is, thus, within the computer science community a divide between "the hacker" and "the professional." By these terms "hacker" and "professional" we are not referring to actual individuals but to constructs of programming constituted in and by the computer science community. The constructs of "hacker" and "professional" are used within the community of computer programmers to identify a way of approaching writing a computer program. Consequently when someone is referred to as a "hacker" it is not just his or her program that is in question but also how he/she has written out the organization of the program.[9] Thus to say that a program has been "hacked" is in part to say that it has not been written out in ways that anyone but its composer could relatively easily, if at all, understand.[10]

In the quotations above, Abelson et al., and also Knuth, offer the community a way of distinguishing a hacked program from a professionally written program. A hacked program may run but it may not be intelligible to other programmers. The "hacker" will write a program that will process information, the "professional" will, *in addition*, write a program that can be understood by other professionals. It is the intelligibility to others of a program that is at issue, not the technical "quality" of the code. This means that there is a distinction between good quality code and a good program, for although a programmer may write "good code" in the sense of code that means that the machine can execute its processing with optimal efficiency, he/she may not write a "good program" because it cannot be understood by other programmers.

This issue can be examined with reference to a particular program written by Nicolas Graube.[11] Graube's program, although recognizable within the community of computer scientists as a rare feat of programming skill, can nevertheless be evaluated within that community in two different ways, according to different sets of criteria. According to one set of criteria it is found within the computer science community to be an example of "good code" whilst according to another set, though still recognizable as a highly skillful feat, it is judged, even by its own author, to be a "bad program." The difference between the sets of criteria resolves around the intelligibility of the program. In order to find it to be good code computer scientists point to its "efficiency" in solving a problem. These criteria take on their meaning in their particular references to code, thus in this instance "efficient" refers to the fact that the program develops a solution to a processing problem in its most essential form. This makes the program "small," "compact" and "concise" which means that the programmer has achieved a most economical deployment of information processing resources. Thus to find that it is good code professionals point to its *intellectual qualities.* It is a virtuoso performance that displays to other professionals the considerable reasoning power of its writer.

However, on other criteria it is a "bad program." In order to substantiate this description computer scientists point out how hard it is for others to understand. That is, readers of the program, no matter how expert, will find it very difficult to follow because, for example, the assumptions that it embodies are not available in and from the program itself. The program is hard -- if not, for all practical purposes, impossible -- to understand because the rationale for it having been written as it has cannot be recovered from its writing. Above all, the "structure" of the code is concealed from readers by the way in which the program has been written and presented.

Thus professional computer scientists recognize a generic problem in writing computer programs which is the practical limitations of esoteric code. On the one hand, no matter the intellectual craftsmanship and skill in a program, and on the other, no matter that a "hack" works, it is the intelligibility of the program for other professionals that is the issue. In this respect, the "virtuoso performance" and the "dirty hack" are of a piece: they are esoteric code. The code makes the machine run but the structure of the program cannot be found in the program itself, but only in the "programmer's head." No matter how clever the code might be in solving a processing problem, its esoteric nature is a limitation upon the practical use of the program within the community of computer programmers, for if it cannot be understood it cannot be used or maintained or in other ways worked on by other programmers. A computer program thus has a community and practical utility and a professional program is built under these utilitarian auspices.

Part of the attempted professionalization of programming has been to devise methods for building into a program the intelligibility of its operation. These are methods for taking the "how" of the program from out of the head of the programmer and putting it into the program itself. Thus computer science students are not just taught computer languages but how to write programs in those languages that satisfy the practical and community constraint of utility. Part of this is to visually organize the code so as to make explicit the way in which the program will process information and display the reasons for processing information in a particular way. Thus it is not just the formulation of the operationally effective lines of code that contributes to the production of the acceptable program, but also and most importantly, the way the layout and format of the sequential lines of code exhibit the structure of the program. It was considered -- in some circles at least -- a revolution in programming methodology to orient toward the delivery of "structured code."

It is the professionalization of programming which accounts for the obsession with the structure of a program in books and courses in computer science. It is the structure of the code that is used as a resource for understanding how the program works. Thus, getting the rationale and organization of the program out of the programmer's head and into the text of the program itself involves methods for writing out the code in such ways that the structure of the program is transparent. Students are taught to structure their code and to structure it in such a way that the structure can readily be followed by a reader. Writing intelligible code that has practical and community utility then involves practices that are designed to make the structure of the code visible. In this respect the problem of writing computer code is not to produce a seamless sequence of lines of code. If computer code were seamless its internal structure would be obscured. Writing computer code, professionally, is to produce a transcription in which the sequence of lines is segmented and the seams between the different segments made manifest.

In order to transfer the rationale and organization of a program from out of the programmer's head and into the written program, computer scientists have developed a number of techniques of formal representation for use in programming work. These take the form of methodologies for writing computer programs. That is, they take programming practices and embed them within a framework for their standardized re-enactment.

These methodologies apply at many levels. For example, within the domain of software engineering, methodologies have been introduced to structure the overall development and design of software. These methodologies provide for a structured approach to program development by providing a sequentially organized model of development. One of the most influential and widespread has been the Yourdon Structured Method.[12] The principle behind this methodology and similar ones is to abstract a description of a system from its implementation. This involves various stages of modeling. Thus under Yourdon methodology, the developer first models the feasibility of a system which involves an analysis of any current system and the environment in which it is used. This phase is followed by essential modeling, which is to model how the system should be organized in terms of the architecture of its data flow. The third phase is implementation modeling which is the integration of customer requirements with the essential model. Thus the methodology provides for a structured -- in the sense of "staged" -- approach to the whole of the software system development cycle; it provides a framework for a standardized sequencing of phases and for a standardized integration between those different phases. Thus developing a system is supposed to be done in the same way whatever the system.[13]

This methodology has consequences for the way in which code is written so as to display its structure. Before actual code writing begins, various models should be produced that the code will then embody. Thus before coding begins a graphical representation of aspects of the system, such as the flow of data, will be constructed. The code should thus be written so as to embody the structure of the graphical representation. The graphical representation and the lines of code can then be read in conjunction to find the structure of the program.

Another methodological practice not just associated with Yourdon methodology is to "comment the code," which is to add textual comments to the code that provide a context for a particular coding instruction. Commenting the code is a way of building into the code an explication of its organization. Thus in the following extract the italicized text is not a processing instruction to the computer; it is *a comment* that furnishes readers with a resource for understanding particular processing decisions. If these comments are removed it will make absolutely no difference to the efficient running of the code, but all the difference to the accessible understanding of the code.

```
(defun check-symmetry-requirements (observer source & aux observers-source)
;; Check symmetry requirements of source. If requirements are met,
;; return nil. If observer isn't willing to give enough information,
;; return an explanatory string.
(if (and (source-symmetry source)
         (eq (source-state source))
```

The fact that computer scientists and software engineers have had to develop practices such as documenting the code displays a decisive feature of a computer program as a document that distinguishes it from some other sorts of documents and which distinguishes the work of producing a computer program on the screen from the work of producing, for example, a mathematical proof on the white or blackboard. That is, a computer program as a document of the work of computer programmers stands in an interesting contrast to other documents of the work of those who have constructed them. Livingston describes how the activities through which mathematical proofs are produced cannot be found in the proofs themselves. Further, developing Livingston's observation, Suchman suggests in her examination of the work of cognitive science that "...the inscriptions on a white-board -- lists, sketches, lines of code, lines of text and the like -- are produced through activities that are not themselves reconstructable from these 'docile records' (Garfinkel and Burns 1979)" (Suchman 1990: 314). In contrast, computer programmers (operating under the auspices of the professional community) attempt to make computer programs animated documents that are designed to read so that the activities through which they were produced can be resconstructed. Thus, making the structure of a computer program visible orients to the fact that a computer program is professionally written for a community of practitioners and accounts for the development of community methods and practices. These are formalized methods and formalized practices and result in formal homilies about and formal criteria for judging computer code. Consequently, for example, students are advised to document their code and admonished for insufficient documentation. As far as the text-books are concerned, if a computer programmer follows the formal methods and practices and attends to the formalized homilies in the production of computer code, then it is possible sufficiently to animate the document and organize the visibility of the structure of the code. Thus in formal representations of computer programming an attempt is made to organize a computer program as a document of the work of programming that reveals, rather than conceals, the practices through which it was produced.

## 3. STRUCTURE IN PRACTICE

In the actual practices of writing and reading computer programs, computer programmers can indeed be observed to orient to the visibility of the structure of a program. However, observations of the "lived work" of computer programmers writing programs at the computer terminal and on the computer screen and the "lived work" of computer programmers reading and interpreting programs written by others, reveals a domain of practices utilized by and known to programmers through which the structure of the code is attended to and through which a program is produced as an animated document, but which do not appear in the manuals for and courses on professional programming nor in the formal representations of programming. Further, these practices cannot always be found in the completed program. This means that despite the fact that writing computer programs under the auspices of writing professionally requires that programmers make the practices through which the program was produced an explicit feature of the program, in the actual situated course of the screen-based work of writing a program, an order of work practices through which the program is produced is concealed. In this respect, computer programs, even those written under the strictures of writing programs professionally, may in practice, resemble the documents produced by scientists and the proofs produced by mathematicians: they are organizational objects that can conceal aspects of the work through which they were produced. Thus, in the situated course of the writing of a computer program, the situated screen-based work practices of writing programs are crafted and folded into the program and in that process may be lost to view.

Computer programmers are thus faced with a paradox. On the one hand the formal methodologies and practices require that the structure of a program is made visible. Yet, on the other, the screen-based practices of writing programs are crafted into the code and are thus invisible in the finished program. Consequently, the attempt by computer scientists as a professional community to differentiate a computer program as a document of the work of programming from other documents by explicitly attending, in their formal methods and formal practices, to making the practices of the production of the program a visible feature of the program is only partial. What is missing from the completed document and what is not attended to in the formal representations of programming is what we could call the *enabling screen-based practices of code writing.*

These enabling screen-based practices are everyday practices of programming, and although programmers would find little news in having these shown to them, they are not found in the professional instructions for programming. Yet they are practices that programmers use to attend to the very issue of the visibility of the structure of a program that the professional literature and the methods exhort. Without these practices, programmers would be unable to write professional programs, yet they do not figure in the professional literature on how to write professional programs. They are practices known to and used by programmers. Indeed they are practices that every programmer has to know and is reliant upon in order to write programs, but they are practices that are conjured out of existence in the professional literature. These enabling practices are the *vulgar competencies*[14] of programming and they interplay with the professional competencies as portrayed in the professional literature. This interplay takes the form of trading in the vulgar competencies of programming in the structuring of a program. However, whilst these are vulgar competencies of programming they are not exclusive to programming. They are vulgar competencies that are recognizable to writers and readers of text as well as computer programs. We will now turn to some of these practices.

## i) Keeping the unfolding structure in view

### a) The Simplest Possible Case

In order to draw out these competencies it is possible to notice some features about the following lines of code. It is some code that is in the process of being written and is a simple filter.[15]

Fragment 1a

```
1    (defun filter (sequence filter)
2          ;; sequence is a flat filter
3          ;; filter is a flat list with * (match any)
4          (if     (and (null sequence)
5                       (null filter))              ; End of filter and sequence
6                  ;                                : This is a match.
7                  (if (eq '* (car filter))
8                      ;; This must deal with the filter
9                      ;; The first car of the filter is not a * this must be
10                     ;; true character :
11                     (if  (eq (car filter) (car sequence))
12                     :
13                         nil ) ) ) )
```

Compare the above code with the code further into its development.

Fragment 1b

```
1    (defun filter (sequence filter)
2          ;; sequence is a flat filter
3          ;; filter is a flat list with * (match any)
4          (if     (and (null sequence)
5                       (null filter))              ; End of filter and sequence
6                  ;                                : This is a match.
7                  (if (eq '* (car filter))
8                     ;; This must deal with the filter
9                     ;; We have to look for the end of the filter
10                    ;; this will give us a upper limit for the filter
11                    ;; ( i.e. :((upper limit (find end - star filter))))
12                 (if      ( null upper limit
13                            ;; typical this must be (...*) thus anything
14                            ;; match
15                            :
16                            ;; otherwise the upper limit exists
17                            (if  (eq upper limit (car sequence))
18                            ;; match the first char continue
19                                (filter (cde sequence
20                 ;; The first car of the filter is not a * this must be
21                 ;; true character :
22                      (if   (eq (car filter) (car sequence))
23                       :
24                          nil ) ) ) )
```

Writing this filter is a routine matter for the programmer who has written many of them over the course of his career. However, although routine and although, in this case the filter is quite crude, it does, nevertheless require that the design is *worked out* for *this* occasion. Also, the programmer is not using, as he certainly would for some programming work, notes and sketches that he would have previously made as he prepared for his code writing and in order to think through the problems and issues involved. In this case the programmer is working the code out from scratch on the screen as he goes along. We have chosen to take this example for precisely this reason, because it highlights the screen-based activities of the programmer's work. That is, the code is being produced from out of the constitutive practices of his screen-based work.

In order to draw out some of these practices, we can first notice that the last line of the code in Fragment 1b is the last line in Fragment 1a and that working on from the point encountered in 1a has involved filling in lines of code (lines 8-19 in 1b). In 1a the programmer had completed "the simplest possible case" of the filter and in 1b the programmer had started to fill in other cases. As the "lived work" of writing code on the screen, writing code does not consist of writing the complete code straight off. Rather, the work of working out the unfolding structure of the code on the screen involves successively building up the code. A programmer will use what he/she has just written on the screen as a resource for writing more.[16] What comes next is, in part, the product of what has just been written, and programmers use a number of mundane and ordinary practices to relate what comes next to what went before. That is, they use a number of mundane devices to order the code. The simplest possible case is, in this instance, one of these devices that is used to order the writing of the code. A question that we may ask, then, is what problem of ordering is the use of this device a solution to?

We have been talking about the way in which the writing of code can be oriented to the intelligible display of its structure for a putative reader, but the perspicuous exhibition of the structure is something that may also be of practical value to the one who is writing the code. In working out a long and complex sequence of lines of code the writer will be concerned to keep track of the structure he/she is developing, to keep both the order of the code actually written out and its projected order "in mind."

If programmers lose sight of that structure they lose sight of where they are in the process of writing, they lose sight of how what they are now writing relates to the program as a whole and to what they have just written. Losing sight of the structure of the code means that they are unable to continue to write intelligible code. Writing out the simplest possible case first is thus a device that is used to keep track of the unfolding structure of the code. It does so by organizing a visual resource that the programmer can refer to in subsequent elaborations of the code, subsequent writing that builds up the code. Thus in writing the first sequence of code above (Fragment 1a), the programmer wrote out a draft of the simplest possible case which he could then use as a basis for developing more complicated cases, which he then proceeded to do by inserting new lines into the original template. Though we cannot tell the difference between the two operations, the programmer's elaboration on the "simplest case" template involved both refining, correcting and smoothing that simplest case and also elaborating it into a structure representing more complex cases.[17]

In writing the simplest possible case first, and then using that as a resource to elaborate the code, the programmer was using a technique familiar to other fields of work. For example, in wood-turning the turner will begin to fashion a bowl by first shaping the outline of the structure. Thus rather than attempting to craft the details of the bowl from the outset such as the form of the base, or the precise turn of the lip, the turner will initially fashion a shape that is then used to guide the shape of the finished article. The work of shaping the finished article involves transforming the first shape, through finer and finer cuts and more and more precise detailing, into the final object. However, the original shape still lurks within the bowl, and although worked on, the practiced eye can still find it.

Writing the simplest possible case of the filter first, in part resembles this process. As described in note 17, writing the simplest possible case is established procedure, and it is later used by readers of a program as a resource that they may look for as part of their practices for making sense of the code. The practice we have been describing is the use made of writing the simplest possible case, *first*, as a screen-base resource for keeping the structure of the code in view as it is being written. Writing the simplest possible case first, thus trades in the established practice of writing the simplest possible case. Like the wood-turner, the programmer can use the simplest possible case as a first shape from out of which to craft the final artifact. The simplest possible case, although it has been worked on, still lurks, however, within the elaborated structure that it has, in part, provided for. In the process of the evolution of the code it is folded into the code, to be, however, possibly found later by readers of programs in order to make sense of the program.

Writing the simplest possible case first is, though, but one screen-based practice that programmers use in building code.[18] It is possible to find within code that is in the process of being written numerous devices that are serving different functions with respect to the crafting of the code. The simplest possible case is a practice that makes the structure of the code visible to the programmer in the course of his/her screen-based work. In a manner of speaking it pegs out the ground. Other screen-based practices can act as shuttering which holds the structure of the code together until it has hardened and are then removed or crafted into the structure.

## b) Temporarily Naming Variables

An example of this order of practice is temporarily *naming variables*. The programming language LISP utilizes, amongst other components, the concepts of "function" and "variable." In the example of the filter program which filters lists of numbers this function would have to be *defined*. So a simple filter program written in LISP with this function would start off:

```
(defun filter (list-of-numbers)
```

A simple example defining a function and a variable may help to clarify matters. In Chapter One of her introduction to LISP programming, Deborah Tatar (1987) provides an example of a program that will model a gum-ball dispensing machine. A way of starting to write the program would be to define a function:

```
(defun gum-machine (supply-of-gum)
```

A function is a state of art term in LISP and can be understood as a processing routine. Thus, in building a representation of a gum-ball machine, one of the routines, or functions, will be "supply-gum." Another term of art in LISP is "variable." For example, there may be different gum-ball machines: one in the barber's shop and one in the grocery shop. It is a requirement of LISP that functions and variables are defined. Thus the above would define the function gum machine and the following defines the two variables of barber's shop machine and grocery store machine:

```
(defvar *barber-shop-machine*
     (gum-machine (generate-gum-supply 4)))
(defvar *grocery-store-machine*
     (gum-machine (generate-gum-supply 6)))
```

Defining a function or variable in LISP creates a value that the LISP programming language can deal with. Obviously, LISP does not "know" what a gum-ball machine is, nor what a barber's shop or grocery shop is. LISP works on lists of functions and variables by "evaluating" them. Then in defining these variables by giving them different values, for example "the grocery shop" and "the barber shop" machines, the programmer can write instructions that incorporate them.

We can further illustrate this by considering the gum that goes into the machine. The gum can be made to vary according to color. Thus, if the programmer wishes to have the gum-ball model randomly dispense a brown or a blue or a orange or a purple or a green or a yellow or a speckled gum, it will be necessary to define the variable gum colors:

```
(defvar *gum-colors* (brown blue orange purple
 green yellow speckled))
```

Consequently LISP will be able to evaluate gum-colors because gum-colors has been identified as brown, blue, orange, purple, green, yellow, speckled. However, again, LISP does not "know" what, for example, "brown" means. LISP "knows" it is a value that has been given to a variable and LISP can consequently work with it. It returns a value but what that value is has to be defined by the programmer.

Thus for a program written in LISP to run it does not really matter what name has been give to the variable or to the function. The name "gum-colors" is not relevant to the evaluative processes of LISP. The defined variable could have been given any name, for example: "chewing-gum-colors," or "tooth-rot-colors," or "foo," or "blardy-blar," or "temp-1." The important issue is that at a certain juncture a variable will have to be defined and given some sort of a name so that it has a value that can be called.

However, whilst the name that is given to a variable or to a function is not important for LISP processing it can be important for other reasons having to do with *making the code intelligible to others*. That is, one way in which the mutual intelligibility of code is achieved is through a naming convention that it is possible to observe programmers using and which furnishes the guideline: *make the name relevant to the process.* Thus, naming is done according to a *relevancy rule.* Knowing that the relevancy rule operates in writing computer programs, then, the reader of a program can interrogate the name of a function or a variable on the assumption that it has been produced according to the relevancy rule in order to understand the process. Thus a resource that a reader of the gum-ball program will use in trying to understand the program is the name given to the function and the variable; operating upon the assumption that the names have been selected according to the relevancy rule, a reader will attempt to find that the program has something to do with gum-ball machines.[19] Shorn of that resource the intelligibility of the program will be altogether more problematic. Thus explicitly acknowledging the provisional status of a name by using names such as "Temp-1" or "Blardy-blar" may conceal rather than reveal the structure of the code, for "Temp-1 or "blardy-blar" have no detectable reference to the function or the variable that may be part of the process.

However, in the course of writing a program, programmers face a dilemma with respect to the relevancy rule for naming. A programmer will reach a place in the unfolding code where it is necessary to define a variable or a function and thus give the variable or the function a name. Until the variable is named it is not possible to call it. Under the conditions of the relevancy rule the programmer will select a name relevant to the process of the function or the function that the variable is involved with within the overall structure of the code. However, in as much as the name is selected by reference to the process it performs within the overall structure of the code, but given that the structure is not itself at any moment of writing a finished object, it is not always possible to be sure just how the variable needs to be defined and just what name would be a fully suitable one to clearly indicate its meaning within the overall structure of the program.

A solution to this problem resides in assigning a *temporary name* to the variable or the function by calling it something like Temp-1 or blardy-blar. The temporary name acts as a place holder in the unfolding organization of the code. It can hold the structure in place as it is forming and it can be returned to later and crafted into the structure in such a way as to explicate that structure by its final naming. Thus temp-1 may be re-named in the final structuring of the programming in such a manner that the name (as we turn to describing in more detail below) provides a semantic clue as to its meaning.[20] The *temporary name* is thus another screen-based practice that programmers can use in their work of keeping the unfolding structure of the code in view, for the occurrences of the name within the written program can be picked out easily and the recurrence of the same name and their inter-linkage with different names enables a reader to trace the way segments of code might be related to the structure of operations which the code is designed to engender. Like the simplest possible case it acts as a visual screen-based resource to keep the unfolding structure of the code in mind, and like the simplest possible case it cannot be found in the finished program.

## ii) Naming

Temporarily naming variables is a screen-based practice that keeps the unfolding structure of the code in view as it is being elaborated. But naming functions and variables is, in itself, a domain of programming activity that is oriented to providing semantic clues about the structure of a program. Thus like T. S. Eliot's naming of cats, naming variables and functions for a program is a serious business, and we will now address it in more depth. As we have noted above, a function or a variable is named according to a process-relevance convention where the name is selected for its readily recognizable relevance to the process of the function or the process that the variable is involved in. However, writers of programs are not just concerned with finding a name that describes the process, but one that *specifies* the process within the logic of the program structure. The reason for this is that for any one process there are often a variety of names that might relevantly describe the process. For example, "fault indicator" may seemingly be as relevant as "problem indicator" for describing a process that lights up a warning light on the control panel of a photo-copier. However, different warning lights may indicate different non-running states that a machine may be in and calling them all fault indicators or problem indicators will just confuse the different faults. Thus a photo-copier may stop working for a variety of reasons: it may be out of paper, there may be a paper jam, or one of its drive motors may have burnt out. Also there may be some state that should be remedied but will not immediately stop it working, such as being low on toner. However, is being out of paper the same as having a burnt-out drive motor? For some purposes it is because it stops the running of the machine. Yet, for other purposes it is not because running out of paper is a routine expected occurrence that can be remedied by the operator, whereas a burnt out drive motor is not expected and will require an engineer. Is running out of paper best described as fault or a problem, or neither? Is the burnt out motor or the low toner best described as a fault or a problem?

Programmers are then faced with a semantic problem which is one of analyzing differences of meaning between words or one of disambiguating the meaning of words. Thus they may distinguish operating faults from breakdowns. The fault system may be constructed to relay detected routine faults for which there are specified courses of remedial action to be taken by an operator. Thus the fault system may be the name that is assigned to a system that monitors paper jams, the state of paper trays and toners, feed problems; initiates recovery procedures; clears stacked instructions and the like. Within the parameters of the program a burnt out motor may not be classified as a fault but as a breakdown and a different system may exist to cover such contingencies. In the naming of the system and the processes within a system, software engineers *assemble domains of meaning*. In this respect they may be observed to engage in *practical componential analysis* by constructing what is, amongst other things, a taxonomy of a semantic domain, for their practical and situated purposes.

An example of componential analysis is Tyler's (1969) example of a taxonomy for furniture which is made up of components that go together "as furniture" such as chairs, sofas, desks, tables, but can be distinguished from one another. These components in turn are made up of components that share the feature of being, for example, tables but which are distinguished from each other by being end tables and dining tables. Thus a taxonomy of a semantic domain in our culture may be constructed and this is often represented as a tree diagram thus:

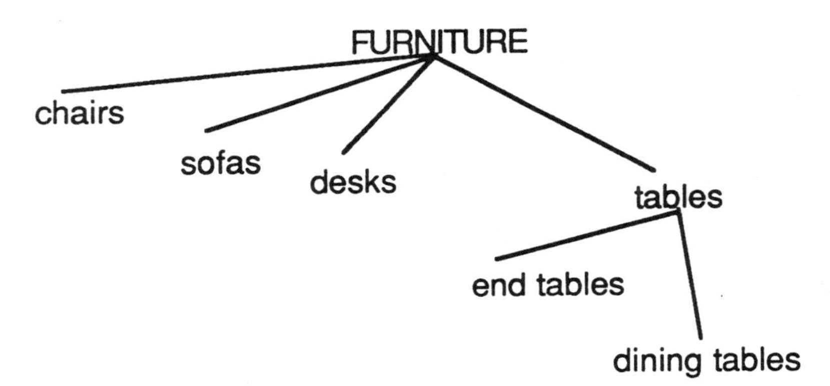


Branching diagram (Tyler, 1969:8)

In software development one software engineer or group of engineers, may deal with one "semantic domain." Thus a software engineer may have responsibility for developing the code that signals a state of non-running to the operator and issues instructions on what to do. Prior to writing the code a model of the fault process will be produced and the processes named. The named processes relate to one another within the semantic domain of faults. Faults will thus be defined in relationship to the named processes that make them up. Different processes can be found to be related to one another in terms of shared components. Thus like the professional componential analyst the programmer or software developer acting as a practical componential analyst is involved in the attempted assembly of a semantic domain.[21]

Whilst a writer of programs may be a practical componential analyst, the reader of programs might be described as engaged in *practical hermeneutics*. That is, readers of programs treat programs as documents or texts, the meanings of which are unclear or fragmentary. The structure of a computer program is viewed as being "a web of meaning" or "a field of meaning" which the reader of a program has to uncover and reveal. However, the text books on computer programming do not furnish programmers with objective procedures and methods for determining the meaning of the document. Thus the reader of a program as a practical hermeneutician has to interpret the program as a historically located or historically contexted document. Like early hermeneutics the context is a culture, the culture of professional programming constituted amongst other things in a community of practices for writing the program. Thus the reader of a program has to reveal the meaning of the program by placing it within the history of the screen-based writing practices through which it was constituted. Without objective methods to do this the readers of programs rely upon their vulgar competencies and practices of document or text reading.

We can illustrate this by reference to the way in which readers of programs can use names that are used in and for a program in order to reveal the meaning of the program. The names are used by readers of a program in order to build a sense of the operation of the program. In conjunction with the name given to the program readers will use the names of functions to move through a program.

In LISP an index of functions can be created, as in the following:[22]

```
{Newton: EuroPARC:RX} <Borning> AWARNESS-SERVICE: 2  22-Aug90 16:32:13
-----Listed on 7 -Nov-90 17 23 05 ---

FUNCTION INDEX

add-observer port           4   find-free-area              8   setup-animation            16
add-port                    4   freemenu-source-updater     8   shell-command              17
all-available-sources       4   grab-image                  9   shot-frame                 17
animate                     4   image-file                  9   symbolconc                 17
auto-reshape                5   kill-observer-port          9   turn-off-feed-back         17
awarness-block              5   kill-port                  10   turn-off-feedback          17
awarness-filepath           6   logfile                    10   turn-on-names              18
awarness-filepath-unix      6   make-observer-window       10   turn-on-video-feedback     18
awarness-service-warn      15   make-source-window         11   update-feedback-window     19
check-sym-requirements      6   maybe-get-new-image        12   update-observer            19
clear-image                 6   maybe-grab-image           13   update-port                19
concatenate-file-paths      6   maybe-handle-mouse         13   update-port-positions      20
create-feedback-process     6   maybe-read-source-file     14   update-source              20
create-observer-process     7   observer-mouse-handler     14   update-view                21
display-image               7   observer-updater           15   watcher-file-paths         21
empty-log-files             8   read-image                 16   window-writable            21
feedback-mouse-handler      8   restore-images             16   write-source-file          22
```

In order to attempt to understand the program, a reader can use the index guide to move around within the program. However, a program is not like a novel but more like a guide to a city. In the novel it typically matters where a reader begins and the chapters are usually to be read sequentially. By way of contrast, with the city guide it is often the case that one section can be read independently of other sections. Having said this, it may, however, be easier to develop a working sense of the layout of the city by starting with a section that deals with a strategic point such as the center, rather than just picking a section at random. Following this principle it might then be possible to explore the city by moving out from the center.

A computer program, at least one written in LISP, is similar to the city guide. It does not necessarily help a reader develop an understanding of the structure of the program to read it as a sequentially organized document. Rather, it is usually better to understand the operation of each of its functions and the points at which those functions are specified may be distributed throughout the program. In this respect it may not matter which function a reader starts with. However, like reading a city guide, it may be best to start with one rather than another.

One order of function that may be examined first is what is described as a *higher level function*. In writing a program a programmer will often break down a function into a number of constitutive processes. The constitutive processes are described as lower level functions and the function they constitute as a higher level function. Should one of the constitutive process itself be broken down into parts, then the program would have another and even lower level of functionality. A typical example that first year structured programming students are given is to devise a program to check a bank account balance. Rather than rushing headlong into writing code they are exhorted to develop an understanding of what is involved by breaking the operation into a number of processes. This makes it simpler to both develop the program and for a reader to understand the program. Thus checking the balance of a bank account may be organized into a number of processing steps such as checking the privileges or credentials of the person requesting the balance, validating the account number, and retrieving a data base. Each of those functions would be defined, and thus in enacting the function of "check balance," other lower level functions would be called on.

In this respect a programmer who is attempting to understand a program by attempting to understand how the different parts of the program fit together may start off by examining one of the higher level functions in a program. By examining that function and seeing how it calls other functions it may be possible to begin to assemble a picture of how the parts of a program hang together, and thus understand the structure of the program. The question remains, however, as to how programmers select which is the appropriate function to begin with. One resource that they use is the name that is given to a function. Thus knowing the name of the program "Awareness-Service" it is possible to find that the function index contains a number of functions that have "observer" in their name. A place to start in the program is thus one of the functions that through the reference to "observer" seems to have something to *do* with awareness. However, as can be seen from examining the index above there are a number of functions with "observer" in their names. A reader may then face the problem of which one to pick. The function that is listed in the index as appearing on page 10 of the program "make-observer-window," however, suggests that it will put a window on the screen through which observation (awareness) may take place. Consequently "make-observer-window" may be the highest level of functionality. It is then possible to see which other functions it calls and thus begin to untangle the logic of the program.[23]

However, whilst these are practices of reading a computer program they are reading practices that are very familiar to readers of other sorts of documents. For example, not all text books are read straight off from beginning to end. Readers will often select parts of a book to read and leave other parts, or may want to become familiar with the make up of the book before embarking upon it, or want to read some parts of it before other parts even if that does not match the ordering of the chapters. To accomplish these sorts of activities, readers of text books will use various combinations of contents, chapter titles, and indexes to acquaint themselves with a book.

Thus although the text-books on computer programming may emphasize the utilization of formal devices such as documenting the code in order to make the structure of the code intelligible to readers, the professional programmer relies upon unstated yet crucial enabling vulgar competencies of document reading. Not only do readers of programs make use of these competencies in familiarizing themselves with the structure of code, but writers of programs orient to the fact that these competencies will be brought to bear upon a program by their readers. They display that orientation in the selection of the names they give to functions and variables. Writers and readers of programs thus depend upon the presumed relevances of the professional community in the intelligible production of computer programs. The writer of programs utilizes the relevancy rule in the naming conventions orienting to the fact that a reader of programs will work on the assumption that it has been used, and a reader of programs will utilize the relevancy rule on the assumption that it has informed the naming conventions in the writing of the program. The designers of languages also orient to these practices as community practices, for designed into the print function of some LISP programs is the facility to produce an alphabetical list of function names.

That is, the printer program for LISP automatically prints off an index of functions when a program is printed.

These vulgar practices of document reading are thus used as a swarm of contextual relevances within which writing code takes place and through which the crafting of the intelligible structure of code is in part achieved. In turn the relevancy of these competencies for making sense of the document is the discovery of readers, for in bringing them to bear upon the document, readers of code find that the document becomes tractable in their presence. This is the instanciation of a general method of sense assembly that has been described for other activities and interactions, that of the prospective-retrospective assembly of sense.[24] For computer programs this method organizes the production of intelligible code through the projection that these enabling vulgar competencies of document reading will be used to make sense of the code, so the code is written in such a way that it is readily amenable to their application, and in their application it does turn out that the intelligibility of the code unfolds, in part, upon their application. These enabling vulgar competencies are cultural competencies and provide the cultural and historical context for the document. In this respect readers of computer code display themselves to be adept at practical hermeneutics.

## iii) Visual Representation

In the following part of a program which has been written in C rather than in LISP, there is a procedure which has a definite beginning and a definite end. The beginning is marked by the left hand bracket "{" and the end by right hand bracket "}". The body of the procedure lies between.

```
/* * Create object 'files_menu' in the specified instance.
*/Xv_opaque graphical_files_menu_create (ip, owner) caddr_t *ip; Xv_opaque owner;
{ Xv_opaque obj ; obj = Xv_create 9XV_NULL, MENU_COMMAND_MENU,
XV_ITEM, XV_KEY_DATA, INSTANCE, ip, MENU ITEM, XV KEY DATA
INSTANCE, ip, MENU_STRING,"Load", NULL, MENU_ITEM, XV_KEY DATA,
INSTANCE, ip, MENU_STRING, "Save", NULL, MENU_ITEM, XV KEY_DATA,
INSTANCE, ip, MENU_STRING, "New", NULL, MENU DEFAULT, 1, NULL);
return obj ; } / * * Intitialize an instance of object 'base_wind'.
```

Contrast the above code with the following code:

```
/*
     * Create object 'files_menu' in the specified instance.
                                                        */
Xv_opaque    graphical_files_menu_create      (ip, owner)
caddr_t *ip;
Xv_opaque              owner;
{
             Xv_opaaque         obj ;
             obj = Xv_create (XV_NULL, MENU_COMMAND_MENU,
                          _XV_ITEM, XV_KEY_DATA, INSTANCE, ip,
                          MENU _ITEM,
                          XV KEY DATA        INSTANCE, ip,
                          MENU_STRING,       "Load",
```

```
                    NULL,
                    MENU_ITEM,
                    XV_KEY DATA,        INSTANCE, ip,
                    MENU_STRING,        "Save",
                    NULL,
                    MENU_ITEM,
                    XV KEY_DATA,        INSTANCE, ip,
                    MENU_STRING,        "New",
                    NULL,
                    MENU DEFAULT, 1,
                    NULL);
          return obj ;
}
/ *
    * Intitialize an instance of object 'base_wind'.
                                                   */
```

Although the visual appearance of the code is markedly different, it will nevertheless run just as efficiently as the previous piece of code. Indeed, although the visual organization of the code differs, the code is indistinguishable "to the computer." Both pieces will probably be processed by the computer in exactly the same way. It is the brackets, "{" and "}", that determine how the computer will process the code. Within C, "{" and "}", are instructions to the computer. Thus as far as processing instructions are concerned the two examples are exactly the same and will probably result in exactly the same computational processing operations.

However, although they have the same computational organization, their visual organization is markedly different. The visual organization of the second piece has been designed to reflect the computational organization and to make *that* organization accountable. Computer programmers use visual *organization as an account of the computational organization of the program.* Through the visual representation of the computational organization, programmers are able to make the computational organization, or some aspects of the organization of the program available for seeing.

In order to elaborate upon this we can give a simple example in LISP. In LISP, code is built up through a series of lists to be evaluated. In a LISP program these lists are in parentheses. Thus typing a list structure, putting objects within parentheses, is an instruction to the LISP program to evaluate the expression. For example, ( + 4 4) is an instruction to evaluate that expression by adding 4 to 4 and LISP will respond to that command and will "return" the value 8. Thus on the screen, a programmer will type (+ 4 4) and underneath it LISP will type up 8. LISP has evaluated 4 + 4 and accordingly returns the value 8 to the programmer:

```
(+ 4 4)
8
```

It is possible to write very complicated procedures in LISP because LISP allows programmers to nest expressions within one another. Thus writing ( + (+ 4 4) ( - 12 2) ) in LISP will result in the returned value of 18. The reason for this is that ( + (+ 4 4) ( - 12 2) ) is an instruction to LISP to add 4 and 4 together, "(+ 4 4)" subtract 2 from 12, "( - 12 2)" and then combine the values, (+ ), thus combining 8 and 10.

The following is a more complicated example taken from Tatar's (1987) introduction:

```
(* (/ (+ 64 11149) (- 466 4.58 )) (/ 7 9) (+ 10039 234900
(sqet 4)))
```

In LISP this is an instruction to add 64 and 11149, subtract 4.58 from 466, divide the value of adding 64 and 11149 by the value of subtracting 4.58 from 466. Then divide 7 by 9. Then add 10039 to 234900 to the square root of 4. Then multiply the three values obtained by each other. It is the evaluative process that constitutes the structure of this code. That is, the code is organized as a series of evaluative processes or *arguments*.

In order to represent the structure of the evaluative process, the code can be *formatted*. Thus, in practice, the code would not be written as above. It will, rather, be formatted around the evaluative processes:

```
(*  (/       ( + 64 11149)
             (- 466 4.58))
    (/ 7 9)
    (+ 10039 2349
                (sqrt 4)))
```

The visual organization of the code on the screen and on paper is an account of the computational organization in as much as it is designed to coincide with that organization. That is, the visual organization of the code is organized around the computational arguments or processes of the code. Writing the code using a formatting convention is done in order to *bring out or extract* the structure of the code from out of the obscurities of its writings. Formatting is thus a practical device for making the structure of the code visible, a device for "extracting the animal from its foliage" (Baccus, 1986).

The visual arrangement of the code is a varying collage of *metaphorical representations* and *literal depictions* of the structure of the code. This is because although the evaluative process is represented sequentially, the evaluative process itself does not necessarily coincide with this sequential organization. Thus on one occasion, depending upon the electrical state of the machine, 64 may be added to 11149 before 4.58 is subtracted from 466, and on other occasions this may be reversed. Either way it does not affect the evaluative outcome; the selection of which argument to evaluate first may only optimize the performance of the machine. Thus the sequential descriptions "then" of the evaluative process above, and the sequentially ordered visual organization of the code is in part a metaphorical gloss of the computational operation. However, on other occasions it will be a literal depiction of the process, for there will be occasions when one evaluative process must precede another. Thus the visual representation of the structure of the code is constituted both metaphorically and literally.

The visual organization of a computer program in this way is a method used in the transformation of *seeing* a computer program into *knowing* a computer program. Knowing that the code will be formatted around its evaluative process and in such a way as to make those processes readily visible, readers of programs can *know* about a program by just *seeing* a program. For example, the reader of a program may be drawn to the following function because it displays that the writer may have had a problem in working out the code.

```
(defun Observer-mouse-handler (window)
      (let*  ((observer   (il : windowprop window 'observer))
             (position          (il : cursorposition nil window))
             (name   (observer-name-observer))
              choice)
                  (il: with.monitor (observer-lock observer)
                          (when (il : mousestate il : left)
                                  (dolist (port (observer-who-observed observer))
                                     (when (maybe-handle-mouse port position     observer)
                                     (return-from observer-mouse-handler))))
                          (setq choice (il: menu (il :create il:menu
                                              il: title: (format nil "operate on observe for A"
                                  name

                                              il : item il
                                              '(     ("update all images" : update-now)
                                                     ("change who observed" : change-who)
                                                     ("change default update interval"
                                                           :change-default-update-interval)
                                                     ("change display parameters"
                                                       nil nil (il: subitems (,(if(observer-auto-
                                                           add-source
                                                                                   observer)
                                                                                   "Don't automatically
                                                                               add
                                                                                   sources"
                                                                                   "Automatically add
                                                                               new
                                                                                   sources")
                                                                                   :toggle-add-new-
                                                                                   sources)
                                                                     ("...................")
                                                                     ("No Auto-reshape": no-auto-
                                                             reshape)
                                                                     ("Rows" : rows)
                                                                     ("Columns" : columns)))))))
                                          .
                                          .
                                          .
```

By just seeing this code an experienced programmer will know that the code involves a problem that has not been elegantly solved. That is, just by seeing the code they can know some things about it, even though they have not yet read through it. The reason for this is that it can be *seen* that community principles for writing code have been violated. The principles involved here concern the way in which functions should be comprised of "manageable" processing operations. That is, in order to make code intelligible to others, and also to help a programmer keep the unfolding structure of the code in mind, programmers are exhorted in the methodologies for programming to break up programming problems into smaller "manageable" functions. Thus, in the example we gave above of a program that allows a customer to check his or her bank balance, a programmer would be advised by the methodologies to break the problem up into a number of parts and write the code for each part. In small parts a programmer will be better able to keep the structure of the code he/she is writing in mind, and a person reading the program will be better able to make sense of the code if he/she has only a few lines of code to deal with.

Breaking the problem into parts is also a feature of programmers' screen-based work. That is, programmers display a preference in their writing practices to keep a function in view, on the screen, at all times if they possibly can. This enables them to see the whole function without having to scroll the screen and lose sight of other parts of the code. It also enables readers to see the code at a glance. Thus it is easier to keep the structure of the code in mind if the code is kept in view on the screen and it is easier to make sense of the structure of the code if the code is in view as it is being read. Thus if a function is going off the screen as it is being written, a programmer may decide that the function is becoming too complicated and re-order the problem by breaking it down into more functions.[25]

Consequently, just by seeing the above function an experienced programmer will be able to tell that the programmer who wrote the code may not have sufficiently thought through the problem. If the programmer had broken the function down into a number of less complicated functions it would have made it easier to understand. The clue to knowing that the function is too complicated is the visual arrangement of the format of the code. As the programmer has continued to elaborate the function rather then closing it off, he/she has had to continue to indent the lines of the code further and further to the right.[26] If the programmer could have closed off the function then he/she could return to the left hand side of the page. But because he/she has not yet closed off the function each next line is further indented, according to programming convention. Thus, visually, the code slopes off to the right and there is a lot of white space to the left. Consequently, just by seeing the code and observing the white space to the left and the sloping code to the right, an experienced programmer will be able to know that there may be a problem here; the programmer should have broken the function down into more manageable parts. The visual structuring of the code is then a method for transforming seeing the code into knowing the code.[27]

However, formatting code is not just a practice that is used to provide access to the structure of the code for readers of code. It is also a device used by code writers as part of their working out of the code on the screen. That is, it is another practice, like the practice of writing "the simplest possible case" and the practice of "the temporary naming of variables" that code writers use as part of a repertoire of screen based work practices to keep the unfolding structure of the code in view as they elaborate it. For example, as we have seen, in LISP the parentheses "(", ")" mark an argument, an expression to be evaluated. In complicated code, it is easy for a programmer to lose track as to which functions they have closed off. That is, writers can find that they may not have closed off one evaluative process when embarking upon another. To illustrate this we can note that the following line of code involves closing down seven evaluative processes, indicated by the parentheses ")":

```
(update-view view : fast)))))))
```

In the course of writing code it is a simple matter for a programmer to lose sight of just where he/she is in the code. For example, has he/she closed off all the arguments that were open? Formatting the code on the screen is thus a practical screen-based working practice for keeping the unfolding structure of the code in place. It allows writers to keep track of the unfolding computational processes, for quite simply it allows writers to be able to better understand where they are in their writing by being able to better see what right hand parenthesis goes with what left hand parenthesis.

However, although a consequential resource in making code intelligible, formatting is not a practice that is exclusive to computer science and software engineering. Formatting, like other computer science practices that we have described, relies upon an enabling vulgar competence for its effectiveness. In this case it is the simple practice of *laying-out*. Model-making enthusiasts are well acquainted with this practice. In *laying-out* the pieces of the model aircraft before commencing to glue it together, enthusiasts can transform the obscurely packaged bits into an intelligible structure. Laying-out enables them to see if any bits are missing, to see what goes with what, to identify the pieces described in the instructions, to make sense of the sequential instructions for assembly. Laying-out enables the modeller to see what he/she has in front of him/her. Laying-out in part transforms seeing the bits that make up the model to knowing how the model should fit together. Laying-out also informs the work of groups other than computer scientists and software engineers and aircraft modellers. For example, the stories, columns, photographs, captions, etc. that go to make up the page of a newspaper or magazine are first laid out to better organize and better see the organization of a page. Accordingly, formatting code is the instanciation of the vulgar competence of laying-out that is commonly available which, indeed, is a resource that is used in the ordering of quite different work to that which computer scientists and software engineers might be regarded and regard themselves as being involved in.

However, in the work of computer science and software engineers it is possible to see that *this* vulgar competence is organized as a formalized account of the professional work of computer programming for the visual organization of the code as a method for transforming "seeing the code into knowing the code" is a method that testifies to the fact that the work of computer programmers is accountable to a community of practitioners and is indeed the accomplishment of that community. As a community, computer programmers have methodically built into the work of writing and reading code the visual organization of code, for they have built themselves computational devices that automatically format the code around the computational processes. So doing is both an acknowledgment that the achievement of the intelligibility of the structure of a program is reliant upon enabling vulgar competencies and an attempt to transform one of these competencies into a formal account of the work of programming. This can be seen in the use of one device which is oriented to writing code on the screen, *the screen-structure editor*, and another device which is oriented to reading code, *pretty printing*, are put in developing the unfolding structure of the code on the screen, and in making sense of the structure of a computer program as a document.

Screen-structure editors automatically lay out the code on the screen as a programmer is writing code. The screen-structure editors vary in how they accomplish their task, but in laying out the code they are all oriented to keeping the computational process that is being worked on and which is unfolding, in view for the writer. They may do this by alternately flashing the parentheses of a computational process that is in the course of being worked on so that the writer can disentangle that process from others of which it is an unfolding part. Thus, in the example above where there were seven processes being closed down, a writer can use the flashing parenthesis to keep a track of where he/she may be in the code. If the left-hand parenthesis that encloses one argument is clicked on, then it and its right-hand counter-part may flash, enabling the writer to bring to the fore that process in order to work on it.

Other screen-structure editors will indent the arguments to pre-assigned tab marks, and thus a writer can see that he/she has completed a process, for the cursor will skip back to the margin default, or skip from the right-hand parenthesis of a process to the left-hand parenthesis.[28] However, whatever procedure the particular screen-structure editor enacts, it provides a visual resource that is used by the writer of code to keep the unfolding structure of the code in view as it is being elaborated. Keeping the changing character of the unfolding structure of the code in view is thus the achievement of methodic community practices.

Practices of formatting code in order to read the structure of the code from its visual representation are not esoteric individualized practices. They are constituted as standardized community practices in the automating of the formatting process in pretty printing. This is a program that prints out code in a standard format and the code is automatically formatted in its printing. Pretty printing is a device that automates, and thus standardizes, the method for transforming "seeing code into knowing code." Pretty Printing achieves for the visual organization of code its status as a professionally available method for making the structure of code tractable upon the occasions of its reading, and is an attempt to render the meaning of the code transportable across situations and persons, and locate the meaning of the structure of the code within a community of professional practices.

## 4. CONCLUSION

The development of screen-structure editors and pretty printing to standardize formatting procedures throughout the community of professional programmers is a recognition by the community of the relationship between professional and lay practice. This is because both developments are an attempt to formally build enabling vulgar competencies into the formal practices of the community. This partly distinguishes computer science and software engineering from both the natural sciences and the social sciences on the stance a community of practitioners takes on the relationship between its professional knowledge and commonsense knowledge.

Within both the natural sciences and the social sciences the relationship between scientific knowledge and commonsense knowledge, and between the methods and practices of the science and the methods and practices of common sense, is understood in a particular way. In order to engage in natural or social science it is conventionally argued that it is necessary to adopt the formal practices of the science and abandon the practices of common sense. Within both the natural sciences and the social sciences the reliance that is made upon the vulgar competencies of common sense thus go largely and systematically unrecognized.[29] Indeed, to judge by the reactions of a great body of social science, ethnomethodologists have not been thanked for acknowledging this relationship.

The acknowledgment of the reliance that is made upon the vulgar competencies of common-sense knowledge and practical reasoning by computer scientists and software engineers, at least as far as the design of screen-structure editors and pretty printing for LISP is concerned, suggests that computer scientists and software engineers can, on occasions in their professional practices, systematically differ from natural and social scientists over the relationship between professional and mundane practice. The acknowledged attempts within computer science to transform the mundane practices of programming into professional practices recognizes the role of mundane practices in the professional work of programming. It is the professional community's recognition of what any programmer knows. Acknowledging this relationship, if only in one respect, may provide the opportunity for a different relationship between ethnomethodology and the "science" under study to the relationship between ethnomethodology and the natural sciences and the social sciences. If computer science can recognize its reliance upon enabling vulgar competencies in some areas of its professional practice, it may, in principle, be amenable to having its reliance in other areas explicated, and in that explication it may find ethnomethodological studies of its work a resource for the development of its professional practices. An interesting thought indeed.

---

* We are indebted to Paul Luff, Nicolas Graube, Paul Dourish, Lennert Lövstrand, Steve Freeman, and Mathew Chalmers, for introducing us to the work of computer programming and responding to what must have often seemed strange and naive questions and requests with patience and good humor. We are also grateful to Bob Anderson, Paul Dourish, Paul Luff, and Paul ten Have for their comments on an earlier draft; and to Paul Dourish for checking, and on numerous occasions correcting, our understanding and descriptions of computer code and computer processing. Randy Trigg helped us to understand the idea of the simplest possible case but should bear no responsibilities if our description is less than adequate. We would also like to thank Alan Borning for allowing us to reproduce parts of one of his programs. The research for this chapter was supported by the Economic and Social Research Council, grant No.: R000232521.

1 See, for example, Garfinkel (1986).

2 See Lynch (1985); Lynch, Livingston, and Garfinkel (1983); Garfinkel, Lynch and Livingston (1981); Garfinkel, Livingston, Lynch, Robillard and MacBeth (1989).

3 See Livingston (1986).

4 Garfinkel (1990) uses the term haecceities to refer to the particulars, the details, the "thises" and "thats" of situated work.

5 There are a number of programming languages available to computer programmers and although there are generic ways of working, it is the case that different languages can be worked with in different ways. This paper is particularly concerned with the work of computer programmers who are using the programming language LISP (though there is also passing reference to another language, C). LISP is one of a number of programming languages that make up a genre of languages known as functional/applicative languages. The terms "functional" and "applicative" derive from mathematics. A function in mathematics is a way of relating elements of one set to the elements of another set. So a function for finding the square of a number associates x with $x^2$ i.e. f(x) =

$x^2$. A LISP program is built by creating and evaluating functions. Not all computer languages work in this way, and part of the work of programming in LISP is to work in LISP expressions such as "function." Other languages may utilize the same process or have equivalent process. Thus C utilizes the concept of function whereas Modula-3, for example, works with procedures. Therefore phrases such as the "work of programmers," and "work practices" is a surrogate for "the work of programmers working in LISP," and "LISP programmers' work practices." The relationship of this work to the work of programmers using other languages is a matter for further research, though it is interesting to note that computer programmers do not regard learning a new language to be learning how to program. The position seems to be that learning a new language is to learn its ways of approaching programming problems that are encountered in using any language.

6 How a computer program is organized in order to display its intelligibility is part of the work of structuring the code. Thus structure is a gloss for the work practices through which a program is organized as an intelligible document. In this respect our use of structure at this juncture is a gloss for the as yet unexplicated work practices of writing a computer program. We can note here, however, that the structure of a computer program implicates both a computational structure and a visual structure. Computational structure refers to the way in which the program processes information or data and to the way in which its parts hang together. Thus computer programs are often written as modules and the computational structure of a program consequently implicates the ways in which those modules fit together. However, structure also has a visual dimension and thus structure also refers to the visual layout of the program. One of the issues we attend to later on is the way in which the organization of the visual structure of a written program is used to make the computational processing structure more accessible to a reader. However, although the idea of "structured programming" addresses the issue of intelligibility, it also impacts upon other matters such as run-time performance, code size, provable correctness and reuse.

7 We introduce the issue of professionalization here not because we are interested in the professionalization of an occupation in the traditional manner of the sociology of work and occupations but because the professionalization of computer programming has involved the development of certain work practices and development methodologies such as that of structured programming. Thus, an orientation to the structure of a computer program in the work of writing computer programs is both a result and a constitutive feature of the professionalization of computer programming.

8 Computer science lecturers often regard their first task in teaching new students to be that of "unteaching" their previous bad habits and practices that they will have developed on home and school micro-computers. Often, they will use the Abelson, et al., book, or it will figure on their reading lists as it has achieved a high reputation amongst computer science lecturers.

9 Of course how they have approached writing the program may be used to criticize the program.

10 In this respect "hack" can at times be a disparaging expression which is used by "professionals" as they seek to distance themselves from hackers, although at other times it is used with some reverence to venerate the *singular* ability of a programmer. In this respect "the hacker" is a construct that pervades computer science and which is used in many different ways. On some occasions it is used to mystify code writing, on others to deride ways of writing it. Much has been written about the "hacker" -- see Levy (1984) for an interesting example.

11 The program was written by Nicolas Graube in 1989 and called "Fully Optimized Version of ObjVLisp in Common Lisp" and was published by the Universite Paris VI. It takes up three A4 pages and is a program that makes the programming language LISP behave as if it were a language from another genre of languages knows as "object oriented languages." This is an exacting and demanding programming problem requiring a high degree of proficiency, a degree few programmers could aspire to. Unlike LISP which is a functional/applicative language, object oriented languages are structured around "objects." An object is an area of computer memory which serves as a basic unit of storage or execution. Examples of object oriented languages are SIMULA and Smalltalk and these work very differently to LISP. Thus, to develop a program that can transform the logic of the operation of one language into the logic of the operation of another in such a concise way as to fit onto three A4 sheets is recognized by professionals as a rare feat of programming skill.

12 See Yourdon and Constantine (1979).

13 See Button and Sharrock (forthcoming) for an examination of the use of Yourdon methodology in the work of software engineering.

14 See Garfinkel et. al. (1989) for a description of the "vulgar competencies" of science.

15 A filter is designed to filter some designated numbers from a list of numbers. For example, it may be written to filter negative numbers from a list of numbers so as to leave only positive numbers. This filter is written in LISP and the process of structuring the code is particularly interesting for LISP because LISP is not a traditional structured language. In Modula-3, for instance, which is strongly structured, procedures have sub-routines, and so on, and blocks of procedures can be grouped into modules which are themselves a unit of structure. Although this can be done in LISP it rarely is, and the result is often a program made up of an almost unstructured list of functions. Thus to order the structure of a LISP program the programmer has to explicitly attend to the structure by, for example, grouping the functions onto files, or, something we describe in more detail, naming the functions in such a way as to give structural cues. The important issue for our purposes is that these practices are not supported directly by the language itself and are therefore not practices that are articulated in the language as a formal representation; they are vulgar enabling practices which are not part of the formal practices of writing code in LISP.

---

16 Fragment 1b does not constitute the completion of the code for the filter. The programmer goes on inserting more lines of code using what he now has in hand for the development of those lines. He corrects lines he had written previously in the light of what he goes on to write, as well as correcting the obvious errors and typing mistakes that he made. He progressively elaborates and builds up his code using what he has before him as a resource with which to do so. "The simplest possible case" is thus an example of devices used for the purposes of elaboration.

17 It is important to note that writing the simplest possible case is not a practice that the programmer developed for this particular code but is a practice that accords to a general form for "recursive" functions (functions which call themselves in order to accomplish some part of the work) which is that they should have a test-for-base-case, base-case handler, and a recursive-call-for-complex cases. Thus writing the simplest possible case first dovetails with well-established practice.

18 We need to note that although a screen-based practice used by programmers, it is not a practice that is deployed in the production of any program. It is part of a repertoire of screen-based practices available to programmers, to be used or not in conjunction with other practices, in writing a program.

19 One of our informants recalls an occasion when the names of functions and variables in a program were substituted for random dictionary entries and the program then passed around. Not surprisingly, no one could make head-nor-tail of it, although the program still processed the information as efficiently as it had previously done.

20 Some variables such as "temp" and "blardy-blar" may however remain in a program. This is because calling them "temp" or "blardy-blar" may be used explicitly to convey the information that they are unimportant, for example, they may be artifacts of the algorithm, and can be ignored for the purposes of understanding the program. When a programmer knows, from the outset that they are writing such a function or variable they often name it "foo" and have no intention of returning to it and renaming it.

21 Attempts have been made to formalize a naming process, thereby abstracting it from the contingent and program sensitive nature of practical componential analysis. For example the Hungarian Method was introduced by Charles Simony (see Lammers, 1986). It requires that names be in part compiled using letters that indicate what is to be found in the location assigned to a function. For instance an "i" is used to indicate that an integer is to be found. This method has not, however, been widely adopted because it is not sensitive to the context of a particular program. Thus a program may provide a context in which it may be appropriate to use "i" to designate more than one type of location. Such a proscriptive method does not provide the same level of sensitivity that practical componential analysis displays for the situated nature of selecting names.

22 An index of functions is not an intrinsic feature of LISP, it is a feature of one implementation of LISP; InterLISP and other implementations may not offer it. Other languages can have their

equivalents, cross referencing is used in Modula-3, and UNIX provides "Cref" which produces a similar index for C. In InterLISP other indexes are also generated such as an index of variables, templates and macros. For our purposes we will confine ourselves to an index of functions for a program.

23 Some languages embody devices for recognizing the top-level function. Thus C, Pascal and Modula-3 have defined "start" points within the program text. For example, within C, the top-level function must be called "main" and has a particular set of arguments which represent the command-line arguments when the program is run.

24 See Garfinkel (1967).

25 The fact that programmers prefer to write functions that fit into the screen of the computer they are working on means that some programmers also have preferences for certain types of machines. A computer that is particularly favored by many programmers we have associated with is the SUN 4. This is because the quality of the high resolution of the screen enables programmers to use small font sizes without losing clarity. Thus they can write more lines of code to the screen, and thus keep more lines of code in view.

26 The indenting is the result of a formatting convention in LISP that is normally automated by the computer's screen editor and by a program called "pretty printing" that prints the code in a conventionally formatted way, an issue we will return to later. We should also note that the fact that the function may be overly complicated does not mean that it will not result in the efficient processing of information. The point is that it creates a problem of intelligibility for other programmers, not a problem of processing.

27 Upon a detailed inspection of the code it turns out that there are extenuating circumstances for writing the code in this way that absolve the programmer.

28 The screen editors do not seem to serve all the needs of programmers working on the screen, for we have observed programmers working on their screens with their fingers. One of these screen-fingering practices is to place a little finger on a left hand bracket and search for it right hand bracket with a hovering thumb that eventually traces out the correct right hand bracket or slaps against the screen at a point where a bracket seems to be missing.

29 See Lynch (1991) and Benson and Hughes (1991) for recent detailed expositions of this reliance.

# Appendix: Transcription Symbols

With a few exceptions, the transcription symbols are those developed by Gail Jefferson to capture those phenomena relevant to the organization of conversation. The system specifically notes the location of silence, onset of speech, overlapped speech and phenomena relevant to interactional units such as turns, turn transitions, and turn completions. Although the system obviously does not capture all the distinctions that can be made in the analysis of talk, it aims to provide the reader with a description of those features most relevant to the analysis of the organization of talk-in-interaction.

Researchers do not use all of the symbols since they may be interested in different aspects of interaction and some add new symbols in order to describe those phenomena to which their study may be oriented. Nevertheless, most researchers within the conversation analysis tradition have found the basic aspects of this notation system both useful and adequate.

The major sources relied upon for this listing are Sacks, Schegloff, and Jefferson (1974:731-734 -- also reprinted in Schenkein 1978); Psathas (1979); Goodwin (1981); Atkinson and Heritage (1984); and Psathas and Anderson (1990).

Certain conventions used in the presentation of research reports are also included here.

I. Sequencing

1. Simultaneous utterances

   Utterances starting up simultaneously are linked together with double left-hand brackets.

   Tom: [[I used to smoke a lot when I was young
   Bob: [[I used to smoke Camels

2. Overlap

   A. Beginning of overlap

   When utterances overlap but do not start up simultaneously, the point at which the overlap begins is marked by a single left-hand bracket.

   Tom: I used to smoke [a lot
   Bob: [ he thinks he's real tough

   An alternate notation for beginning of overlap is to use double oblique markers to indicate the point at which the overlap begins.

   V: Th'guy says tuh me-- .hh my son//dided.
   M: Wuhjeh do:.

A multiple-overlapped utterance is followed, in serial order, by the talk which overlaps it. Thus, C's "Vi:c" occurs simultaneously with V's "left," and C's "Victuh" with V's "hallway."

V: I//left my garbage pail in iz//hallway
C: Vi:c
C: Victuh,

B. End of overlap

The point where overlapping utterances stop overlapping is marked with a single right-hand bracket.

Tom: I used to smoke [a lot] more than this
Bob: [I see]

An alternative notation for end of overlap is an asterisk to indicate the point at which two overlapping or simultaneously started utterances end, if they end simultaneously, or the point at which one of the ends in the course of another or the point at which one utterance component ends vis à vis another.

M: [[I mean no no n'no*
V: [[P't it back up*
M: [[Jim? wasn' home* uh what.
V: [[Y'know;W?

3. Latching of contiguous utterances

Equal signs indicate latching (i.e., no interval between the end of a prior and the start of a next part of talk).

A. Latching with change of speakers

Tom: I used to smoke a lot=
Bob: =He thinks he's real tough

B. Latching by more than one speaker

Two speakers begin simultaneously and with no interval between their start and the end of the last speaker's talk.

Tom: I used to smoke a lot=
Bob: =[[He thinks he's so tough
Ann: =[[So did I

C. Latching at the end of overlapped speech

Two utterances end simultaneously and are latched onto by a next.

Tom: I used to smoke [a lot]=
Bob: [I see]
Ann: =so did I

D. Latching within the same speaker's talk

V: well my son did it = I'm gladjer son didn't get hurt ...

E. Latching as a transcription convenience

When a speaker's lengthy utterance is broken up arbitrarily for purposes of presentation, especially when overlap occurs, the equal sign is used to indicate continuity in the same speaker's utterance.

V: my wif//caught d'ki:d,=

R: yeh
V: =lightin a fiyuh in Perry's cellar

Tom: I used to smoke [a lot more than this=
Bob: [you used to smoke
Tom: =but I never inhaled the smoke

II. Timed intervals, within and between utterances

1. Numbers in parentheses

The number indicates in seconds and tenths of a second the length of an interval.

Lil: When I was (0.6) oh nine or ten
(0.4)
Joe: Are you talking to me

A. One alternative is to use dashes within parentheses. Each dash is a tenth of a second; each full second is marked with a plus sign.

J: How's uh, (- - - - - - - - - - + - - ) Jimmy

B. A second alternative is the use of plus markers within parentheses. Each plus mark is one tenth of a second; each full second may be marked by a space.

J: How's uh, (+ + + + + + + + + +   + +) Jimmy

2. Untimed micro-intervals

More or less than a tenth of a second is indicated by a dot within parentheses.

J: barges are struck (.) stuck that it

3. Untimed intervals of longer length

If timing is not achieved, a pause, silence, or gap may be noted as untimed.

John: who all is there.
Kitty: Oh, Marcia and Judy stopped by
((gap))
John: who else
Kitty: oh, what's his name ((pause)) Tom.
John: oh.

III. Characteristics of speech production

Punctuation marks are used to describe characteristics of speech production. They are not to be interpreted as referring to grammatical units.

1. Sound stretch

A colon indicates that the prior sound is prolonged. Multiple colons indicate a more prolonged sound.

V: So dih gu:y sez
M: I Ju::ss can't come
T: I'm so::: sorry re:::ally I am

2. A single dash indicates a cut-off of the prior word or sound (i.e., a noticeable and abrupt termination).
   C: Th' U:sac-- uh:, sprint car dr-- dirt track ...
3. Intonation
   A. A period indicates a stopping fall in tone.
      F: So with every (.) economic failure. (0.5) they turn (0.5) more viciously. (0.5) on the local authorities.
   B. A comma indicates a continuing intonation (e.g., the kind of falling-rising contour one finds after items in a list).
      A: There was a bear, a cat, enna dog.
      P: now if ya have thirteen points:, (1.0) counting: voi:ds?
   C. Question mark indicates a rising intonation. Question mark/comma indicates rising intonation weaker than that indicated by a question mark/period
      V: A do:g? enna cat is different.
      P: Yih ever take'er out again?
      P: t'morrow er anything?,
   D. Upward or downward pointing arrows immediately prior to the rise or fall mark rising or falling shifts in intonation.
      T: I am however (0.2) very fortunate (0.4) in having (0.6) a ≠marvelous deputy.
   E. Exclamation point indicates an animated tone.
      C: An that! so what he sez.
4. Emphasis -- pitch or stress
   Emphasis is indicated by italics or underscoring. The larger the italics, the greater the relative stress.
   Ann: It happens to be mine.
   Ben: Its not either yours it's MINE.
   V: I sez y'know WHY, becawss look.
5. Pitch
   The relationship between emphasis and prolongation (stretch) indicate pitch change (or non-change) in the course of a word.
   A. Word stressed but with no change in pitch:
      To indicate stress (and here stretching as well), the stress-mark is placed on the first letter of the stressed syllable. Of course, if the stressing is greater, then the underscore is longer.
      J: it's only a venee:r though,
   B. Pitch drop:
      J: it's only a venee:r though,
      To indicate pitch-drop, the underscore should be placed at the vowel immediately preceding the colon. Again, for more pronounced emphasis, the underscore is longer.
      J: it's only a venee:r though,
      The idea is not to have the colon underscored and an immediately preceding vowel underscored.
   C. Pitch rise:

J: it's only a venee:r though,

To indicate pitch rise, the stress is marked upon the prolongation. If the rise occurs somewhere in the course of a prolongation, that can be shown as follows:

J: it's only a venee::::r though,

And one can show rising and falling:

J: it's only a venee:::::r though,

6. Volume -- loudness or softness
   A. Upper-case letters are used to indicate increased volume.
      V: In it dint fall OUT!
   B. A degree sign is used to show a passage of talk which has a noticeably lower volume than the surrounding talk.
      J: An' how are you feeling? (0.4) °these days,°

IV. Aspiration -- audible inhalation and exhalation

An h or series of hhh's is used to mark an out-breath unless a dot (period) precedes the hhh's in which case an in-breath is indicated.

1. Out-breath
   J: I'm not sure hh- who it belongs to
2. In-breath
   Marge: .hh Okay, thank you Mister Hanys'n
3. Plosive aspiration as in laughter, breathlessness, or crying is indicated by placing the h in parentheses.
   Pam: An th(hh)s is for you hhh
   Gene: So that shook up the old (h)house(h)hold up fer a(h)whi(h)le heh
   Joyce: ehh [hhhhhhh!
   C: [oh(hh)h hah huh!

V. Transcriptionist doubt

Other than the timings of intervals and inserted aspirations, items enclosed within single parentheses are in doubt.

Ted: I ('spose I'm not)
(Ben): We all (t-- )

Sometimes, multiple possibilities are indicated.

(spoke to Mark)
Ted: I ('spose I'm not)

When single parentheses are empty, no hearing could be achieved for the talk or item in question.

Todd: My ( ) catching
( ): In my highest ( )

On occasion, nonsense syllables are provided in an attempt to capture something of the produced sounds.

R: (Y' cattuh moo)

VI. Verbal descriptions

Double parentheses are used to enclose a description of some phenomenon which the transcriptionist does not want to contend with. These may be vocalizations that are not easily spelled, details of the conversational scene, or various characterizations of the talk.

Tom: I used to ((cough)) smoke a lot
Bob: ((sniffle)) He thinks he's tough
Ann: ((snorts))

Jan: This is just delicious
((telephone rings))
Kim: I'll get it

Ron: ((in falsetto) I can do it now
Max: ((whispered)) He'll never do it

VII. Presentation Conventions

1. Arrows or dots in the left-hand margin of the transcript may be used to call the reader's attention to particular parts of the transcript. The author will inform the reader of the significance of the referent of the arrow (or dot) by discussing it in the text.

Don: If I had the money I'd get one for her
--> Sam: And one for your mother too I'll bet
Don: I like the blue one very much
• Sam: And I'll bet your wife would like it

2. Ellipses

A. Horizontal ellipses indicate that an utterance is partially reported (i.e., parts of the same speaker's utterance are omitted).

J: hhh (0.4) hhh we just want to get ...

B. Vertical ellipses indicate that intervening turns at talk have been omitted.

12 Bob: Well I always say give it your all
.
.
.
19 Bob: I always give it everything

3. Numbering of lines or utterance parts in a transcript is arbitrarily done for convenience or reference. Line numbers are not intended to be measures of timing or number of turns or utterances. Silences between talk may also receive line numbers.

11 Tim: Nice hand Chris:,
12 (0.4)
13 Jim: Th'ts a nice ha:nd.

# References


Abbagnano, N. (1958). Four kinds of dialectics. *Rivista di Filosofia* 49(2):123-133.

Abelson, H., Sussman, G.J. and Sussman, J. (1985). *Structure and interpretation of computer programs.* Cambridge: Massachusetts Institute of Technology Press.

Alberts, J.K. (1992). An influential/strategic explanation for the social organization of teases. *Journal of Language and Social Psychology.*

Anderson, W.T. (1989). Dentistry as an activity system: Sequential properties of the dentist-patient encounter. In D. Helm, T. Anderson and A. Rawls (Eds.), *The interaction order: New directions in the study of social order.* New York: Irvington.

Asch, S.E. (1946). Forming impressions of personality. *The Journal of Abnormal and Social Psychology* 41(3):258-290.

Asch, S.E. (1951). The effects of group pressure on the modification and distortion of judgements. In H. Guetzkow (Ed.), *Groups, leadership, and men.* Pittsburgh: Carnegie Press.

Atkinson, J.M. (1982). Understanding formality: The categorization and production of formal interaction. *British Journal of Sociology* 33:86-117.

Atkinson, J.M. (1984). *Our master's voices: The language and body language of politics.* London: Methuen.

Atkinson, J.M. and Drew, P. (1979). *Order in court: The organization of verbal interaction in judicial settings.* London: Macmillan.

Austin, J.L. (1979/1961). A plea for excuses. In J.L. Austin, (Ed.), *Philosophical Papers.* (Third edition). Oxford: Oxford University Press.

Baccas, H.D. (1986). Sociological indication and the visibility criterion of real world social theorising. In H. Garfinkel, (Ed.), *Ethnomethodological studies of work.* London: Routledge and Kegan Paul.

Baccus, M.D. (1986). Multipiece truck wheel accidents and their regulations. In H. Garfinkel (Ed.), *Ethnomethodological studies of work.* London: Routledge and Kegan Paul.

Bacharach, S.B. and Lawler, E.J. (1981). *Bargaining: Power, tactics, and outcomes.* San Francisco: Jossey-Bass.

Baker, C. (1977). Regulators and turn-taking in American Sign Language discourse. In L.A. Friedman (Ed.), *On the other hand.* New York: Academic Press.

Bal, P. (1988). *Dwangcommunicatie in de rechtszaal [Coercive communication in the courtroom].* Arnhem: Gouda Quint.

Bales, R.F. (1969). *Personality and interpersonal behavior.* New York: Holt Rinehart.

Bateson, G. (1972). *Steps to an ecology of mind.* San Francisco: Chandler.

Bauman, R. (1977). *Verbal art as performance.* Prospect Heights, IL: Waveland Press.

Beach, W.A. (1991). Establishing transitional regularities in "casual" "okay" usages. Paper delived at the Annual Meeting of the Speech Communication Association, Language and Social Interaction Division, Atlanta, November.

Bennett, W.L. and Feldman, M.S. (1981). *Reconstructing reality in the courtroom.* New Brunswick: Rutgers University Press.

Benson, D. and Drew, P. (1978). "Was there firing in Sandy Row that night?" Some features in the organisation of disputes about recorded facts. *Sociological Inquiry* 48:89-100.

Benson, D. and Hughes, J. (1991). Method: Evidence and inference for ethnomethodology. In G. Button (Ed.), *Ethnomethodology and the human sciences.* Cambridge: Cambridge University Press.

Berger, P.L. and Luckman, T. (1967). *The social construction of reality.* Harmondsworth: Penguin.

Bjelic, D. and Lynch, M. (1992). The work of a [scientific] demonstration: Respecifying Newton's and Goethe's theories of prismatic color. In G. Watson and R. Seiler (Eds.), *Text in context: Contributions to ethnomethodology.* Beverly Hills: Sage.

Blau, P.M. (1977). *Inequality and heterogeneity: A primitive theory of social structure.* New York: Free Press/Macmillan.

Boddendijk, A. (1991). *Sprekende taal in telefonische interviews? Een exploratief onderzoek naar veranderingen in schrijftaalkenmerken. [Spoken language in telephone interviews? An exploration into the changes of features of spoken language].* Afdeling Taalbeheersing, Universiteit van Utrecht.

Boden, D. (1990). The world as it happens: Ethnomethodology and conversation analysis. In G. Ritzer (Ed.), *Frontiers of social theory.* New York: Columbia University Press.

Boden, D. (Forthcoming). *The business of talk: Organizations in action.* Cambridge: Polity Press.

Boden, D. and Zimmerman, D.H. (1991) (Eds.). *Talk and social structure: Studies in ethnomethodology and conversation analysis.* Cambridge: Polity Press.

Bogen, D. and Lynch, M. (1989). Taking account of the hostile native: Plausible deniability and the production of conventional history in the Iran-Contra hearings. *Social Problems* 36(3):197-224.

Brannigan, A. and Lynch, M. (1987). On bearing false witness: Credibility as an interactional accomplishment. *Journal of Contemporary Ethnography* 16(2):115-146.

Brenner, M. (1978). Interviewing: The social phenomenology of a research instrument. In M. Brenner, P. Marsh and M. Brenner (Eds.), *The social context of method.* London: Croom Helm.

Brenner, M. (1982). Response effects of "role-restricted" characteristics of the interviewer. In W. Dijkstra and J. van der Zouwen (Eds.), *Response behavior in the survey interview*. New York: Academic Press.

Briggs, C.L. (1986). *Learning how to ask: A sociolinguistic appraisal of the role of the interview in social science research*. Studies in the Social and Cultural Foundations of Language 1. Cambridge: Cambridge University Press.

Brun-Cotton, F. (1991). Talk in the workplace: Occupational relevance. *Research on Language and Social Interaction* 24:277-295.

Bruner, J. (1961). The cognitive consequences of early sensory deprivation. In P. Solomon, et al. (Eds.), *Sensory deprivation*. Cambridge: Harvard University Press.

Bruner, J. and Postman, L. (1949). The perception of incongruity: A paradigm. *Journal of Personality* 18:206-223.

Button, G. (1987). Moving out of closings. In G. Button and J.R.E. Lee (Eds.), *Talk and social organisation*. Clevedon: Multilingual Matters.

Button, G. (1987). Answers as interactional products: Two sequential practices used in interviews. *Social Psychology Quarterly* 50:160-171.

Button, G. (1991). Conversation-in-a-series. In D. Boden and D.H. Zimmerman (Eds.), *Talk and social structure*. Cambridge: Polity Press; Berkeley: University of California Press.

Button, G. (1992) (Ed.). *Technology in working order: Studies of work, interaction and technology*. London: Routledge and Kegan Paul.

Button, G. and Casey, N. (1984). Generating topic: The use of topic initial elicitors. In J. Atkinson and J. Heritage (Eds.), *Structures of social action*. Cambridge: Cambridge University Press.

Button, G. and Lee, J.R.E. (1987) (Eds.). *Talk and social organisation*. Clevedon: Multilingual Matters.

Button, G. and Sharrock, W.W. (Forthcoming). Occasioned practices in the work of implementing development methodologies, environments and languages. In J. Goguen, M. Jirotka and M. Bickerton (Eds.), *Requirements engineering*. New York: Academic Press.

Caplow, T. (1968). *Two against one: Coalitions in triads*. Englewood Cliffs, N.J.: Prentice Hall.

Cappella, J.N. (1979). Talk-silence sequences in informal conversations I. *Human Communication Research* 6:3-17.

Cappella, J.N. (1980). Talk and silence sequences in informal conversations II. *Human Communication Research* 6:130-145.

Cappella, J.N. and Planalp, S. (1981). Talk and silence sequences in informal conversations III: Interspeaker influence. *Human Communication Research* 7:117-132.

Carlen, P. (1976). *Magistrates' justice*. London: Martin Robertson.

Carmel, S.J. and Monaghan, L.F. (1991). Studying Deaf culture: An introduction to ethnographic work in Deaf communities. *Sign Language Studies* 73:411-420.

Chafe, W. (1986). Evidentiality in English conversation and academic writing. In W.A.J.N. Chafe (Ed.), *Evidentiality: The linguistic coding of epistemology*. Norwood, N.J.: Ablex.

Cicourel, A. (1964). *Method and measurement in sociology*. New York: Free Press of Glencoe.

Cicourel, A.V. (1973). *Cognitive sociology*. London: Penguin.

Cicourel, A.V. (1981). Notes on the integration of micro- and macro-levels of analysis. In K. Knorr-Cetina and A.V. Cicourel (Eds.), *Advances in social theory and methodology: Toward an integration of micro- and macro-sociologies*. London: Routledge and Kegan Paul.

Clayman, S.E. (1988). Displaying neutrality in television news interviews. *Social Problems* 35:474-492.

Clayman, S.E. (1989). The production of punctuality: Social interaction, temporal organization, and social structure. *American Journal of Sociology* 95:659-91.

Clayman, S. E. (1992). Caveat orator: Audience disaffiliation in the 1988 presidential debates. *Quarterly Journal of Speech* 78(1):33-60.

Clayman, S.E. and Whalen, J. (1988/89). When the medium becomes the message: The case of the Rather-Bush encounter. *Research on Language and Social Interaction* 22:241-272.

Cody, M.J. and McLaughlin, M.L. (1988). Accounts on trial: Oral arguments in traffic court. In C. Antaki (Ed.), *Analysing everyday explanation: A casebook of methods*. London: Sage.

Collins, R. (1981). Micro-translation as a theory-building strategy. In K. Knorr-Cetina and A.V. Cicourel (Eds.) *Advances in social theory and methodology: Toward an integration of micro- and macro-sociology*. London: Routledge and Kegan Paul.

Collins, R. (1981). On the microfoundations of macrosociology. *American Journal of Sociology* 86/5:984-1014.

Coulter, J. (1983). Contingent and a priori structures in sequential analysis. *Human Studies* 6:361-76.

Coulter, J. (1989). *Mind in action*. Oxford: Polity Press.

Coulter, J. (1990). Elementary properties of argument sequences. In G. Psathas (Ed.), *Interaction competence: Studies in conversation analysis*. Washington, D.C.: University Press of America.

Davidson, J. (1984). Subsequent versions of invitations, offers, requests, and proposals dealing with potential or actual rejection. In J.M. Atkinson and J.C. Heritage (Eds.), *Structures of social action*. Cambridge: Cambridge University Press.

Davidson, J. (1990). Modifications of invitations, offers and rejections. In G. Psathas (Ed.), *Interaction competence: Studies in conversation analysis*. Washington, D.C.: University Press of America.

Dijkstra, W., van der Veen, L. and van der Zouwen, J. (1985). A field experiment on interviewer-respondent interaction. In M. Brenner, et al. (Eds.), *The research interview: Uses and approaches*. New York: Academic Press.

Drew, P. (1984). Speakers' reportings in invitation sequences. In J.M. Atkinson and J.C. Heritage (Eds.), *Structures of social action: Studies in conversation analysis*. Cambridge: Cambridge University Press.

Drew, P. (1987). Po-faced receipts of teases. *Linguistics* 25: 219-253.

Drew, P. (1990). Conversation analysis: Who needs it? *Text* 10/1:2:27-35.

Drew, P. (1990). Strategies in the contest between lawyer and witness in cross-examination. In J.N. Levi and A.G. Walker (Eds.), *Language in the judicial process*. New York: Plenum Press.

Drew, P. (in press). Interaction sequences and "anticipatory interactive planning." In E. Goody (Ed.), *The social origin of intellegence*. Cambridge: Cambridge University Press.

Drew, P. and Heritage, J.C. (1992) (Eds.). *Talk at work: Interaction in institutional settings*. Cambridge: Cambridge University Press.

Druckman, D. (1977). Social-psychological approaches to the study of negotiations. In D. Druckman (Ed.), *Negotiations: Social psychological perspectives*. Beverly Hills: Sage.

Duncan, S. (1972). Some signals and rules for taking speaking turns in conversations. *Journal of Personality and Social Psychology* 23:283-92.

Duncan, S. and Fiske, D.W. (1977). *Face-to-face interaction: Research, methods, and theory*. New York: Wiley and Sons.

Duranti, A., Goodwin, C. and Goodwin, M.H. (1991). Communicative acts as socially distributed phenomena. Preliminary remarks prepared for the session "Speech Acts as Socially Distributed Phenomena," American Anthropological Association, Chicago.

Ehlich, K. (1979). Formen und funktionen von "HM": Eine phonologisch-pragmatische analyse. In H.Weydt (Ed.), *Die Partikeln der deutschen Sprache*. Berlin and New York: Walter de Gruyter.

Engestrom, Y. (1992). Artifacts and talk as mediators of medical teamwork. Paper presented at the First Conference on Socio-Cultural Analysis, Madrid.

Erickson, F. (1990). The social construction of discourse coherence in a family dinner table conversation. In B. Dorval (Ed.), *Conversational organization and its development*. Norwood, N.J.: Ablex.

Erickson, F., and Shultz, J. (1977). When is a context? Some issues and methods in the analysis of social competence. *The Quarterly Newsletter of the Institute for Comparative Human Development* 1(2):5-10.

Firth, A. (1991). Discourse at work: Negotiating by telex, fax, and phone. Unpublished Ph.D. dissertation. Aalborg University, Denmark.

Firth, A. (1993). "Accounts" in negotiation discourse. Paper presented at the Fourth International Pragmatics Association Conference, Kobe, Japan.

Firth, A. (1994). Negotiating in the "virtual marketplace": Making sense of telenegotiations. In K. Ehlich and J. Wagner (Eds.), *The discourse of business negotiations*. Berlin: Mouton de Gruyter.

Frankel, R.M. (1984). From sentence to sequence: Understanding the medical encounter through micro-interactional analysis. *Discourse Processes* 7:135-170.

Frankel, R.M. (1990). Talking in interviews: A dispreference for patient-initiated questions in physician-patient encounters. In G. Psathas (Ed.), *Interaction competence*. Washington, D.C.: University Press of America.

Frolich, D., Drew, P. and Monk, A. (1992). The management of repair in human computer interaction. Unpublished paper.

Gadamer, H.G. (1960/1975). *Truth and method.* New York: Continuum.

Garfinkel, H. (1963). A conception of, and experiments with, "trust" as a condition of stable concerted actions. In O.J. Harvey (Ed.), *Motivation and social interaction.* New York: Ronald Press.

Garfinkel, H. (1967/1984). *Studies in ethnomethodology.* Englewood Cliffs, N.J.: Prentice Hall; Cambridge: Polity Press.

Garfinkel, H. (1986) (Ed.). *Ethnomethodological studies of work.* London: Routledge and Kegan Paul.

Garfinkel, H. (1988). Evidence for locally produced, naturally accountable phenomena of order, logic, reason, meaning, method, etc., in and as of the essential quiddity of immortal ordinary society (I of IV): An announcement of studies. *Sociological Theory* 6:103-109.

Garfinkel, H. (1990). Respecification: Evidence for locally produced, naturally accountable phenomena of order, logic, reason, meaning, method, etc., in and as of the essential haecceity of immortal ordinary society (I) -- An announcement of studies. In G. Button (Ed.), *Ethnomethodology and the human sciences.* Cambridge: Cambridge University Press.

Garfinkel, H. and Burns, S. (1979). Lecturing's work of talking introductory sociology. Unpublished paper, Department of Sociology, University of California, Los Angeles.

Garfinkel, H., Livingston, E., Lynch, M., MacBeth, D. and Robillard, A.B. (1989). Respecifying the natural sciences as discovering sciences of practical action, I and II: Doing so ethnographically by administering a schedule of contingencies in discussions with laboratory scientists and by hanging around their laboratories. Unpublished paper, Department of Sociology, University of California, Los Angeles.

Garfinkel, H., Lynch, M. and Livingston, E. (1981). The work of a discovering science construed with materials from the optically discovered pulsar. *Philosophy of the Social Sciences* 11:131-158.

Garfinkel, H. and Sacks, H. (1970). On formal structures of practical actions. In J.C. McKinney and E.A. Tiryakian (Eds.), *Theoretical sociology.* New York: Appleton Century Crofts.

Garfinkel, H. and Wieder, D.L. (1992). Evidence for locally produced and naturally accountable phenomena of order*, logic, reason, meaning, method, etc., in and as of the essentially unavoidable and irremediable haecceity of immortal ordinary society, IV: Two incommensurable, asymmetrically alternate technologies of social analysis. In G. Watson and R. Seiler (Eds.), *Text in context: Contributions to ethnomethodology.* Beverly Hills: Sage.

Gilsinan, J.F. (1989). They is clowning tough: 911 and the social construction of reality. *Criminology* 27:329-344.

Glenn, P.J. (1989). Initiating shared laughter in multi-party conversations. *Western Journal of Speech Communication* 53:127-149.

Glenn, P.J. and M.L. Knapp (1987). The interactive framing of play in adult conversations. *Communication Quarterly* 35:48-66.

Goffman, E. (1959). *The presentation of self in everyday life.* Garden City, N.Y.: Doubleday.

Goffman, E. (1961). *Encounters: Two studies in the sociology of interaction.* Indianapolis: Bobbs-Merrill.

Goffman, E. (1963). *Behavior in public places: Notes on the social organization of gathering.* New York: Free Press.

Goffman, E. (1970). *Strategic interaction.* Oxford: Basil Blackwell.

Goffman, E. (1971). *Relations in public: Microstudies of the public order.* New York: Harper and Row.

Goffman, E. (1974). *Frame analysis.* New York: Harper and Row.

Goffman, E. (1981). *Forms of talk.* Philadelphia: University of Pennsylvania Press.

Goode, D. (1979). The world of the congenitally deaf-blind: Toward the grounds for achieving human understanding. In H. Schwartz and J. Jacobs (Eds.), *Qualitative Sociology: A method to the madness.* New York: Free Press.

Goodwin, C. (1979). The interactive construction of a sentence in natural conversation. In G. Psathas (Ed.), *Everyday language: Studies in ethnomethodology.* New York: Irvington.

Goodwin, C. (1980). Restarts, pauses, and the achievement of mutual gaze at turn-beginning. *Sociological Inquiry* 50:272-302.

Goodwin, C. (1981). *Conversational organization: Interaction between speakers and hearers.* New York: Academic Press.

Goodwin, C. (1984). Notes on story structure and the organization of participation. In J.M. Atkinson and J.C. Heritage (Eds.), *Structures of social action.* Cambridge: Cambridge University Press.

Goodwin, C. (1986). Between and within: Alternative treatments of continuers and assessments. *Human Studies* 9:205-217.

Goodwin, C. (1986). Gestures as a resource for the organization of mutual orientation. *Semiotica* 62:24-49.

Goodwin, C. (1987). Forgetfulness as an interactional resource. *Social Psychology Quarterly* 50:115-131.

Goodwin, C. and Goodwin, M.H. (1987). Concurrent operations on talk: Notes on the interactive organisation of assessments. *IPRA Papers in Pragmatics* 1(1):1-54.

Goodwin, C. (1990). Perception, technology and interaction on a scientific research vessel. Paper presented at Bath 3: Rediscovering Skill in Science, Technology and Medicine. Social Studies Center, University of Bath.

Goodwin, C. and Goodwin, M.H. (1992). Professional vision. Paper presented at the Conference on Discourse and the Professions, Uppsala University, Uppsala, Sweden.

Goodwin, C. and Goodwin, M.H. (in press). Formulating planes: Seeing as a situated activity. In D. Middleton and Y. Engestrom (Eds.), *Distributed cognition in the workplace.* Amsterdam: John Benjamins.

Goodwin, C. and Heritage, J.C. (1990). Conversation analysis. *Annual Review of Anthropology* 19:283-307.

Goodwin, M.H. (1991). *He-said-she-said: Talk as social organization among black children.* Bloomington: Indiana University Press.

Goodwin, M.H. (in press). Announcements in their environment: Prosody within a multi-activity work setting. In E. Couper-Kuhlen and M. Selting (Eds.), *Prosody in conversation: Interactional studies.* Cambridge: Cambridge University Press.

Goodwin, M.H. and Goodwin, C. (1986). Gesture and coparticipation in the activity of searching for a word. *Semiotica* 62(1/2):51-75.

Greatbatch, D. (1988). A turn-taking system for British news interviews. *Language in Society* 17:401-430.

Grice, P. (1975). Logic and conversation. In P. Cole and J. Morgan (Eds.), *Syntax and semantics*, Vol. 3. New York: Academic Press.

Gulliver, P.H. (1979). *Disputes and negotiations: A cross-cultural perspective.* New York: Academic Press.

Gunter, R. (1974). *Sentences in dialog.* Columbia, S.C.: Hornbeam.

Gurwitsch, A. (1959/1966). Contribution to the phenomenological theory of perception. In A. Gurwitsch, (Ed.), *Studies in phenomenology and psychology.* Evanston: Northwestern University Press.

Gurwitsch, A. (1964). *The field of consciousness.* Pittsburgh: Duquesne University Press.

Hall, S. (1983). Train-gone-sorry: The etiquette of social conversations in American Sign Language. *Sign Language Studies* 41:291-309.

Handel, W. (1982). *Ethnomethodology: How people make sense.* Englewood Cliffs, N.J.: Prentice-Hall.

Heath, C. (1982). Preserving the consultation: Medical record cards and professional conduct. *Sociology of Health and Illness* 4:56-74.

Heath, C. and Luff, P. (in press). Collaborative activity and technological design: Task coordination in london underground control rooms. *Journal of Computer Supported Cooperative Work.*

Heritage, J.C. (1984). *Garfinkel and ethnomethodology.* Cambridge: Polity Press.

Heritage, J.C. (1984). A change-of-state token and aspects of its sequential placement. In J.M.Atkinson and J.C. Heritage (Eds.), *Structures of social action: Studies in conversation analysis.* Cambridge: Cambridge University Press.

Heritage, J.C. (1985). Recent developments in conversation analysis. *Sociolinguistics* 15:1-19.

Heritage, J.C. (1985). Analyzing news interviews: Aspects of the production of talk for an overhearing audience. In T. van Dijk (Ed.), *Handbook of discourse analysis,* Vol. 3. London and New York: Academic Press.

Heritage, J.C. (1987). Ethnomethodology. In A. Giddens and J. Turner (Eds.), *Social theory today.* Stanford: Stanford University Press.

Heritage, J.C. (1988). Explanations as accounts: A conversation analytic perspective. In C. Antaki (Ed.), *Analysing everyday explanation: A casebook of methods.* London: Sage.

Heritage, J.C. (1989). Current developments in conversation analysis. In D. Roger and P. Bull (Eds.), *Conversation: An interdisciplinary perspective.* Clevedon: Multilingual Matters.

Heritage, J.C. (1990). Oh-prefaced responses to inquiry. Paper presented to the International Pragmatics Association Conference, Barcelona, Spain.

Heritage, J.C. (1991). Intention, meaning and strategy: Observations on constraints on interaction analysis. *Research in Language and Social Interaction* 25:311-33.

Heritage, J.C. and Drew, P. (1992). Introduction. In J.C. Heritage and P. Drew (Eds.), *Talk at work.* Cambridge: Cambridge University Press.

Heritage, J.C. and Greatbatch, D. (1991). On the institutional character of institutional talk: The case of news interviews. In D. Boden and D.H. Zimmerman (Eds.), *Talk and social structure.* Cambridge: Polity Press; Berkeley: University of California Press.

Heritage, J.C. and Sefi, S. (1992). Dilemmas of advice: Aspects of the delivery and reception of advice in interactions between health visitors and first-time mothers. In P. Drew and J.C. Heritage (Eds.), *Talk at work.* Cambridge: Cambridge University Press.

Heritage, J.C. and Sorjonen, M. (1992). Constituting and maintaining activities across sequences: And-prefacing as a feature of question design. To appear in *Language in Society.*

Heritage, J.C. and Watson, D.R. (1979). Formulations as conversational objects. In G. Psathas (Ed.), *Everyday language: Studies in ethnomethodology.* New York: Irvington.

Hilbert, R. (1990). Ethnomethodology and the micro-macro order. *American Sociological Review* 55:794-808.

Hilbert, R. (1992). *The classical roots of ethnomethodology.* Chapel Hill: University of North Carolina Press.

Hodgson, G.M. (1988). *Economics and institutions.* Cambridge: Polity Press.

Holland, N.N. (1982). *Laughing: A psychology of humor.* Ithaca, N.Y.: Cornell University Press.

Hopper, R. (1989a). Speech in telephone openings: Emergent interaction v. routines. *Western Journal of Speech Communication* 53:178-194.

Hopper, R. (1989b). Sequential ambiguity in telephone openings: "What are you doin'." *Communication Monographs* 56:240-252.

Hopper, R. (1990/1991) (Ed.). Ethnography and conversation analysis after talking culture. *Research on Language and Social Interaction* 24:161-387.

Hopper, R. (1992a). Speech errors and the poetics of conversation. *Text and Performance Quarterly* 12:113-24.

Hopper, R. (1992b). *Telephone conversation.* Bloomington: Indiana University Press.

Hopper, R. and Glenn, P.J. (in press). Repetition and play in conversation. In B. Johnstone (Ed.), *Repetition in discourse: Interdisciplinary perspectives,* Vol. II. Norwood, N.J.: Ablex.

Houtkoop, H. (1987). *Establishing agreement: An analysis of proposal-acceptance sequences.* Dordrecht: Foris.

Houtkoop-Steenstra, H. (1992). *Questioning turn formats in telephone survey interviews.* Paper presented at the meeting of the International Communications Association, Language and Social Interaction Interest Group, Miami.

Hughes, J.A., Shapiro, D., Sharrock, W.W., Harper, R. and Randall, D. (in press). *Ordering the skies: The sociology of coordinated work.* London: Routledge and Kegan Paul.

Hughes, J.A., Randall, D. and Shapiro, D. (1992). Faltering from ethnography to design. *CSCW '92: Proceedings of the conference on computer supported cooperative work.* New York: Association for Computing Machinery.

Huizinga, J. (1955). *Homo ludens: A study of the play element in culture.* Boston: Beacon Press.

Hutchins, E. (1989). The technology of team navigation. In R.K.J. Galegher and C. Egrido (Eds.), *Intellectual teamwork: Social and technological foundations of cooperative work.* Hillsdale, N.J.: Lawrence Erlbaum Associates.

Hyman, H.H. (1954). *Interviewing in social research.* Chicago and London: University of Chicago Press.

Jaffe, J. and Feldstein, S. (1970). *Rhythms of dialogue.* New York: Academic Press.

Jefferson, G. (1972). Side sequences. In D. Sudnow (Ed.), *Studies in social interaction* . New York: Free Press.

Jefferson, G. (1973). A case of precision timing in ordinary conversation: Overlapped tag-positioned address terms in closing sequences. *Semiotica* 9:47-96.

Jefferson, G. (1977). On the poetics of ordinary talk. Paper presented at the Second International Institute on Ethnomethodology and Conversation Analysis, Boston.

Jefferson, G. (1978). Sequential aspects of storytelling in conversation. In J. Schenkein (Ed.), *Studies in the organization of conversational interaction.* New York: Academic Press.

Jefferson, G. (1979). A technique for inviting laughter and its subsequent acceptance/declination. In G. Psathas (Ed.), *Everyday language: Studies in ethnomethodology.* New York: Irvington.

Jefferson, G. (1980a). End of grant report on conversations in which "troubles" or "anxieties" are expressed (HR 4805/2). London: Social Science Research Council.

Jefferson, G. (1980b). On "trouble-premonitory" responses to inquiry. *Sociological Inquiry* 50:153-85.

Jefferson, G. (1984). Notes on the systematic deployment of the acknowledgement tokens "yeah" and "mm hm." *Papers in Linguistics* 17:197-216.

Jefferson, G. (1985). An exercise in the trancription of laughter. In T. van Dijk (Ed.), *Handbook of discourse analysis*, Vol 3. London and New York: Academic Press.

Jefferson, G. (1986). Notes on "latency" in overlap onset. *Human Studies* 9(2/3):153-184.

Jefferson, G. (1988). On the sequential organization of troubles-talk in ordinary conversation. *Social Problems* 35(4):418-441.

Jefferson, G. (1989). Notes on a possible metric which provides for a "standard maximum" silence of approximately one second for conversation. In D. Roger and P. Bull (Eds.), *Conversation: An interdisciplinary perspective*. Clevedon: Multilingual Matters.

Jefferson, G. and Lee, J.R.E. (1981). The rejection of advice: Managing the problematic convergence of a "troubles telling" and a "service encounter." *Journal of Pragmatics* 5:399-422.

Jefferson, G., Sacks, H. and Schegloff, E.A. (1987). Notes on laughter in the pursuit of intimacy. In G. Button and J.R.E. Lee (Eds.), *Talk and social organization*. Avon: Multilingual Matters.

Jefferson, G. and Schegloff, E.A. (1975). Sketch: Some orderly aspects of overlap in natural conversation. Paper presented at the meeting of the American Anthropological Association.

Jefferson, G. and Schenkein, J. (1978). Some sequential negotiations in conversation: Unexpanded and expanded versions of projected action sequences. *Sociology* 11:87-103. Reprinted in J. Schenkein (Ed.), *Studies in the organization of conversational interaction*. New York: Academic Press.

Jirkota, M., Luff, P. and Heath, C. (1992). Making a big deal out of ethnography: A case study utilising ethnography and interaction analysis in a dealing room. Paper presented at the Workshop on Ethnographic Studies of Work and CSCW System Design, CSCW '92: Conference on Computer Supported Cooperative Work, Toronto.

Johnstone, B. (1991). Individual style in an American public opinion survey: Personal performance and the ideology of referentiality. *Language in Society* 20:557-576.

Kahn, R.L. and Cannell, C.F. (1957). *The dynamics of interviewing: Theory, technique, and cases*. London: Wiley and Sons.

Katz, J. (1983). A theory of qualitative methodology: The social system of analytic fieldwork. In R.M. Emerson (Ed.), *Contemporary field research*. Prospect Heights: Waveland Press.

Kendon, A. (1977). Technologies of accountability: Of lizards and airplanes. In A. Kendon (Ed.), *Studies in the behavior of social interaction*. Lisse, Holland: Peter DeRidder Press.

Knuth, D.E (1992). *Literate programming*. Stanford: Centre for the Study of Language and Information.

Komter, M.L. (1990). Dilemma's in de rechtszaal [Dilemmas in the courtroom]. In C. Maris, A. Bos, A. Hoekema and T. van Peijpe (Eds.), *Recht, rechtvaardigheid en doelmatigheid.* Arnhem: Gouda Quint.

Komter, M.L. (1991a). *Conflict and cooperation in job interviews: A study of talk, tasks, and ideas.* Amsterdam and Philadelphia: John Benjamins.

Komter, M.L. (1991b). Discriminatie en Interactie. Macht, culturele verschillen en spreekstijl als mogelijke bronnen van discriminatie in de rechtszaal [Discrimination and interaction. Power, cultural differences and speech-style as possible sources of discrimination in the courtroom]. *Tijdschrift voor Criminologie* 33(3):295-308.

Komter, M.L. (1991c). De verdeling van kennis in de rechtszaal [The distribution of knowledge in the courtroom]. *Recht der Werkelijkheid* 12(2):3-19.

Komter, M.L. (1993). Onderhandelen in de rechtszaal over verklaringen voor geweldsmisdrijven [Negotiating explanations for violent crime in the courtroom]. In C. Bouw and B. Kruithof (Eds.), *De kern van het verschil. Culturen en identiteiten.* Amsterdam: Amsterdam University Press.

Kyle, J. (1990). The Deaf community: Custom, culture and tradition. In S. Prillwitz and T. Vollhaber (Eds.), *Sign language research and application.* Hamburg: Signum Press.

Labov, W. and Fanshel, D. (1977). *Therapeutic discourse: Psychotherapy as conversation.* New York: Academic Press.

Lammers, S. (1986). *Programmers at work.* Washington, D.C.: Tempus Books.

Lane, H. (1992). *The mask of benevolence: Disabling the deaf community.* New York: Knopf.

Latour, B. and Woolgar, S. (1979). *Laboratory life: Social construction of scientific facts.* New York: Sage.

Lave, J. (1988). *Cognition in practice.* Cambridge: Cambridge University Press.

Lave, J., and Wenger, E. (1991). *Situated learning: Legitimate peripheral participation.* Cambridge: Cambridge University Press.

Lee, J.R.E. (1987). Prologue: Talking organization. In G. Button and J.R.E. Lee (Eds.), *Talk and social organization.* Clevedon: Multilingual Matters.

Leiter, K. (1980). *A primer on ethnomethodology.* Oxford: Oxford University Press.

Leont'ev, A.N. (1981). *Problems of the development of the mind.* Moscow: Progress Publishers.

Lerner, G.H. (1987). *Collaborative turn sequences: Sentence construction and social action.* Unpublished Ph.D. dissertation, University of California, Irvine.

Lerner, G.H. (1989). Notes on overlap management in conversation: The case of delayed completion. *Western Journal of Speech Communication* 53:167-177.

Lerner, G.H., (1991). On the syntax of sentences-in-progress. *Language in Society* 20:441-458.

Lerner, G.H. (1992). Assisted storytelling: Deploying shared knowledge as a practical matter. *Qualitative Sociology* 15(3): 247-272.

Levinas, E. (1969). *Totality and infinity: An essay on exteriority.* Pittsburgh: Duquesne University Press.

Levinson, S.C. (1983). *Pragmatics.* Cambridge: Cambridge University Press.

Levy, S. (1984). *Hackers: Heroes of the computer revolution.* New York: Doubleday.

Liberman, K. (1985). *Understanding interaction in central Australia: An ethnomethodological study of Australian Aboriginal people.* London and New York: Routledge and Kegan Paul.

Livingston, E. (1986). *The ethnomethodological foundations of mathematics.* London and New York: Routledge and Kegan Paul.

Livingston, E. (1987). *Making sense of ethnomethodology.* London and New York: Routledge and Kegan Paul.

Luff, P. and Heath, C. (in press). The practicalities of menu use: Improvisation in a screen-based activity. *Journal of Intelligent Systems.*

Lynch, M. (1982). Technical work and critical inquiry: Investigations in a scientific laboratory. *Social Studies of Science* 12:499-533.

Lynch, M. (1985). *Art and artifact in laboratory science: A study of shop work and shop talk in a laboratory.* London and New York: Routledge and Kegan Paul.

Lynch, M. (1985). Discipline and the material form of images: An analysis of scientific visibility. *Social Studies of Science* 15:37-66.

Lynch, M. (1988). The externalized retina: Selection and mathematization in the visual documentation of objects in the life sciences. *Human Studies* 11:201-234.

Lynch, M. (1991). Method: Measurement -- ordinary and scientific measurement as ethnomethodological phenomena. In G. Button (Ed.), *Ethnomethodology and the human sciences.* Cambridge: Cambridge University Press.

Lynch, M. and Bogen, D. (1990). "The very fact of the existence of science": A mere argument on behalf of a post-analytic ethnomethodology. Unpublished manuscript.

Lynch, M., Livingston, E. and Garfinkel, H. (1983). Temporal order in laboratory work. In K. Knorr-Cetina and M. Mulkay (Eds.), *Science observed: Perspectives on the social study of science.* London and Beverly Hills: Sage

Manning, P.K. (1988). *Symbolic communication: Signifying calls and the police response.* Cambridge: Massachusetts Institute of Technology Press.

Marlaire, C.L. and Maynard, D.W. (1990). Standardized testing as an interactional phenomenon. *Sociology of Education* 63(April):83-101.

Maynard, D.W. (1984). *Inside plea bargaining: The language of negotiation.* New York: Plenum.

Maynard, D.W. (1985). How children start arguments. *Language in Society* 14:1-30.

Maynard, D.W. (1991). On the interactional and institutional bases of asymmetry in clinical discourse. *American Journal of Sociology* 97:448-95.

Maynard, D.W. and Clayman, S.E. (1991). The diversity of ethnomethodology. *Annual Review of Sociology* 17:385-418.

Maynard, D.W. and Manzo, J.F. (1992). "Justice" as a phenomenon of order: Notes on the organization of a jury deliberation. Paper presented at the symposium Negotiations in the Workplace: Discourse and Interactional Perspectives, Aalborg University, Denmark.

Maynard, D.W. and Marlaire, C.L. (1987). *The interactional substrate of educational testing.* Paper presented at the Conference on Video Analysis, Guilford, UK.

Maynard, D.W. and Zimmerman, D.H. (1984). Topical talk, ritual, and the social organization of relationships. *Social Psychology Quarterly* 47:301-316.

Mazeland, H.J. (1992). *Vraag/antwoord-sequenties [Question/ answer sequences].* Amsterdam: Stichting Neerlandistiek VU.

McHoul, A. (1978). The organization of turns at formal talk in the classroom. *Language in Society* 7:183-213

McIlvenny, P. (1991). Some thoughts on the study of sign language talk. In K. Sajavaara, D. Marsh and T. Keto (Eds.), *Communication and discourse across cultures and languages.* AFinLA Yearbook 1991. Jyväskylä University, Publications de L'Association Finlandaise de Linguistique Appliqueé.

Meehan, A.J. (1986). Record keeping practices in the policing of juveniles. *Urban Life* 15:70-102.

Meehan, A.J. (1989). Assessing the "police-worthiness" of citizen's complaints to the police: Accountability and the negotiation of facts. In D.T. Helm, W.T. Anderson, A.J. Meehan, and A.W. Rawls (Eds.), *The interactional order: New directions in the study of social order.* New York: Irvington.

Mehan, H. (1991). The school's work of sorting students. In D. Boden and D.H. Zimmerman (Eds.), *Talk and social structure.* Cambridge: Polity Press.

Mellinger, W. (Forthcoming). Accomplishing fact in police records: The case of the "dispatch package." In G. Miller and J. Holstein (Eds.), *Perspectives on social problems.* Greenwich, Conn.: JAI.

Mishler, E.G. (1986). *Research interviewing: Context and narrative.* Cambridge and London: Harvard University Press.

Moerman, M. (1988). *Talking culture: Ethnography and conversational analysis.* Philadelphia: University of Pennsylvania Press.

Molotch, H. and Boden, D. (1985). Talking social structure: discourse, domination, and the Watergate hearings. *American Sociological Review* 50:273-288.

Morley, I. and G. Stephenson (1977). *The social psychology of bargaining.* London: George Allen and Unwin.

Mulgan, G.J. (1991). *Communication and control: Networks and the new economies of communication*. Cambridge: Polity Press.

Mulkay, M. (1985). Agreement and disagreement in conversations and letters. *Text*. 5(3):201-27.

Mulkay, M. (1986). Conversation and texts. *Human Studies* 9:303-321.

Nowell, E. (1989). Conversational features and gender in ASL. In C. Lucas (Ed.), *The sociolinguistics of the Deaf community*. New York: Academic Press.

O'Connell, D.C., et al. (1990). Turn-taking: A critical analysis of the research tradition. *Journal of Psycholinguistic Research* 19:345-373.

Parsons, T. (1937). *The structure of social action*. New York: Free Press.

Peyrot, M. (1982). Understanding ethnomethodology: A remedy for some common misconceptions. *Human Studies* 5:261-83.

Pike, K. (1954). *Language in relation to a unified theory of the structure of human behavior*. Glendale, CA: Summer Institute of Linguistics.

Pimiä, P. and Rissanen, T. (1987). *Kolme kirjoitusta viittomakielestä [Three studies of sign language]*. Department of General Linguistics Publication No. 17, University of Helsinki.

Pollner, M. (1975). "The very coinage of your brain": The anatomy of reality disjunctures. *Philosophy of the Social Sciences* 5:411-430.

Pollner, M. (1987). *Mundane reason: Reality in everyday and sociological discourse*. Cambridge: Cambridge University Press.

Pollner, M. (1991). Left of ethnomethodology: The rise and decline of radical reflexivity. *American Sociological Review* 56:370-80.

Pomerantz, A.M. (1978). Compliment responses: Notes on the co-operation of multiple constraints. In J.N. Schenkein (Ed.), *Studies in the organization of conversational interaction*. New York: Academic Press.

Pomerantz, A.M. (1980). Telling my side: "Limited access" as a "fishing" device. *Sociological Inquiry* 50:186-98.

Pomerantz, A.M. (1984). Agreeing and disagreeing with assessments: Some features of preferred/dispreferred turn shapes. In J.M. Atkinson and J.C. Heritage (Eds.), *Structures of social action: Studies in conversation analysis*. Cambridge: Cambridge University Press.

Pomerantz, A.M. (1984). Giving a source or basis: The practice in conversation of telling "How I know." *Journal of Pragmatics* 8:607-625

Pomerantz, A.M. (1984). Pursuing a response. In J.M. Atkinson and J.C. Heritage (Eds.), *Structures of Social Action*. Cambridge: Cambridge University Press.

Pomerantz, A.M. (1986). Extreme case formulations: A way of legitimizing claims. *Human Studies* 9:219-30.

Pomerantz, A.M. (1988). Offering a candidate answer. *Communications Monographs* 55:360-373.

Prinz, P.M. and Prinz, E.A. (1985). If only you could hear what I see: Discourse development in sign language. *Discourse Processes* 8:1-19.

Psathas, G. (1979) (Ed.). *Everyday language: Studies in ethnomethodology*. New York: Irvington Press.

Psathas, G. (1990). (Ed.). *Interaction Competence.* Washington, D.C.: University Press of America.

Psathas, G. (1990). Some sequential structures in direction-giving. *Human Studies* 9:231-246

Psathas, G. (1990). Introduction: Methodological issues and recent developments in the study of naturally occurring interaction. In G. Psathas (Ed.), *Interaction competence.* Washington, D.C.: University Press of America.

Psathas, G. (1992). Calls and work: Talk and social structure and studies of work. Paper read at the International Institute for Ethnomethodology and Conversation Analysis, Waltham, Bentley College.

Putnam, L.L. and Jones, T.S. (1982). The role of communication in bargaining. *Human Communication Research* 8/3:262-280.

Putnam, L.L. and Poole, M.S. (1987). Conflict and negotiation. In F.M. Jablin, L.L. Putnam, K.H. Roberts, and L.W. Porter (Eds.), *Handbook of organizational communication: An interdisciplinary perspective.* London: Sage.

Rangarajan, L.N. (1985). *The limitation of conflict: A theory of bargaining and negotiation.* London: Croom Helm.

Rawls, A. (1989a). An ethnomethodological perspective on social theory. In D. Helm, W. Anderson, A. Meehan, A. Rawls (Eds.), *The interaction order: New directions in the study of social order.* New York: Irvington.

Rawls, A. (1989b). Language, self, and social order: A reformulation of Goffman and Sacks. *Human Studies* 12:147-172.

Rissanen, T. (1985). *Viittomakielen perusrakenne [The basic structure of sign language].* Department of General Linguistics, Publication No. 12, University of Helsinki.

Rogoff, B. and Lave, J. (1984a). *Everyday cognition: Its development in social context.* Cambridge: Harvard University Press.

Roy, C.B. (1989). Features of discourse in an American Sign Language lecture. In C. Lucas (Ed.), *The sociolinguistics of the Deaf community.* New York: Academic Press.

Roy, C.B. (1992). A sociolinguistic analysis of the interpreter's role in simultaneous talk in a face-to-face interpreted dialogue. *Sign Language Studies* 74:21-61.

Sacks, H. (1963). Sociological description. *Berkeley Journal of Sociology* 8:1-17.

Sacks, H. (1971-1972). *Unpublished lecture notes.* Transcribed and edited by G. Jefferson. University of Irvine.

Sacks, H. (1973/1987). On the preferences for agreement and contiguity in sequences in conversation. In G. Button and J.R.E. Lee (Eds.), *Talk and social organisation.* Clevedon: Multilingual Matters.

Sacks, H. (1974). An analysis of the course of a joke's telling in conversation. In R. Bauman and J. Sherzer (Eds.), *Explorations in the ethnography of speaking.* Cambridge: Cambridge University Press.

Sacks, H. (1975). Everyone has to lie. In B. Blount and M. Sanches (Eds.), *Sociocultural dimensions of language use.* New York: Academic Press.

Sacks, H. (1984a). Notes on methodology. In J.M. Atkinson and J.C. Heritage (Eds.), *Structures of social action.* Cambridge: Cambridge University Press.

Sacks, H. (1984b). On doing "being ordinary." In J.M. Atkinson and J.C. Heritage (Eds.) *Structures of social action.* Cambridge: Cambridge University Press.

Sacks, H. (1992). *Lectures on conversation.* Two volumes, ed. G. Jefferson. Oxford: Blackwell.

Sacks, H. and Schegloff, E.A. (1979). Two preferences in the organization of reference to persons in conversation and their interaction. In G. Psathas (Ed.), *Everyday language: Studies in ethnomethodology.* New York: Irvington.

Sacks, H., Schegloff, E.A. and Jefferson, G. (1974). A simplest systematics for the organization of turn-taking for conversation. *Language* 50:696-735. Reprinted in J.N. Schenkein (Ed.), *Studies in the organisation of conversational interaction I.* New York: Academic Press.

Schaeffer, N. (1991). Conversation with a purpose -- or conversation? Interaction in the standardized interview. In P. Biemer et al. (Eds.), *Measurement errors in surveys.* New York: Wiley and Sons.

Schegloff, E.A. (1968/1972). Sequencing in conversational openings. *American Anthropologist* 70:1075-1095. Reprinted in J.J. Gumperz and D. Hymes (Eds.), *Directions in sociolinguistics.* New York: Holt Rinehart and Winston.

Schegloff, E.A. (1970). The social organization of conversational openings. Unpublished manuscript.

Schegloff, E.A. (1972). Notes on a conversational practice: Formulating place. In D. Sudnow (Ed.), *Studies in social interaction.* New York: Free Press.

Schegloff, E.A. (1973/1987). Recycled turn beginnings: A precise repair mechanism in conversation's turn-taking organization. In G. Button and J.R.E. Lee (Eds.), *Talk and social organization.* Clevedon: Multilingual Matters.

Schegloff, E.A. (1979). Identification and recognition in telephone conversation openings. In G. Psathas (Ed.), *Everyday language: Studies in ethnomethodology.* New York: Irvington Press.

Schegloff, E.A. (1980). Preliminaries to preliminaries: "Can I ask you a question?" In D.H. Zimmerman and C. West (Eds.), *Language and Social Interaction* (special double issue of *Sociological Inquiry* 50:104-152).

Schegloff, E.A. (1982). Discourse as an interactional achievement: Some uses of "uh huh" and other things that come between sentences. In D. Tannen (Ed.), *Georgetown University roundtable on languages and linguistics.* Washington, D.C.: Georgetown University Press.

Schegloff, E.A. (1984). On some questions and ambiguities in conversation. In J.M. Atkinson and J.C. Heritage (Eds.), *Structures of social action.* Cambridge: Cambridge University Press.

Schegloff, E.A. (1986). The routine as achievement. *Human Studies* 9(2/3):111-152.

Schegloff, E.A. (1987a). Analyzing single episodes of conversation: An exercise in conversation analysis. *Social Psychology Quarterly* 50:101-114.

Schegloff, E.A. (1987b). Between micro and macro: Contexts and other connections. In J. Alexander, et al. (Eds.), *The micro-macro link.* Berkeley and Los Angeles: University of California Press.

Schegloff, E.A. (1988). Description in the social sciences I: Talk-in-interaction. *Papers in Pragmatics* 2:1-24.

Schegloff, E.A. (1988/89). From interview to confrontation: Observations of the Bush/Rather encounter. *Research on Language and Social Interaction* 22:215-240.

Schegloff, E.A. (1989). H. Sacks -- lectures 1964-65: An introduction/memoir. *Human Studies* 12:185-209.

Schegloff, E.A. (1990). Comment. *Journal of the American Statistical Association* 85(409):248-250.

Schegloff, E.A. (1990). On the organization of sequences as a source of "coherence" in talk-in-interaction. In B. Dorval (Ed.), *Conversational organization and its development.* Norwood, N.J.: Ablex.

Schegloff, E. A. (1990). Where does theory come from? More rules of turn taking. Paper delivered at Speech Communication Association.

Schegloff, E.A. (1991/2). Reflections on talk and social structure. In D. Boden and D.H. Zimmerman (Eds.), *Talk and social structure: Studies in ethnomethodology and conversation analysis.* Cambridge: Polity Press.

Schegloff, E.A. (1992a). Introduction. In H. Sacks, *Lectures on conversation*, Vol 1. Oxford: Blackwell.

Schegloff, E.A. (1992b). Repair after next turn: The last structurally provided defense of intersubjectivity in conversation. *American Journal of Sociology* 97:1295-1345.

Schegloff, E.A. (1992c). To Searle on conversation: A note in return. In J. Searle, et al. (Eds.), *(On) Searle on conversation.* Amsterdam and Philadelphia: John Benjamins.

Schegloff, E.A., Jefferson, G. and Sacks, H. (1977). The preference for self-correction in the organization of repair in conversation. *Language* 53(2):361-382.

Schegloff, E.A. and Sacks, H. (1973). Opening up closings. *Semiotica* 6-7:289-327.

Schenkein, J.N. (1978) (Ed.). *Studies in the organization of conversational interaction.* New York: Academic Press.

Schiffrin, D. (1980). Meta-talk: Organizational and evaluative brackets in discourse. *Sociological Inquiry* 50:199-236.

Schuman, H. and Presser, S. (1981). *Questions and answers in attitude surveys. Experiments on question form, wording, and context.* London: Academic Press.

Schutz, A. (1962). *Collected Papers*, Vol 1: The problem of social reality. The Hague: Martinus Nijhoff.

Schutz, A. (1964). *Collected Papers*, Vol 2: Studies in social theory. The Hague: Martinus Nijhoff.

Schutz, A. (1966). *Collected Papers*, Vol 3: Studies in phenomenological philosophy. The Hague: Martinus Nijhoff.

Scott, M.B. and Lyman, S.M. (1968). Accounts. *American Sociological Review* 33/1:4662.

Scribner, S. (1984) (Ed.). Cognitive studies of work. *The Quarterly Newsletter of the Laboratory of Comparative Human Cognition* 6 ns. 1-2,1-4.

Shapiro, D., Hughes, J., Harper, R., Ackroyd, S. and Soothill, K. (1991). Policing information systems: The social context of success and failure in introducing information systems in the police service. Technical Report EPC-91-117. Rank Xerox Limited, Cambridge EuroPARC.

Sharrock, W.W. and Anderson, B. (1986). *The ethnomethodologists.* London: Tavistock.

Sharrock, W.W. and Turner, R. (1978). On a conversational environment for equivocality. In J. Schenkein (Ed.), *Studies in the social organization of conversational interaction.* New York: Academic Press.

Shearing, C.D. (1984). *Dial-a-cop: A study of police mobilization.* Toronto: Centre of Criminology.

Siefert, C.M. and Hutchins, E.L. (1989). Learning within a distributed system. *Quarlerly Newsletter of the Laboratory of Comparative Human Cognition* 11(4):108-114.

Simmel, G. (1950). *The sociology of Georg Simmel.* Ed. K. Wolff. Glencoe, IL: Free Press.

Simons, H. (1990). Going meta. Lecture at University of Texas at Austin, November.

Smith, D.E. (1990). *Texts, facts and femininity: Exploring the relations of ruling.* London: Routledge and Kegan Paul.

Smith, D.E., Whalen, J., Whalen, M. and Carter, M. (1992). Texts in action. Paper presented at the International Institute for Ethnomethodology and Conversation Analysis, Bentley College, Waltham, MA.

Stokoe, W.C. (1960). Sign language structure: An outline of the visual communication system of the American Deaf. *Studies in Linguistics Occasional Paper 8.* University of Buffalo.

Suchman, L. (1988/1990). Representing practice in cognitive science. *Human Studies* 11:305-325. Reprinted in M. Lynch and S. Woolgar (Eds.), *Representation in scientific practice.* Cambridge: Massachusetts Institute of Technology Press.

Suchman, L. (1992). Technologies of accountability: Of lizards and airplanes. In G. Button (Ed.), *Technology in working order: Studies of work, interaction and technology.* London: Routledge and Kegan Paul.

Suchman, L. (in press). Constituting shared workspaces. In Y. Engeström and D. Middleton (Eds.), *Cognition and communication at work.* Cambridge: Cambridge University Press.

Suchman, L. and Jordan, B. (1990). Interactional troubles in face-to-face survey interviews. *Journal of the American Statistical Association* 85(409):232-241.

Sudnow, D. (1965). Normal crimes: Sociological features of the penal code in a public defender office. *Social Problems* 12:255-276.

Sudnow, D. (1972). Temporal parameters in interpersonal observation. In D. Sudnow (Ed.), *Studies in social interaction*. New York: Free Press.

Sudnow, D. (1978). *Ways of the hand*. Cambridge: Harvard University Press.

Swisher, M.V., Christie, K. and Miller, S.L. (1989). The reception of signs in peripheral vision. *Sign Language Studies* 63:99-125.

Tatar, D.G. (1987). *A programmer's guide to COMMON LISP*. Palo Alto: Digital Press.

ten Have, P. (1987). *Sequenties en formuleringen; aspecten van de interactionele organisatie van huisarts-spreekuur-gesprekken. [Sequences and formulations: Aspects of the interactional organization of GP-consultations]*. R.I.: Foris.

ten Have, Paul (1990). Methodological issues in conversation analysis. *Bulletin de Méthodologie Sociologique* 27:23-51.

Terasaki, A. (1976). Pre-announcement sequences in conversation. *Social Sciences Working Paper No. 99*. University of California at Irvine.

Tyler, S.A. (1969). *Cognitive anthropology*. New York: Holt, Rinehart and Winston.

Vygotsky, L.S. (1978). *Mind in society: The development of higher psychological processes*. Cambridge: Harvard University Press.

Vygotsky, L.S. (1981). The genesis of higher mental functions. In J.V. Wertsch (Ed.), *The concept of activity in Soviet psychology*. Armonk, N.Y.: M.E. Sharpe.

Watson, G. and Seiler, R.M. (1992). *Text in context: Contributions to ethnomethodology*. London: Sage.

Watson, D.R. (1983). The presentation of victim and motive in discourse: The case of police interrogation and interviews. *Victimology* 8(1-2):31-52.

Watson, D.R. (1987). Interdisciplinary considerations in the analysis of pro-terms. In G. Button and J.R.E. Lee (Eds.), *Talk and social organization*. Clevedon: Multilingual Matters.

Watson, D.R. (1990). Some features of the elicitation of confessions in murder interrogations. In G. Psathas (Ed.), *Interaction competence*. Washington, D.C.: University Press of America.

Watson, R. (1992). The understanding of language use in everyday life: Is there a common ground? In G. Watson and R. Seiler (Eds.), *Text in context: Contributions to ethnomethodology*. London: Sage.

Watson, D.R. and Sharrock, W.W. (1991). On the provision of "ethnographic context" in ethnomethodological and conversation analytic research. Paper presented at the International Conference on Current Work in Ethnomethodology and Conversation Analysis, Amsterdam.

Wertsch, J.V. (1981b). *The concept of activity in Soviet psychology*. Armonk, N.Y.: M.E. Sharpe.

Whalen, J. (1991). Conversation analysis. In E.F. Borgatta and M.L. Borgatta (Eds.), *The encyclopedia of sociology*. New York: Macmillan.

Whalen, J. (1992). The transfer of scripted emergency medical instructions in 911 calls. Paper presented to the Department of Languages and Intercultural Studies, Aalborg University, Aalborg, Denmark, September.

Whalen, J., Zimmerman, D.H. and Whalen, M.R. (1988). When words fail: A single case analysis. *Social Problems* 35:335-361.

Whalen, M.R. and Zimmerman, D.H. (1987). Sequential and institutional contexts in calls for help. *Social Psychology Quarterly* 50:172-185.

Whalen, M.R. and Zimmerman, D.H. (1990). Describing trouble: Practical epistemology in citizen calls to the police. *Language in Society* 19/4:465-492.

Wieder, D.L. (1974/1988). *Language and social reality.* Washington, D.C.: University Press of America.

Wilbur, R.B. (1983). Discourse structure in American Sign Language conversations. *Discourse Processess* 6:225-241.

Williams, F. (1982). *The communications revolution.* London: Sage.

Williams, F. (1987). *Technology and communication behavior.* Belmont, CA: Wadsworth.

Wilson, T.P. (1970). Conceptions of interaction and forms of sociological explanation. *American Sociological Review* 35:697-709.

Wilson, T.P. (1991). Social structure and the sequential organization of interaction. In D. Boden and D. Zimmerman (Eds.), *Talk and social structure.* Cambridge: Polity Press.

Wilson, T.P. (1992). The Rashomon of ethnomethodology. Unpublished manuscript.

Wilson, T.P. and Zimmerman, D.H. (1980). Ethnomethodology, sociology, and theory. *Humboldt Journal of Social Relations* 7:52-88.

Yourdon, E. and Constantine, L.C. (1979). *Structured design: Fundamentals of a discipline of computer program and system design.* Englewood Cliffs, N.J.: Prentice-Hall.

Zartman, I.W. (1989). In search of common elements in the analysis of the negotiation process. In F. Mautner-Markhof (Ed.), *Processes of international negotiations.* Boulder, CO: Westview Press.

Zimmerman, D.H. (1970). On the practicalities of rule use. In J. Douglas (Ed.), *Understanding everyday life.* Chicago: Aldine.

Zimmerman, D.H. (1984). Talk and its occasion: The case of calling the police. In D. Schiffrin (Ed.), *Meaning, form, and use in context: Linguistic applications.* Georgetown University Roundtable on Language and Linguistics. Washington, D.C.: Georgetown University Press.

Zimmerman, D. H. (1988). On conversation: The conversation analytic perspective. In J.A. Anderson (Ed.), *Communication yearbook*, Vol. 11. Beverly Hills: Sage.

Zimmerman, D.H. (1992a). The interactional organization of calls for emergency assistance. In J.C. Heritage and P. Drew (Eds.), *Talk at work.* Cambridge: Cambridge University Press.

Zimmerman, D.H. (1992b). Achieving context: Openings in emergency calls. In G. Watson and R.M. Seiler (Eds.), *Text in context: Contributions to ethnomethodology.* Newbury Park, CA: Sage.

Zimmerman, D.H. and Boden, D. (1991). Structure-in-action: An introduction. In D. Boden and D. Zimmerman (Eds.), *Talk and social structure*. Berkeley: University of California Press.

Znaniecki, F. (1934/1968). *The method of sociology*. New York: Octagon.

# Index

# About the Contributors

GRAHAM BUTTON, Ph.D. 1976 University of Manchester, is a Senior Scientist at Rank Xerox EuroPARC, Cambridge, U.K. His main research interest has been talk-in-interaction and at present he is investigating how technology is socially ordered in the interactions and work of those participating in its production. His recent publications include two edited collections, *Ethnomethodology and the Human Sciences* (1991) and *Technology in Working Order: Studies in Work, Interaction, and Technology* (1993).

STEVEN E. CLAYMAN received his Ph.D. from the University of California at Santa Barbara, and is currently in the Department of Sociology at the University of California, Los Angeles. He is interested in various forms of talk and interaction designed for mass audiences, including news interviews, press conferences, speeches, and talk shows. His recent publications have appeared in *Annual Review of Sociology* (1991), *American Sociological Review* (1993), and *Text* (1993). He is currently working on a book (with David Greatbatch and John Heritage) called *The News Interview: Studies in the History and Dynamics of a Social Form.*

MAREK CZYZEWSKI is Lecturer in Sociology at the University of Lodz in Poland, where he received a Ph.D. in Sociology in 1980. He was awarded the Heinrich Hertz Scholarship, University of Bielefeld and University of Bochum, for 1988/89. His research interests include therapist-client interaction, intercultural stereotyping in discourse, and the analysis of mass media and political discourse. His recent critique of John Heritage's *Garfinkel and Ethnomethodology* appears in the journal, *Theory, Culture, and Society.*

ALAN FIRTH, is Assistant Professor at the Department of Languages and Intercultural Studies, Aalborg University, Denmark, where he received the Ph.D. in sociolinguistics (1992). He holds an M.A. in applied linguistics from the University of Birmingham, U.K. He was Visiting Fellow at the East-West Center, Honolulu during 1989-90. His research interests include the discourse of negotiations, communication via new technologies, and conversation analysis. He is currently editing a volume entitled *Negotiation in Workplaces: Discourse and Interactional Perspectives.*

PHILLIP J. GLENN is Associate Professor of Speech Communication at Southern Illinois University at Carbondale. He holds an M.A. from the University of North Carolina at Greensboro (1977) and a Ph.D. from the University of Texas at Austin (1987). His research interests include the organization of laughter in everyday talk, argument structures, and conversation. He has recently published in *Research on Language and Social Interaction, Text and Performance Quarterly*, and in an edited volume entitled, *Repetition in Discourse: Interdisciplinary Perspectives.*

MARJORIE HARNESS GOODWIN is Professor of Anthropology at the University of South Carolina. She received a Ph.D. in Anthropology at the University of Pennsylvania in 1978. Her principal areas of interest include conversation analysis, language in the workplace, and gender and language. In her monograph, *He-Said-She-Said: Talk as Social Organization among Black Children* (1990), she analyzes how children use talk to construct their social organization in peer groups. She has recently been investigating work-relevant talk in tool-saturated environments.

ROBERT HOPPER, Ph.D. University of Wisconsin, is the Charles Sapp Centennial Professor of Communication at the University of Texas at Austin. Conversation analysis, children's speech, telephone communication, and the social construction of gender are among his research interests. His most recent book is *Telephone Conversation* (1992).

HANNEKE HOUTKOOP-STEENSTRA is an Assistant Professor in the Dutch Department of Utrecht University, The Netherlands. She has published a variety of studies in conversation analysis, including articles in the *Journal of Pragmatics* and *Sociology of Health and Illness*. She has recently become interested in the relevance of conversation-analytic findings to the prescriptive literature on verbal interaction, especially with respect to medical interaction and survey interviewing.

MARTHA L. KOMTER is lecturer in criminology at the Bonger Institute of Criminology, University of Amsterdam. Her work has concentrated on the analysis of interaction in institutional settings. She has recently published *Conflict and Cooperation in Job Interviews: A Study of Talk, Tasks, and Ideas* (1991).

DOUGLAS MAYNARD, Ph.D. 1979, University of California, Santa Barbara, taught in the Department of Sociology, University of Wisconsin, and is now in the Department of Sociology at Indiana University. His recent publications have appeared in *Annual Review of Sociology* (1991), *American Journal of Sociology* (1991), and *Qualitative Sociology* (1992). Maynard has two main current interests: the general topic of "bad news in everyday life," in which area he has published a variety of investigations concerning the delivery and receipt of diagnostic news; and a collaborative project concerned with interaction in survey interviews.

PAUL McILVENNY obtained his Ph.D. in Artificial Intelligence and Linguistics from Edinburgh University in 1991. He is presently lecturing in the English Department of Oulu University, Finland. His research interests currently encompass computer-supported collaboration and interaction, sign language talk, public discourse, humor and comedy, difference and cultural identity, and the nature of improvisation in human life and culture. He has recently published in an edited collection entitled *Computers and Conversation*, and in *Intelligence Systems Journal*.

GEORGE PSATHAS, Professor of Sociology at Boston University since 1968, holds a Ph.D. from Yale University and has taught at Indiana University and Washington University, St. Louis. He has lectured on ethnomethodology and conversation analysis at various universities and international conferences since 1967 and has published numerous papers in books and journals. He is Editor-in-Chief and founder of the international journal, *Human Studies*. His most recent work is *Conversation Analysis: The Study of Talk-in-Interaction* (1994) and the edited collection *Interaction Competence* (1990).

EMANUEL A. SCHEGLOFF, M.A. and Ph.D. 1960, 1967, University of California at Berkeley, has taught at Columbia University and the University of California at Los Angeles. His work is preoccupied with the understanding of human conduct in interaction and its import for understanding humans and conduct more generally. He has recently published articles in *American Journal of Sociology* and *Research on Language and Social Interaction*, as well as chapters in two edited volumes, *Rethinking Context: Language as an Interactive Phenomenon* (1992) and *Talk at Work* (1992).

WES SHARROCK has been at the University of Manchester, where he is now Reader in Sociology, since 1965. His interest in ethnomethodology developed in the late 1960s and has informed much of his work since. He has had a long standing interest in the study of work which is currently directed towards software engineering. He has published numerous papers in books and journals as well as several books that develop ethnomethodological themes.

PAUL TEN HAVE is an Associate Professor in the Department of Sociology at the University of Amsterdam. He teaches qualitative research methods, ethnomethodology, and medical sociology, and has published widely in these fields. His current interests include questioning and negotiation in medical consultations and computer work practices. Among his recent publications are contributions to two edited volumes, *Text and Talk as Social Practice*, and *Talk and Social Structure*.

JACK WHALEN is an Associate Professor of Sociology at the University of Oregon. He received his Ph.D. from the University of California at Santa Barbara. Currently he is working on a book on police and fire communications centers, and on related studies of technologically- and textually-mediated communication. He has published recently in *Social Problems*, *Research on Language and Social Interaction*, and the *Encyclopedia of Sociology*.